JEAN PAUL

Jean Paul Friedr.
Richter

Jean Paul

A READER

Edited, with an introductory essay and
commentary, by Timothy J. Casey

Translations by Erika Casey

The Johns Hopkins University Press
Baltimore and London

© 1992 The Johns Hopkins University Press
All rights reserved
Printed in the United States of America

The Johns Hopkins University Press
701 West 40th Street, Baltimore, Maryland 21211-2190
The Johns Hopkins Press Ltd., London

The paper used in this book meets the minimum requirements of American
National Standard for Information Sciences — Permanence of Paper for Printed
Library Materials, ANSI Z39.48–1984.

Library of Congress Cataloging-in-Publication Data
Jean Paul, 1763–1825.
    [Selections. English. 1992]
    Jean Paul : a reader / edited, with an introductory essay and
commentary, by Timothy J. Casey ; translations by Erika Casey.
        p.   cm.
    Includes bibliographical references and index.
    ISBN 0-8018-4153-4. — ISBN 0-8018-4154-2 (pbk.)
    1. Jean Paul, 1763–1825 — Translations into English.   I. Casey, Timothy
Joseph, 1927–   . II. Title.
PT2455.A13C37   1992
838'.609 — dc20   90-25478

For Margaret, Markus, Timothy, and Brigitte

Contents

Preface   xi

PART ONE   COMMENTARY

Introduction   3

Life and Works   8

The Invisible Lodge   11

Hesperus   15

Quintus Fixlein   18

Siebenkäs   19

Titan   22

Fledgling Years   27

Preschool of Aesthetics   30

Levana   31

Schmelzle and *Dr. Katzenberger*   34

Life of Fibel   37

The Comet   39

Narrative Practice   43

Philosophy and Politics   57

Inwardnesses   69

PART TWO TEXTS

The Invisible Lodge (1793)
Introduction 81
Life of the Merry Masterkin Maria Wutz in Auenthal:
A Kind of Idyll 83

Hesperus; or, 45 Dog Post Days (1795)
Introduction 115
On the Desert and the Promised Land of the Human Race 116

Quintus Fixlein (1796)
Introduction 120
History of My Preface to the Second Edition of Quintus Fixlein 122
Life of Quintus Fixlein unto the Present Time Extracted from
Fifteen Slipboxes 142
Outing of Headmaster Florian Fälbel and His Primaner to
Mount Fichtel 153

Siebenkäs (1796)
Introduction 158
Flower- , Fruit- , and Thornpieces; or, the Married Life, Death, and Wed-
ding of Advocate of the Poor F. St. Siebenkäs 161

The Vale of Campan (1797)
Introduction 184
The Vale of Campan; or, on the Immortality of the Soul, together with an
Explanation of the Woodcuts under the 10 Commandments of the
Catechism 185

Palingeneses (1798); *Jean Paul's Letters* (1799)
Introduction 193
Palingeneses 196
Jean Paul's Letters and Biography to Be 197

Titan (1800–1803)
Introduction 203

Titan   208
Comic Appendix to Titan   210
Airshipman Giannozzo's Logbook   217
Clavis Fichtiana seu Leibgeberiana   227

Fledgling Years (1804)
Introduction   236
Fledgling Years   237

Preschool of Aesthetics (1804)
Introduction   241
Preschool of Aesthetics   244

Levana (1807)
Introduction   269
Levana; or, Doctrine of Education   271

Schmelzle (1809)
Introduction   275
Army Chaplain Schmelzle's Journey to Flätz   276

Dr. Katzenberger (1809)
Introduction   282
Dr. Katzenberger's Spa Journey   283

Political Lenten Sermons during Germany's Week of Martyrdom (1811)
Introduction   286
*The Twin Military Review in Grosslausau and in Kauzen, Complete with
    Campaigns*   287

Life of Fibel (1812)
Introduction   288
Life of Fibel, Author of the Bienrodian Primer   289

The Comet (1820–1822)
Introduction   300
The Comet   303

Contents

Self-Life Description (1826)
  Introduction 322
  Self-Life Description 323
Selina (1826)
  Introduction 360
  Selina; or, on the Immortality of the Soul 362
Index 365

Preface

"NOTHING TORMENTS ME ABOUT MY WHOLE BOOK," says Jean Paul in *Hesperus*, "but fear of how it will be translated." The way in which the work passes through an intermediary reminds him of the poor people in Lappland. "In that country," he says, "when the rich sit in their drinking-rooms, getting drunk on the liqueur brewed from the costly fly fungus, the poor folk lurk at the door of the house, until a well-to-do Lapp comes out and p-ss-s; the coarsened beverage, the Vulgata of distilled water, greatly benefits the poor devils" (*W* 2.1006).

For the translations in this volume, no use was made of earlier English versions. If one is attempting a fresh translation, consulting earlier versions is counterproductive. Not that there is much material available. The nineteenth-century Anglo-American preference was for the solemn and sentimental Jean Paul. Even when a major work like *Titan* was translated by one of the best American translators, Charles T. Brooks, the *Comic Appendix*, from which the excerpts here are mainly taken was simply left out.[1]

---

1. *Titan. A Romance. From the German of Jean Paul Friedrich Richter*, trans. by Charles T. Brooks, vols. 1–2 (Boston, 1862).

Apart from any bias in the choice of passages, presenting an author by way of selected reading is a procedure to which one may well feel very opposed in principle. Authors and works should be read whole, and one complete work is preferable to any number of excerpts. Unfortunately, Jean Paul has to be the exception. It is not a question of age but that he is antiquated in a way that Sterne or Swift, say, are not. He can be brilliantly inventive, and again and again the reader will come across passages of astonishing modernity and prescience. But the reader also has to reckon with Jean Paul's collector's mania, cope with the overladen language, and find a way through the labyrinth of melodrama. The greatest barrier are the many hundred pages of monotone pathos. If Jean Paul is to have a present-day readership, it can only be by way of selected readings. This seems an acceptable compromise provided the selections are extensive enough and representative enough to be an introduction and reference work to the whole of Jean Paul, not just an anthology of choice paragraphs, aphorisms, bon mots, and quotable oddities.

Every translation is a compromise: one must choose between being faithful to the German at the risk of awkward English and presenting a smooth English version at the risk of departing from the German. One tries for the best of both worlds, but where concessions had to be made, then the bias has been, in most cases, toward keeping as closely as possible to what Jean Paul wrote and, certainly, not modernizing him. The difficulties are great. Jean Paul is a mannerist, and his mannerisms know no bounds. Of all the major German writers, he is probably the most difficult to read, let alone to translate. Jean Paul himself suggests, both in *Preschool of Aesthetics* and again in a letter to Thomas Beddoes, that any work that is capable of, is not worth, being translated. (*W* 9.352; H-KA 3.5.84). This is discouraging, but it is only acting in the spirit of Jean Paul to say that the dictum is equally true if you stand it on its head: the more untranslatable the work, the more it merits translation.

The standard edition of John Paul's works is *Sämtliche Werke, Historisch-kritische Ausgabe*, which began to appear in 1927. It was published in Weimar and later in Berlin under the auspices of the Prussian Academy of Sciences. Most of the volumes were edited by Eduard Berend. The *Historisch-kritische Ausgabe* is in three sections: works that appeared in Jean Paul's lifetime, posthumous works, and letters. This work is referred to here as *H-KA*, followed by the relevant section and volume numbers.

Based on that critical edition is the excellent Hanser edition (Munich, 1959N), which was republished in 1975 as a twelve-volume paperback edition, *Jean Paul: Werke in Zwölf Bänden*, edited by Norbert Miller, with postscripts by Walter Höllerer. This is the edition used here and referred to as *Werkausgabe*, or *W.*

Useful basic reference works are Uwe Schweikert's *Jean Paul*, in the Metzler series (1970), and his *Jean Paul Chronik*, in the Hanser series (1975). Among the sources of bibliographical material are Eduard Berend's *Jean-Paul Bibliographie* in the expanded edition by Johannes Krogoll (Stuttgart, 1963) and the special Jean Paul volume of *Text und Kritik*, edited by Heinz Ludwig Arnold (Munich, 1983).

Two recent and easily accessible publications on Jean Paul's life and work are Günter de Bruyn's lively biography *Das Leben des Jean Paul Friedrich Richter* (Halle, 1975; Fischer paperback, 1978) and the essays of the president of the Jean Paul Gesellschaft, Kurt Wölfel, collected in the Suhrkamp paperback edition *Jean Paul Studien* (1989).

Jean Paul's oeuvre is such that any comprehensive study must stretch over several years. Many people have helped us along the way, but our thanks in particular go to Eva Anselm, for help in preparing the manuscript, to University College, Galway, for the study leave without which it could not have been finished, and especially to Wolfgang Wierscheim, without whom it would not have been begun.

PART ONE

COMMENTARY

Introduction

THE CONSENSUS ON JEAN PAUL SEEMS TO BE THAT HE IS both one of Germany's greatest writers and one of its least known. There was a time when he was the most popular novelist in Germany, not least for his sentiment; his work was thought to be more affecting than *Werther*, itself. For a period, he was prominent in the English-speaking world, the "most extraordinary, original, and difficult writer in the German language," to quote one of the earliest English translators.[1] In the later nineteenth century, his popularity at home and abroad waned; he became for the most part a writer — in fact *the* writer — for connoisseurs and enthusiasts. It would not have surprised him. He wrote, he said, not so much for a minority as for a minimity.[2]

But then the understanding of Jean Paul, what his readers respond to or react against, has changed much over the years. He is often cherished for the idyllic element in his work, the snug domestic scenes, the quirky

---

1. A. Kenney, *The Death of an Angel and Other Pieces. Translated from the works of J.P.F. Richter* (London, 1839), p. v.
2. Letter to Christian Otto. *H-KA* III 1 p. 397.

characterization of the humble and the homely. This has led to accusations of escapism. Later nineteenth-century histories of literature, while admitting all manner of isolated gifts and fine passages, deplore a weakness at the core, a flight from real life into an artificially contrived, make-believe world.[3] To some extent, the view persists. Emil Staiger sums up one attitude toward Jean Paul by saying that the man who estranges us from life cannot accompany us through life.[4] Readings of Jean Paul, even among those who are looking at, perhaps even for, the same thing, vary widely. Georg Lukács represents the older Marxist attitude when he accuses Jean Paul of petit bourgeois reconciliation with the miserable German reality.[5] On the other hand, the most significant book to appear on Jean Paul in recent years is the massively detailed *Jean Paul's Poetry of Revolution*, by Wolfgang Harich, who sets out to prove the opposite — that Jean Paul was a radical revolutionary and that his work is precisely a confrontation with and denunciation of the German social and political *misère*.[6] That all of this is in Jean Paul and that none of it is in Goethe is one of the book's refrains. Harich wants to end once and for all the false image of Jean Paul's idyllic contentment and reveal the real face of his humanistically divine discontent. The study is that of a brilliant advocate, marshaling in a masterly way such evidence as suits the thesis. In the end, Harich's picture is as one-sided as the idyllic one.

But these are later arguments, and whatever their rights and wrongs, the historical fact is that during the nineteenth century Jean Paul was regarded as representative in particular of the supposedly characteristic German inwardness. He was regarded in this manner as much if not more so abroad, where he became known in England and America through De Quincey, Carlyle, Longfellow, Coleridge, George Eliot, and in France above all through Madame de Staël. The images differed between the two language areas. The Anglo-American image emphasizes the humorous, sentimental, and religious aspects. Madame de Staël emphasizes the bizarre and what she called Jean Paul's somber talent. Most influential is her translation of *Speech of the Dead Christ from the Universe*

3. For example, Otto von Leixner, *Geschichte der Deutschen Literatur* (Leipzig, 1893); or Robert Koenig, *Deutsche Literaturgeschichte* (Bielefeld and Leipzig, 1910).

4. Emil Staiger, *Meisterwerke deutscher Sprache aus dem 19. Jahrhundert* (Zürich, 1957), p. 98.

5. Georg Lukács, *Skizze einer Geschichte der neueren deutschen Literatur* (1964), pp. 59ff.

6. Wolfgang Harich, *Jean Paul's Revolutionsdichtung. Versuch einer Deutung seiner heroischen Romane* (Reinbek, 1974).

that There Is No God, so that, far from promoting the idyllic image, her presentation comes rather under the heading of the romantic agony. This Jean Paul became the main source of that death of God concept that a French writer, Nodier, commenting at the time on Madame de Staël's work, refers to as the most daring idea of the romantic spirit.[7]

If one asks who was the real Jean Paul, idyllic or nihilistic, revolutionary or conservative, sentimental or satirical, the obvious answer is that he is all of these things. He represents inwardness while at the same time being one of the main social and political commentators and satirists of his age. To discount the inwardness for the sake of politics would be a misconceived attempt. It is not the fact of Jean Paul's inwardness that is in question but its nature, which is certainly debatable.

All this seems to assume that Jean Paul is a romantic, which begs many questions. In histories of German literature, he generally has a section to himself and seems to be regarded as the outsider, by definition. He could be assigned to the Enlightenment; but with so many qualifications, it is easier to say he is *sui generis*. All the same, it seems fair enough as an introduction to his style of writing to say that it is romantic in an archetypal sense, whether it is romantic in the historical sense or not. His extreme subjectivity, open-ended fragmentariness, bewildering shifts of perspective, and willful and wayward style can be said to represent the romantic spirit, at least in contrast to literature that is more classical in spirit: objective, ordered, disciplined, and contained. Nobody would call Jean Paul objective, ordered, disciplined, or contained.

If there is one thing that all critics agree on, it is that Jean Paul is eccentric. Adjectives like *quaint, quirky, odd,* or *bizarre* describe his style of writing, which seems to be a succession of conceits. It is, of course, mannered and can sometimes be tiresome. But it is not a veneer; rather, it is an expression of an essentially eccentric experience, of a disorientation and dislocation that is always present, at least as a possibility, in Jean Paul. In this he represents that aspect of romanticism that is a forerunner of modernism, with its alienations and anxieties. The more classical spirit seems to recoil from this, or at least keep its distance. Among the *Xenien*, the aphoristic parting gifts of Goethe and Schiller to friend and enemy, is the one by Goethe on the Chinaman in Rome, who is out of place in the classical world; this is Goethe's metaphor for Jean Paul. In a letter to

---

7. Cf. Byron R. Libhart, "Madame de Stael, Charles de Villiers, and the Death of God in Jean Paul's *Songe*," *Comparative Literature Studies* 9 (1972): 141–51.

Goethe (28 June 1796) Schiller speaks of meeting Jean Paul for the first time and finding him, as he expected, strange, as if he had dropped from the moon.

More especially, Jean Paul can be called romantic if we are using the term as René Wellek and Austin Warren use it in their distinction between the objective mode of narration and the "romantic-ironic" mode, with a narrator who plays up his own presence and parades his artistry and, indeed, the artificiality of the work.[8] If the extreme example of this in English is Laurence Sterne, in German it is Jean Paul. Not only does he pile reflection on reflection or digression on digression; not only does he constantly interfere with his characters and interrupt their stories; at any moment in a Jean Paul novel one might meet Jean Paul himself wandering through the book, perhaps composing another book or in the company of characters from other books, who may themselves be composing books that elsewhere seem to be Jean Paul compositions. Sometimes the effect is intimate and homely, calmly reflective. Sometimes it is quite the opposite, for the reflections only serve to put us out of countenance, with an eerie sense of the doppelgänger – Jean Paul, after all, coined the term – that seems to violate the integrity of the individual.

With his quirky vocabulary, his wayward syntax and conceits, and his endless metaphors – that he had thought up the greatest numbers of metaphors was the epitaph he wanted to appear on his tombstone – Jean Paul is the most taxing of German writers. This is a matter of quantity as well as quality. Quite apart from the long novels and other sprawling works of fiction, Jean Paul was a compulsive writer. He not only had a vast correspondence but, from his school days, filled copybook after copybook with thousands of excerpts from his equally compulsive reading – notions, fancies, curiosities, and stray bits of information or insight, his own or others. He started collections under a variety of headings, such as Dreams, Coincidences, Ironies, Pathetic Scenes. Under the heading of Ironies alone, he filled twenty copybooks.

Jean Paul's material will probably never be published in full, although ever since the first edition of sixty-five volumes in the 1820s, there have been several other editions, above all the *Sämtliche Werke, Historisch-kritische Ausgabe*, which has been in progress since 1927. Jean Paul said his ambition was to do what no author had ever done: to record for posterity every thought that ever came into his head. He must have nearly succeeded. So one is faced with trying to beat into shape in a short space

---

8. René Wellek and Austin Warren, *Theory of Literature* (New York, 1956), pp. 212ff.

a work both qualitatively and quantitatively unwieldy. The first chapter of the following survey relates briefly the facts of his life, the sequence of his works, and the plots of his main stories. In the following chapters, an attempt is made to analyze his method and his subject matter.

Life and Works

JOHANN PAUL FRIEDRICH RICHTER WAS BORN 21 MARCH 1763, the eldest son of Johann Christian Richter, the Tertius (Third Teacher) and organist and later Lutheran clergyman in Wunsiedel, in Upper Franconia, now northeastern Bavaria. He later changed his name to Jean in homage to Rousseau, and he ultimately published under the name by which he is usually known, Jean Paul. (Scholars, bibliographers, and librarians have failed to agree on a convention of reference, so that researchers must make a triple search under *J*, *P*, and *R*.) He came, there-fore, from a teaching background — his grandfather, too, was a teacher — and from the Protestant parsonage, which has been such a fruitful source in German cultural life. (Martin Luther's sarcastic prophecy about him-self, that he would be, like Abraham, father of a mighty race, has thus been fulfilled.)

Education and religion remained Jean Paul's abiding interests; he had in great measure the eighteenth-century appetite for knowledge and mental and moral improvement, and he wistfully recreated the domes-tic atmosphere of the small-town parsonage and schoolhouse. Hence he has been accused of having idealized what was in reality frequently a

wretched existence, not only because of the poverty and subservient position of teachers and parsons but often because of their own narrowness.
Jean Paul's father was one of the more severely orthodox, and Jean Paul's
book on education, with its progressive and enlightened ideas, was partly
a reaction against the pedagogy of his father.

But even in the more idyllic works, the reader is made aware of the
underlying realities. Moreover, it is basic to Jean Paul that experience is
one thing, the relating of that experience is another, and it is the pleasures
of the latter that he exploits. Put in his fashion: "No adventure, not even
the worst, can ever be so blissfully experienced as related" (*W* 4.938). To
be sure, his work includes many idyllic scenes of childhood, lamplight,
firelight, Christmas, and he often mocks himself as a domestic snail,
speaking of his inglenook disposition and his spiritual nest making. And
although his work is wide ranging, he is a regional writer. His whole life
was spent in one remote area of Germany, in a picturesque landscape,
beginning with the little market town of Wunsiedel — where, he says, he
was "gladly born."

In 1765 Jean Paul's father was appointed to a ministry in the village
of Joditz on the River Saale, near Hof. Jean Paul recorded one of his
decisive experiences there, his second birth, as it were:

> I shall never forget that epiphany within myself, which I had never men-
> tioned to a living soul, where I was present at the birth of my self-
> consciousness, and I can yet quote place and time. One morning, when I
> was a very young child, I stood on our doorstep looking toward the wood-
> pile on my left, when, all of a sudden, the inner vision, "I am an *I*" de-
> scended from the sky like a flash of lightning in front of my eyes, and it
> has remained aglow ever since: my *I* had beheld itself for the first time
> and forever (*W* 12.1061).

This central experience reappears again and again in the work as both
the miracle of human consciousness and the threat of alienation. Jean
Paul's practice was to draw on a store of anecdotes and analogies, and one
of the more frequent references is to the supposed last words of Jonathan
Swift, "I am I." They are echoed, for example, by the dying Schoppe, in
Titan; Schoppe is half playactor, half the crazed victim of his philosophic
egoism. The theme is elaborated upon in the appendix to *Titan*, which
includes *Clavis Fichtiana*, or the key to Fichte, Jean Paul's parodistic *re-
ductio ad absurdum* of the *I* philosophy.

In 1776 Jean Paul's father became pastor in Schwarzenbach, and from
there, a few years later, Jean Paul began to attend the gymnasium in Hof.

He was already an omniverous reader, encouraged by various teachers and, particularly, by Pastor Vogel in the neighboring village of Rehau. In the same year that he went to Hof, 1779, his father died, leaving the widow and five sons in very poor circumstances. Eventually, Jean Paul was issued with the *testimonium paupertatis*, entitling him to a scholarship. At school, in what he called his Mulus-time, he was already writing first works typical of the Age of Reason, which was also the Age of Sentiment. He wrote, for example, *Exercises in Thinking* and a sentimental novel in letters on Abelard and Heloise. Of particular importance in Jean Paul's life, and built into his works in a variety of ways, were friendships, beginning with the friendships in Hof with Johann Bernhard Hermann, Adam Lorenz von Oerthel, and Christian Otto.

In 1781 he went to Leipzig University to study theology, but theological studies became less important than his philosophical studies and both less important than his reading of Shakespeare and Swift, Pope and Young. He cultivated especially the satirical authors, Horace, Voltaire, Erasmus, and he wrote his own imitative first satire, *Praise of Foolishness*. The 1780s were the years he later came to call his vinegar factory. He was very conscious in himself of the combination of, or even conflict between, reason and sentiment. It is perhaps because he felt that he too easily erred on the side of sentiment that in his apprenticeship years he stressed the satirical side and the cultivation of "wit." He wrote scores of essays on aesthetic, philosophical, and theological matters, on people and places, things and events, on life, and on the art of living. His first publications were a collection of such essays, entitled *Greenland Lawsuits*, published under the signature *R* in 1782, and later, in 1787, a collection under the pen name J. P. F. Hasus called *Selection from the Devil's Papers*. But he was gradually moving away from the satirical to the moral and the narrative.

In Hof, Jean Paul began to be surrounded — and remained so until the end of his life — by admiring women, young and old, his *tutti* love, as he called them, or his Erotic Academy. Mostly they were the charming daughters of well-to-do families; later there would be many princesses and persons of title. He was briefly engaged to Sophie Ellrodt in 1783 and to Karoline Herold in 1794. Jean Paul's work during these years is based directly on life experience. His work on education is based not only on his childhood experiences but also on his work as a private tutor, which was his source of income. Again, he made copious notes. *The Anthology of My Students* were notes on the children he taught in Schwarzenbach.

He had been tutor to the younger brother of his school friend Adam Lorenz von Oerthel, who had just died. Oerthel's death marked the beginning of Jean Paul's life-long preoccupation with death. Soon afterward, in 1789, Jean Paul's brother Heinrich committed suicide at the age of nineteen, and the year after, a second of the school friends, Johann Bernhard Hermann, died. Jean Paul composed essays like "What Death Is," "Description of My Epitaph," "Life after Death," and "My Funeral Sermon at the Grave of a Beggar." Some of these formed the basis of later works. "My Living Burial" anticipated the idea of pretended death in *Siebenkäs*, and the first version of *Speech of the Dead Christ* is "Lament of the Dead Shakespeare."

Like the awareness of the self, this awakening to an awareness of death is also told in terms of sudden revelation. It is dated 15 November 1790 and is noted in his diary as "the most important evening of my life." (He was to die on the eve of a 15 November.) It reminds one of the date of greatest importance to Tess of the d'Urbervilles, the unknown date of her future death. "She suddenly thought one afternoon, when looking in the glass at her fairness, that there was yet another date of greater importance to her than those; that of her own death, when all these charms would have disappeared; a day which lay sly and unseen among all the other days of the year, giving no sign or sound when she annually passed over it; but nonetheless surely there."[1] On that evening of 15 November 1790, Jean Paul had a vision of himself with sunken face and glassy eyes on his deathbed, heard the last "battling fantasies" of his mind, and experienced once and for all the brevity of man's "little bit of life." This moment is often recalled in his work as the "unforgettable November hour." It introduces, for example, Ottomar's experience of death in *The Invisible Lodge*, the first of a number of similar scenes.

The Invisible Lodge

Jean Paul's first idyll, *Wutz*, followed from that November experience, and it is indicative of its nature that it did so. Why Jean Paul called it "a kind of idyll" has been variously explained, sometimes with technical or formal reasons. Probably the qualification "kind of" has to do with content, with undertones and undercurrents, while on the surface *Wutz* conforms to Jean Paul's own definition of the idyll, namely the "representation of complete happiness within limits" — itself a sufficiently par-

---

1. Thomas Hardy, *Tess of the d'Urbervilles* (Aylesbury, 1978), p. 149.

adoxical definition. *Wutz* appeared as an appendix to his first major novel, *The Invisible Lodge*, and since this was a novel of education and concerned with the achievement of harmony and happiness, one can, if one tries hard, relate the idyll to the novel. But it is doubtful if one should try too hard. Jean Paul himself was skeptical about the nexus between the two and said later that they were held together by the binding. The novel itself remained a fragment, and he quickly gave up hope of finishing it, referring to it as "a born ruin." We learn little or nothing about the secret society to which the title seems to refer, which might be something like the secret society that directs affairs in *Wilhelm Meister*. The idea of a secret society was probably prompted by contemporary interest in Free-masonry as well as by Jean Paul's own love of mystification and all manner of romantic apparatus. In his letters he more often refers to it by the subtitle, *Mummies*, which, as he said to Emanuel Osmund, suggested its "egyptian sermonizing on mortality" (*H-KA* 3.2.28).

To familiarize oneself with the world of Jean Paul it is necessary to follow the story line in his works, for there is always a story. His style may be one of digression, of playacting in the narrator role, and of conversation with the reader, and one could say that, while there are many influences, his main model was Sterne. But the digressions in Sterne are different since in a sense he is all digression and no story. With Jean Paul, one has to cope with fantastically complicated plots in novels that are nothing like the average nineteenth-century novel. Even if they resemble the eighteenth-century novels of education and political intrigue, they are really more old-fashioned than that. They are baroque; or perhaps one could say they are monstrous offspring of a marriage between the gothic and the baroque. It follows that it is well-nigh impossible to relate the plot, particularly since the more one clarifies, the less the result resembles the bewildering original.

In *The Invisible Lodge*, the colonel-forester von Knör has promised his daughter Ernestine in marriage to the man who can beat her at chess. Ernestine's mother, for her part, demands that when Ernestine's first child is born it should be brought up for the first eight years under the earth — an experiment after Rousseau, one might say — and in the care of a Moravian Brother. Through an accident brought about by Ernestine herself, the cavalry captain von Falkenberg wins at chess. The child Gustav is born and spends the first years of his life in a cave together with the Moravian teacher, Genius, and a dog. When, at the end of this period, Gustav is brought up to the surface of the earth, he thinks he is dying, that earth is heaven, the sun is God, and human beings are blessed spirits. This purple resurrection passage made a deep impression on contemporaries and was much anthologized.

The novel has many dream sequences, dreams merge into reality and reality into dream, and there is even a kind of anticipation of the blue flower of Novalis. In his waking moments, the older Gustav tends to forget his early teacher but remembers him in dreams. In one dream he is changed into a dewdrop lying in a blue flower, which carries him into a room where Genius stretches out his arms to him. Even apart from the dreams, there are many mystical, musical night scenes in poetic prose. Passages like these have been selected and published separately, for example by Stefan George, who presented Jean Paul as the precursor of impressionism. Equally, one could regard Jean Paul as anticipating expressionism or surrealism, if only to give respectability to the coincidences and counterfeits, intrigues and mysteries that surround the identities of so many. But then, Jean Paul ridicules the reader who expects a clear plot, digresses into so-called extras, and lectures on topics like education, adultery, and female popes. However, there is a story. And Jean Paul reminds us that readers, like liars, must have good memories. So to return to the plot:

After his resurrection, the child Gustav is lost in the forest and is rescued by Frau von Röper, the former mistress of his father. She sees a resemblance between Gustav and her long-lost son, Guido, and she sends Gustav to the Falkenberg family in the principality of Scheerau. Here Gustav undergoes a new course of education, a more artistic one, under the guidance of the tutor, Jean Paul.

Then, in accordance with the wishes of his father, who is hostile to pietism, Gustav is sent to the military academy and schooled in the manlier disciplines under the regime of the courtier von Oefel. Oefel introduces him to the court at Scheerau, where he meets Beata, the daughter of Herr von Röper and the supposed sister of the missing Guido. She, too, has been educated by Jean Paul. Gustav falls in love with her, to the grief of his best friend, Amandus, who is also in love with her. Amandus fortunately falls ill and dies. On his deathbed, he joins the hands of Gustav and Beata.

Gradually, Gustav becomes more involved in court life. Eventually, he succumbs to the wiles of the prince's mistress, Bouse, whereas Beata rejects the advances of the prince. Stricken with remorse, Gustav confesses all in a letter to Beata and leaves the court to live in retirement with his parents in the country. However, he and Beata meet again in the romantically named spa of Lilienbad. Needless to say, the tears and pieties of these scenes, once so affecting, are now a barrier to the reader.

Another strand in the plot is Gustav's friendship with Ottomar, the illegitimate son of the prince, which brings in the more political aspects of the story. Ottomar is involved in a conspiratorial secret society, into which Gustav is apparently initiated and which, if the novel had been finished (it breaks off with the news that Gustav is imprisoned), would doubtless have played an important role, possibly directing Gustav's future development. Ottomar is an actively revolutionary idealist, determined to overthrow despotism, although he, too, has an uncanny presentiment of death. He becomes cynical and resigned or, at least, at some remove from his original revolutionary enthusiasm. In different ways, Ottomar and Gustav both represent Jean Paul's ideal of the "high man." But equally important as these high-minded heroes are the satirical foil figures, who are introduced into almost every Jean Paul story: the critical and bitter idealists.

The first of such figures appears in this novel, the physician Dr. Fenk. He comes into the plot first by way of the story of Amandus, his illegitimate son, and later in the course of the Ottomar story. When Gustav is imprisoned, Ottomar, before he commits suicide, reveals the conspiracy to Dr. Fenk in order to save Gustav. So Fenk in the end becomes, as similar characters often do in Jean Paul, the point of reference and observation. Like many of his successors, he is a distorted and distorting figure, but he too is a "high man" and what Jean Paul calls a "moral optimist," much preferable to the metaphysical kind. The moral optimist is open to all and has a "higher tolerance" — meaning, in the context, higher than the Peace of Westphalia. So Dr. Fenk is meant to be a truthful observer of affairs. For example, his diagnosis of hypochondria in the case of the Jean Paul figure is exact and true. Whole chapters are given over to reporting this sickness, until Jean Paul eventually becomes too ill to continue and his sister Philippine has to take over.

Moreover, the fictional Jean Paul is apparently waiting for the publication of another book on Gustav, being written by another character in the novel, against which to check his own facts. In the end, we may feel that the real Jean Paul has so complicated matters as not merely to confuse the reader but to prevent himself from providing a coherent conclusion. In any case, he gave up the endeavor, or rather he transferred it to his next novel, *Hesperus*, which is something between a continuation and a revision of *The Invisible Lodge*.

Hesperus

It need hardly be said that *Hesperus* is not a simple novel. Among the unpublished remains in the Jean Paul archives there are some six and a half thousand notes on *Hesperus*. Still, it could be said to have a consistent story line, which is not to say that it is less baroque than its predecessor. Not only do we have a secret society once more, we now have several kidnapped illegitimate sons of a prince. These are a source of great confusion to the reader, although less so than the legitimate sons of the prince and those of Lord Horion and the clergyman Eymann, for none of these sons lives with his real parents, and they are all mistaken as to their true identity.

The hero is Viktor. Viktor can to some extent be taken as a self-portrait, perhaps Jean Paul's one and only such. He does not represent, as most Jean Paul characters do, one aspect of Jean Paul but combines conflicting, but nonetheless coexisting, moods and characteristics.

Viktor has grown up in the house of Pastor Eymann in the little spa of St. Lüne. He becomes a doctor and, when the book opens, has returned to St. Lüne to operate upon — and restore the eyesight of — his supposed father, Lord Horion. Lord Horion is cured and sets off for England to find the missing fifth son of Prince Jenner von Flachsenfingen, the other four sons being apparently untraceable. In St. Lüne, Viktor renews his old friendship with Flamin, the supposed son of Eymann, and Flamin having just been appointed counselor at the court, Viktor goes there also, as court physician. Again the two friends fall in love with the same girl, Klothilde, the supposed daughter of the courtier Le Baut.

Viktor is unhappy over this rivalry and is further troubled when Lord Horion reveals that Flamin is in fact one of the prince's sons and therefore a brother of Klothilde. Viktor seeks distraction at court but gradually realizes that Klothilde returns his affection, and they experience spiritual union in the paradise landscape of Marienthal, in the company of the Oriental teacher Emanuel Dahore, who has been, under different names, the mentor of both Klothilde and Viktor. This period of bliss is interrupted by the story of Flamin, by his jealousy, and by the intrigues that entangle him, leading to his duel with Le Baut, Klothilde's supposed father. Flamin is accused of killing Le Baut, as he mistakenly believes he has done, and is imprisoned.

Meanwhile, Viktor learns from the dying Emanuel that he himself is the son of Pastor Eymann, not as he had thought, the son of Lord Horion. Thereupon, he feels obliged to renounce Klothilde. She, however,

would not hesitate to marry a commoner, and the various misunderstandings are cleared up when Lord Horion returns, enlightening and reconciling them all before his voluntary death, as they meet on the Island
of Union. Three Englishmen appear and are revealed to be sons of the
prince. And finally, the narrator discovers himself to be the long-lost fifth
son of the prince.

In spite of such intrigue and mystification, the novel has a kind of
unity as a novel of education. At least, it is clearly concerned with the
ideas and ideals of friendship, of political freedom, and of attitudes to
life, death, and the afterlife, and with the development of the hero, who,
although a sufferer from romantic melancholy, ends in salvation rather
than suicide.

It is all sentimentally told; *Hesperus* is the most emotionally charged,
not to say self-indulgent, of Jean Paul's works. It appealed to the public
of his time and was his best-seller, rivaling *Werther.* It appealed (as Jean
Paul's early biographer, Paul Nerrlich, said) to all who have pure hearts
and deep feelings. H. A. Korff called *Hesperus* a book of consolation for
Weltschmerzler.[2] Christoph Wieland read it, he says, three times in quick
succession. Johann Herder said he was so transported he could not pursue his normal activities for days. Goethe and Schiller were impressed,
Goethe remarking in a letter to Schiller (10 June 1795) with a barbed
compliment, that it was a first-rate Tragelaph (half deer, half goat).

Doubtless the response was mainly to its sentimental and "spiritual"
qualities, but for Harich the political and revolutionary aspect is dominant. There is certainly a political dimension, for example in the story of
Lord Horion, who directs operations behind the scenes. He kidnaps the
prince's sons and oversees their development toward the overthrow of
despotism and the establishment of a just order. Jean Paul was writing
Hesperus during the French Revolution, and if one can say only that he
favored its ideals up to a point, it would be a point beyond that of most
of his contemporary peers. But the sympathies of the novel are with the
moderates rather than the extremists, and *Hesperus* is not marked by enthusiastic radicalism, although it is resigned to revolution.

Jean Paul was a tireless propagandist for cosmopolitanism, for what
he called the higher philanthropy of whole-earth patriotism. This long-
term, long-view perspective gives the novel its strikingly prophetic quality. In the four quarters of the globe there are, everywhere, enchained

2. H. A. Korff, *Geist der Goethezeit* (Leipzig, 1949), 3:33.

races: "Their chains grow daily thinner — time loosens them — what des-
olation, at least what upheavals, must they not bring about on the little
bowling green of our cultivated countries?" (*W* 2.869)

But it is other matters, more inward and "religious," that dominate
in *Hesperus*, in intensity as well as in extent. Much of Harich's thesis applies better to Flamin than to the hero. Consequently, his interpretation
demotes Viktor. Similarly, he plays down the role of Emanuel, who is so
important to Jean Paul. Korff says that Emanuel is the "real hero" of the
novel, its "spiritual center."

Emanuel is a reincarnation of Genius in *The Invisible Lodge* but is a
more complex and complete example of Jean Paul's superior man. He is
a tribute partly to his friend Emanuel Osmund ("The person who commands the greatest love of the author and perhaps of the reader bears
your lovely name") and partly to its model, Karl Philip Moritz.[3] A major
element in the novel is Emanuel's view of life, largely seen as a matter of
his attitude toward death. He determines the day of his own death, lives
calmly toward it, invites Viktor to be present at it, and brings him to the
grave, where he has planted flowers. But Jean Paul characters never come
to rest. And Emanuel, although he preaches Providence and a God who
conceives the man who conceives Him, is overcome, when the midnight
of his predicted death approaches, with fears of an empty and unanswer-
ing eternity.

This ever-recurring obverse of Providence is the specter that stalks
through all of Jean Paul's works. Here, instead of a serene death scene,
there is a melodramatic explosion. It has to do with the subplot of the
English sons, who have returned and are about their revolutionary business. Emanuel is hurtled into the open grave. When he regains consciousness, the earth appears to him once more as a God-filled paradise.
But immediately, there is another abrupt transition, for at this moment a
maniac passes by, uttering maledictions and waving his bleeding arm
stump, having cut off the hand by which death was holding him. Once
more, Emanuel has a change of heart. Now he is determined to pay less
attention to death and future life and more to the present. But before
this can develop, he dies — of pneumonia, it seems, not surprisingly.

The political dimension is present, therefore, in such themes as not
neglecting life for the afterlife. But it is equally clear that the "second
world" and the problems of theism, deism, and atheism are central to

3. *H-KA* 3.2.29. Korff, *Geist der Goethezeit*, 3:33.

When the story begins — and the straightforward opening is un-usual — advocate of the poor, Firmian Stanislaus Siebenkäs, is in Kuh-schnappel impatiently awaiting the arrival of his bride, Lenette, from Augsburg, from whence she is being fetched by his friend, school super-intendent Stiefel. What develops thereafter is, after a brief period of do-mestic harmony, a story of incompatibility. For Siebenkäs, like his friend and alter ego Leibgeber, is an outsider, little mindful of middle-class val-ues and practices, as careless of public opinion as of money matters. Le-nette is concerned with convention and appearance, proud enough of her bookmaking husband, although unable to read his work — not unnatu-rally, since he is writing Jean Paul's *Devil's Papers*. She secretly fears her husband is "an atheist, or at least a philosopher." She is ultimately worn down by his demands and, before she is aware of it, finds consolation with Stiefel, his theological holy water being more to her liking than the Al-pine spring of Siebenkäs. And Siebenkäs is worn down by her demands and finds consolation with Natalie. Neither is indifferent to the other's needs, and they both try to salvage their marriage, but from the view-point of this story, intimate domestic detail, elsewhere idyllic, is now sti-fling and frustrating.

Early in the story we learn that Siebenkäs and Leibgeber, physically so alike as to be almost indistinguishable, had in their student days ex-changed names. (Jean Paul has so contrived that one must continue to refer to them, even outside the novel, by the "wrong" names, unless one is to get totally confused, particularly at the later stages of the novel, where Siebenkäs is pretending to be Leibgeber.) This is discovered by the Privy Blaise, the guardian of Siebenkäs (as one must call him), and Blaise thereupon refuses to disburse the expected inheritance. Leibgeber takes up the cause of his friend, quarrels with Blaise, and has to leave the country. Siebenkäs himself takes legal action against Blaise.

The lawsuit and the increasing poverty gradually undermine the mar-riage, and Lenette, although impervious to the advances of the dissolute Everard Rosa von Meyern, becomes more and more dependent on Stie-fel. Siebenkäs is more concerned with his writing and does little to alle-viate their lot, apart from taking the prize at the carnival shooting match and taking her furniture piece by piece to the pawnshop: "Censeo Car-thaginem delendam," he says of one piece after another. Feasts like Christmas only serve to highlight their poverty. "We are Christians after all," says Lenette, "when all Lutherans have goose, but you believe in nothing." And when Siebenkäs pawns Lenette's calico dress, there is a bitter quarrel, in which Stiefel sides with Lenette. Eventually husband

and wife communicate only by letter, and Siebenkäs loses his court action.

However, there is a sharp turn in events, for Leibgeber sends Siebenkäs money for the *Devil's Papers* and an invitation to come to Bayreuth. Siebenkäs sets out in a mood responsive to the Maytime season. On the way he is captivated by the sight of a strange lady, and when he meets Leibgeber is told by him of this beautiful niece of Blaise, Natalie, who is expecting the arrival of her fiancé, Rosa. Siebenkäs meets her and warns her of Rosa's true nature. Meanwhile, Siebenkäs has told Leibgeber of his own plight, and Leibgeber devises a plan. Siebenkäs is to pretend to die — Leibgeber suggesting a list of diseases and their several advantages — thereby not only freeing himself but providing for Natalie, as well as Lenette, out of the death benefits. Later, Siebenkäs is to take Leibgeber's place in a new appointment as inspector in the service of Count Vaduz.

When Siebenkäs returns to Kuhschnappel, Lenette is less well disposed than ever, being jealous of Natalie and ready to believe Rosa's slanderous account of Siebenkäs. When Siebenkäs plays sick, tender feelings return to them both. Before his supposed death, Siebenkäs entrusts Lenette to the care of Stiefel and leaves instructions that only Leibgeber shall see him in death. Leibgeber so arranges affairs that an empty coffin is buried. He helps Siebenkäs escape to Vaduz. There, he acts the part of Leibgeber, with some difficulty, for he is less the satirical prankster than his friend. Later, he learns that Lenette has married Stiefel and that Blaise, frightened by the ghostly appearance of Leibgeber as Siebenkäs, will pay out the inheritance. He also learns that Natalie was in love with him and is mourning his death. He reveals himself to the Count and seeks permission to revisit Kuhschnappel. There he finds the grave of Lenette, who has just died in childbirth, but he also finds Natalie, and they are reunited at the graveside. The implication is that they live happily ever after, although the planned sequence on the marriage of Siebenkäs and Natalie was never written.

Uwe Schweikert comments: "The representation of the marriage of Siebenkäs and Natalie could only have been the repetition of that of Siebenkäs and Lenette; for fantasy and reality are, for Jean Paul, irreconcilable opposites."[4] But Jean Paul's happy-ever-after has to be seen in the context of what he means by being "not happy, but happier" and what he means by "eternity." "Eternity is in this world," says Natalie, and in the

---

4. Uwe Schweikert, *Jean Paul* (Stuttgart, 1970), p. 32.

kind of eternity and the kind of happiness that Jean Paul presents, flower, fruit, and thorn are interdependent. It is said that the famous flower piece *Speech of the Dead Christ* should not be seen as it so often is, in isolation, but in the context of the novel. Similarly, one could say that the novel should be seen in the context of that passage, which on the one hand is an expression of despair but which also claims that fear is a quickener of hope.

Nowhere in Jean Paul is doubt banished. It is an ever-recurring, exorcising nightmare. To a large extent, Jean Paul remains as agnostic as in his early essays "On Man" (1781), where he says both that man is the creature that can reconcile opposites and that man knows as little of his end as of his origin (*H-KA* 2.1.182, 273). In *Siebenkäs*, Siebenkäs alone does not represent man any more than Leibgeber does. The bewildering resemblances and substitutions in Jean Paul are part of his romantic stock-in-trade, but they are also a reflection of dualism and precarious balance. For the purposes of the story, Siebenkäs and Leibgeber are two different persons, but the truth of the story can only reside in both together.

How much Jean Paul is concerned with problems of faith and feeling, of immortality and otherworldliness, and how constantly these matters are presented two ways at once (by way of sentiment and by way of satire) are no less evident in the smaller works. These were written in the years of and between *Siebenkäs*, and the next major novel, *Titan*, and in the years between *The Parson in Jubilee*, his most conventional idyll, and the work that marks the end of the eighteenth century, *The Marvellous Company of New Year's Night*. He put forward his philosophy, whether directly or by way of parody, in a variety of publications at this time, the most important being *The Vale of Campan* and its appendix, *An Explanation of the Woodcuts under the 10 Commandments of the Catechism*, *Palingeneses*, and *Jean Paul's Letters and Biography to Be*.

Titan

One expects to find the same concerns and the same mixture in *Titan*, his "general and cardinal novel," as he called it, in which Jean Paul reviews the age of the titanic genius and passes judgment on it for its "partiality" or one-sidedness, for its lack of purpose, and for its cult of energy and creativity for their own sake. That at least is the gist of his letters to Friedrich Jacobi (*H-KA* 3.3.129f., 156f., 4.236f).

The novel should really be called *Anti-Titan*, Jean Paul says. Mere aestheticism is rejected and mere geniuses come to grief, whereas the hero, Albano, who "comes close" to being titanic and suffers as a result, wins through to some kind of harmony and to union with his beloved. Not that the critics have agreed that this was, or was convincingly, the conclusion, any more than they have agreed that the novel is as much directed against the aesthetics of Weimar as it appears to be. But then, the most characteristic formal aspect of *Titan* is the extent of, and the weight attached to, the appendix, where once again Jean Paul seems to give of his best and most of himself. Besides, one should not look in the main story for too partisan a consistency. Jean Paul's feelings in the novel are as mixed as were his feelings for the *Titaniden* in his own life. These were Charlotte von Kalb and Emilie von Berlepsch. Both were divorced and interested in Jean Paul. Ultimately, he escaped, first into the brief engagement at the turn of the century with Karoline von Feuchtersleben and then into the lifelong, if not always untroubled, marriage with Karoline Mayer in 1801, in which he sought the domesticity he had known in his parents' home. For he was, as he said to Johann Gleim, no "Hero" and sought no "Heroine" (*H-KA* 3.3.342).

Given Jean Paul's practice and given that *Titan* is a four-volume work (his longest), one does not expect the story to be other than exceedingly complex. Its cast of characters is bewilderingly large, even without the many cases of obscure origins and mistaken identities. The only possibility of synopsis is to isolate the central figure and consider the other characters in relation to his story.

This hero is Albano Cesara, in reality the son of the Prince of Hohenfließ and Princess Eleonore. Albano's twin sister is Julienne. His elder brother, Luigi, is the Crown Prince, who, in the course of the story, is seduced into a dissipated life by Monsieur de Bouverot as part of the wicked designs of the rival principality of Haarhaar. To save Albano from these Haarhaar intrigues, he is transported immediately after his birth to Isola Bella, where he is brought up with Linda, who is the same age as himself. She is the daughter of Count Gaspard de Cesara and his wife, Princess de Lauria. Albano believes, therefore, that he is the son of Gaspard and that Linda is his twin sister. (Linda is one of the titanic characters, and Jean Paul gives her features, physical as well as psychological, of the *Titaniden* in his own life.) After the death of her mother, Linda is brought to Spain and given out to be, not Gaspard's daughter, but his ward. Gaspard's plan is that Albano and Linda be separated in early childhood and later meet and fall in love, so that his daughter shall marry into the princely house, as he himself once vainly hoped to do.

So Albano spends the first three years of his life on Isola Bella with his supposed twin, Linda. Afterward, he grows up in Blumenbühl, near Pestitz (Leipzig), the capital of Hohenfließ, in the house of the landscape architect Wehrfritz, his wife, Albina, and his daughter, Rabette. As the story mainly concerns Albano's education, there is a large cast of mentors, including Magister Wehmeier, the Lector, von Augusti, the music and dancing master, von Folterle, the titular librarian, Schoppe, with his crucial comedian role, and the so-called harmonist or architect and Greek artist, Dian — to say nothing of their several entourages. In the course of this education, Roquairol, the son of Prime Minister von Froulay, is held up to Albano as a model. Albano's dearest wish is to be become acquainted with Roquairol and Roquairol's sister, Liane.

Events begin to move when Albano reaches the age of twenty and is finally permitted to go to the capital of the principality, Pestitz, where he gets to know Luigi (who is, in fact, his older brother), Liane, and later Roquairol. In Tartarus he makes a pact of friendship with Roquairol, and he falls in love with Liane in the royal garden of Lilar. But in the interest of Gaspard's plans to unite Albano and Linda, Liane's teacher and the court preacher, Spener, enlightens Liane as to Albano's true, princely parentage, and she feels obliged to renounce her love. Albano misunderstands and accuses her falsely, whereupon she goes blind and finally dies. Albano collapses in remorse, but at that moment Schoppe leads in Idoine, the sister of Princess Isabella of Haarhaar, who is the image of Liane and who, playing the role of Liane, forgives Albano so that he recovers. At the same time, there has come to be a break between Albano and Roquairol, after the latter confesses to having seduced Rabette, Albano's foster sister.

Roquairol is, in fact, decisive to the action of the novel from the time Albano makes his acquaintance. He is one of those heaven stormers of whom Jean Paul says (in a letter to Jacobi) that in *Titan* each of them finds his own hell. Others, too, become victims of their excesses. One could say that Liane is too sentimental, Linda too willful, and Schoppe too egoistic; they all come to grief appropriately. But Roquairol in particular is Albano's counterpart and from the beginning behaves titanically, that is to say, immoderately. At twelve years of age, he fell in love with Linda at a masked ball (she as Lotte, he as Werther), and when he was rejected, he shot and wounded himself, as Albano later admiringly learns. Now he has seduced Rabette and later will seduce Linda.

But before this happens, Albano, together with Princess Isabella, is sent by Count Gaspard on an educational journey to Italy. The Princess, the former mistress of Albano's father, tries in vain to win Albano for herself. But he is planning to join the cause of the French Revolution. On Ischia he meets Linda, without recognizing her as his supposed sister, and Linda returns his love. He also meets the lady to whom Linda is companion and who is, in fact, his sister Julienne. It would appear that Gaspard's plan to unite Albano and Linda is being realized.

But after the return to Hohenfließ events take a different turn, largely because of Roquairol's intrigues. He is still in love with Linda, jealous of Albano, and intent on revenge. He announces a stage presentation entitled "The Tragedian" and, before this production takes place, plays a theatrical tragic villain role himself in real life. He makes use of the fact that he is able to imitate Albano's voice and handwriting, of the fact of Linda's night blindness, and of the fact that her love of Albano is so titanic that she is prepared to give herself to him without benefit of convention. His plans succeed, and in the same park in which Albano and Roquairol swore eternal friendship, Roquairol seduces Linda. On the next evening, he plays out the same scene in his theatrical presentation, which he ends by shooting himself on stage. Linda now regards herself as his widow and departs with Gaspard.

The comedian Schoppe, too, comes to grief, in part because, understandably, he misunderstands so much. Thus he has warned Albano from the beginning against falling in love with Linda, believing her to be Albano's sister. Schoppe becomes increasingly frantic in his attempt to unravel the true facts and in the end goes mad at the sight of his former friend and doppelgänger, Siebenkäs (which would make Schoppe Leibgeber, no great problem in the world of Jean Paul). But the legacy he leaves to Albano, together with a letter from Albano's deceased mother, Eleonore, finally resolves the confusion of portraits and persons, and Albano learns his true identity.

Meanwhile, Albano's elder brother, the sickly Luigi, has ascended the throne and has married the heiress of Haarhaar. Now Luigi dies, and the succession falls to Albano, who abandons his French plans and takes over the government of the state. He marries Idoine of Haarhaar, who resembles Liane and loves him no less, and so he unites the two principalities. The novel ends with an appeal to universal brotherhood and confidently anticipates an improved state of government.

Not unexpectedly, this ending has been regarded by many, Helmut Widhammer, for example, as utopian, compromising rather than harmonizing. Uwe Schweikert finds the ending illogical, since Albano, too, is titanic.[5] (Jean Paul himself, however, seems to except Albano in the antititan letter to Jacobi.) Many critics have felt that in *Titan*, Jean Paul, while appearing to intend Goethe and Schiller as targets of attack, in fact approaches ever closer to Weimar classicism. Walter Höllerer sees the novel as a perhaps unwitting victory for Weimar (*W* 6, 1140). It is true that Jean Paul is not in the end proposing a radical social revolution. But then, that was hardly ever his priority. To Emilie von Berlepsch he wrote: "Ah, if only my *Titan*, could present as clearly, as it appears within me, that the whole ideal world can only be entered upon and beheld by the inner and not by the outer man." Jean Paul's promised land is one of inwardness, and even as a politically critical writer he remains idyllic. What he wrote to Christian Otto is no less valid for *Titan:* "The word 'idyll' is the proper term for all Jean Paul's histories: I conduct within myself the history of my own life idyllically" (*H-KA* 3.2.67, 352).

One will not expect in *Titan* a straightforward novel of development with an unambiguous political program. Even the synopsis above is misleading, for in reality the novel is much more complex. Many more characters would have to be accounted for, above all the ubiquitous Jean Paul, who wanders through this novel as the son of the Governor of Flachsenfingen. Then there is the apparatus of masques and mysteries and *Konterfeis*, of misunderstandings and mistaken identities; the grotesque testamentary directions of the deceased mother, leading to the key to her coffin and its secrets; and the diverse apparitions, the bodiless heads, and headless voices, all of which are hardly less bizarre because they turn out to be the elaborate tricks of Gaspard, aided by his ventriloquist brother.

And as if *Titan* were not complicated enough, there remains finally the *Comic Appendix*, an all-important element, which doubtless makes the greatest appeal to the modern reader. Apart from shorter satirical sketches, the appendix mainly comprises *Airshipman Giannozzo's Logbook* and, as appendix to the appendix, *Clavis Fichtiana seu Leibgeberiana*. It was saying something when Jean Paul remarked to Christian Otto: "In the Comic Appendix I am wilder than elsewhere" (*H-KA* 3.4.42). Gianozzo is a fantast, striving for the absolute and ethereal. From his airship he looks down on Germany, passes harsh judgment on it, and comes to a violent end when his airship is struck by lightning.

In a different way, but no less wildly, Jean Paul passes judgment on Johann Fichte by carrying the *I* philosophy *ad absurdum* and into insanity

5. Schweikert, *Jean Paul*, p. 42.

in a work whose fictive author is the crazy Schoppe. It is often objected that Jean Paul was too influenced by his friend Jacobi into misunderstanding Fichte's philosophy as solipsism. But, apart from the fact that in real life Jean Paul warmly defended Fichte, his concern was with the possibilities of the *I* experience, including the aberrations of an *I* experience become titanically exaggerated and "partial." Above all, Fichte was for Jean Paul a vehicle for humor, which was his own mode of philosophy and his way of preserving balance. Hence his basic narrative form was the humorous idyll, whereas the traditional idyll, it is not unfair to say, is a markedly humorless genre.

Fledgling Years

Jean Paul's next major work, *Fledgling Years*, developed out of the *Titan* material and was originally intended as an appendage to the appendix. It took on independent life and became his most popular novel in Germany. In the English-speaking world, some of the most frequently translated and reprinted Jean Paul passages were taken from it, in particular the "Opening of the Will" scene, as an example of the comic style, but also such descriptive passages as the summertime excerpt included here.

The book does not make as extravagant demands on the reader as the usual Jean Paul. As one of the more realistic German-style novels, it does not attempt to sustain the high Italian style; in addition, it seems to have a single center of interest throughout, at least if one reads the story in the manner suggested by the title of the nineteenth-century English translation *Walt and Vult; or, the Twins*.[6] (*Flegeljahre* is, incidentally, the most difficult title to translate. *The Callow Years* is another possibility and perhaps closest in meaning. *The Awkward Age* and similar possible titles have associations unsuited to Jean Paul, and Carlyle's *Wild Oats* is hardly true to the novel.)

Jean Paul incorporated in the twin brothers the contrasting elements in his nature, the implication being that some synthesis should be achieved, whatever conclusion one draws from the fact that in the story this does not happen. To some extent the pattern is as heretofore. The protagonist, Walt, poet and dreamer, man of feeling and inwardness, and an innocent abroad, is successor to the protagonists of the earlier novels, to Gustav, Viktor, and Albano, even perhaps to Siebenkäs. Moreover, his

---

6. *Walt and Vult; or, the Twins. Translated from the Flegeljahre of Jean Paul by the Author of the "Life of Jean Paul,"* Eliza Buckminster Lee (Boston, 1846).

twin, Vult (the bizarre name derives from his father's exclamation, when it appeared at the birth that a second baby was emerging: "Quod Deus Vult"), rationalistic and rebellious, sarcastic and misanthropic, has his predecessors in Fenk and Leibgeber, Schoppe and Gianozzo.

But the honors are divided more equally in this novel. It is significant for Jean Paul's development as a whole that the satirical side steadily progresses toward a higher status and that the hero is less idealized. Walt may to some extent resemble Viktor in *Hesperus,* but rather more does he anticipate the Don Quixotelike figure of Jean Paul's later hero Nikolaus Marggraf. Vult is no longer a mere accompanying foil, still less can he be relegated, as an appendage, to an appendix. It is significant, too, that Vult, although the realist and man of reason, is also musician and artist.

Originally, Jean Paul intended "Jean Paul" to be the twin of Walt, and to a large extent Vult is his mouthpiece. Vult himself says that realism is the Sancho Panza of idealism and comments that poetry is like a pair of skates, fine for skimming smoothly over the crystal floor of the ideal, but clumsy out on the street. In Tonio Kröger fashion, he dismisses the amateurishness of emotional art: if you mix moods and tears into your music, then it becomes their servant, no longer their creator. In his "Vita-Book" Jean Paul says: "relate how you wanted to present yourself as Vult and Walt."[7] The hoped-for harmonization between Walt and Vult is given its narrative correlative in the twins' undertaking to write together their book, "Hoppelpoppel." (It is a pity Jean Paul did not retain the original title, *The Book of Judges,* with the allusion to his name. *Fledgling Years* is, incidentally, the only novel in which the name Richter appears on the title page.)

At any rate, the undertaking fails, and the twins must remain apart, as Vult recognizes: "Fare thee well; thou are not to be altered, I am not to be reformed." As if it were a foreshadowing of Kafka's *On the Gallery,* Schweikert speaks of *Fledgling Years* as necessarily fragmentary, reflecting the unbridgeable gap between a reality that is unbearable and a utopia that is unreal.[8]

But it is again the case that the reader does not take his bearings so much from the story as from the storyteller, who is as obtrusive as ever, both in his role as, according to the terms of the testament that opens the novel, officially appointed biographer and in comment and footnote,

7. *Wahrheit aus Jean Paul's Leben,* ed. Christian Otto and Ernst Förster (1826–33), 2:10.
8. Schweikert, *Jean Paul,* p. 46.

interlude and digression. If this has been always true of Jean Paul, it has become increasingly so, as the unresolved dichotomies in the material are reflected and, on the page at any rate, resolved in their narration. More than ever, in the later Jean Paul synthesis was found in the imagination, in a utopia that was, therefore — in one sense — nowhere. It was also concrete and localized, ending, as it were, where Jean Paul's last novel was to end, in the room where he was composing it in the Rollwenzelei, the inn outside Bayreuth where he spent his writing hours.

Fledgling Years begins with the reading of the will of the wealthy and eccentric Van der Kabel, attended by seven prospective heirs, police inspector Hauprecht, churchman Glanz, court agent Neupeter, court treasurer Knol, bookseller Pasvogel, preacher Flachs, and painter Flitte. To their bitter disappointment, they are left nothing but the house, which is left to whoever of them first weeps for the deceased, a competition won by the preacher. Named as sole heir of the rest of the large fortune is the unknown young dreamer and student of law from Elterlein, Gottwalt Peter Harnisch, called Walt. However, Walt must fulfil a variety of conditions: relive *in nuce* the various careers of the deceased — as piano tuner, gardener, hunter, notary — lead a morally irreproachable life, and stay in the house of each of the seven disappointed heirs in turn. They thus become at once his seven guardians and his seven enemies. For each mistake, Walt forfeits to them a part of his inheritance. (In the event, these terms are not followed through in the novel, which thus does not have even the absurd cohesiveness this would afford.)

The terms of the will are revealed to Walt on the day of his examination for admission as notary. The examination takes place at his parental home, to which his twin brother, the wandering flautist Vult (who ran away from home at the age of fourteen) has just secretly returned. From his hiding place in the apple tree, Vult watches the oddly conducted but successfully completed examination of his poetic brother. When Walt, hearing of his inheritance, sets off for the capital city, Vult follows him and contrives a meeting in an inn on the way. Their reunion is ecstatic. Vult, with his experience of the world, will help Walt fulfil his tasks. Together, as sentimentalist and satirist, they will write their twin novel, "Hoppelpoppel; or, the Heart."

In his innocence, Walt makes various mistakes that cost him portions of his inheritance. But he is little concerned by this and more concerned with his disappointments in friendship, as with Count Klothar, or in love, as with Wina, the daughter of General Zeblocki. These relationships are complicated by crossed letters, assignations, and masked meetings. True to his promise, Vult does protect him, rescuing him from the seductive designs of the actress Jacobine. But Vult is also Walt's rival for Wina. He exchanges masks with his brother, and when he meets Wina succeeds merely in confirming that she loves only Walt.

In the final scene, Walt enthusiastically relates his latest dream to Vult, who, unknown to Walt, has already taken his leave by letter and whose commentary on the dream takes the form of a flute melody, fading in the distance, as he departs from his unsuspecting brother. "Walt still listened enraptured to the fading notes from the street below, for he did not notice that with them fled his brother."

Preschool of Aesthetics

Jean Paul's main theoretical work on his craft was written in the same year as *Fledgling Years*. In *Preschool*, while it is universally applicable and full of acute observation, Jean Paul argues *pro domo*. Ludwig Tieck was not altogether unfair in suggesting that it is simply a prescription for writing in the manner of Jean Paul. It is probably most often recalled for such basic distinctions as that between plastic Greek and musical romantic, or between the three types of novel, the sublime Italian, the lowly Netherlandish, and the median German, such as his own *Titan,*, *Fixlein*, and *Fledgling Years*. ("No creature likes so much to classify as man," says Jean Paul, "especially if he is German" [*W* 9.67].)

But on the whole, the work is not so much systematic and abstract as discursive and detailed, if not to say passionately partisan, both in its hero worship of Herder and its implied rejection of what Jean Paul saw as the all too sublime rival aesthetics of poetry as autonomous play. The play of poetry is a means, not an end. One plays in earnest, not in play. One cannot "rise above elevation" (*W* 9.444f). For Jean Paul, the role of poetry is essentially mediatory, and poetry is ideally located midway between the nihilism of contempt for reality and the materialism of mere imitation of reality. Jean Paul keeps returning, by a variety of paths, to different aspects of humor, that "converse sublime," at once destructive and liberating. It creates greatness out of the experience of smallness: "When man looks down, like in the old theology, from the supernatural to the earthly world, the latter passes by, insignificant and vain; when, like humor does, with the little world he paces out infinity, there arises that laughter in which there is pain and greatness" (*W* 9.129).

It is striking how much Jean Paul stresses the "annihilating" effect and the subjective nature of humor, those aspects related to his seminal ex-

periences of selfhood and mutability. It is a common observation in the
history of fiction that humor is peculiarly subjective. Jean Paul clearly
belongs in the obtrusive tradition of novel writing. Like Alfred Döblin,
Jean Paul demands that the narrator should, like King David, himself
dance in the arena, and it is his own practice to stage-manage his presence. "For every humorist, the *I* plays the leading role; wherever he can,
he even brings his own personal circumstances onto the comic stage, albeit only to annihilate them poetically" (*W* 9.132). Annihilation, while
referring here in the first place to poetic transformation, also relates both
to humor as a cutting down to size and to an experience of the self that
is inflated and deflating at the same time.

By the time the *Preschool* and *Fledgling Years* were published, Jean Paul
had settled in Bayreuth, where he was to spend his last twenty-one years.
His adult life had begun with the comparative obscurity of tutor and
struggling writer in Hof and Schwarzenbach. In the middle period of his
career, in the closing years of the eighteenth and the first years of the
nineteenth centuries, he played his part on the larger stages and with
more celebrated characters, in centers like Leipzig, Dresden, and above
all, Weimar and Berlin.

Typically, one thinks of Jean Paul in Berlin, not only in the company
of Fichte and Friedrich Schleiermacher, Tieck and Friedrich Schlegel,
but as much, or more, in the company of Henriette von Schlabrendorff
and Josephine von Sydow, Rahel Levin and Henriette Herz, and Queen
Luise, herself.

After their marriage in 1801, Jean Paul and Karoline Meyer settled
first in Meiningen, where their first daughter, Emma, was born, then in
Coburg, where Max was born, and finally, in August 1804, in Bayreuth,
where their third child, Ottilie, was born the same year. The move to
Bayreuth was largely in order to be near Emanuel Osmund and Christian
Otto. Most readers probably picture Jean Paul as he was in the last years,
walking with his manuscripts and his Pomeranian dog to the Rollwenzelei, the inn outside Bayreuth, where Frau Rollwenzel mothered him,
fed him, and provided him with the private room where, away from
home, he could write undisturbed his idylls of domesticity.

Levana

The volume of output in the last period hardly decreased, although
for the most part the works were smaller in scope, such as the several
political booklets, beginning with the *Freedom Booklet* in 1805, expressing

Jean Paul's basically republican and democratic sympathies. He became less revolutionary with the years and was later much embarrassed by the fact that his fellow Wunsiedler K. L. Sand, who assassinated Kotzebue, appealed for justification to Jean Paul's essay in 1801 on Charlotte Corday. But he continued to place his hopes, not in Prussia, still less in Austria, but in France and the ideas of the French Revolution.

More considerable than the political essays, however, and a companion piece in the field of education to his work on aesthetics is *Levana; or, Doctrine of Education*, which appeared in 1807 as a memorial to the pedagogical eighteenth century. This work is no more a systematic work than *Preschool*, and it is presented in a variety of forms: essays, aphorisms, fictitional letters or speeches, and even verse. Jean Paul resolved to aim at "much enthusiastic disorder, in order to stimulate" (*H-KA* 1.12.xix).

For all the fragmentariness, for all the subdivisions into religious and secular, male and female, moral, intellectual, and aesthetic, the unifying principle is clear: education is a process of liberation toward a state of independence (*W* 9.528). Being based not only on his decade as a practicing teacher but on a lifelong experience of education and educators — and given the cast of his mind, with his eye and ear for detail and his fund of facts — *Levana* is anything but impractically abstract. At the same time, its principles and premises are as ideal as one could imagine. For Jean Paul, education was nothing less than the liberation — with the help of a liberated teacher! — of the "ideal man" latent in every child. One should, he claims, have the temerity to call this ideal man the God-man, for the discovery of the self is also the discovery of God. He speaks in almost Berkeleyan terms, suggesting that, just as there is no material world without the *I*, there is no spiritual world of the *I* without God. Jean Paul's work on education, like all his work, is religious — meaning, to be sure, religion as unsystematic as possible and one with which all those are in communion who seek the other world. In that sense, religious concern was a constant in his life, although his agonizing never came to rest.

In any case, as a preeminently epic writer, meandering and open-ended, with little sense of lyric single-mindedness or dramatic conclusiveness, he would probably have found the state of rest as inhuman and as little to his liking as Voltaire did. He was fond of mocking his fellow countrymen for their lethargy. He claimed that Germans have a gift for immobility, evidenced by the fact that they turn over in bed less often than the volatile French (*W* 10.941). This is further related to Jean Paul's emphasis on feelings and thus on changing moods. He says in a letter in 1796: "The ancients sought their happiness in principles, we in sentiments; the former afford a small one, the latter, an uncertain one: nothing remains but to unite them, the lasting with the great" (*H-KA* 3.2.275f.).

Perhaps inevitably there is a suggestion of resignation in the Jean Paul of the Bayreuth years. There is often a sense of disappointment in his letters, sometimes over personal matters, sometimes over political developments, or lack of them. In his private life he had, to be sure, worked out a satisfactory, if unconventional, *modus vivendi* with the help of the Rollwenzelei. And in spite of ups and downs, of occasional quarrels with those closest to him — his wife and Emanuel — he retained a passionate attachment to family and friends. In his last years he made many journeys beyond Bayreuth and made many new contacts, such as with E. T. A. Hoffmann. A crisis was brought about by his visit to Heidelberg in 1817 and 1818, where he not only found a new friend in Heinrich Voß, son of the Homer translator, but also fell in love with the young Sophie Paulus. He even considered divorce, but it came to nothing.

His output in these years continued unabated, even if it was only a few major works and very many minor ones. This was largely due to his personal troubles, for in spite of his fame he had no financial security and was forced to spend much of his time on a variety of quick commissions. However, with whatever constraints and difficulties, he continued to explore aphoristically and anecdotally, essayistically and narratively the fields of politics and education, aesthetics and religion. Much of the later work is, therefore, scattered through a variety of journals, with collections of one kind or another appearing from time to time.

In 1810 he published the anthology *Autumn Flora* (*Herbst-Blumine*) and, in 1814, *Museum*, which included among its more significant contributions an essay on magnetism and the grotesque *Nightthoughts of Midwife Walther Vierneissel on His Lost Fetus Ideals*. In 1819 appeared *On the Evergreen of Our Feelings*, partly inspired by the Sophie Paulus affair and, in 1820, the curious example of misguided energy *On the German Compounds*. Influenced by a contemporary language purist, Christian Wolke (who was responsible for the term *Blumine* as a Germanization of the goddess Flora), Jean Paul began to correct his own language, particularly by eliminating the so-called linking *s*, all the more time consuming because of his own fondness for compounds.

The last work published in his lifetime was the collection of prefaces and reviews, together with a postschool to the preschool, the *Little Bookreview*, in 1825. More important were the works published posthumously in 1826: the fragment of autobiography *Self-Life Description* and the also unfinished *Selina; or, on the Immortality of the Soul,* his last variation on that *Vale of Campan* theme that comes more than ever to the fore in the closing stages of his work.

That body of work that can be characterized as religious or spiritual is a very large part of Jean Paul's output, and while it can be explained in different ways, it cannot be explained away. Robert Minder, not one to underestimate the political and with a preference for the skeptical, rightly says: "Il est vrai qu'au dessus de la révolte, il y a toujours chez lui l'union mystique . . . la ferveur religieux prime la passion politique."[9]

Together with *Self-Life Description* and *Selina,* the most important works of the later Bayreuth years are the narratives: *Army Chaplain Schmelzle's Journey to Flätz* and *Dr. Katzenberger's Spa Journey,* both published in 1809, *Life of Fibel,* published in 1812, and the last novel, the unfinished *The Comet,* of which the first two volumes appeared in 1820, the third in 1822.

Schmelzle and *Dr. Katzenberger*

Army Chaplain Schmelzle's Journey to Flätz, a mixture of the satirical and the idyllic, takes the ironic form of Schmelzle's self-defense, in a letter to his friends, against the slanderous rumors of his cowardice. The faint-hearted Attila Schmelzle is an endearing character, representative of all those for whom daily life, from daybreak to nightfall and beyond, is a succession of choices and problems.

The source of Schmelzle's trouble is his fearful imagination, always several stages ahead of himself in anticipated danger, whether he is nervously conversing in the coach with the "very probable harlot," keeping at a safe distance from riverbanks in case he should see somebody fall in, trying to avoid familiar greetings from the jailbirds as he passes the prison windows, or taking precautions against sleepwalking by attaching himself to his wife by a string, which, as he says in his Pooterish manner, "I laughingly refer to as our conjugal bond."

His rebuttal of the charge of cowardice is by way of elaborate explanations for his caution. For example, the fact that he promenades with an umbrella on a sunny day probably seems foolish to those who do not realize that the umbrella serves as a lightning conductor in case of summer storms. In *Schmelzle,* Jean Paul parodies his own parade of learning,

9. Robert Minder, "Le problème de l'existence chez Jean Paul, romancier et visionnaire," *Études Germaniques* 18 (1963): 88.

for that, too, is a further source of worry to Schmelzle, as he reflects on electricity in the atmosphere or is frightened by what he reads about chemistry in Lichtenberg. Jean Paul as narrator obtrudes here more than ever, for in *Schmelzle*, short as it is, he has more footnotes than in any other work. They are numbered at random and with no reference to anything in the text.

Schmelzle is, as well as ironic, idyllic in its domestic setting, although the domesticity, too, has a satirical secondary purpose. Jean Paul is parodying German attitudes when he attributes to Schmelzle violent and visionary dreams of Lutheran proportions, or when he has Schmelzle refer to his Bergelchen as his Teutoberga. (One is reminded of Heinrich von Kleist's *Die Hermannsschlacht*, unfortunately not a parody, in which the bloodthirsty Cherusker addresses Thusnelda, his blonde Germanenweib, as his Thuschen.) Hence the work can also be read as political satire on German pretensions and evasions in the Napoleonic period.

All the same, *Schmelzle* is gently sentimental, whereas the other journey report of that year, *Dr. Katzenberger's Spa Journey*, comes from Jean Paul's vinegar factory and is characterized by a cynicism that many of his contemporaries found distasteful. Katzenberger is a professor of anatomy, author of "De monstris epistola," and a passionate collector of abnormalities. He is father of a normal daughter, Theoda, whose normalcy he blames on his wife. He is a house tyrant and sparing of any outlay of time or money that does not advance his theories or career.

> It was pleasant to see, when any stranger, distinguished neither by learning nor illness, showed no sign of departure, with what capers he attempted to lead him to farewells; how he wound up his watch, sank into silence or into a listening attitude toward a nearby noiseless room, or how he twisted the most innocent movement of the stranger on the sofa into a preliminary of leave-taking, himself jumping to his feet and inquiring whence the hurry. (*W* 11.100)

Katzenberger is about to set off with his daughter to Bad Maulbronn, partly in order to chastise his rival and reviewer, the Spa physician Dr. Strykius, and partly because a friend of his daughter's is shortly expecting a child and he wants to avoid the expense of being godfather. As he also wishes to reduce the expense of the journey, he has advertised for a paying traveling companion. So they are joined by Theudobach von Nieß, who is in fact the writer Theudobach to whose sentimental works — *Dr. Katzenberger* is in part a parody of the sentimental school — Theoda is so passionately attached. The writer, however, is calling himself merely

Nieß. He claims to be a friend of the writer, his secret plan being to arrive incognito in Bad Maulbronn, give readings from his works, and at a suitable moment reveal himself.

During the journey, Nieß talks to Theoda about his writer friend — that is to say, about himself — and arouses her interest and enthusiasm even more. However, when he does arrive in the spa and gives his readings to much acclamation, his plans go awry. A handsome young officer enters at the critical moment (as Jean Paul says, if someone had come onto the scene while Christ was delivering the Sermon on the Mount, everyone would have looked around at the newcomer). The officer's name is Theudobach, and he is an author, albeit of works on fortification. He reaps the rewards, to his own surprise, both of the general acclaim and of Theoda's love, which remains unchanged even after the truth is revealed.

Meanwhile, Katzenberger's plans, too, do not work out as he wished. He does, for the most part, enjoy himself in his own fashion, indulging his interest in all that is supposed to be disgusting. Thus he lectures at table on the act of eating, deriding the illogicality of aversion to spittle, present in everybody's mouth, or of eating snipe but not the excrement of snipe, which he compares to being prepared to eat *brutto* but not *netto*. (Katzenberger is a grotesque "spiritualist." The fascination with the physically disgusting is related to his contempt for the material world, which he likes to abuse in his mind — for example, imagining a world in which people's hair stands on end for love, who go green for shame, or who vomit for joy.)

The course of Katzenberger's feud with Strykius is less successful, and in the end the office of godfather catches up with him, too, as the baby has meanwhile arrived and the father has come to Maulbronn with the invitation. However, this also introduces the happy end. Theoda, accompanied by Theudobach, returns home to be with her friend. Katzenberger stays on to confront Strykius, but before he wreaks final revenge, he is mollified by a gift from Strykius of a six-fingered hand and, when he does return home, he is reconciled to the union of Theoda and Theudobach on learning that on the estate of his future son-in-law there is a cave full of promising bones.

"For the sake of brevity," says Jean Paul in one of the appendixes to *Dr. Katzenberger*, "permit me to expand a little" (*W* 11.321). Even apart from the many "improved worklets" appended or interpolated, *Dr. Katzenberger* is particularly discursive and includes such matters as reflections on the social and political scene at the turn of the century. It is charac-

teristic of Jean Paul generally, and consonant with the "scurrility" of Dr.
Katzenberger in particular, that light is trained on solemn subject matter
in a refracted manner. Thus much of *Dr. Katzenberger* is concerned one
way or another, if only by way of ugliness, with aesthetics — with disquisitions, for example, on the laxative effect of comedy, such that
comedy is in the end the necessary catharsis of tragedy.

Still more dominant in the work, as they are a still more urgent concern in Jean Paul, are the religious themes — God, death, immortality —
and *Dr. Katzenberger* includes both a visionary essay on annihilation and,
as a mock-heroic celebration of immortality, a funeral oration on the resurrection of the transfigured stomach.

Life of Fibel

By contrast with *Dr. Katzenberger*'s digressions and appendixes, *Life of
Fibel* is a more uniform work, even if that can only mean in the case of
Jean Paul a very convoluted uniformity. The occasion of the work was
the detailed and, in Jean Paul's opinion, doubtless all too hagiographical
biographies of Kant and Schiller, which appeared in these years after
their deaths. *Fibel* is a parodistic counterpart, being the mock-heroic biography of Fibel. Fibel is revealed to be the real name of the author of
the Fibel, the German term (a corruption of bible) for a child's first book
or primer — the illustrated ABC with which Jean Paul himself had learned
to read.

Jean Paul presents Fibel's *Bienrodian Primer* as fit for biblical exegesis
or the care of a learned academy, such as the Edinburgh Ossian Society.
His own study of the primer has involved years of research and the collection throughout the countryside (helped by an army of children) of
scattered records that had meanwhile been used for making and mending, wrapping and measuring, for coffee and for fish, for fidibuses and
for paper kites; hence the haphazard chapter headings.

Fibel's work is shown to be inspired. In a dream, he is riding a rooster
that crows like the cock of St. Peter. He obeys the command to pluck a
quill from the rooster and commence to write. In the opinion of his academy commentators, his childhood foreshadows his messianic mission. If
he at first appears simpleminded, then this is no more than the law of
nature — the more blossoms, the less fruit — and of human nature, as witness the oxlike childhood of Aquinas and the mediocre performances of
Swift in Oxford and Leibniz in Leipzig.

If Jean Paul does not stray very far from the story in *Life of Fibel*, this is because the focal point, the primer with its random collection of objects described and depicted in alphabetical sequence, allows him to go off in many different directions, whether in terms of geographical areas or areas of literary genre, discussions of the pre-Homeric and post-Homeric, or conflicting opinions on canon law. Fibel himself is credited with the invention of that favorite punctuation sign of Jean Paul, the proliferating — or one might say, propagating — thought dash. Hence his many Malthusian critics.

And of course, Jean Paul is as obtrusive as ever, as narrator, as the biographer of the Fibel biographers, as a reviewer of Fibel's work (taking exception, for example, to Fibel illustrating X with a slander on the virginal Xantippe: "Xantippe was an arrant whore / X Xs is one hundred and no more"), and as researcher in search of Fibel's present whereabouts in order to finish his story before the next Book Fair. At last he finds him and accepts the parting present of Fibel's dog, Alert, the Pomeranian dog of the real-life Jean Paul. This brings full circle the story of Fibel, which is contained within the framework of his first and second childhoods. For *Life of Fibel* is essentially, once again, an idyll and one that finally shades over into a kind of mysticism. Max Kommerell says of Jean Paul that at the end of his life he became with *Fibel* "perhaps the only genuine mystic" of Germany's classical literature.[10]

According to one of Jean Paul's notes, he intended Fibel as a combination of Wutz and Walt, with a kind of innocent vaingloriousness (if that is what he means by the term *Ehrgeck*) (*H-KA* 1.13.xciii). The first chapters are the idyllic story of Fibel's childhood in his village home, of his parents and his sweetheart Drotta. As always, it is an idyll interspersed with scenes of grotesque realism, as when the coffin is delivered to Fibel's father, old Siegwart, the thrifty bird catcher. He tests it out for size and finds he has been cheated by the carpenter. The dying Siegwart has no more claim to an answer to life's questions than his phlegmatic "that's the way."

The last section, the after chapters, is so strange, says Jean Paul, he wouldn't believe it, if he hadn't written it himself. Jean Paul finally meets Fibel. Having experienced a rebirth at the age of 100, he is now 125 and living among his fruit trees in the company of his many animals, playing his music, and reading his Bible. He is not in flight from life to the afterlife but experiencing eternity's presence in time. So the story comes to rest in the evocation of Fibel's "calm of soul." The last word, however,

---

10. Max Kommerell, *Jean Paul* (Frankfurt, 1967), p. 285.

has to relate to the narrator and be a more restless one: "Then I went on my way down the road."

The Comet

As happens so often, Jean Paul has it both ways in *Fibel*. Fibel is a genuine visionary but also a quixotic fantasist. As such, he is a precursor of Jean Paul's last hero, Nikolaus Marggraf, the protagonist of the last novel, *The Comet*. Of all Jean Paul's novels, this has the most complicated genesis, ideas for it going back as far as 1806, although Jean Paul did not really begin writing it until 1813. On the one hand it was to be, even more than the rest of his work, an autobiography and apologia. "As if *The Comet* were not my own story," he remarked once, although he also said that he had written it several years before, noting the parallel to his own life.[11] But then, he was used to the fact that his art mimicked his life, and vice versa.

For a time he intended to couple *The Comet* with the autobiographical *Self-Life Description*. Yet he also spoke of the novel as if it were, even for him, unusually open and unstructured. It was to be his "opus magnum," his "great comic work," his "purely comic pan theon," a panoramic survey of the world in the form of a thousand and one fooleries. Various vehicles were considered: an angel would come to collect inhabitants for another planet and would choose Jean Paul characters, or alternatively Goethe would spend the money he won on a lottery to engage Jean Paul's characters to people the court at Weimar. Claiming to have been all too regular and orthodox in his writing in the past, Jean Paul says in a letter to Paul Thieriot that this time he would let himself go and finally catch up with his youth in his old age (*H-KA* 1.15.viiiff.).

In reality, *The Comet* has a relatively simple story structure and, to a large extent, a single unifying theme. In the comic hero, with his dreams of nobility and sanctity, Jean Paul is parodying artistic solipsism, both generally in the sense of what Gottfried Keller calls the "irresponsibility of the imagination," and doubtless also with a specific reference to Jean Paul's time and place, to a lack of realism as a tendency in romanticism and as a tradition in Germany.

The hero is Nikolaus Marggraf, from the little German country town of Rome. He is marked by two "medical peculiarities," the twelve pock-

---

11. *Jean Pauls Persönlichkeit, Zeitgenössische Berichte*, ed. Eduard Berend (Munich/Leipzig, 1913), p. 266. Cf. *W* 12.1365ff.

marks on his nose and a kind of halo that sometimes appears above his head, especially when he perspires. His apothecary father, eavesdropping on the confession of his dying Catholic wife, learns that Nikolaus is really the son of a prince. Nikolaus, too, becomes an apothecary — indeed, an alchemist in search of the formula for making diamonds. Diamonds are discovered in the furnace, whether a result of his experiments or a hidden legacy from his mother. This permits him to set off in search of his unknown father. He carries with him the wax bust of the Princess Amanda, with whom he is in love — a love at a very romantic remove: "He could no more have touched her than he could have feathered and fried the dove of the Holy Ghost" (*W* 11.636).

Nikolaus travels in courtly style, of a sort. He acquires a *Residenz*, his Nikolopolis, when he purchases a prefabricated wooden town from traveling Jewish traders. Among his retinue are an army of invalids, a court painter, and a court musician, both nonpracticing. Also along are his Sancho-Panzalike laboratory assistant, Stoeßer Stoß, and the majordomo of his court, the voluble and volatile Peter Worble. And then there is Jean Paul himself. A "Jean Paul" has always wandered in and out of the writings, but he is introduced most corporeally in this last novel.

> When Worble stopped on a hill at the frontier inn for all to have breakfast, he spied on the roadway opposite a lean youth with bare breast and flowing hair and a tablet in his hand, coming at a trot and singing as he went. The fellow also stopped in front of the inn above and gazed down at the new harvest home of poverty. He seemed ever more pleased at the scene and in the end even burst into tears. (*W* 12.832)

They get into conversation about the weather, and the stranger makes an unlikely forecast, which presently proves correct, for he is indeed a weather prophet. (Forecasting was one of Jean Paul's hobbies.) Asked his name, he replies: "Who else should I be but Candidate Richter from Hof in Voigtland?" So Jean Paul enters the story and enters into the employment of Nikolaus as weather official.

They do finally reach the city that is their goal, but here they are enveloped by the "densest fog of the last century," and Nikolaus now finds himself shadowed by a sinister figure, clothed in leather, the lanky, fleshless, colorless Leather Man, the Prince of the World and Wandering Jew, who calls himself Cain and identifies with the devil. He represents destructive reasoning and has thought himself into a state of hatred and hopelessness. In the end, the resourceful Peter Worble hypnotizes

Leather Man into a healing sleep, in which he confesses and repents, if only momentarily.

Here the novel breaks off, and one can only speculate on the ending. A sobering process seems to be going on all the time. Berend believes that a dispelling of fantasy is implicit from the beginning. Others, like Schweikert, stress rather the inevitability of the novel's fragmentariness, once again a born ruin, demonstrating the impossibility of a happy conclusiveness within Jean Paul's terms. It may be too much to find fitness in the accidents of composition. It seems likely that, through figures of mediation like Peter Worble and through the medium of humor, the follies of *The Comet* would be exorcised in the end. From the notes, it appears that Nikolaus and his entourage were to have continued their journey to various symbolic cities — the City of Poets, the City of Scholars, the City of Bigotry — until finally they would find refuge in an inn outside Bayreuth — in fact, in the Rollwenzelei, where Jean Paul was writing the novel.[12] In that sense, admittedly very metaphorical, Jean Paul's characters would come at last to rest.

Even apart from his age and ailing health at the time he wrote *The Comet*, Jean Paul always found it hard to contain the material of his imagination and to bring his work to some kind of conclusion. In *The Comet* as in all Jean Paul's novels, there are a score of passages peripheral to the story, although central to Jean Paul's concerns. There is the visionary *Dream upon the All*, for example, known in English through De Quincey's translation. There are the passages of social and political comment, like the attack on censorship or the sermon that Jean Paul, in the person of theology candidate Richter, preaches on the death of a maidservant, who has slaved for forty years without respite and without even escape into dream. This passage is at once sentimental and savage, a striking example of *saeva indignatio*. Even when he still had hopes of completing *The Comet*, Jean Paul seems to have despaired of finding sufficient room within it. Even the foreword to *The Comet* is both the foreword to that work (among other things, relating the title to the erratic character and career of the hero) and also a foreword to his next and "last" comic work. This last work was to be itself but an infinite digression, a work that could more justly be called a comet, hyperbolically extending into eternity. This would be his "paper kite," which (thereby giving us one way of defining the purpose of his art) he would finally let fly "for the fun of it, for

12. Cf. *H-KA* 1.15.liiff.; Schweikert, *Jean Paul*, p. 59.

the sake of scientific experiment, and as a lightning conductor" (*W* 11.569f.).

But Jean Paul did not live to publish "Paper Kite," and *The Comet* remained unfinished. Painful illness and his rapidly failing eyesight handicapped him, and although he remained active almost to the end, his energies were either dissipated in detail work of all sorts or, insofar as they were concentrated, concentrated rather on *Selina* and on the ever-present problems of his religious beliefs. These latter were now more pressing than ever after several deaths in his circle, particularly the death of his only son, Max, in 1821 and of Heinrich Voß in the following year.

If it is natural enough that these events made Jean Paul more religious, it is characteristic of him that they also made him more than ever opposed to religious excesses. He had observed in his son the consequences of what he regarded as an unhealthy and hysterical religiosity, which he therefore proceeded to attack in one of his last works, *Over-Christianity*. Like the main religious work of his last years, *Selina*, this was not published until after his death. He died on 14 November 1825. The memorial address was delivered by another writer of republican sympathies (*pace* Heine) Ludwig Börne and included the prophecy, which must have been quoted in every Jean Paul study since then: "but he stands patiently at the gate of the twentieth century and waits with a smile for his sluggish countrymen to follow."[13] Soon the image will apply to the twenty-first century. Jean Paul's old-fashioned modernity is doubly demanding, and it can hardly be said that the public has caught up with him even now.

13. Ludwig Börne, "Denkrede auf Jean Paul," *Iris*, no. 241, 4 December 1825.

¿ *JEAN PAUL'S*

Narrative Practice

THE FIRST THING THAT STRIKES ONE ABOUT JEAN PAUL'S manner of narration is how mannered it is. In the preface to *Clavis Fichtiana*, he suggests that ever since the *Xenien*, the satirical verses of Goethe and Schiller to which he so much took exception, we have become bad mannered. If we want to be rude, at least we should be rude with rhetoric, he says, adding that he himself uses such figures as *asteismus, charientismus, diasyrmus*. In a letter to Christian Otto, he claimed that for any author the material is no more than a vehicle to talk about everything else. Years later, he confessed to Friedrich Oertel that he hated all storytelling, even in a novel, unless the story became new for the teller himself "through ten thousand reflections and conceits" (*H-KA* 3.1.375; 3.3.177).

In the preface to *Siebenkäs* he apologizes to those readers of his first opus, who had been unable to say what it was they were reading, an epic poem or a ready reckoner, a kind of dictionary or a work on heraldry. Not that Jean Paul does not tell stories. Respect for the story is basic to his ethics and aesthetics. In that same first novel, we read that education begins with stories, stories from natural history and stories from the story that is human history, best understood by way of biography. For "only as an *I*" can the truth of the world be imaginatively understood (*W* 1.125; 8.778ff., 782). He is forever defending the individual and the particular (and his particularism was to make him heretical vis-à-vis many orthodoxies) against the abstract and the universal. He finds the universal in the particular, rather than vice versa. He quotes Plotinus or Scaliger to the effect that the greater understanding is by the lower in station of the higher, and he quotes the theologians who say that men comprehend the angels, but angels do not comprehend men (*W* 7.465).

Yet it is remarkable that when Jean Paul, after a lifetime of storytelling of the most narrator-intrusive kind, came in the end to write his own story, his letters are full of dispirited reference to the task. It gave him little pleasure; since it was all there, there was nothing to make up. He was averse to stories unadulterated by comedy or sentiment, and to nothing was he so indifferent as to himself (*H-KA* 3.7.238; 3.8.135).

This indifference does not conflict with, is rather a logical consequence of, Jean Paul's preference for self-parading narration. Autobiography was the one form that could not be a vehicle for the pretended interplay of art and life, which he otherwise enjoyed and exploited. In *Palingeneses*, "Jean Paul" goes to Bayreuth, staying where Siebenkäs and Leibgeber had lodged, and commenting that he likes this introduction of his books into his life and likes to direct and act at the same time (*W* 8.776).

The actual entry onto the stage of a Jean Paul is only the most obvious element in the obtrusive narrative method, which is as characteristic of Jean Paul as it is of comic writing, generally. Jean Paul says "You will find the oftener *I* in all comic authors" (*H-KA* 3.3.208). From the beginning, this *I* intrudes on the reader. He writes around the reader at such length and will so enmesh him, says the narrator in *The Invisible Lodge*, that he can pull him in any direction he pleases. In Jean Paul's jotter notes of the same time, we find him reminding himself that he "must express many false conjectures in order to confuse the reader" (*W* 1.37; *H-KA* 1.2.xxii).

Even before that, he introduced himself to the reading public in a manner that illustrates the way in which he turns the facts of life to fictional account. In one of his periods of depression at the end of the 1780s, he consulted his medical student friend, Johann Hermann, who told him he was a hypochondriac. Thereupon, Jean Paul presented himself in the role, such a severe hypochondriac that he believed himself dead (*H-KA* 2.3.xviiif.). From then on, the figure of Jean Paul appears in most of his major works.

A particularly elaborate example is *Titan*, in which "Jean Paul" is a court official, maintaining a network of spies throughout the cities and courts of Germany, whose dispatches provide him with the material for his story. The character Jean Paul complains bitterly at the disadvantages of this kind of storytelling. If he does not have the trouble of inventing his material, all the more does he have to so cloak and cipher it that it retains a masonic mysteriousness, the aura of an invisible church. Above all, he has to cope with a wealth and weight of material, particularly from those, like his ambassador in Hohenfließ, Hafenreffer, who are excessively scrupulous and report in the pettiest detail.

> One does not hold a post like mine just for the sport of it: the whole legation writing-and-reading society addresses letters and writes to me; both *chiffre banal* and *chiffre déchiffrant* are in my hands, and I appear to know the ropes. Indescribable is what I learn — were I to hatch, feed, and reel off the whole silkworm cocoonery of new supplements dispatched to me in strong bagfuls each mail day by the *corps diplomatique*, man could not read nor horse pull it. Nay (and to use a different metaphor), the biographical timber dumped into the rivers Elbe or Saale or the Danube up there by my rafting inspectorate has risen to such a pile in my carpenter's yard that I could not use it up, even supposing I were to continue with my ships of fools, fancy dress ballrooms, and magic castles day and night, year in and year out, and went neither dancing nor riding, nor ever talked or sneezed. . . . Verily, often enough when I compare my ovary with many another roe, it is with a certain vexation that I must put the question why one man who for lack of time and space cannot deliver, should be thus burdened, while another one barely lays and hatches a wind egg. (*W* 5.61ff.)

The weight of material and the endless stream of reports are not only elements of Jean Paul's comedy. They also relate to his social, political, and religious attitudes and to his peculiarly epic view of life, which involve a championing of details over design, of matter over form, even of quantity over quality. He distrusted uniformity and accepted open-endedness or the fact that the work, like life, will end when it happens to end.[1]

The passage quoted continues in similar vein for several pages and then concludes:

---

1. Cf. Timothy J. Casey, "Digressions for Future Instalments: Some Reflections on Jean Paul's Epic Outlook," *Modern Language Review* 85, 4 (1990), pp. 866–78.

Enough! This discursive inaugural program was somewhat lengthy, but so was the celebratory period; the longer St. John's Day lasts in a country, the longer lasts its St. Thomas's Night. — And now let us all together skip into the book, into this gratuitous ball of the world — myself ahead, leading the dance, and the readers galloping after in their Highland fling —, so that to the peal of the baptismal and funeral bells of the Chinese house of the universe — sung to by the singing school of the Muses — and played to by Phoebus's lyre — we shall merrily dance from tome to tome — from cycle to cycle — from one digression to another — from one dash to the next — until either the work comes to an end or the workman or both!

In the passage headed "On Egoism" in *The Parson in Jubilee*, Jean Paul expounds his "higher comparative anatomy," describing his translocations and transfigurations as he tries out different civilizations and centuries, electing himself Holy Roman Emperor or appointing himself governor of the Bastille, becoming a leper, a knight, a negro, a cardinal, the Wandering Jew. The end effect is "humility and justice," the lessons of resemblances, although these are rarely admitted — just as the butterfly, the chrysalis, and the caterpillar, could they consider the matter, would as little admit their relationship as would the three estates (*W* 7.468f.).

Jean Paul rings the changes on this role playing in all his novels, culminating in the last, *The Comet*. This novel is indeed about the imagination: the quixotic apothecary, Nikolaus, has inherited from his mother the fertile imagination Jean Paul likes to attribute to Catholics, particularly to Catholic saints. Nikolaus has the rare gift of "being many," and can be a second Frederick the Second, or a concert pianist, or simply a native speaker of French, depending on what books he is reading. His Kantian categories are expanded, for he inhabits the vast spaces of distance, the rich Indias of past and future, so many square miles greater than the proximate and present.

The narrator would have us accept the truth of this imagination. At one stage of the novel, when Nikolaus is in the seventh heaven of love, the narrator, coming back to the garden in Bayreuth where he is writing the story, says that if he were to doubt such happiness all he need do is listen in to the little girls playing their make-believe game beside him. The narrator of *The Comet* also identifies with the hero's lively and imaginative companion, Peter Worble, the Polincinello and Bajazzo, Pickelhering and Buffo, who was "born to be a J.P." (a Jean Potage, Jack Pudding, John Bull). But the focus of the novel is Nikolaus himself, and the passage on the hero's imagination concludes: "To myself as epic histor-

ian—for what is history other than an epic in prose—Nikolaus' multi-
and magni-mannery most suits my book, for if in a heroic poem, like the
Homeric one, every science must be found, it is a great help if they all
reside in the hero himself" (*W* 11.601ff., 12.738, 963).

Jean Paul makes it clear that he is going to tell his stories at great
length. Judged by the criteria of the so-called epic law—epic lingering
and epic breadth—Jean Paul is the most epic of writers. In *Fledgling
Years*, he announces his intention of holding lectures at the next Leipzig
Fair on the reasons why the epic is "endlessly long" and the epic day like
an Imperial Diet. In one of the several prefaces to his first novel, he pro-
fesses to abhor what he calls the French manner of narration and says, as
might Thomas Mann, that only the long drawn out is interesting. The
death of a mouse, says the narrator in *Hesperus*, is more interesting than
the defeat of an army "because I relate it at length"(*W* 4.924f.; 1.29, 561).

Inevitably, he cites Cicero, who, when asked which of Demosthenes'
speeches was the best, answered: the longest. This again is a matter of
principle for Jean Paul, for whom quantity itself is qualitative. The more
the better, seems to be his motto, and in *The Invisible Lodge* he advises the
tutor of his future children: never speak to them shortly and generally,
rather sensually and in detail (*H-KA* 3.1.147; *W* 1.127).

But of course he also means the more the merrier, and like the role
playing, the prolixity is incorporated into the comedy of narrative. In the
preface to *Siebenkäs*, the narrator, in order to enjoy the company of his
namesake Johanne Pauline, must first put her father to sleep—as he is
well able to do with "lengthily stylized holding forth." Sometimes he pro-
fesses to be annoyed, as narrator, over so many characters—who appear,
only to disappear; more often, he must remind the reader, perhaps in
footnotes, who is who; or he complains about his German readers, who,
from whatever disease or disability, cannot be trusted to remember from
one chapter to the next. In a more hopeful moment, with a kind of per-
verse logic: "The reader will probably remember, or at least have forgotten that . . ." (*W* 1.607f., 153, 164; 12.981).

Occasionally, Jean Paul has to confess defeat, himself. In *Dr. Katzenberger*, he makes a remark he says he has read elsewhere in his writings,
although he cannot remember where: he cannot be expected to retain
everything from such a volume of work, which in any case he rarely
reads, except when he writes it—although he has read *Hesperus* three
times, "twice in the eighteenth century and once in the nineteenth." In
Dr. Katzenberger, he divides all readers into two classes. Some are valedictory readers, frog eaters, interested only in the tail end, staying with

the philosophizing narrator only as long as he is storytelling, as North Americans listen to the sermon only as long as the brandy lasts. These epilogists are bid begone, and the narrator remains with the second class of reader, "my own people, people of a certain cast of mind, whom I draw behind me on the long lead of love" (*W* 11.104f., 214f.).

Jean Paul insists therefore on material as diverse and an overview as total as may be. That is not to say that a sense of design and direction is lacking. He said himself to Thieriot: "I have more plan and purpose in my work than people usually believe."[2] But comprehensiveness takes priority over comprehensibility; and life, as he sees it — multifaceted and multicolored, a piecemeal patchwork — is expressed in such favorite Jean Paul terms as "crazy" (*toll*) or, as in a passage translated below, in such objects as the quodlibet drawing Walt buys for Vult in *Fledgling Years* (*W* 4.877). The typical Jean Paul narration is punctuated by lists of people, places, and things, introduced in a variety of ingenious ways, and often held together by no more than his most characteristic punctuation mark, the dash.

In Jean Paul's *Biographical Entertainments*, the narrator sits in a closed carriage and, just as he used to guess where he was when he was carried around with his eyes closed as a child, imagines all those persons outside, whose paths might chance to cross his own (*W* 7.278ff.). In *Fledgling Years*, we find the hero sitting in the inn "in that epic mood in which he regards the comings and goings." The following chapter, headed "Life" and recounting Walt's next journey (in Jean Paul, the journey motif is less the romantic one of homesickness than one of observation and incident), illustrates the way in which Jean Paul puts order and form second, the first concern being to include all — and all equally. Hence the paratactic manner in which paragraphs follow on one another: "He saw ... He heard ... He went ... He came to ... He met. ..." In the same chapter, in the paragraph beginning "The magic lantern of life," the elements are again held together by little more than punctuation dashes (*W* 4.870, 874ff.).

The motto (taken from his own earlier *Selection from the Devil's Papers*) that Jean Paul chose to place at the beginning of his first novel is the aphorism that, using printers' terminology, one might translate: "Man is the great em rule in the book of nature." What is called in German the thought dash is the most characteristic symbol of Jean Paul's

2. *Jean Paul's Persönlichkeit, Zeitgenössische Berichte*, ed. Eduard Berend (Munich/Leipzig, 1913), pp. 19f.

epic syntax. The aphorism is also characteristically bookish. The *I* that Jean Paul constantly parades is, in the first place, the book maker. The printer in *The Parson in Jubilee* carries in his pocket, as well as a quarter pound of punctuation dashes, a particularly large quantity of capital *R*s, that being Jean Paul's initial — although of course the narrator, in Jean Paul fashion, has several other associations and reflections in train: the months without *R*, the passage without *R* in Barthold Brockes's *Earthly Contentment in God*, descriptive of calm after the storm, and still more obscurely, the poem "L'R sbandita" by the neapolitan Dominican Vincente Cardone.

The first foreword to *Levana*, particularly confusing in that the characters pass in and out of each other's dreams, is a disquisition on errata and on the many people who were responsible for them, not only author and printer, but transcriber and corrector, to say nothing of readers' own mistakes and of the wayward heavenly powers of various patrons: St. Luke or St. Catherine, Apollo or Thot, the Egyptian god of the alphabet (*W* 7.528f.; 10.1285ff.).

The joyful, sorrowful, and glorious mysteries of the writing passion are a major Jean Paul theme. When death comes to call him from his writing desk, he says in *The Parson in Jubilee*, he will plead for time for one more sequel. Death may find him replete with life, but not with writing. When all else fails, his writing finger will retain its *motus vitales*, like the little finger that was all of Atys that Jupiter was prepared to revive. The most endearing portrayal of the joys of authorship is in *Life of Fibel*. Describing Fibel's enthusiasm over his first publication, Jean Paul remarks that the thrill of seeing one's efforts in print for the first time is difficult to convey to those who have never had even a mourning card printed (*W* 7.458; 11.461).

Given Jean Paul's emphasis on the narrator and the narrative framework, the forewords and appendixes are often a major and sometimes the choicest part of Jean Paul's works. One of his most felicitous shorter works is *History of My Preface to the Second Edition of Quintus Fixlein*, an elaborate account of the reasons that prevented Jean Paul from writing a preface. Forewords are essentially the author's apologia, the *prodromus galeatus*, as he calls it in the case of *The Parson in Jubilee*. He obviously enjoys best arming himself and dressing up for this role. In the prefaces, the reader is confronted by the author in person who, in his multiplicity of roles, personifies man. Hence it is, as we read in the "Preface to Prefaces" in *The Secret Lament*, that, while light is created by the work on the first day, the preface is created on the last day, the author coming in at the end like a Roman general on his chariot—although he is also the grumbling mob at his feet and the servant whose office it is to repeat: "remember, thou art but man" (*W* 8.1085).

In his last novel, Jean Paul repeats that authors write the preface last. This time he refers to this fact as a happy conjunction of interest between authors and readers. For readers make a beeline for the story and its outcome, so that when they come to the end of the story, they will surely run into the narrator as he writes the preface. With the same kind of convolution, the foreword to *Jean Paul's Biographical Entertainments* begins with the sentence: "I am writing this foreword so that the reader doesn't mistake the first chapter for it and skip that instead of this" (*W* 11.656ff.; 7.265).

But important as are forewords and appendixes in Jean Paul, they are only a fraction of the material brought about by his policy of digression. In the foreword to the appendix (!) to *Jean Paul's Biographical Entertainments*, Jean Paul is accused of being unable to narrate in a straightforward manner, of interposing interminable sermons before the audience reaches the sacred music, and of constantly changing course so that his delicate readers, after being immersed in steam baths of sentiment, are plunged into cold baths of satire. The court is petitioned to oblige him to narrate without digression, but the petition fails—not unnaturally, since Jean Paul himself appears for the petitioning readers, like the thrifty Swiss farmer who was defendant in a civil action but was so busy haymaking that he requested the plaintiff to represent him.

In his own defense, Jean Paul points out that his readers are not obliged to read his digressions, which are signposted throughout. He questions the plaintiffs' credentials, relating the office of reader to that of lector in the Greek Church, and is doubtful if his readers are validly ordained. Besides, his work is like life itself, with its beautiful pattern of alternating black and white, or like the Koran, which, because the angel was dictating too quickly, is acknowledged to be interspersed with passages inspired by the devil. Playing the roles of litigant, lawyer, and judge simultaneously, Jean Paul defends his work as *simultaneum* and himself as a College of Cardinals, acting quite as legally as did the German Emperor, who as Hungarian King made war against himself as Austrian Duke, while preserving his imperial neutrality (*W* 7.347ff.).

There are many other hardly less elaborate examples of Jean Paul's defense of his method and of digression, generally. In the *Palingeneses*, he dilates on the advantages of slow occidental justice, likening it to the River Seine, meandering over fifteen miles to cover the quarter mile through Paris, to the great benefit of local inhabitants. Or it is like Dr. Radcliffe, who wisely evaded his hypochondriac patient, so that the latter was cured by the time he caught up with him. In Jean Paul's last novel, the narrator congratulates himself on having introduced a character without beating about the bush, but the self-congratulation takes the form of a digression on the crablike procedures of writers, all too prone, like Walter Scott, to the preambles of prehistory. Even historians, like Thucydides, take an erratic to-and-fro course. Thus, as the narrator reflects, the "Blücher forward" is forever threatened by the "Scott retreat." One is hardly surprised to learn that the last article submitted to press by Jean Paul bears the title *Digression for Future Instalments* (*W* 8.895; 12.994ff., *H-KA* 1.18.xxxviii).

But then, references to digressions in Jean Paul are really references *passim*. His preference is for the proliferating detail that reflects life itself. Life consists of many bagatelles, says the narrator in *Outing of Headmaster Florian Fälbel*, and greatness is a great number of smallnesses. His work is a collection of "notions." If he left them out, he says in the preface to *Hesperus*, there would be little left of the work but the binding. In his passion for similes and associations, Jean Paul vowed to write uninterruptedly for forty years, marrying ideas day in day out, as intertwined and within forbidden degrees of kindred as European royalty (*W* 7.232; 1.483; 8.1066f.).

It need hardly be said that the associations are often farfetched, dragged in by the hair, like those associations occasioned by the incident in *The Comet*, where Nikolaus is lifted by the hair, reminding the narrator of fish dangling from a line, criminals from the rope, Loyola's levitations, Mohammed's coffin. In the frivolous eighteenth century, double meanings came particularly readily to mind, Jean Paul remarks in *Explanation of the Woodcuts*, recalling that he once invited a lively gentleman of his acquaintance to point out a single piece of furniture in his room that did not remind him of something else, and that he was unable to do so.

In the sexual sphere, Jean Paul is proper to the point of prudery. But he gave offense to many, including Queen Luise, otherwise his admirer, by his juxtaposition of the sacred and the profane — all the more frequent since so much of his material came from the theological area (*W* 11.600; 8.669f; *H-KA* 1.17.xxxvii). Thus he refers to the notorious whores in Christ's family tree. Or in speaking of the helpfulness of the schoolmaster in *Fibel*, he says that he was one who, like Simon, would willingly help another to carry the cross as long the latter was the one to be crucified. In *Titan*, the resemblance between Albano's mother and Linda is said to be a veritable *homoousion*, rather than a mere *homoiousian*. Or he speaks of the minister able to preach a sermon of the warmest kind without effecting any change in himself — like God, according to the philosophers, in the act of creation.

Jean Paul explains his own mixture of styles in terms of his two natures, divine and human. And when, much to his annoyance, the pirated anthology of extracts from his works appeared under the title "Jean Paul's Spirit," he referred to it as the Son that had proceeded from Himself (*W* 7.134; 11.442; 6.703; 7.391; 8.563; 10.1295). He was partial to the kind of religious references that Italy in particular provided. Among the more frequent are references to the liquefaction of the blood of San Gennaro in Naples and to the *casa santa*, the Blessed Virgin's home in Nazareth, flown in to its present site in Loreto. From theological lexica he extracted such information as the teaching of the Church Fathers that women, on the Last Day, would arise as men.

Often, the associations from whatever sphere are, for modern readers anyway, rather too obscure. When Dr. Fenk expounds in *The Invisible Lodge* on the soul-reflecting physiognomy of the different sorts and sizes of kitchen pots, one is supposed to recognize references not only to Lavater but to the practice of the young Melanchthon of trying out his preaching before an audience of kitchen utensils (*W* 3.521; 12.718, 874; 3.472f.; 1.392). From the beginning, Jean Paul collected out of the way "facts": that Louis XIV was "born dentated"; or that by Royal Danish Decree of 1707, in order to prevent depopulation, the women in Iceland were allowed six illegitimate children each. In an early letter to Christian Oerthel he dilates on a work by J. Christian Henke, "Newly Discovered Secrets Regarding the Propagation of Man," according to which the right testicle produces males and the left, females. He considered the constitutional problems raised, how society itself might be manipulated by gentle pressure on the proper testicle at the proper time, and how the discovery might help to liberate women from their Babylonian captivity (*W* 4.872; 7.456; *H-KA* 3.1. 213ff.).

This proliferation of associations and ideas, notions and conceits, facts and figures as diverse and disparate as possible, was not only Jean Paul's constant practice, he stubbornly defended it as a method, as opposed to a method too concerned with connections and ending with more mortar than bricks. So one might relate to Jean Paul himself the passage in *Hesperus*, where Viktor, in his funeral oration over himself, recalls his variety of interests and says: "Who sought less than he that strict connection of ideas that misleads the German into cementing good ones with bad ones and using more mortar than blocks?" (*W* 2.937f.). It was Jean Paul's implicit contention throughout that this epic method, meandering and lingering, with its byways of pointillistic detail and its magpie acquisitiveness and inquisitiveness, best represents life — what Siebenkäs calls "our mosaic of minutes and specks, of drops and points and vapors." In the same novel, the narrator is critical of his novelist colleagues, with their dramatic presentation of sudden ruptures and reconciliations, which, he claims, is less true to nature and life than his own slow circumlocutions.

Throughout Jean Paul there is a mistrust not only of the simple story line but of any single-mindedness that misrepresents life. Life is characterized by "a lack of *unisono*," however regrettable it might be that we do not all live and die uniformly. The sort of allusions and analogies Jean Paul tends to favor suggests the variety of life patterns, like the Catholic rosary ritual with its Joyful, Sorrowful and Glorious mysteries (*W* 3.107, 339f., 445f., 152). His passion is for comprehensiveness. If only he could learn all languages and all sciences, he says in an early letter, in which he confesses a preference for total tolerance and a reluctance to dismiss anything as nonsense. The most useful book, he declares, would be one that showed the sense of all nonsense (*H-KA* 3.1.297).

Jean Paul put his trust in this variety and totality, and his favored heroes are those who do the same. After voicing his depression of the moment, Siebenkäs adds: "Yet do not think that I say, because total eclipse is on me, it is also in America; or that I believe, because snowflakes fall on my nose, that winter has set in on the Gold Coast. Life is beautiful and warm, and even mine was once." The proliferation of ideas, notions, and conceits are a matter not only of technique but of optimistic attitude. Like all such Jean Paul heroes Siebenkäs marvels at the inexhaustibility of the mind. Not only will something occur to Siebenkäs, he knows beforehand that it will. And when he is miserable, he says: "I wonder what help I will think of now, for one will certainly occur to me, as surely as I accommodate four brain chambers" (*W* 3.352, 209, 81).

Epic variety and variability, as not only the spice of life but as the only experience appropriate to the human being, are particularly emphasized in *Siebenkäs*. "Sleep, riches, and health are only enjoyed when they are interrupted," says the narrator. And of Siebenkäs we read that he leaves a company in order to join it again. In general, he practices the art of interrupting his pleasures in order to savor them, as Montaigne had himself roused from sleep in order to experience it. The emphasis is on the deliberate practice of an art. The reflections of Siebenkäs on the human need for paragraph division, for intervals of sleep and death — as the light of solar systems needs the deserts of darkness between — these reflections are introduced with the remark: "He sought to dispel the melancholy in his breast with philosophic observations" (*W* 3.256, 264, 266).

Jean Paul often refers to his own mixture of moods and modes and to his preference for the shifting perspective. In this connection, the most famous passage is a paragraph in *Billet to My Friends* (the first publication he issued under his own full name), which appears "instead of a foreword" to *Quintus Fixlein*, describing the three ways of becoming, not happy, but happier:

> I could never detect more than three roads to being happier (not happy). The first one, which rises, is: surging high enough above life's clouds to behold from afar the whole external world, with its pitfalls, charnel houses, and storm conductors spread out below one's feet like a dwindled, little, child's garden. — The second one is: dropping straight down into that little garden and nestling so snugly in a furrow there that, again peeping from one's cozy nest, one will not set eyes on pitfalls, charnel houses, and rods, but only spikes of corn, each of them being tree, umbrella, and sunshade in one to the fledgling. — And lastly, the third one — which I consider the most arduous one and the wisest — is to alternate the other two (*W* 7.10f.).

If, as Jean Paul went on to suggest, the first way is too much for most and the second too little for some, his own preference is clearly for the mode that alternates between the faraway and the close at hand, the macrocosmic and the microscopic. The mode that, as the passage quoted implies, best reflects life as it is, its sunshine and its shadow. The most striking term in the passage is the comparative "happier," which nowadays reminds one most of Kafka and his variations on all those comparatives — which throughout his work, up to the "higher salvation" of the mouse Josefine, take the place of the positive and, under the appearance of improving matters, in reality relativize what would otherwise be absolute.

In Jean Paul the sentiment is different, even where the scene is the same. In *Siebenkäs*, there is a Kafkaesque passage on the indefinite postponements of the law and on the advocates who see to it that the action never ends and who forever present petitions preventing one another from coming to a conclusion. In the Jean Paul text there is, as well as satire, also implied approval. The lawyers behave like Simonides, who, on being asked by the tyrant Hieron of Syracus what God is, asked for a day to think it over, and then for another, and another, and another. In every sphere of work and life, Jean Paul seems to prefer the rambling epic to dramatic definitiveness. An interpolated passage in *Siebenkäs* on the consolations of philosophy is typical. We should not expect sudden and radical transformations from philosophy. It is enough if it transforms the total mourning of the soul into half mourning. It is enough if we can say of our philosophy: without it the pain would be greater (*W* 3.214f., 199).

So although Jean Paul is — at any rate, he almost stridently claimed to be — an optimistic writer, it is never a matter of happy ends. Rather, as in *Siebenkäs* itself, it is a matter of happier ends. The history of the world is an unfinished novel, Jean Paul says in the preamble introducing his first novel, *The Invisible Lodge*. In the same work, he takes leave of one of his characters with the remark: "We shall not hear of her again, and so it will continue throughout the book, which, like life, is full of scenes that do not reappear" (*W* 1.13, 145).

Jean Paul specifically departs from Walter Scott's principle: "It is a part of the author's duty to account for everything." This was precluded by the very ambition to follow every linking idea and to be as comprehensive as possible, which necessarily resulted in loose ends. In *Preschool of Aesthetics*, Jean Paul talks of the danger for the writer of motivating too much, which would only serve to remind the reader of the writer's arbitrary despotism. The reader would demand an ancestor to every motivation, and the writer would have to go back through all eternity *a parte ante* (a favorite phrase of Jean Paul's, referring to past eternity, as opposed to the coming eternity of *a parte post*). As a creator, the writer should, says Jean Paul, like God himself, be answerable to none (*W* 9.246).

Jean Paul novels can only be open-ended. Some, of course, are simply uncompleted, like his first, the born ruin, although it is brought to a kind of conclusion in *Hesperus*. "At rest" are the last words of that novel, the words on the tombstone of Horion, and they have a finality with respect to his story. But the focal figure of *Hesperus* is not Horion but Viktor, and if there is any coming to rest in *Hesperus* or anywhere else in Jean Paul's work, it is in the only form in which Viktor himself can find it: "Peace! Neither joy nor pain can give that, only hope alone" (*W* 2.1235).

Perhaps the best example of not being able to finish, or rather of finishing with variations on the theme of not being able to finish, is the work that, on the face of it, seems not only untroubled but to come indeed to a happy end: *The Parson in Jubilee.* "Now the reader sits in front of the completed Sunday piece," says the narrator, observing that, having brought his characters to their resting place, he really now should get up and go. But he finds himself unable to do so and lingers on as a guest, much troubled by thoughts of the impermanence of joy and fearing that, if he stays long enough, he will end with corpses on his hands. In the end, he takes refuge, as Jean Paul so often does, in the appendix, or rather — in this case — in what is called "Appendix of the appendix; or, My Christmas Night." Here, he steps outside the story and out of his role as narrator, ending with the twin eternities of nostalgia for the past and hope for the future, rather than with any conclusion within the fictive present (*W* 7.540ff.).

"Nobody who has a system," said Jean Paul, "thinks freely any more." For his heroes he chose examples of what he called "quicksilver man," who carries little weight with the leaden philistines of Krehwinkel — although in reality (for after all, he tells us, the weight of lead is only 11,352 as against the 13,568 of quicksilver), weightier than they. A wild hero like Vult claims that man, made in the image of God, should aspire to be a "little own-causelet" (*H-KA* 2.5.64; *W* 8.1090; 4.999). These restlessly creative heroes obviously suit the wayward course of events — but then, nothing is so consistent in Jean Paul as the multiplicity and contradictoriness conveyed in his mixed styles, mixed characters, and mixed-up plots. His practice seems to accord with the view of man he put forward in the 1781 essay *Something Concerning Man:* "We are able to be everything, but not to be anything completely or for long; we live on change" (*H-KA* 2.1.182).

JEAN PAUL'S

Philosophy and Politics

OVER THE YEARS, JEAN PAUL'S INTERPRETERS HAVE held widely differing views on the question of his philosophy and politics. His work is a record of mixed feelings, and readers can choose between a bewildering number of dicta and contradicta, so that it can seem to be revolution art or restoration art. That is not to say that the various facets cannot be reconciled. He represents the eighteenth century not least in the complementary coexistence of Enlightenment and Sentiment.

A large part of his attraction lies in the self-conscious parading of himself and his century, at once committed to and parodying its pedagogical ideals. Typical is the way he refers in his first novel to one of the characters getting a fright; and then adding that, to be sure, many people got a fright in the eighteenth century: the Jesuits, the aristocrats, Voltaire. He parodies in text and learned footnotes the search for scientific certainties. He considers, for example, the dating of the world's birth, whether it began on 20 March — as Lipsius, the historiographer of Philip II, maintained — or on the Forenoon of 22 October — as claimed by Petavius in "De doctrina temporum." Side-by-side with the mockery is the commitment to ideals of intellectual and moral enlightenment — just as

Jean Paul's novels are all novels of development, of the apsis line of the hero's moral being, as it is called in *Titan* (*W* 1.166; 5.101; 6.1071; 5.234).

In an early fragment, probably dating from 1781, Jean Paul welcomes the waning of superstition and the free thinking of the eighteenth century. It is a striking feature of his work that he so often, through sympathetic characters, flirts with atheism but never with orthodoxy. He would rather be an atheist than an "enthusiast," he wrote in his diary, and expresses the same sentiment in his essay *Comparison of Atheism and Fanaticism*. It is an essay in the spirit more of Voltaire than of Rousseau, essentially a defense of enlightenment against the religious fanaticism that makes a hell of this world for the sake of a future heaven. "The brightness of the Enlightenment banishes this creature of darkness." (*H-KA* 2.1.157, 279; 1.18.40ff.).

It is true that these are early references, but Jean Paul remained a rationalist to the end, as he was religious from the beginning. He had much to find fault with in the Enlightenment for its lack of religious sentiment, but he had no use for what he saw as a resurgence of religious obscurantism. In one of his last letters, he deplores the "newest age, which brings us, instead of light, a chaotic infusion of Indian-poetic-mystical-supercredulous Christianity." When Johann Kanne, after visiting Jean Paul in 1823, asserted that Jean Paul would yet become converted, Jean Paul commented that, on the contrary, he was becoming less orthodox with age.[1] He had a horror of Protestant orthodoxy, not to say of Catholicism, and the bitterest blow was the religious melancholy of his son Max, whom he had tried to influence by way of models – Lessing, Kant, Jacobi, Hamann, Herder – who represented the kind of religion and the kind of enlightenment he favored.

At the same time, Jean Paul was out of sympathy with the Enlightenment as represented by Friedrich Nicolai. He could never resist caricaturing the "Nicolaites" and the organ of the Berlin Enlightenment, the *New Universal German Library*. Jean Paul opposed the Berlin Enlightenment in the name of his religion, although in fact they had much in common – not just because Jean Paul was "enlightened," but because the Enlightenment in Germany, less antireligious than in France and more

---

1. *H-KA* 3.8.225, 232f. On the question of Jean Paul's theology, see T. J. Casey, "Der tolle Mensch in der Pfarrhausstube. Jean Pauls Stellung zu der Gretchenfrage und seine Auseinandersetzung mit der Theologie," in *Die deutsche literarische Romantik und die Wissenschaften*, ed. Nicholas Saul and Eda Sagarra (Munich, 1990).

theistic than in England, was so much a matter of religious concerns. This is evident in the *New Universal German Library,* itself, and even more so in Nicolai's own *Sebaldus Nothanker.*

The hero of that novel is a pastor, and everything he stands for, all the theses of the work — and it is very much a thesis novel — are such as might have been formulated, however different the tone, by Jean Paul himself. Nothanker's struggle is against the orthodox clergy, with their dogma of eternal punishment, which "teaches children not to sympathize with the damned," and with the Pietists, for whom human nature is depraved. Nothanker prefers atheism to such a God. It might be Jean Paul himself, when Nothanker says: "I pray the Our Father, and there is nothing there about a covenant of blood and *sola gratia.*"[2] Nothanker's humanitarianism is regarded as heresy. He is lukewarm on the priority of the Bible and Revelation. Not without some reason, the Lutheran pastor accuses him of not being Lutheran at all, but Pelagian. During all of this, Nicolai's hero is almost a model of Jean Paul's thinking on these subjects, for all that the Nicolaites so often appear as the adversaries in Jean Paul's world.

The actual relationship between Jean Paul and Nicolai was partly a matter of accident, being colored by unfortunate experiences, from the first refusal by Nicolai to publish the unknown writer to the later unfavorable reviews of Jean Paul in the *Library.* But Nicolai and Jean Paul were also different in temperament — as different, say, as is the grim and loveless picture of the parsonage milieu one gets in Nicolai from the parsonage idyll of Jean Paul. But then, Jean Paul's own parsonage background cannot be called grim, and the domesticity he idealizes had, as the reports of other family members bear out, a real enough basis. Jean Paul would find none of this "warmth" of religion, or religion of warmth, in Nicolai, so that in one sense *enlightened* can be a term of abuse in Jean Paul.

In that sense, too, he was glad, he said, that he grew up in an age of superstitions, of poetic truth, when the world was explained theologically rather than mechanistically. It is true that in the later Jean Paul there is increasing emphasis on the pieties of the heart and the need for warmth as well as light. But as early as *Hesperus* he was critical of the "heartless"

---

2. Friedrich Nicolai, *Das Leben und die Meinungen des Herrn Magisters Sebaldus Nothanker,* ed. Fritz Brüggemann (Darmstadt, 1967); see esp. pp. 118ff. and editor's introduction, pp. 5ff.

Enlightenment, which was like the empty houses of Potsdam, lit at night by decree of Frederick II, so that they might seem inhabited (*W* 9.95; 1.685). So Giannozzo denounces the "enlightened eighteen-hundreders" in general and the Nicolaites in particular.

In the *Palingeneses*, Jean Paul observes Germany at the end of the eighteenth century, ironically celebrates the machine age of machine man, and looks forward to a superhuman development in the nineteenth century, when human beings will no longer be encumbered by their own limbs, ideas, and memories. The *natura naturans* will have disappeared and only the *natura naturata* will remain, to the great benefit of the earth, which is now so full of rubble and gaps. Here, Jean Paul was looking at the world from outer space. For just as, he says, Cardinal Richelieu, in his sick phases, imagined himself to be a horse, so Jean Paul likes to imagine himself as tutor to the Dauphin of the Milky Way, giving geography lessons to his pupil. Together, they look down at the earth of the eighteenth century, the dark ship of fools, counting the gallows and the galleys, the drunkards and the thieves, the book reviewers and the ex-Jesuits, the court chaplains and the libertines — on all of whom, to be sure, the "sun of the Enlightenment" shines, but as yet its light was only refracted and "without much warmth."

It was a century of supersititous unbelief, of "ninety-niners," as Jean Paul put it; here the obscure reference is to the thrifty custom, as he claims, of East India shipowners keeping to a complement of ninety-nine, since, according to English law, they would have had to take on a chaplain for every hundred souls (*W* 8.907, 865, 880). The same version of a world without warmth, because it is heartless and godless, is conjured up in the foreword to his future biography, where he foretells a titanic age, when physicists and chemists, geologists and politicians would declare that there was nothing behind the veil of Isis. There would be bloody revolution, and it could indeed be said that man had awoken, but he was still lying face down on the earth — and what was needed was a religious and moral revolution.

Speaking in a letter to Emanuel Osmund on the limited influence of schools and schooling — which may make men more learned, but hardly happier and better — Jean Paul says that what is needed is a life-long "Pädagogium," namely, a state. "As long as our form of government does not so change that slaves become men and egoists friends of the fatherland, so long will humanity remain a miserable, abject, frightened swarm." Wolfgang Harich rightly highlights this letter in support of his political interpretation, but the same passage is highlighted by Dr. Caselmann of the *Jean Paul Gesellschaft* in 1934 to demonstrate Jean Paul's anticipation of the National Socialist state.[3]

The misuse of Jean Paul texts during the National Socialist period does not invalidate Harich's argument, and the letter to Emanuel certainly documents Jean Paul's concern with the state and political structures. Harich plays down, however, what is in Jean Paul the far more frequent emphasis on the inward revolution, as in the foreword to the future biography. "Let each improve and revolutionize, instead of his age, his self." Jean Paul's assent to revolution, and to enlightenment otherwise, is qualified, like the half-celebration of the Enlightenment in Leibgeber's panegyric on Frederick the Great, who did indeed storm the Bastille within himself, and who, even if gallic philosophy robbed him of belief in virtue, did not lose his own. Yet his world could not be harmonious because it lacked "the gentle belief in a second world" (*W* 8.929f.; 3.524).

If Jean Paul particularly disliked what he saw as the atheism and materialism of the Encyclopedists, he was hardly less critical of Germany's critical philosophy, the subjectivity of which he saw developing into a godless — because objectless — solipsism. He deplored the fact that, as he wrote to Friedrich Jacobi, the philosophical and the religious so rarely come together. With Jacobi, he found himself most in sympathy, and he suggested a study of Jacobi as a cure for the century.

Most often, Jean Paul's judgments are couched in terms of coldness and warmth. And whether he did or did not applaud the Enlightenment varied according to whether he did or did not believe that in the particular case heat as well as light was generated. His most basic objection to his time was, as he wrote at the end of the century to Jacobi, its "lack of warmth." Writing to another friend a decade later, he was in more sanguine mood and detected a growing warmth in the Enlightenment, even of Berlin (*H-KA* 3.4.22ff.; 3.3.294, 250; 3.6.77).

In political affairs, Jean Paul's sympathies generally were on the progressive side, and his satire was directed against the forces of restoration, which he compared to the regular restoration of Luther's inkblot by the castellan of the Wartburg. The guiding principle of his politics was hope. Since this hope was based on faith in providence and since there was so much emphasis on piety, he might well seem to counsel more submission than reform, let alone revolution (*W* 3.76; 10.1072).

---

3. *H-KA* 3.2.130; Wolfgang Harich, *Jean Pauls Revolutionsdichtung. Versuch einer Deutung seiner heroischen Romane* (Reinbek, 1974), pp. 392ff.; *Jean Paul Blätter* 9 (1934): 4ff.

In fact, however, the demand for social reform is a constant in Jean Paul's work and is not contradicted by the piety, which has a different reference. In *Siebenkäs*, we read that the wounds of fate heal quickly, while the wounds of human injustice fester. Here he is making the same distinction as, in the first version of the novel, Green Henry makes in his reflection on beautiful and ugly, moral and immoral suffering. "An orphan weeping at the graveside is beautiful and its grief beneficial for life, but a child that grovels in hunger and neglect brings shame upon the whole landscape."

A strikingly similar distinction is made by Walt in *Fledgling Years* when he says: "Truly, I will endure the death of a child but not its misery."[4] In this sense, Jean Paul remained an activist. The later Jean Paul, by this time himself courted by nobility, appeared more conservative and seemed to pin his hope on reform from above. But when he addresses the nobility, as in *Dusks and Dawns for Germany*, the main emphasis is on the dangers of uniformity and the tyranny of the straight line. Nothing is more dangerous for human well-being, he says, than subordination to the will of one. The line of freedom is as curved as the line of beauty, and only death achieves an even uniformity. He continues to urge action, as in the aphoristic "polymeter" entitled *Advice:* "Do not say: let us suffer, for you have to. Say rather: let us act, for you do not have to (*W* 10.955f.; 11.362).

Jean Paul's political comments naturally vary with changing circumstances and his immediate concerns. The area in which he is most consistently rebellious is the area of censorship. He had often enough to contend with it himself, although it became less of a problem in the later years. Even *The Parson in Jubilee*, which might seem his most innocuous work, was at first forbidden. When, on appeal, a different censor permitted publication, it was only on condition that such Böll-like changes were made as substituting "good spirit" for "holy Spirit" (*H-KA* 3.6.11; 1.5.xlvii).

A recurring satirical motif is the free speech the German enjoys when he is asleep. Jean Paul deduces from the grumbling he overhears from the children in an orphanage that they are asleep, since, awake, they are perforce content with their lot. In the foreword to the second volume of *The Comet*, he speculates on the free dissemination of dangerous ideas from pillow to pillow. He suspects a conspiratorial League of Dreamers, for dreams have the power to convert a heathen into a Father of the

---

4. *Der grüne Heinrich. Erste Fassung* (chap. 2); *W* 4.911.

Church, as in the case of Arnobius. The sinful dreams of monks are induced either by malicious Protestants or by cunning Catholic penitents. Dreams are seditious cracks of light in a system in which the state keeps everything under one ecclesiastical and military roof. The danger is that "the night dreamers of the Enlightenment" will begin to make corresponding demands by day and eventually will have to be, as in the training of falcons, hindered by the police from sleeping (*W* 8.756ff.; 12.692ff.).

If censorship is welcome grist to the mill of Jean Paul as satirist, there are few matters on which he privately wrote so impatiently. In a letter to Christian Otto, he expresses his disgust with a work called "Mémoire sur l'état actuel de l'Allemagne," in which the author, Alexander Stourzda, attacking the German universities as hotbeds of the revolutionary and atheistic spirit, demands censorship of the press and the subordination of theological research to church authority (*H-KA* 3.7.244).

So although Jean Paul's radicalism became more restrained, his political attitude was on the whole remarkable for its constancy. Naturally, one does not expect the same constancy in detail and in his day-to-day reactions to particular people and events. Thus he was for the most part an anglophile, and in a letter to Otto declares himself to be "a real Englishman," for freedom is only to be found in England. The French Revolution itself said nothing that had not already been said in the British Parliament. Not that he was an uncritical observer. In *Levana*, he gives as an example of the dissolving agency of distance the way in which British freedom dissolved by the time it reached Ireland (*H-KA* 3.4.216f.; *W* 10.760). During the later power struggles in Europe, he became disillusioned with England, and refers to "blood- and money-suckers of Europe." Often the remarks are cryptic. When he says in a letter to Otto, for example, that nothing in England is bad except its Minister, he may have implied his own sympathy for the French Revolution, in contrast to Pitt's opposition (*H-KA* 3.5.152, 159; 3.3.45).

Jean Paul was so very prolix, delivering judgments right, left, and center, and his letters in particular are so spontaneous and dependent on his own mood and the identity of the recipient, that it is all too easy to extrapolate material purporting to show his support for whichever political creed the interpreter favors. The publications of the Jean Paul Society show how easily Jean Paul can be edited to suit National Socialism, including even — although this is quite baseless — antisemitism.

More serious is the fact that some volumes of the Critical Edition (but not those edited by Berend) similarly attempt to establish a Jean Paul image acceptable to the National Socialists. Undoubtedly, some of Jean Paul lends itself to this, provided one is satisfied with half-truths. In volume 14, for example, the editor, Wilhelm von Schramm, is at pains to show that Jean Paul was no politician and certainly no Realpolitiker. He was rather "an inner patriot," "a pastor of souls," concerned with religious and ethical matters. It would be a great mistake, we are told, to regard Jean Paul as a pacifist, for his *Declaration of War on War* had only a very limited Napoleonic reference. The editor deplores the misinterpretation, ever since Börne, of Jean Paul's *Peace Sermon* by pacifists, Marxists, and others opposed to the national movement, who would make of Jean Paul a prophet of human rights in a sense hardly distinguishable from treason. The editor welcomes the interest of Moeller van den Bruck in Jean Paul and notes how his true German substance is revealed by Fritz Klatt in his *Jean Paul and War.* In much the same way, the editor of volume 17, Kurt Schreinert, deplores the misunderstandings that led the journalists of Young Germany to claim Jean Paul for themselves, whereas, as Schreinert puts it, "their spirit was not his spirit, least of all were they blood of his blood" (*H-KA* 1.14.x, xxiv, xxvii, lv; 1.17, vi).

If the National Socialist claims on Jean Paul are not well-founded, neither are they wholly unfounded. An anthology of Jean Paul's pronouncements on war, for example, would, without elaborate explanations of the context in each case, make confusing reading. It is difficult to reconcile his *Peace Sermon* and *Declaration of War on War* on the one hand with, on the other hand, an essay like *The Beauty of Dying in the Flower of Youth*, on the need to "sacrifice time to eternity," the pathos of which is all the more difficult to relish since at the same time Jean Paul was objecting to having people billeted on him. If he more often demythologizes war, sometimes he glorifies it. In *Levana* he denounces all war as civil war and the betrayal of the ideals that give rise to states in the first place. In his *Peace Sermon* he rejects justifications of war as the price of heroism. And in *Dusks and Dawns for Germany* he observes that there is nothing enervating about peace, which, rather than war, strengthens and elevates (*H-KA* 1.17.301ff.; *W* 10.751f., 883, 964ff.).

In *Titan*, Gaspard's counsels to Albano on the educative nature of war — irrespective of its rights and wrongs, which are no concern of theirs — does not necessarily carry the approval of the author. But in the later letters we find Jean Paul saying: "Present humanity needs to be strengthened by war rather than by peace." He said this at a time when he was writing many letters in search of accommodation away from the scenes of war. There is, besides, the tendency of the later Jean Paul to identify with the establishment. In another letter, he suggests that only the educated realize the imperative of war, for only they can recognize the moral force of bloodshed, whereas "the poor people," in their narrowness of vision, can only see in war a struggle for land or money (*W* 6.725; *H-KA* 3.5.126, 238).

Politically, therefore, Jean Paul is not as clearly on the side of the angels as Harich suggests. Granted that Harich is less concerned with the later Jean Paul, the politics of even those works, like *Titan*, that Harich depends on are questionable enough. When Albano declares his intention of taking part in France's freedom war, this is in the first place for personal reasons: "War — that word alone gave Albano peace." We hear little in *Titan* about tyranny and liberty, while many pages of exalted prose celebrate heroic deeds. Albano adopts a lofty tone: "Only take the higher view of war." He speaks of entering the service of destiny and glorifies the battlefield with its "portals of death and honor" for its divinely spiritual "contempt for the body." There could hardly be a more ecstatic celebration of the "tragic stage" that binds friend and foe together in a common act of valor. Nor is there much suggestion of political or social purpose when Linda later asks Albano his reasons for going to the French wars. His concern is for self-fulfillment and the development of a manly destiny, which no woman must be allowed to curtail (*W* 5.584ff.; 6.662ff.).

There is, therefore, on war as on so much else, plenty of material in Jean Paul for a conflict of exegesis. But then it is less the fluctuation of mood, in response to changing circumstances, that matters than the inventiveness of his imagination. In *Declaration of War on War*, for instance, he speculates:

> Finally it is not seven-year wars reduced to seven-day wars that we need, as at present, but thirty-year wars condensed into thirty hours. Henri, the Paris artificer, invented — approved — flintlocks, which, after *one* loading fire 14 shots in a row; — oh, how much murdering time can be saved here and taken from life-time! — And who guarantees that with those giant developments in physics and chemistry they will not hatch out a murder machine in the end that will give and conclude battle in *one* shot, like a mine, so that the enemy fires no more than the second, and the campaign will be over before nightfall?

As is clear from satirical passages, like the excerpt from *Outing of Headmaster Florian Fälbel*, Jean Paul was basically in sympathy with the democratic ideas of the French Revolution. There is nothing unusual in the fact that his attitude toward later developments was like that of the progressive Count Lismore, who initially identifies with the French, but who leaves France in a mood of disillusioned resignation in 1793, when the temple of the Goddess of Freedom is taken over by the "evil" Robespierre. Jean Paul dated his own change of mind from the same year in the essay *On Charlotte Corday,* where he speaks of his revulsion against the bloodlust of 1793 and of his support for the storming of the Bastille until Paris itself was turned into a greater one (*W* 7.297f.; 11.332).

In *Siebenkäs* both Viktor, the hero of *Hesperus,* who reappears here, and the fictive Jean Paul identify with France, and the bloodshed is spoken of as a necessity. In a later work like *Levana,* the French Revolution is an object lesson in man's terrible potential for cruelty. References to the French generally become less flattering, as in *Fibel,* where Jean Paul speaks of their attractive politesse and repulsive egotism. By the end of the century he lost most of his sympathy for the Revolution. Referring to his Corday essay, he complained to Jacobi about the research he had to undertake in the almost illegible, because blood-stained, books of the Revolution, about which he "seeks to know ever less" (*W* 3.436; 9.626, 11.465; *H-KA* 3.3.227). He began to see France as humanity's enemy and reacted like St. Peter to the crow of the gallic fighting cocks, as he says in a later letter to Jacobi. To Christian Otto, he wrote that he did not hate Bonaparte so much as he despised the French; "and Goethe was more farseeing than two-thirds of the world in that he held in contempt the beginning of the Revolution as we do its end." He became increasingly cautious and assured his publisher, Cotta, that he would refrain from any political allusions (*H-KA* 3.5.94; 3.4.301; 3.5.116).

No doubt there were many factors influencing Jean Paul, but the kernel of his case against the contemporary world in general and the Revolution in particular was that it lacked the religious dimension, the "sense of the supernatural." This he expounds at length in *Levana* — just as the educational advice of the fictive Jean Paul to his foster sister is that she be taught to see the world beyond, be taught astronomy rather than French. In the end, his judgment on the Revolution was that it had "fallen away from God," had sacrificed God instead of sacrificing to the gods, as he says in *Dusks and Dawns for Germany.* So unenthusiastic about revolution had Jean Paul become by this time that in the preliminary notes to that work he says that, whereas France needed a revolution and a Napoleon, the Germans only needed the latter (*W* 9.570ff.; 7.51; 10.1024; *H-KA* 1.14.xvi).

Jean Paul was to become disillusioned with Napoleon, too. But over and above his fluctuating reactions to particular people and events there is a consistent preference throughout the later Jean Paul for reform from above rather than for revolution from below.

That this was related to his own change of status is all too obvious, particularly as he so often drew attention himself, with a humble kind of vanity, to the favor he later found at this court or that. "The Queen of England reads me," he said. He told repeatedly of the adulation of the princesses at Hildburghausen (*H-KA* 3.3.213, 345; 3.4.29). He was in correspondence with a score of princes and courtiers, with Kaiser Alexander of Russia, King Max and Queen Karoline of Bavaria, with Metternich and Hardenberg. Sometimes the correspondence was a question of petition and was of necessity in the flowery language of obeisance. (When, exceptionally, he was unsuccessful in the case of Duke Emil August von Sachsen-Gotha, the latter was thereafter referred to by Jean Paul as His Lowly Highness [*H-KA* 3.6.108ff., 377ff.; 3.7.8ff., 31ff.])

Characteristic of the earlier Jean Paul are Vult's cynical attack on the aristocracy and Jean Paul's plan, outlined to Nicolai in 1784, for an essay in which he would demonstrate the divinity of kings by way of a Manichaean theology. Or again, his remark in a letter to Christian Otto that he had as little taste for Erasmus as the latter had for fish. For the early Jean Paul, Erasmus was an establishment figure, suggesting moderate reforms that were to no avail, since, says Jean Paul here, princes are well able to confess to crimes and commit them at the same time (*W* 4.791, 796ff.; *H-KA* 2.2.xx; 3.1.375ff.).

There is no denying the later change of tone. In a letter of petition to Friedrich Wilhelm III, he appeals on the grounds that he has sacrificed everything — time and money, health and career prospects — to the task of reestablishing belief in warmth in a coldly egoistic and revolutionary age. This was not written under duress; still less is it hypocritical. The suggestion that religious considerations have priority is nothing new in Jean Paul. And he invariably made value judgments in terms of coldness and warmth. But now he was also distancing himself from the revolutionary attitudes of his youth: "I am horrified that I should have approved even for a minute," he wrote later, when there was a question in Bayreuth of opposition to the Prussian administration. His counsel was: "We must suffer force, not use it against authority" (*H-KA* 3.4.68; 3.5.109ff.). The gesture of piety, of humanity's face raised in reverence to the heavens, was a recurring element from the beginning.

Increasingly, Jean Paul tends to celebrate authority and to assign to the people their proper role of admiration. That is the spirit, for example, of the essay *Wishes for Luther's Memorial*, in which he quotes Chateau-briand at the end to the effect that admiration is the greatest sentiment on earth. For the New Year of 1800, Jean Paul delivered an homage ser-mon, in which the eighteenth century is seen as the criticizing century, the century that was "cross with princes." The term *homage sermon* is meant half in jest, but also wholly in earnest (*W* 11.310ff., 330, 138ff.).

In the *Political Fasting Sermons*, he praises that "German love of princes" that inspired his countrymen to sacrifice for the sake of hero princes, whose good deeds are greatest, as honey from the hills is sweet-est. "In short, the states, like the bees, must begin to build their cells *from above.*" If it is the duty of the people to venerate the princes, it is the duty of the princes to trust the people, who in the past made such sacrifices for them as other peoples made for a republican constitution. The princes have nothing to fear from the Germans, who are of all peoples the least rebellious and who are given to banding together in brother-hoods and guilds rather than in conspiracies of civil disobedience. Of course, the tribute to a harmless people from whom nothing is to be feared is half satirical, but it is a wholly serious appeal to authority and betterment from above (*W* 10.1147ff., 1185ff.).

# *JEAN PAUL'S*

Inwardnesses

AS JEAN PAUL INCREASINGLY CELEBRATED AUTHORITY, so he increasingly emphasized the interior life and betterment within. In the essay *On the Natural Magic of the Imagination*, he comes to the conclusion that we should be content. We should not demand the "precious substitute for reality" and reality itself at the same time, nor forget that the rainbow of poetry is highest when the sun is lowest. Fulfillment is only to be found in the "heavenly" reality of the otherworld of dream. The whole essay celebrates the happy dispensation whereby "we fantasize forever." We all idealize in our imagination, he says, and this is what he himself has done in *Fixlein*, the work to which the essay is appended. He bathes in "idealizing moonshine . . . what is to me the otherwise hateful dungeon and debtor's tower," the realities of a pastor's life (*W* 7.195, 199, 205).

Taken in isolation, this would seem to divert attention from social and political realities. But of course it cannot be taken in isolation. Not only does this idealizing inwardness coexist with criticism of the social and political realities, but the latter seems in Jean Paul to flow from the former. That one is a man first and a citizen second and that humanity comes before motherhood were the sort of principles that lead him to very practical reflections on freedom and civil rights. However, while remaining critical and satirical, Jean Paul became ever less inclined to encourage any revolution other than an interior one. Writing to Friedrich Perthes, he faults the latter's use of the word *subjugated* with respect to present German conditions, a word that was "much too hard and untrue." At the same time, he congratulates Perthes for counseling the people to "come to themselves" (*W* 9.558; 10.694; *H-KA* 3.6.79f.).

Jean Paul is at all stages a sentimental writer. In the moral as in the physical world, he says in *Fixlein*, there are more tear lakes than there is dry land. And in *Palingeneses* he says: "O, whoever does not sometimes feel too much and too tenderly, always feels too little" (*W* 7.107; 8.917). Sometimes he mocks his sentimentality, referring to himself as a native of Damp Cheeks (the nearby town of Feuchtwangen). Mostly, he makes a virtue out of sentiment and rejects the cold moralism of the Kantians, whose disinterested virtue is without material content and without good works apart from those they write (*W* 6.1148; 8.812f.).

For those who are religious, as Jean Paul understands it, morality is not a matter of "moral law," and he has as little liking for "torture morality" as for its blood relation "blood theology." He advises the sundial policy: *horas non numero nisi serenas* (*W* 9.579; 10.1284; *H-KA* 3.5.163). When he distributes praise or blame, it is generally in terms of warm or cold, the warmhearted Arnim, for instance, as against the cold intellectualism of Tieck or Schlegel. He finds this warmth above all in the Herder household, and among the most effusive of his many emotional letters are those that tell of the happiness of their tearful meetings (*H-KA* 3.6.121; 3.7.218, 228; 3.2.206ff.).

Jean Paul is very insistent on the truth of feeling, basing on it his arguments for God or immortality. Yet often enough in his own life he experienced fickleness of feelings. So he both admits the fallibility of feelings and at the same time insists that "there are no truths but felt ones." Feelings change, and yet our so-called reasoning, if we are not to pursue arguments *ad infinitum*, must end with a felt truth (*H-KA* 3.3.351; 3.6.202; 3.1.305ff.). In a later letter to Counselor von Dobeneck who wrote a book on folk belief, he congratulates him for presenting his theme in the "old believing tone . . . without destroying it with explanations." Jean Paul not only believed in the holiness of the heart's affections, he equates the heart's affections with religious belief itself — which is "not the knowledge of the understanding" (*H-KA* 3.6.154; 3.7.55).

The religious argument in Jean Paul, the affirmative answer to the question of God and immortality, depends on the fact that the question is put in the first place. Man would be a desert, were it not that he feels that he is. "This feeling is our immortality." The positive characters in Jean Paul, like Fenk and his friends, are moral optimists, big hearted enough to attribute immortality to the universe. Jean Paul emphatically relates religious belief to instinct, with its feeling of a creator and an infinite future. Since nature does not lie, we must accept this as a true instinct, the object of which is "as remote as it is certain" (*W* 2.1090; 1.228; 9.59ff., 64).

Religion in this sense is the heart of man, and God is deduced from and defined as, "an inexpressible sigh in the depth of the soul." The existence of God is as axiomatic as the existence of existence. The *I* seeks a "primal *I*," which it could not do if it did not instinctively apprehend it. From all of this, Jean Paul, in *Levana*, draws the practical moral that religious education is a matter of communicating the feeling for religion, not bolstering it up with reasons (*W* 9.577ff., 580, 637ff.).

The emphasis on feeling is related to Jean Paul's increasing antipathy toward orthodox religion. Where he is satirical, he pities, for example, the scrupulous clergymen of Switzerland, who are enjoined by the helots there to acknowledge not only that the Hebrew consonants are inspired, but the divinity of the vowels also. In his early essay *On the Religions in the World*, his attitude is to respect the propriety of each religion in its own time and place and to recognize in Lessing fashion the gradual growth, improvement, and refinement of religious sensibility. This remained his attitude, but in later years he came more positively to dislike the "petty-mindedness" of the overorthodox, whether Jewish or Christian, preferring the natural miracle of life itself to biblical miracles. Wherever he talks of the subject it is in terms of freeing oneself from the restrictions of organized religion, from its "swaddling clothes," "bandages," "compresses" (*W* 7.391; *H-KA* 2.1.55ff.; 2.4.50ff.).

On the Bible itself he is seldom complimentary, except as ammunition against the established churches, remarking that if one gave the Bible to a savage to read, he would scarcely deduce from it anything resembling the orthodoxies, whether Lutheran or Catholic. In any case, the Bible, which is "only historical," was of less concern to Jean Paul than the principles that preceded it. One could see some of his remarks — for example, that the tears of Christ are more important than the blood of Christ — as part of a process of secularization. His own brand of religion became progressively less christocentric and Biblecentered. Revelation reveals only the historical, he suggests, whereas his concern is with something at once more remote and more immediate, with the inward and metaphysical. When he says, for example, that the madonna corresponds among the Italians "to Christ with us," this is not, as one might think, Protestant German prejudice against Catholic Italy. On the contrary, it has more in common with Rilke's Catholic prejudice when he speaks of Protestantism as "stuck fast in Xto" (*H-KA* 2.4.50, 52, 55f., 61f., 64f., 156, 173).

There is often a sense in Jean Paul of being in a post-Christian era. Praising his friend Christian Otto for his work on Loyola and Luther, he remarked that the history of a sect cannot really be written by a member, adding that only now could the history of Christianity be written. The work he particularly recommended to his son as a confession of faith was *Dream upon the All.* Yet what that work most graphically evokes is the nightmare of solitude in a godless universe. Nietzsche's theme of the "growing desert" is preechoed in *Dream upon the All:* "I become too lonely in creation, I shall become lonelier still in its deserts; the full world is great, but the empty world is greater, and with the All the desert grows" (*H-KA* 3.2.201f.; 3.8.96; *W* 11.684f.).

Of course this is, in Jean Paul, the obverse side of a faith or a hope that he continued to profess while acknowledging its fragility. To retain belief, we must look upward in trust to Providence. But, he adds, the upward gaze must not falter and fall upon the earth: "otherwise the whole proof wavers" (*H-KA* 2.4.26). It need hardly be said that Jean Paul himself often enough looked down, like his Giannozzo, and in his work the dream of Providence is invariably accompanied by the nightmare of nihilism. His epic restlessness reflects the nature of faith as an enduring hope. Jean Paul confesses an aversion to ideas of a fixed eternity, which seems to him like a stagnant expanse of standing water. Our nature is such that even in the second world the only blessed state is the prospect of a third. We need a new God and a new immortality, more suitable to the age of astronomy. Our ideas of heaven and its static bliss are all too much a product of the Orient, where to walk around was a troublesome exertion. His own heaven, he suggests in one of his later letters, consists of a perpetual journey through it (*H-KA* 3.2.173f., 280; 3.1.400; 2.4.156, 168).

The most extended examination of belief and unbelief is in *The Vale of Campan,* in which the arguments for and against belief in immortality are presented in letter form, in an eighteenth-century setting of sentiment, and in a framework of friendships that is central to the subject matter. Immortality, it is suggested there, is something to which man is morally entitled. His nature depends on the otherworld, for which he is intended.

Philosophically, the argument is presented on the basis of that "realism" to which Jean Paul invariably subscribes, insisting on the real originals of our ideas and images and rejecting the "idealism" of the atheist. In his very last work, *Digressions for Future Instalments*, he speaks of the timelessness of our inner life, of the "eternal moment" within: "Is not then an eternal world an unshakeable certainty? Or what else is an eternity in man for?" Such is, as it were, the official argument of *The Vale of Campan*. Taken as a whole, however, the work is much more a matter of conflicting emotions. At one point in the friends' discussions, the fictive Jean Paul interrupts to say that in his experience few people either decisively believe in or decisively deny an afterlife and that most, according to the impulse of alternating emotions, "waver poetically" between the two (*W* 8.608, 611; *H-KA* 1.18.402). In the sequel to *The Vale of Campan*, *Selina; or, on the Immortality of the Soul*, friendship and sentiment are once again central to the main issue. The only conclusion is within the framework context, for in the end the friends are in agreement "only in their affection for one another." For the rest, Jean Paul "wavers poetically." Insofar as there is a concluding attitude to the afterlife, it includes both the open question of the future and the prayer for the present as expressed by Liane in *Titan:* "Will the human breast be able to breathe in your ethereal Spring? O . . . let me live here as if I walked already in your heaven" (*W* 12.1226; 5.212).

In that sense, Jean Paul's religion is very earth centered, and he could hardly be accused of neglecting this world by escaping from it. But he does take refuge within it. An otherworld of the inward and the imagined has priority. One cannot say of Jean Paul, for all his particularism, that his truth is concrete. In the first flowerpiece of *Siebenkäs*, in striking contrast to Brecht, Viktor's letter to Cato extols philantrophic, or inner, love against mere practical love of neighbor and love of enemy, which is expressed in deeds that are "easily done" (*W* 3.421). More than most of his contemporaries, Jean Paul is a social satirist and a political commentator, but there is a sense in which memories and dreams, past and future, have priority over the present. The *I* of the idylls exploits and enjoys all the epic possibilities of the imagination, living in the past and the future, which are more congenial to the imagination, as the narrator in *Hesperus* says, than the constraints of the present. The heaven of man, he says in *Titan*, has to be at a distance. May the reader encounter memories and hopes, from which all enjoyment derives, says the narrator in the preface to *Jean Paul's Biographical Entertainments*, for like the night owls we are only at home in those twin twilights (*W* 2.1060; 5.390f., 511; 7.265f.).

The theme is turned into narrative in idylls like *The Parson in Jubilee:* "Yesterday's Christmas Eve I enjoyed, in the expectation that I would describe it this Christmas Day; this I enjoy now, in remembering yesterday." That memory is the gift that gives meaning to life, that present joy is the enjoyment of future memories, that man seeks his future by gazing into the past — these and similar variations on the one theme keep recurring in Jean Paul, for whom indeed it is a religious theme, for memory is a presentiment and a present afterlife. "Memory is the second world of joy" (*W* 7.547; *H-KA* 2.4.190; 2.5.360; 3.2.260; 3.3.200).

In the world of Jean Paul, this is all the more reason why it should be parodied in bizarre manipulations of memory. In the last novel, *The Comet*, for example, the narrator — having found a book that fascinates him — skims through it as fast as he can, because he wants to read it at leisure as soon as he gets it back from a friend, to whom he must therefore lend it as soon as possible. The narrator of *Titan* admits that the present experience can never compare with the experiences of the past and the future, the mind's paradise lost and paradise regained. If poetry ever did become reality, it would only prove to be a higher poetry, with still more distant memories and expectations (*W* 12.788; 5.221f.).

Central to Jean Paul's work, then, are idyllic scenes like the winter pleasures in *Quintus Fixlein:* the frost and snow outside; within, the stove and the coffee, the poodle and the pipe. Often they involve such juxtapositions as Fixlein reading of the Thirty Years' War while he listens with half an ear to the dinner preparations in the kitchen. Appended to *Fixlein* is the *Natural Magic* essay, in which the imagination, concerned with the happy isles of the past and the promised land of the future, is said so to transfigure that even the wicked characters of drama have a charm they would not have in the cold light of real life. Poetry vouchsafes to the imagination what is denied to the senses. In poetry, country folk idealize the life of the court; and the people of the city make a pastoral idyll out of the life of the land. The whole essay is a defense of these conjuring tricks of poetry, which responds to the innate longing for eternity with its own "make-believe infinity." Our reaction to this should be to abandon the bad habit of desiring at one and the same time the dream and the reality.

In assessing statements like that, one should remember not only the irony of the idylls and their satirical content but also Jean Paul's claim that the idyllic is not an escape from reality but rather a circuitous approach to it. In his "Open Letter to Leibgeber" in the *Palingeneses*, he speaks of poetry's ideals and images of freedom and happiness, again observing that the domestic and pastoral idylls delight the courtier rather than the countryman. Merry haymaking songs are for the amusement of princes, not of harvesters. Poetry deals in such illusions. Yet, he concludes, just as the dream that we are drinking serves to prove the reality of thirst, so the seductive poetic imaginings lead us back by a roundabout route and restore to nature, to freedom, to domestic life, to reality followers more faithful than they had been at the outset (*W* 8.730). Jean Paul's projections into the past and the future are not vain nostalgia and utopias but a progressive "dreaming ahead."

In any event, the emphasis is invariably on the inner life. "Country life is within us, not outside of us." His own biography, he says, would be more an internal one like Moritz's than an external one like Goethe's (*H-KA* 2.5.130; 3.6.297). Nothing was more cultivated by Jean Paul than his local patriotism, but, he wrote to Emanuel, the *patria* he meant was the poetic one, not the real one in the mire. Even the enjoyment of nature he regards in the same fashion. "The feeling for nature is in reality the fantasy for nature," he says in *The Invisible Lodge*. Viktor, the hero of the first novel, is, like many to follow, oppressed by the emptiness of life but open to another, inward world (*H-KA* 3.4.291; *W* 1.396, 545).

As novels of development, Jean Paul's works expand on this theme ever more elaborately up to the last hero, the apothecary who is the "busy architect" of his own castles in the air. The narrator of *Titan* addresses his beloved Albano as the deceived one, for confusing the real world with the world of the mind's eye. This must surely have bearing on the moral of the book. There is social satire and even political purpose in *Titan*, but at the same time the novel demonstrates, according to that letter to Emilie von Berlepsch, that the ideal world can only be inwardly entered upon (*W* 12.745; 5.77; *H-KA* 3.2.352).

If the later Jean Paul becomes more religious, it is in the sense that his religion, too, becomes more inward, moving farther and farther away from the revealed religions of the churches, which were not inner- and other-worldly enough. Only the craven Hanseatic soul idealized this world, he says in a letter to Friedrich Oertel. The real world is "in us" and "over us." Why should that second world exist less, he says in that letter, because it only exists in the *I* (*H-KA* 2.4.61ff.; 3.2.136ff.).

In the light of the Jacobian philosophy to which Jean Paul keeps returning, what is "only in the *I*" reflects realities, and he claims to be realistic in choosing as his subject matter the world of the imagination and, specifically, the world of books, writers, printers, and readers. The best world is in the microcosm, he says in *Hesperus*, and Arcadias are contained within the four chambers of the brain. "Why is man sometimes so happy," he asks there, and replies: "It is because he is sometimes a *literatus*" (*H-KA* 3.2.302; *W* 1.509, 512).

Comic inventiveness sustains itself. Let no one speak disparagingly about the web that supports us and our happiness, he says in *Siebenkäs;* we spin it out of ourselves, yet it bears us up and withstands the storms. Goethe, one notices, does not share this faith. In a letter to Karl Zelter (30 October 1808) Goethe refers to Jean Paul's just published *Dream of a Mad Person* as one of the most "dreadful examples" of the way in which the humorous, because it has in itself no law and support, easily degenerates into melancholy and ill humor. For his part, however, Jean Paul rejected such support. The comic genius is like a bell, he says in *The Comet* — dull when it touches the earth. It must hang free in order to give a full sound (*W* 3.330; 11.571).

There is, of course, irony and social comment in the idea of the *literatus* and his happiness. In *Siebenkäs* there is a passage that nicely illustrates the combination of the idyllic — the alleviation of the inner life — with the satirical. For nothing in the lot of the actors has been altered and still less, as Jean Paul added in characteristic afterthought, in the lot of their wives:

> If a threadbare persecuted schoolman, a lean *magister legens*, if a penitent parson with five children or a harrassed tutor lies there in misery, exposed in every nerve to instruments of torture, along comes his brother in office, beset by as many instruments, debates, and philosophizes with him all evening long and tells him the latest opinions from the literary journals: why then, the sandglass of torture is turned around, and Orpheus with the lyre of science brightly descends into the physical hell of the two colleagues, and all their torment is interrupted, the melancholy tears fall from brightening eyes, the snakes of the furies twine into curls, Ixion's wheel rotates melodiously, and the two Sisyphi settle down on their two stones and listen. But the good wife of the penitent parson, of the wandering *magister legens*, of the schoolman, what consolation has she in her similar misery? None but her husband, who should show her the more forbearance for that. (*W* 3.180)

Jean Paul keeps intruding as a character in his stories because the inward *I* experience is the centerpiece of his narrative. He likes to present it as a particularly troublesome experience for his countrymen, envying the self-assured English for being able to capitalize their *I*s without being regarded as egoistic. They can even, without stumbling over the phrase in embarrassment, say "I myself," quite naturally, as indeed the French can say "moi même." The Germans, however, have a distorted relationship to themselves, either denying the *I* or inflating it in Fichtean selfishness (*W* 9.135).

Jean Paul's stories ring the changes on the *I* experience, which at the one extreme can mean idyllic scenes of the intimate and familiar and at the other extreme the isolation and alienation of an *I* unrelated to any reality outside itself. He clung subbornly to realism as his chosen creed and claimed that the insights, dreams, and wishful thinking of man's inner world "must be" true reflections. But the fear that the images may be, as a modern poet like Gottfried Benn would say, "endogenous" remained a perpetual threat in a work that "wavers poetically." The signs can always be read differently. "The zero of nought and the circle of perfection have the same sign," he says in *Siebenkäs*. The options remain open, and if there is any conclusion it seems to be something like an anticipation of the Thomas Mann theme of man as "master of counterpositions." As far back as 1781 Jean Paul defined man as "that creature able to unite the irreconcilable" (*W* 3.479; *H-KA* 2.1.182).

Doubtless, Jean Paul himself would prefer a happier end than one in which art seems only to play with life; and wherever he sermonizes, as he often does, he puts forward a belief in a final reality as a guiding principle. We play for real, not for play, is the gist of his argument in *Preschool*'s final *cantate* lecture, with its implied criticism of Schlegel irony and Schiller play and with its homage to Herder. Appearing there as Jean Paul, he lectures his hero Albano: "We have something within us that irresistably posits an eternal earnestness, the enjoyment of an ineffable union with an unknown reality." Even the crazy Schoppe is a realist at heart. In *Titan*, he is finally accorded a happy end, the *bona mors* he deserved, for, says the narrator, he always sought something more than himself. Jean Paul expresses similar concern for the immortal souls of his readers. He recommends the reading of his friend Jacobi, which would surely convert us from the "chirographic" to the "hypothecarian" philosophy (*W* 9.444; 6.1029). The reference is to a distinction in Roman law between debts that are merely certified and debts covered by security. It is the sort of out-of-the-way analogy that Jean Paul liked and that Jean Paul readers are likely to remember, even if they are not moved to read Jacobi, or to be converted if they do.

TEXTS

The Invisible Lodge

THE STORY OF SCHULMEISTERLEIN WUTZ APPEARS IN *The Invisible Lodge* (*W* 1.422ff.). *Wutz* is the first work in the present volume purely for reasons of chronology. One might almost wish this were not so, because of the danger, in spite of the suggestive subtitle — *A Kind of Idyll* — of establishing an image of Jean Paul such as led to Georg Lukács's impatience with petit bourgeois evasions and accommodations. Even Max Kommerell, from a very different standpoint, speaks of Jean Paul as someone who introduced "a great, almost dubious interiorization of art."[1] The tendency in the past was to identify Jean Paul with his blithely oblivious little schoolmaster, somewhat in the quaintly endearing Spitzweg manner.

In recent years, more sophisticated readings are the norm, beginning with Ralph-Rainer Wuthenow's "Endangered Idyll" in the 1960s and up to Richard Hannah's Derridaian essay "The Fortunes of the Idyll" in the 1980s. Nevertheless, even modern discussions of Jean Paul's inwardness, like Hartmut Vinçon's *The Innerworld and Outerworld in Jean Paul*, seem

---

1. Max Kommerell, *Jean Paul* (Frankfurt, 1967), p. 98.

to suggest a Jean Paul imprisoned in his inwardness.[2] *Wutz* in particular remains a problem, not least to its most sympathetic interpreters.[3]

In the most influential recent work on Jean Paul, Wolfgang Harich appears uncomfortable with *Wutz*.[4] The aim of his study is, after all, to demolish the image of the idyllically contented Jean Paul, whose work expresses, unlike that of Goethe and Schiller, precisely discontent. Harich labors the point that Wutz is no model hero, and he interprets as much as possible subversively, perhaps overinterprets; is Wutz's longing for sleep really a reference to the churches' indoctrination of a death wish? But in the end, Harich is mainly concerned lest *Wutz* be given too much attention. Anyone who places *Wutz* or *Fixlein* above *Titan*, he says, merely demonstrates his incompetence to talk about literature at all.

One can be heavy-handed about Jean Paul's idylls, as about his humor, and there is a danger of overintellectualizing the topic. In a letter to Emanuel Osmund, Jean Paul, speaking about the difference between an intellectual and a moral or poetic understanding in human relationships, went on to exemplify by saying: "Only on the printed page and in the all-embracing heart is Wutz a good Wutz" (*H-KA* 3.5.161).

Besides, looking for comprehensiveness within the idyll is contrary to its nature, as presented in paragraph 73 of *Preschool of Aesthetics*, where Jean Paul says of it that it must not include the passions or storms of life. There he offers his own definition. It is a mistake, he maintains, to define the idyll in terms of the pastoral life or the golden age of humanity; rather, it is "the epic presentation of perfect happiness within limits." As well as the place of the idyll in his work, one might also bear in mind Jean Paul's practice of the art of contentment. Eduard Berend reminds us how often and how insistently Jean Paul wrote on the need to be happy — or rather to resolve not to be the opposite — and that it was at a time of deep depression and disappointment, of money and marriage problems, that he set about constructing his *Booklet of Joys*, for which he

2. Ralph-Rainer Wuthenow, "Gefährdete Idylle," in *Jahrbuch der Jean-Paul-Gesellschaft* 1 (1966):79–94; and Richard W. Hannah, "The Fortunes of the Idyll: Jean Paul's *Wutz* and the Loss of Presence," *Germanic Review* 56, no. 4 (1981): 121–27. See also Jens Tismar, *Gestörte Idyllen* (Munich, 1973). German studies of *Wutz* are too numerous to list. A useful English annotated edition is that by Eva Engel in the Anglica Germanica series (S-Gravenhage, 1962). Hartmut Vincon, *Topographie: Innenwelt-Außenwelt bei Jean Paul* (Munich, 1970).

3. For example, Kathleen Blake, "What the Narrator Learns in Jean Paul's Wutz," *German Quarterly* 48, pt. 1 (1975): 52–65.

4. Wolfgang Harich, *Jean Pauls Revolutionsdichtung. Versuch einer Deutung seiner heroischen Romane* (Reinbek, 1974), pp. 154ff.

intended the title *Theodicy or the Art of Joy* (*H-KA* 2.4.viff.).

The accent is on the "art" of being content. Obviously, *ars* semper *gaudendi* can hardly apply to Jean Paul's work as a whole, with its medley of moods.But then, that work is not about being happy, but about being *happier*. So it is that most modern discussions of *Wutz* highlight the ambivalences, the indulgent tone, and the satirical indictment of the status quo, the tensions between hero and narrator or between the idyllic subject matter and the omnipresence of the death motif. The balances are delicate. There is a way of so emphasizing the narrative reservations as to devalue the world of Wutz, which is hardly in the spirit of the author.

And if it is usually assumed that the death motif is not consonant with the nature of the idyll, that may not be as self-evident as it seems. One might find in *Wutz*, as indeed is intimated in the opening lines, the kind of acceptance of the natural order personified, for example, in the figure of Dortchen Schönfund in Keller's *Green Henry*. Not that *Wutz* was likely to be Jean Paul's last word, either. The idyll is brought to a restful conclusion, but there are treacherous undercurrents in the closing paragraphs — just as throughout Jean Paul's writings there are undertones of unbelief in the most exalted and fervent professions of faith.

Life of the Merry Masterkin Maria Wutz in Auenthal: A Kind of Idyll

Oh how gentle and sea calm was thy living and thy dying, thou merry little schoolmaster Wutz. The still, clement sky of an Indian summer did draw no clouds but a haze around thy life; thy seasons were like the swaying of a lily and thy dying like its decline, its petals wafting onto standing flowers — and even this side of the grave thou sleptest gently.

But first of all, my friends, let us pull up our chairs around the stove and have the table with the water jug at my side; the curtains must be drawn and our nightcaps donned, and not a thought be wasted on the grande monde across the way and the Palais royal, for I am now going to tell you the peaceful story of the merry little schoolmaster — and you, my dear Christian, whose bosom is receptive to the only fireproof joys of life, the domestic ones, sit on the arm of the grandfather chair, from which I shall tell my tale, and lean against me a little now and again! You will not disturb me a whit.

Ever since the days of the Swede, a Wutz had been schoolmaster in

Auenthal, and I believe not once did pastor or parish have reason to complain. Eight or nine years after the wedding, a Wutz and son would hold
this office with perception — our own Maria Wutz teaching the alphabet
in the very week in which he himself learnt that art of spelling, which
profits naught. Our Wutz was somewhat playful and childish of character, as is the teaching of other schoolmasters; although not in trouble,
but in joy.

Even in childhood he was a little childish. For there are two kinds of
children's games, the childish ones and the serious ones — the serious
ones are imitations of grown-up people, playing at being a grocer, a soldier, an artisan — the childish ones, the mimicking of animals. Wutz at
play was never anything but a hare, or a turtledove, or her chick, a bear,
a horse, or even the wagon attached to it. Believe me, not even a seraph
can find any business in our universities and lecture halls but games, and
if he looks hard enough, these two kinds of games.

Yet Wutz also, like all philosophers, had his serious concerns and
hours. Did he not overcome deep-rooted prejudices — long before
grown-up Brandenburg clerics would be seen wearing as much as five
threads of colored stuff — by donning a blue apron in the forenoon,
which is rarely the gown of the cleric but rather the Dr. Faustus mantle
of the good candidate, which will bear him into a living, and in this vest-
ment, the color of heaven, hold up to his father's serving girl the many
sins that might deprive her of heaven and hell? — yea, he attacked his own
father, although that was in the afternoon; for when he read *Cober's*
"Family Preacher" to him, it afforded him a deep delight to slip in a few
occasional words or even lines of his own ideas and to read these inter-
polations with the rest of the text as if Herr Cober himself were addressing his father. I think that with this personal note I throw much light on
him and on a jest that he perpetrated later from the pulpit when, also in
the afternoon, he stood in for the pastor and read the postil to the devout,
intertwined, however, with so many editorial notes and fabrications of his
own that Satan was diminished and his servants moved. "Justel," said he
afterward at 4 o'clock to his wife, "you have no idea in your pew down
below how glorious it feels up above, especially during the hymn before
the sermon."

We can easily learn what he was like in his fledgling days from his
older years. In the Decembers of these he had his lamp brought in an
hour later, for he recapitulated his childhood during that hour — each day
a different day. While the wind darkened his windows with a snow curtain
and the fire winked at him through the chinks in the stove, he would shut

his eyes and let the long-perished spring thaw on the frozen meadows. Then he nestled into the hayrick with his sister and rode home on top of the mountainous dome erected on the hay wagon, eyes closed and guessing from above where they might be on their journey. In the cool of the evening, with the swallows skirmishing overhead, he would enjoy his nether bareness and the déshabillé of his legs, while he darted about like a vociferous swallow and, with the help of a wooden beak, built a mud rotunda for himself and his chick — a wooden Christmas cock with feathers glued to it — and afterward carried bed straw and bed feathers to the nest. A splendid Trinitatis (I wish there were 365 Trinitatisses) was kept for the palingenesis of another winter dusk hour, when he stalked with his jingling bunch of keys — spring ringing without and within — through the village to the garden, cooled himself in the dew, and thrust his glowing face through the dripping currant bush, measured himself against the tall grass, and with weak fingers twisted off the roses for the Herrn Senior and his pulpit. On that very Trinity Sunday, and this was the second course for the same December evening, with the sun shining on his back, he squeezed the hymn "Glory Be to God on High" into or out of the organ keys (that is all he can manage as yet), seeking in vain to reach the pedals with his short legs, while his father pulled out the correct organ stops for him. — He would have jumbled together the most disparate things had he remembered the activities of his childhood December during those two imagined evenings; but he had the wisdom to wait for a third before recalling the way he used to look forward to the locking of the shutters, for now he would be safely sitting inside the brightly lit room, wherefore he did not care to look long into the room, which the reflective windowpanes transposed beyond the shutters; how he and his brothers and sisters spied on, assisted, and interrupted his mother while she was cooking their supper, and how he and they, eyes tightly shut and hiding between the ramparts of their father's legs, eagerly awaited the dazzle of the tallow light to come, and how sheltered they were in the enclosure of their room, carved out of or built into the boundless vault of the universe, how warm, how well provided for, how snug. . . . And each year when he staged this return journey of his childhood and its wolf's month, he forgot, and it would take him by surprise — as soon as the lamp was lit — that he was at that moment sitting in the very room that he had fetched like a little Loreto house from the childhood Canaan. At least this is how he himself describes these *high opera* of memory in his *Rambles à la Rousseau*, which I have placed in front of me so as not to tell lies. . . .

But I shall let my foot be hampered by roots and brambles if I do not extract them by cutting a certain extremely important circumstance out of the years of his manhood and recording it without further ado; afterward, though, we shall begin a priori in an orderly fashion and accompany our little schoolmaster step-by-step along the three *ascending signs* of the stages of life and down again on the other side along the three *descending* ones — until at the foot of the lowermost step Wutz will tumble into his grave before us.

I wish I had not chosen this simile. Whenever I looked at the lamentable scaffold of the Seven Stages of Life, be it in Lavater's Fragments, or Comenii orbis pictis, or on a wall — whenever I watched the depicted creature, stretching and straining himself as he climbs the pyramidical anthill, looks about him on the summit for all of three minutes and, contracting, creeps downhill again and tumbles, curtailed, on the forebears surrounding this Golgatha — and whenever I turn to the face so vibrant and glowing, full of spring and thirsting to drain a whole heaven, and I ponder the fact that it was decades not chiliads that shrank and shrivelled this face into that parchment of long outlived hopes. . . . But while I grieve over others, the steps rise and fall for myself, and anyway, let us not make each other so solemn!

The important circumstance, which, as we stated, we are so eager to hear in advance, is namely this, that Wutz wrote in his own hand — how could the man buy it? — a complete library for himself. His inkstand was his pocket press; each new fruit of the Book Fair whose title our little master clapped eyes on was now as good as written or purchased: for he would sit down at once and produce it and donate it to his handsome collection, which like the pagan ones, consisted of manuscripts only. Lavater's physiognomical fragments, for instance, had hardly appeared when Wutz began to gain on the fertile brain ahead by folding his scribbling paper in quarto and not quitting his chair for three weeks on end until he had delivered his own brain of the physiognomical fetus (— he bedded the fetus on the bookshelf —) and in writing drew level with the Switzer. He labeled the Wutzean fragments Lavater's, with the annotation that "he had nothing against those in print; but he hoped that his hand was equally legible, if not an improvement on some median Gothic print." He was no confounded pirate who, with the original in front of him, often copied the greater part of it; *he* did not touch the original. Therein lies the capital explanation of two facts: firstly, the fact that there are certain flaws, and that in the whole of Feder's Treatise on Space and Time he treats of nothing but the *space* in the holds of ships and the *time* that among womenfolk is called menses. The second fact is a matter of his faith: having for some years stacked and thoroughly studied his bookcase in this fashion, he came to believe his manuscripts to be the true canonical sources and the printed works merely plagiarisms of his own handwritten ones; for the life of him, he complained, he could not fathom how and why the book haulier forever falsified and altered the printed text to such an extent that if you did not know better you would truly swear that print and manuscript had two different authors.

It was naive of an author to hope to steal a march on him by writing an opus profoundly, namely in traverse folio format, or wittily, in sextodecimo shape, as his comaster Wutz would leap at it instanter, placing his sheet traversely or folding it sextodecimowise.

Only the catalogue of the Book Fair was allowed to darken his threshold; for the best items of the inventory had to be indexed with a black hand in the margin by the Senior, permitting them to be written swiftly enough for the hay of the Spring Fair to be fed to the ruminate bookshelf before the Michaelmas aftermath sprouted. I would not fancy writing his masterworks. It brought the man nothing but damage — constipation for weeks and head colds at the other end — when the Senior (his Friedrich Nicolai) marked too many good books to be written, inciting his hand through the hand in the margin; and his son oft complained that there were years when the literary travails hardly allowed his father time to sneeze while giving birth to the triplets of Sturm's Contemplations, the improved edition, The Robbers by Schiller, and Kant's Critique of Pure Reason, for instance. This took place in the daytime; furthermore, the good man had to row around the South Pole in the evenings, after supper, and during this Cook's Tour of his he barely managed to address three intelligent words to his son up there in Germany. For as our encyclopedist had never set foot in the interior of Africa, not to mention the stable of a Spanish mule, or conversed with the inhabitants of either, he had all the more time and competence for furnishing magnificent travel accounts of both of these and, indeed, any country — I mean, such as the statistician, the chronicler of mankind, and I myself can rely on — firstly, because other traveling journalists, too, often proceed with descriptions but not with the journey — and secondly, because any other production of travel accounts is plainly impossible, seeing that no travel writer ever did stand within or in front of the country he was about to silhouette: for even the dumbest remembers enough of Leibniz's predestined harmony to know that the mind, or let's say the minds of a Forster, a Brydone, or a Björnstähl, for instance — altogether sedentary on the insulating stool of the petrified pineal gland – can describe nothing of southern India or Europe but what each one thinks up by itself about them and which, with a total lack of external impressions, it reels and twines from its *five spinning mamillae*. So Wutz, too, extracted his travelogues exclusively out of himself.

He writes on any topic, and if the learned world is amazed to see him, five weeks after The Sorrows of Werther appeared in print, remove a hardy quill from an old feather duster and, stante pede, write them down, the Sorrows – the whole country was later to copy his Sorrows – no one is less amazed than myself at the learned world, for how could it have perceived and perused Rousseau's Confessions recorded by Wutz, and still hidden among his papers? In these, however, J. J. Rousseau or Wutz (it makes no difference) says the following of himself, merely accoutered in different words: "Truly he would not be so stupid as to take up his pen and produce superior works if all it needed was for him to dip into his purse and purchase them. Alas, it contained but two tarnished collar studs and a dirty creutzer. Consequently, should he have the wish to read something intelligent, like for instance from the practical pharmacopia or the universal medical history, there was nothing for it but to settle down beside his weeping window and invent the stuff. Whom was he to turn to if he wanted to sound out the enigma of the Masonic secret, which Dionysian ear, did he think, if not his own two? He listened intently to those inserted in his own head, and as he read closely and strove to understand the Masonic speeches that he wrote, he noticed several wondrous things, made great strides, and in general smelled a rat. As he knew about as much chemistry and alchemy as Adam after the fall, when he had forgotten everything, he had truly done himself a great favor by forging this Annulus Platonis, this silver ring around a leaden Saturn, this ring of Gyges, which is said to bestow invisibility upon many an object, minds as well as metals; for this book, once he could fully perceive it, was to provide him with his striking knowledge of the lie of the land." And now let us return to his childhood.

In the tenth year of his life, he appeared in the mulatto-tinted chrysalis of alumnus and pupil of the higher Quinta in Scheerau. His examiner there must bear witness that I present my hero unvarnished if I pluck up the courage to report that he had arrived at the fourth declension, except for one page, and he was able to reel off like clockwork the entire gender exception of thorax caudex pulexque, and it was only the rule he missed out on. And of all the seminarians' cubbyholes none was as scoured and ordered as his; it gleamed like the kitchen of a hausfrau of

Nurenberg; proving again that contentment breeds order. With a penny's worth of nails he studded his cell and provided a nail for each item of his possessions — his notebooks he stacked with their backs in a line to pass muster on a Prussian parade ground, and in the light of the moon he got out of his bed and, taking their bearings again and again, he ensured that his shoes were aligned in impeccable manner. Once all was symmetric, he rubbed his hands, hitched his shoulders over his ears, leapt aloft, shook his head almost off, and laughed uncommonly.

Before I continue to prove how happy he was in the school I shall show you that this kind of life was no joke, but a herculean task. A hundred Egyptian plagues are counted for nothing merely because they befall us in the years of our boyhood, when compound fractures and wounds of the mind as speedily heal as those of the body — young wood not breaking as lightly as dry. A school such as this is designed from its early beginnings as a *cloister* for Protestant *boys*, as its regulations will tell us; yet we should leave things alone and not wish to convert such a preventive prison into a château de plaisance, making philanthropy govern where misanthropy reigneth supreme. Do not the fortunate inmates of such a school fit for princes take the three vows of the monk? Firstly, the vow of *obedience*, as the guardian of scholars and master of novices presses the spur wheel of the most frequent and odious orders and mortifications into his dusky novices' sides. Secondly, the vow of *poverty*, as it is not cruditées and leftover morsels but hunger that they preserve and carry over from one day to another; and *Carminati* would be able to cure whole invalid houses with the overflow from the gastric seminarian juices of alumni. The vow of chastity fulfills itself if a man must fast and run all day long and lack no motion but the peristaltic. A citizen has to be badgered into important office. But is only the Catholic novice to be hammered into a friar, the mean messenger in Bremen smoked into a merchant's assistant, the uncivilized South American native hammered and smoked and, by a variety of torments described in my excerpts, sized and sublimated into a cazique? Is then, I ask you, a Lutheran pastor of lesser importance, or is his future appointment not worthy of similar tortures? Fortunately, he has them; perhaps it was only for his sake that the ancients bricked up the school portals so that their conclavists were verily slaves of the slaves: for certainly other faculties gain very little from this crucifixion and wheel breaking of body and spirit. — Hence the much-faulted choir- or street- or funeral-singing of the alumni is a right good means to make of them Protestant friars — and even their black overall, the canonical blackamoor wrap of their mantle, resembles the cowl of the monk. And in view of the fact that later they shall be bewigged with their clerical dewlaps, the St. Thomas's pupils in Leipzig sprout betimes the germ leaves of wiglets, peering about on their heads like desk flaps or the wing halves of beetles. In the cloisters of old, learning was penance; learning the psalms off by heart or copying authors in Latin was assigned to the sinner; in the good poor-schools, such punishment is not neglected, and thrift in teaching is ever practiced as the innocent means of chastising and mortifying the poor pupils.

Except that our master was hardly put out by this cross-school. All day long he enjoyed and looked forward to something. "Before I get up," said he, "I look forward to breakfast, and during the morning to dinner, to my vesper bread at vespers, and at night to my supper — and this way alumnus Wutz has ever his expectations." On taking a deep draught, he would say, patting his stomach: "This tasted good to Wutz," and "Bless you, Wutz my dear," when he sneezed. — Out-of-doors in shivery, frosty November he would quicken himself by keeping his inner eye firmly fixed on the stove and the foolish delight of having first one then the other hand cozily lodged in his coat. And should such a day be altogether too wild and too squally — we manikins know harry days of such a nature, when the whole world is a harry house and plagues splash and drench us like jocular fountains at every step — our masterkin had wit enough to sit down under the weather without taking notice; it was neither submission, which accepts the evil that is *unavoidable*, nor callousness putting up with the evil *unfelt*, nor philosophy digesting the evil *diluted*, nor religion reconciling itself to evil *rewarded:* nay, 'twas the thought of his bed that sustained him. "Tonight," he would think, "no matter how hard they will harry and hunt me all day long, I shall snuggle under my cover with my nose on my pillow and have peace for eight hours." — And when he did at the close of one of those passion days creep under his featherbed, he settled himself and curled up like a baby and said to himself: "See, Wutz, it has passed after all."

Another paragraph in the Wutzean Art of Ever Being Content was his second trick, always to awake in a good humor — and he achieved this by means of a third, namely never facing the morrow without something pleasant in store from the previous day, be it baked dumplings or an equal number of highly dangerous pages from Robinson, of whom he was fonder than of Homer, — or it might be fledglings or seedlings that had to be checked in the morning in order to see how feathers or foliage had grown overnight.

Only when he had reached the Sekunda did he develop paragraph three of his Art of Being Content, which may be presumed to be the most thoroughly reasoned:

he fell in love. —

Such a development would be just what I fancy. . . . However, I have to break off here this minute, for as I have never before in my life attempted the charcoal portrait of love in a flowerpiece, we shall continue the sketching tomorrow at six when the fire is burning more brightly.

If the cities of Venice, Rome, and Vienna and the entire conglomerate of pleasure cities were to grant me a shrovetide to equal the one in the precentor's black parlor in Joditz where we children danced from 8 to 11 (this is how long our carnival lasted when we were skipping away our appetite for the Shrove Tuesday porridge): those capital cities would attempt the impossible and the ridiculous, and yet not quite as impossible as it would be should they try to repeat for alumnus Wutz the Shrove Tuesday delights when he, the visiting pupil of the Lower Sekunda, at 10 o'clock in the morning and in his father's dancing- and school-room, fell in love with a vengeance. Such a Shrove Tuesday delight — my dear little master, what can you be thinking of? He was thinking of nothing at all but Justina, whom I shall seldom or never call Justel, as the people of Auenthal did. As the alumnus grasped in an instant and while he was dancing (not many grammar school pupils would have deigned to take part, but Wutz, although ever vain, was never proud) what was pertaining to Justel — not counting himself — that is to say that she was lissome and comely and already versed in letters, proportions, and fractions, the goddaughter of the Mistress Senior, 15 years old, and only a guest in the ballroom, our own guest dancer proceeded for his part with what is required on such an occasion, he fell, as we've said, in love — in the first round of the dance the fever already flew to him, and while taking his place for the second, he stood and considered his right hand's thermic enclosure; it climbed to inordinate heights — and he visibly danced himself into love and was netted. — And when she allowed her red ribbons to part and enfold her bare throat into the bargain in an uncommonly negligent manner, he could no longer perceive the bass viol — and finally when, seeking coolness, she waved her red kerchief and it fluttered before and behind him, he was irretrievably lost and even the 4 major and 12 minor prophets combined would have preached in vain. For he was totally helpless and succumbed on the spot when faced with a kerchief in a feminine hand, just like the lion in face of the rattling cartwheel or the elephant faced with a mouse. For do not the village coquettes make the same cannons and war engines out of their kerchiefs as the city coquettes make out of their fans? But the waves of the kerchief are ever more pleasing than the strident club of the turkey fan spreading its tail with a rattle.

In any case, Wutz may plead the excuse that to the best of his knowledge places of public enjoyment open our hearts to all sentiments standing in need of space, to selfless devotion, to courage, and also to love; — in confining workrooms and offices, town halls and privy chambers, our hearts lie as on so many *drying beds* and *ovens* and shrivel.

Wutz carried his heart balloon, afloat and replete with the gas of love, happily back to the school without breathing a word, least of all to the lady handkerchief-standard-bearer herself — not that he was bashful, but because he never desired anything but the present; he was happy being in love, without any further concern. . . .

Why is it to youth that heaven assigned the lustrum of love? Perhaps because it is then that one gasps in classrooms, clerical offices, and other poisonous furnaces: there love rises like a burgeoning rambler about the windows of the said chambers of torture and shows in flickering shadows the great Spring from outside. For let you, Reverend Prefect, and myself, and also yourselves, esteemed janitors, wager that should you wrap our merry Wutz into a hair shirt (he wears one already, when all's said and done) — should you force him to move Ixion's wheel and Sisyphus's philosophers' stone as well as your baby's perambulator — should you starve him, or beat him within an inch of his life — should you (and I would not have thought it of you) because of so wretched a wager show yourselves to be devils incarnate — Wutz will be Wutz and ever manage to slip his bit of amorous happiness into his heart, especially during the dog days! —

Perhaps nowhere have his canicular holidays been depicted more lucidly than in his very own *Pleasures of Werther,* which his biographers need do scarcely more than transcribe. — There he returned after the Sunday evening worship to the village of Auenthal and pitied the people he passed in the streets that they had to remain behind. Once abroad, his bosom expanded with the skies unfolding before him, and as in a dream he listened twice blessed in this avian concert hall, now to the feathered sopranos and now to his fancies. In order to free some of his gushing vitality, he would strike an occasional gallop. As he had always been filled with a certain voluptuous, rapturous yearning just before and after the sunset — man is exalted by night as by a longer death and divested of earth — : he retarded his landfall in Auenthal until his blue tunic was embroidered in gold with the filaments threaded over the ears of the cornfields outside the village by the sun dissolving behind them and until his shadow stalked like a giant across the river and over the hillside. Then he would, with the vesper bells ringing as if from yore, sway into the village brimful with charity toward all mankind, even the Prefect. Stepping around the house of his father and perceiving the moon's reflection in the dormer window above and his Justina in a window below at her Sunday's instruction in the art of letter composing . . . oh if only in this elysian quarter of an hour of his life he could have blasted the room and the letters and the village away from himself by about fifty paces and instead have drawn around him and the letter composer a secluded Tempean vale in the gloaming — if in this valley he with his rapturous soul, which on the way had enfolded every being, could have embraced his most beautiful being as well, and he and she and heaven and earth have receded and melted before a moment ablaze, a flashpoint of earthly ecstasy. . . .

He did nevertheless manage it at eleven o'clock of the night and did not do too badly before then. He told his father, although really Justina, of his syllabus and of his political influence; he opposed the criticism his father employed in correcting her letters with all the weight such an expert commands, and having freshly arrived out of town he fair sparkled with wit — in short, while he fell asleep he heard in his giddily whirling fantasy nothing but the music of the spheres.

To be sure, thou, my dear Wutz, art well able to compose The Pleasures of Werther, thine outer and inner worlds being ever soldered together like the two halves of a shell enveloping you as their oyster; but with us poor buffoons, sitting around the stove here, the outer world rarely provides the choral accompaniment to the merry tuning within us; or at most only when our tuning board breaks down entirely and we start creaking and croaking; or to use another metaphor: it is when our noses are blocked that we are presented with an entire Eden of flowery bowers whose perfume we cannot get wind of.

Also, on every visit our dear schoolmaster gave his Johanna-Therese-Charlotte-Mariana-Klarissa-Heloise-Justel a ginger cake and a potentate as a present; I shall give satisfaction on both those counts.

The potentates came out of his own publishing house; however, whereas the Imperial Stationer's princes and counts are made of a portion of ink, parchment, and wax, he fashioned his potentates much more preciously, from soot and tallow and some twenty colors. In his seminary, the fires were lit with the frames of a deal of potentates, all of whom, with the aforementioned artist's materials, he knew how to copy and represent as ably as if he had been their ambassador. He would daub a quarto sheet first with the stub of a candle and then with soot from the stove — this he would put, black side down, on a white page and top both with some royal portrait — take up a broken-off fork and, with its point pressing down, travel all over the sovereign gentleman's visage and body — this pressure duplicated the potentate, who transferred himself from the black to the white sheet of paper. Thus he took right clever copies of anyone wearing a crown within Europe; mind you, I never denied that his grafting fork scratched and abraded the Russian Tsarina (the late one) and a lot of crown princes to such an extent as to render them suitable only to follow their frames. However, the sooty quarto sheet was merely the praiseworthy sovereigns' etching trough, or if you like, their stroking and *spawning pond* — the potentates' *stretching pond* or finishing machine, though, was the little paint box he used to illuminate entire dynasties, the whole range of shells dressing a single grand duke, while one and the same shell would furnish rouge and makeup and modesty's blush for the royal princesses. — These reigning beauties he presented to her who reigned over him and who was at a loss as to what she should do with this hall of historical portraits.

Regarding the gingerbread, she knew enough to eat it. Giving a ginger cake to one's beloved I rate a difficult thing, as it is apt to be consumed by oneself just before the donation. Had not Wutz paid the three kreutzer for the first one already? Had he not carried the brown rectangulum in his pocket and traveled to within an hour of Auenthal and the appointed awarding? And had he not taken the sweet *votive tablet* out of his pocket again and again in order to check if it still was rectangular? Therein lay its undoing; for during this inspection and taking of evidence, he would knock a couple of insignificant almonds out of the cake; — a habit of his — then he would tackle, not the squaring of the circle, but rather the problem of restoring the squared circle to its pristine condition by biting off neatly the four right angles, producing an octagon, a hexa-histagon — for a circle is an infinite polygon — and after all these mathematical elaborations, the polygon was no longer in a condition to be offered to a young lady — when Wutz skipped and said "Ah well, I'll gobble it up myself," and out came the sigh and in went the geometrical figure. — There will be few Scottish masters, academic governing bodies, or aspiring Masters of Arts who would not be mightily pleased to be told by which deus ex machina Wutz extricated himself in this matter — 'twas with a second gingerbread that he did it, which he would put in his pocket side by side with the first. While he munched number one, number two disembarked without lesions in the charge of the twin, its sentry and fire wall. One thing he learned by experience: in order to transport more than a torso or atom to Auenthal he would have to augment the auxiliary forces or ginger cakes from one week to the next.

He would have transferred to the Prima had not his father transferred from our planet on to the next or to a satellite. Hence he proposed matching his father's amelioration by exchanging his seat in the Higher Sekunda for the schoolmaster's chair. Herr von Ebern, the patron in charge of the living, inserted himself between those two structures, holding his former cook by the hand whom he wished to instal in an office he would be well able to handle, for here also were suckling pigs[1] to be whipped and dressed, albeit not to be eaten. In my review of the school system I have already noted, and earned Herrn Gedike's praise for it, that each peasant boy carries within him an embryo schoolmaster whom a few ecclesiastical years could well embellish — that not only could ancient Rome raise world consuls, but present-day villages could raise school consuls straight from the plough and the furrow — that here one could just as well be *educated* by one's peers as one is *adjudicated* by them in England, and that he to whom one owes most of Scibile one most resembles, namely oneself — that if a whole town (Norica at the foot of the Apennine Mountains) is content to be ruled by four unlettered members of the magistrate (li quatri illiterati), surely the youth of a village could be ruled and birched by a single unlettered man — and that due attention ought to be paid to what I said in the text above. As in this case the memorandum itself is the text, all I will say is that I declared that a village school is staffed satisfactorily. There are (1) the gymnasiarch or pastor, who from one winter to the next dons his canonical coat to visit and startle the schoolhouse — (2) the rectorate, conrectorate, and subrectorate in the person of the master himself — (3) installed as teachers of the lower forms, the schoolmaster's wife, who is, if any human being can be, charged with teaching the girls' school deportment, as well as her son, who is Third Teacher and rascal in one, and exacts sundry tributes and legacies from his pupils before he lets them off saying their lessons and on whose shoulders oftentimes during the regent's absence from home rests the territorial curacy of the entire Protestant school district — (4) finally, a whole caterpillars' nest of collaborators, namely some schoolboys themselves, because there, just as in the Hallean Orphanage itself, the pupils in the higher forms have already turned into teachers of the lower. — As there was such a clamor for practical schools from so many

---

1. Which, it is well known, taste better if flogged to death.

seats of study, *parishes* and *principals* could not but hear it and were only too willing to do their bit. The *parishes* selected for their chairs of teaching only such pedagogical bottoms as had already graced the stools of weavers, tailors, and cobblers and of whom therefore great things could be expected — and indeed do such men by producing in the presence of an attentive institute coats, books, fishing baskets, and all the rest easily convert a nominalistic school into a realistic one, where you are introduced to manufactures. The *schoolmaster* carries things a step farther still in pondering day and night on realistic schoolmastering; there are few tasks of the paterfamilias or his servants in which he does not exercise his village Stoa, and all morning long you see the dispatchers' seminary rushing to and fro, hewing wood and drawing water, etcetera, so that apart from the realistic school he teaches hardly any other and earns his crust in the sweat of his school's brow. . . . No need to tell me that there are poor and neglected country schools as well; suffice if the majority does exhibit the virtues I have just ascribed to it.

I will not apologize for my satellite aberration by embarking on what would be only another. Herr von Ebner would have installed his cook as schoolmaster if only a gifted successor could have been found for the cook, but none was obtained; and as the squire suspected it might be an innovation having both kitchen and school in the charge of *one* subject — although separation and duplication of the servants to school and squire was a much greater and older one; for in the ninth century it had been the task of the pastor of the patronate church even to attend as a servant to the needs of his patron and saddle his horse[2] and the like, and it was only later that those two offices, and others as well, had been sundered — he held onto the cook and summoned the alumnus, who had all along had the good sense to remain in love.

I am guided completely by the creditable certificates that are in my hands and that Wutz had obtained from the Superintendent, for his examination was perhaps one of the most rigorous and felicitous that have latterly come to my attention. Did not Wutz have to recite the Our Father in Greek while the examinatorial board was brushing his velvet trousers with a glass brush; — and later the Symbolum Athanasii in Latin? And was not the examinee able to enumerate the Books of the Bible correctly one after the other without tripping once over the painted flowers and cups on the coffee-drinking examinant's breakfast tray? And was he not asked to catechize a poor beggar boy who was only after a penny and

2. Lange's Ecclesiastical Law, p. 534.

did not pass like his underexaminer but stood like a dumb beast? And was he not asked to dip all his five fingertips into five vessels with water and select the correct one whose water was neither too warm nor too cold for a baby about to be baptized? And last but not least, did he not have to tender three gulden and 36 kreutzer?

On the 13th of May he stepped out of the school a scholar and into his private house a public teacher, and out of the broken black alumnus pupa burst forth a gaily colored cantor butterfly.

On the 9th of July he stood before the altar in Auenthal and was wed to his Justel.

But oh, what an elysian interval between the 13th of May and the 9th of July! — No mortal man will ever again receive such a golden age of eight weeks' duration from heaven; for our wee master alone did the heavenly dew glisten on earth's *star-spangled* pastures. — Weightless thyself and floating in ether thou didst behold through diaphanous earth heavens and suns in their orbits around thee; but no such eight weeks are granted to us alumni of nature, not even one, hardly *one* day when nought but the glow of sunrise and sunset is painted across its pure azure by the heaven *above* and *within* us — when we soar above life, blithely transported as in a dream — when the wild torrent of life does not toss us and shake us and rack us through its whirlpools and cataracts, but rocks us gently on shimmering ripples and bears us along under floral cascades — a day the like of which is not to be found among those that have passed and will leave us lamenting at the end of all others: there wasn't one like it ever again.

I daresay 'twill do us all good if I enlarge on those eight ecstasy weeks or two ecstasy moons. They were made up of days that were all of a kind. Not a cloud overhead. The night sky was skirted by the bewitching glow where the setting sun like a rose had incandesced and faded. At 1 o'clock in the morning the larks started warbling, and all through the night nature played and extemporized her nightingale harmonies. The airs outside pervaded his dreams, and on their wings he soared over blossom trees, which borrowed their fragrant breath from the true ones outside his window. The *dawning* dream carried him tenderly, like the whispering mother her babe, from slumber to waking, and with gulping breast he stepped forth into the clamor of nature, where the sun once again created the earth and both merged in a billowing ocean of bliss. From this early flood tide of exultation and life he returned to his dark little chamber seeking renewed vigor in lesser delights. There he took pleasure in everything, the sunny and the shady windows, the newly swept room, breakfast, which was defrayed by his pastoral revenues, 7 o'clock, because it no longer called him to his Sekunda, his mother, who was happy each morning that he was the master and she had not been called on to vacate the familiar house.

While drinking his coffee, he cut not only his rolls but also the pens for his Messiad, which he fully completed at the time, excepting the three final cantos. The greatest care he expended on cutting the epic pens faultily, be it like stakes or without slits or with an extra slit, which would splutter; seeing that all was to be set in hexameters that must not be intelligible, the poet who, try as he might, could not accomplish the slightest unintelligibility — he ever attained in an instant every verse, meter, and pes — had to resort to achieving it by writing *illegibly*, and a good idea, too. Through this poetical license he forestalled comprehension in a fashion unforced.

At eleven o'clock he would set the table, which had four drawers, and more *in* it than *on* it, first for his birds, then for himself and his mother. He cut the bread, cutting his mother the white crust although he did not care for the brown himself. Oh, my beloved, how can it be that dining at the Hôtel de Bavière or the Römer is not half as merry as at the Wutzean table with its four drawers? — Straightaway after dinner he fashioned not hexameters but wooden spoons; my sister has a dozen of them in her possession. While his mother washed what he carved, the two of them did not neglect feeding their souls; she told him anecdotes about herself and his father, which his academic career had prevented him so far from learning — and he humbly unfolded to her his plan of campaign and blueprint of domesticity, for he loved to ruminate over the thought of his being a paterfamilias. "I shall," said he, "be quite a sensible housekeeper — I'll fatten a piglet for the feast days, and with all the potato and turnip peels, it won't cost us a penny — and for winter Justel's father will have to deliver a cartload of brushwood, and the door will have to be properly lined and upholstered, for, Mother, the likes of us have their pedagogical duties in winter and one can't cope with the cold then." — On the 29th of May a christening followed after these conversations, his first, bringing in his first revenue — a large cashbook to go with it he had already stitched himself at the school — and he studied and counted the few groschen twenty times as if they were new. — He stood at the font in full panoply, and the audience stood on the gallery and in the seignorial pew in their workaday rags. — "tis the sweat of my brow," said he half an hour after the function, imbibing part of his fee in a half pint of beer at this unusual hour. — I am looking forward to some pragmatic pointers from his future biographer as to why Wutz stitched himself a book for the takings but not the expenses, and why he put Louis d'or, Groschen, Pennies at the top when he never took in the first kind of coin at the school.

The function performed and the beer digested, he had the table moved out under the cherry tree and sat down in order to shape some more illegible hexameters in his Messiad. And even while he nibbled and polished off his ham bone for supper he would polish an epic foot or two; and I know full well that it is because of the grease that several cantos appear somewhat oily. As soon as he noticed the sunbeams climbing up from the street to the houses, he handed his mother the requisite house-keeping monies and ran outside in order to fancy in peace what his life would be like in future, in autumn, in winter, on feast days, among his schoolchildren and his own. —

These are merely the weekdays; the blazing splendor of Sunday, how-ever, shines more brightly than even an altarpiece. — And indeed the con-cept of Sunday held by cantors and masters is unrivaled in the souls of this century; it does not surprise me at all if they cannot stay modest during such gala days. Even our Wutz could not but feel the importance of playing the organ, alone among a thousand people — of the custodi-anship of draping the sacred coronation robe around the Senior's shoul-ders, being his valet-de-fantaisie and his blackamoor-de-chambre — or exercising territorial sway over a whole sun-drenched gallery and being enthroned as the officiating lord of the choir on his organ bench, in greater command of the parish's poetry then the pastor was of their prose — of leaning over the balustrade after the sermon, completely sans façon, and in a loud voice proclaiming rather than reading right royal commands. . . . Surely here, if at all, one should think I should admonish dear Wutz: "Remember thy state but a few months ago! Consider that few can be cantors, make use of the inequalities of estates but do not abuse them looking down on us here by the stove." — Of course not! upon my soul, the kindly wee master would not dream of it anyway; if only the peasants had wit enough to look into thy gall-less, sugar-drenched heart, thou waggish, smiling, tripping, gleeful wight: what would they have spied there? Merriment in both thy ventricles, and merriness in thine auricles. Thou didst but count up there on the gallery, thou lovable thing of whom I get more fond by the minute, thy future schoolboys and schoolgirls in their pews and place them all, in anticipation in thy school-room, around thy diminutive nose, wherewith thou hadst decided to sneeze each day, once in the morning and once in the afternoon after a dose from the snuffbox, to make thine entire institute leap to attention and call: Bless thee, Sir! The peasants would further have found in thy heart the mirth that filled it at thy being a setter of folio numerals the size of those on the church clock, for thou didst publish each Sunday upon the black hymn board the number of the next hymn — we authors appear with worse stuff — ; and again thy delight in parading thy musical talents in front of thy father-in-law and thy betrothed; and last but not least, thy hope of swigging the sour-tasting dregs of communion wine all by thyself. A Superior Being must have loved thee as fondly as the present reporter as He caused thy benevolent patron to go to communion during thy eight weeks' lustrum of Eden: for he had the discernment of exchanging the altar wine, a fair imitation of Christ's *potion* on the cross, for Christi *tears* from his cellar; oh, what heavens suffused thy limbs after the cup had been drained. . . . Forsooth, I am tempted to sing his praises each time; I wonder, why is it that I, and possibly all of you, too, derive from this schoolmasterly merry heart so much delight? Might it not be because we ourselves never receive it as fully, for we are weighed down and choked with the thought of the world's vanity and have had a glimpse of the black earth of God's Acre under the swards and flower pieces on which the wee master is frisking his life away? —

He could feel the above-mentioned altar wine bubbling away in his veins until evening; and this part of his Sabbath day needs to be sketched yet. He could only walk out with his Justel on Sunday. First, he would sup at his father-in-law's, though with poor profit; during grace his ravenous appetite weakened, and it disappeared altogether during the merrymaking afterward. If I were able to read it, I could draw on his Messiad for a complete rendering of this evening, as he had woven it into the sixth canto, just as all major scribes braid their curriculum vitae, their kith, kin, and kine, into their opera omnia. He thought to himself, there was surely such an evening in the printed Messiad. In his own, I expect, he set forth in true epic style how the peasants trudged over the banks of their fields, scanning the growth of their haulm, and saluted him from the other side of the water as their duly ordained cantor — how the children made music on leaves and penny whistles, and how every shrub, blossom, and calyx provided a fully cast orchestra, all of whose members sang, hummed, or buzzed — and how, finally, all became festive as if Earth herself observed Sunday, while hills and woods waved their censers around this magic circle, and the sun made his way toward the West through a brilliant triumphal arch, while the moon rose in a pale arch from the East. Oh the hues and the rays and the luminous spheres in which thou settest thy pallid earth, Father of Light! And now the sun shrank to a single red beam, which joined with the reflected evening glow on the brow of his betrothed; and she who had known only silent emotions said to Wutz that as a child she had oftentimes longed to stand on the red hills of sunset and to descend with the sun to those rose-tinted lands lying beyond the evening glow. While his mother rang the Vesper bell, he laid his hat on his knees and, without folding his hands, gazed at the red spot in the sky where the sun had been last and down where the river flowed, bearing deep shadows; and he felt as if the evening bell rang the world and, once more, his father to rest — for the first and the last time in his life his heart transcended the earthly scene — and something seemed to call to him from those evening sounds that he was now to die of joy. . . . Filled with passion and rapture, he embraced his betrothed, saying: "Oh how fond I am of thee, how eternally fond!" From the river came sounds of flutes and singing and drew nearer; beside himself, he pressed himself to her bosom longing to die united, believing the heavenly sounds would waft their two souls away and breathe them like sparks of dew upon the river banks of Eden. The voice sang:

> O God, how lovely is Thine earth
> How worthy of a man's content
> So may I evermore with mirth
> Rejoice in field and firmament.

'Twas a gondola from town with some flutes and young fellows in fine voice. He and Justina walked with the floating gondola along the river path, hand in hand, and Justina tried to sing softly; sundry heavens walked with them. When the gondola floated around a wooded promontory, Justina stopped him gently so that they would not follow, and when the vessel had disappeared behind it, she threw her arms around his neck in the first blushing kiss. . . . Oh never to be forgotten first of June! he writes. — They accompanied and hearkened afar to the floating music; and dreams played around them until she said: "It is late and the evening glow has moved on, and all is quiet in the village." They walked home. He opened the windows of his moonlit room and with a whispered goodnight tiptoed past his mother, who was already asleep. —

Each morning the thought that he had slept himself one night nearer to the wedding day, the 8th of June, shone on him like a dawn; and during the day, the joy of not yet having passed through the elysian days, which had interposed themselves between him and the bridal bed, skipped along with him. Thus, like the metaphysicians' ass, he held his head between the two bundles of hay, between the present and the future; yet, not being an ass or a scholastic, he browsed and plucked from both bundles at once. . . . Indeed, human beings should never be asses, be it of the indifferentistic, the wooden, or the Balaamitic kind, and I have my reasons for saying this. . . . I am going to break off here as I wish to consider whether I shall depict the wedding day or not. And by the way, I have more than enough colors for the mosaic. —

To tell you the truth, I did not attend his day of honor, nor any such of my own; I shall therefore describe it as best I can and — else I am like to have none — compose me a pleasure trip.

I can't think of a more suitable place or page for it, anyway, than this here for making the readers aware of my sufferings: the magic scenes in Switzerland where I lay myself down — the forms of Apollo and Venus on which my eyes feast — the glorious fatherland for which I lay down my life, the life that was ennobled by it before — the bridal bed into which I climb, all of it has been, alas, painted only or printed by a strange hand or by my own; and if only thou, thou heavenly one to whom I shall remain true, who shall remain true to me, with whom I saunter through arcadian nights in July, with whom I gaze on the setting sun and the rising moon, and for whose sake I love all thy sisters, if only thou — werest; alas, thou art an altarpiece, and I seek thee in vain.

It is true that the god of the River Nile, Hercules, and other gods were, like myself, offered merely manufactured maidens; but they had received real ones first.

We'll have to take a peep into the school- and wedding-house on Saturday, for there will be no time left on Sunday to study the premises of this eve of the nuptials; it was for the same reason that the world (according to the older theologians) was created during six days and not in *one* minute, so that the angels could peruse the Book of Nature as it unfolded in easy stages. On Saturday, the bridegroom is conspicuously running hither and thither between two corporibus piis, viz, the parsonage and the schoolhouse, heaving four settles out of the former and into the latter. He borrowed these constructions from the pastor in order to offer them to the accommodator himself as his prince bishop, to the pastor's wife as the godmother of the bride, to the subprefect of his seminary, and to the bride herself. You don't have to tell me that this borrowing luxury on the part of the bridegroom cannot be wholly defended; however, those colossal leased chairs (people and chairs have shrunk nowadays) had put fillets of blue cloth over their whorls of false cow hair on armrests and seats, and yellow nail galaxies darted along yellow braid like chained lightning, and sitting on the *edge* of those chairs was like wearing a double posterior — as I said, I never extolled this posterior luxury of either debtor or creditor as a model; although, on the other hand, anyone who has seen something of the *Schulz of Paris* must admit that the extravagance at the Palais royal, and indeed any court, seems to be greater. And how can I fully convince those Methodists of the stricter observance of the merits of Wutz's grandfather- and easy-chair that takes hold of the ground with four lion's paws, linked by four wooden crossbars — the perches of chirpy finches and linnets — whose chignon is more than gorgeously sheathed in a flowery hide, and that reaches out for an occupant with two hirsute arms — scraggy with age? . . . This question mark may come as a surprise to those readers who have lost track of the paragraphs.

The pewter dinner service that the groom also fetched from his prince bishop can be more thoroughly studied under the auctioneer should it ever be put to the hammer, but this much the wedding guests know: the salad bowl, sauce boat, cheese dish, and mustard jar were all represented by one single platter, which was, however, scrubbed clean before it took on each new role.

A whole Nile and Alpheus gushed over each floorboard, which had to be rinsed of good honest garden soil, against each bedpost and up the windowframe, leaving behind the usual sediment of a flood, to whit, *sand*. According to the rules of the novel, our little schoolmaster should now be arraigning himself and stretching himself out in a meadow beneath a rippling coverlet of flowers and grass and engulfed by dream upon dream of love — alas, he was plucking hens and ducks in the kitchen and carving firewood for the coffee and roasts, and even the roasts themselves, and serving the Sunday on Saturday by decreeing and performing fifty kitchen orders at once, clad in the blue apron of his mother-in-law, and skipping hither and thither and everywhere, with his head horned by curlers and his hair tied up like the tail of a squirrel: "for 'tisn't every Sunday that I get married," said he.

There is nothing more distasteful than seeing and hearing a hundred forerunners and outriders to one tiny enjoyment; yet nothing is sweeter than doing the forerunning and outriding yourself; for the activity that we not only see but partake in turns the enjoyment into a fruit that we ourselves have sown, watered, and gathered; and we are spared the terrible tension of waiting, into the bargain.

Heavens, I would need a whole Saturday for a thorough report: for I cast only a glance into the Wutzean kitchen in passing — oh the writhing! and the reeking! — Why are murder and marriage so closely related, as

are the pertaining commandments? Why is it that a royal wedding is to
folk so often what a bourgeois one is to fowl, viz, a St. Bartholomew's
Massacre?

Yet nobody in the wedding house spent these two days of rejoicing in
a more discountenanced and disconsolate state than the two finches and
three linnets: these the bridegroom, a lover of cleanliness as well as of
birds, arrested — after much flapping of aprons and throwing of nightcaps — and drove out of their ballroom and into a couple of Carthusian
wire cells and, thus suspended, they hopped about in an attic.

Wutz narrates both in his "Wutzean Ancient History" and his
"Reader for Intermediate Children" that at 7 o'clock in the evening,
when the tailor tried the new trousers, waistcoat, and frock on our Hymen, all had been newly born, burnished, and in metrical order, excluding himself. An ineffable calm rests on each chair and table in a newly
arranged and polished room! Whereas one feels under notice to quit
without further delay in chaotic surroundings.

His night (as well as the next) myself and the sun shall pass over, and
we meet him again on the Sunday morn as, flushed and electrified by the
thought of today's paradise, he comes rushing downstairs and into the
radiant room on which we spent so much labor and ink yesterday, doing
it up with lotions — mouchoir de Venus and makeup tissue (floor cloth) —
powder case (sandbox), and sundry toiletry tubs and utensils. He had
awoken seven times in the night and had seven times rejoiced at the morrow; also arisen two hours early in order to feed on them both minute
by minute. Methinks I am stepping through the door with the master to
whom the minutes of this day are as honey cells, to be drained by him
one by one, and each bearing a further chalice of honey. Not for a pension for life could our cantor have conceived of a house in the whole wide
world where today did not dwell Sunday, sunshine, and happiness. — The
second thing he opened downstairs after the door was a transom in order
to let a fluttering butterfly — a floating sequin of silver, a winged petal
and image of *Cupid*, out of *Hymen's* chamber. He went on to feed his choir
of birds in their cages in advance of the turbulent day, and at the open
window he played on the paternal fiddle the dance tunes to which he had
danced himself from Shrove Tuesday night to the wedding night. It is
only striking 5 o'clock, dearest friend, and there is no great hurry. Let us
have the two yards of cravat (into which, like formerly into the arms of
the bride, you are dancing while your mother is holding the other end)
and also the band for the pigtail tied smoothly two full hours before the
bells ring. I would gladly exchange the grandfather chair and the stove,

whose assessor I am for the secret of turning myself and my audience into transparent sylphs, so that our entire brotherhood might wing their way into the garden after the fidgety bridegroom and not break into his secret happiness as he cuts for a female heart, which is neither adamantine nor false, natural flowers to match — where he shakes glistening beetles and dewdrops from petals, gladly awaiting the bee to be suckled a last time at the flowery breast — where he remembers the Sunday morns of his boyhood, when his legs barely spanned the flower beds, and the chilly pulpit that was to receive the nosegay. Go home, son of thy forebear, and look not back on this eighth of June to the west where the silent six feet of God's acre cover many a friend, but look forward, to the east where thou wilt catch a glimpse of the sun and the door to the parsonage and Justina slipping through in order to have her hair done and be laced into her wedding dress by her godmother's hand. I can feel how my audience is eager to be turned into sylphs again to flutter around the bride; but she does not care for that.

At last the cerulean coat — the livery color of millers and schoolmasters — its buttonholes blackened, and the smoothing hand of his mother, easing all wrinkles, rest on the Masterkin's body, and his hat and his hymnal are all that is missing. And now — to be sure, I, too, know the meaning of splendor, royal splendor at royal weddings, their cannonades, fireworks, parades, and apparel, yet I would not speak of the likes of that in the same breath as the Wutzean nuptials: just follow the man with your eyes as he is taking the path of sunshine and heaven to his betrothed, looking across at that other path to the seminary while thinking to himself: "Who would have thought it four years ago"; I say, look at him! Does not the maidservant of the Auenthal parsonage gaze likewise, though she be carrying water, and fold away that splendid full dress down to the last fringe in the clothes compartment of her mind? Is he not powdered from the tip of his nose to the top of his toes? Are not the red wings of the gate at his father-in-law's thrown wide open, and does he not stride through them just as his betrothed, adorned by her hairstylist, steals through the lych-gate? And do they not, thus rigged out and bepowdered, bump into each other and not have the courage to bid each other Good Morning? For have either of them ever before in their lives beheld a sight more sumptuous and noble than each other this morning? And is not in this pardonable embarrassment the long splint a godsend, which her young brother has cut and holds out to the sister that she might wind around it and fasten like to a vine stake the bunch and nosegay for the precentor's buttonhole? Will envious lady friends speak to me ever again if I now dip my paintbrush and color for them the finery of the bride, the trembling gold in her hair replacing her hairpin, the three gold medallions on her breast with the miniature German Emperors,[3] and below them the silver ingots, now cast into buttons? . . . I could throw my paintbrush at somebody's head at the thought that my dear Wutz and his bride might, when this is printed, be ridiculed by coquettes and a similar Satan's brood: think ye, ye townish distilled and tattooed sellers of souls who measure and prize in a man all but his heart, that this would leave me and my readers indifferent or that we would not gladly exchange your drawn cheeks, twitching lips, eyes singeing with wiles and desires, arms compliant to every chance, and even your sentimental declaimings for one single scene where love's rays are reflected in the dawning blush, when the innocent soul is baring herself to every eye but her own, and when a hundred innermost struggles ensoul the transparent countenance, and where, in a word, my loving pair were themselves the actors as the jolly old prankster of a father-in-law caught hold of the befrizzed and bepowdered heads of the two of them and smartly guided them to a kiss? Oh, thy happy blush, my dear Wutz! — and thy shy one, darling Justina! —

Who would, shortly before his marriage contract, consider more keenly these and related matters and afterward act them more subtly than the present biographer himself?

This is where the din made by the children and coopers in the street and by the reviewers in Leipzig prevent him from setting down things in detail, like the magnificent cornerpieces and treble rosettes with which the groom at the organ embellished each line of the hymn — his best hat saluting the choir on the wing of a wooden angel — the name of Justina gracing the pedal pipes — his pleasure and joy as they joined their right hands before the ordinance (the Golden Bull and Imperial Charter of matrimony), and he with his ring finger tickled the palm of her hand under a screen as it were — their entrance into the banqueting hall, where perchance the grandest and most prominent personages and authorities of the village were assembled, a pastor, a pastor's wife, a subprefect, and a bride. But I expect it shall be met with approval if I stretch my legs and step over the whole of the wedding-breakfast and -pasture and also the afternoon to drop in again in the evening when the subprefect stretches his legs in a dance or two. In fact, things are pretty hectic already. — Battleclouds of tobacco smoke and a steam bath released from the soup

---

3. In some German regions, girls wear three ducats around their necks.

bowls swirl around the three candles and create fogbanks between the folk. — The violoncellist and the violinist do not so much bow strange guts as fill their own. — All Auenthal supplies the gallery, jostling on the sill and peering through the window, and the village youth dance outside thirty yards from the orchestra, and very handsomely, too. — The old village Bonne shouts her most interesting personal tidbits into the ear of the pastor's wife, who in turn gets her own off her chest with sneezing and coughing, each eager to follow her historical call of nature and begrudging the other's being ensconced on the stool. — The pastor looks like the bosom disciple of the bosom disciple John, whom the painters portray holding a cup in his hand, and his laugh is more stentorian than his sermons. — The prefect flits around like a dandy, leaving them all behind. — My Maria paddles and splashes in all four rivers of paradise and is mightily lifted and rocked by the swell of the ocean of joy. — Only one of the bridesmaids (with a skin and a soul too tender for the calluses of her profession) hears the drumbeat of joy as if it were muffled by echoes and swathed in crape like at a royal interment, and the hushed rapture pervades her bosom in the shape of a sigh. — My Schoolmaster (he is allowed to appear twice in the kitchen piece) steps with his connubial half under the doorway, which has a swallows globe as its dessus de porte, and looks up to the silent star-spangled heaven above him, thinking that each large sun there was looking down and into his window just like the people of Auenthal. . . . Sail thou merrily over thine evaporating droplet of time, thou canst do it; though not all of us can: the solitary bridesmaid cannot, for one. — Oh, had I, like thee, on a wedding morn encountered a frightened butterfly enticed away from the flowers, like thee met the bee enclosed in the calyx, like thee noted the church clock run down at 7 o'clock, like thee beheld a silent heaven above and a noisy heaven below: I should have remembered that it is not on this tempestuous globe, where the winds buffet our flowers, that the resting place should be looked for, where their fragrance enfolds us unhindered, or an eye might be found free from dust, an eye *without* raindrops hurled at us by those tempests — and had the blazing goddess of joy stood as close to my bosom I should yet have glanced yonder at the ashes into which she who hails from the sun and not our glacial zones has already calcified other poor mortals by her embrace; — and oh, if even the foregoing description of a great pleasure left me so sad, I should, if, oh hand reaching from infinite heights low down into this earth! thou borest one down for me from above, like a flower brought forth by the sun, I should let tears of joy flow on this fatherly hand and with too feeble an eye turn away from mankind. . . .

Now, while I say all this, Wutz's wedding is long over and past, his Justina is old, and he himself in the graveyard; the current of time has submerged and buried him, and all these bright days under its four- and fivefold layers of sediment; and the selfsame interring deposit is mounting higher and higher around ourselves; only another three minutes and it will have reached our hearts and smoothly settle over myself and ye.

While this mood is upon me, let no one expect me to impart the Masterkin's many delights out of his Manual of Delights, his Christmas-, Kermess-, and School-Delights in particular — it may come to pass, possibly in a posthumous postscript by and by, but not today. Today we had better take a last look at the happy Wutz, alive and dead, before we take our leave.

I should not have known much at all of the man, in spite of passing his door dozens of times, had not last year on the 12th of May the old Justina stood in it and called over to me when she saw me filling my slate in passing: was not I, too, a maker of books? "To be sure, dear lady," said I, "I make these things year in and year out and afterward give them away to the public." — Would I then, she continued, kindly come in for a while to her husband who also made books but who was in a sorry state?

A stroke had paralyzed the old man's left side, either because a thaler-sized eczema had healed inward or because of old age. He sat up in his bed, supported by pillows, and with a hoard of objects, which I shall specify presently, in front of him on the counterpane. A sick man, like a traveler — and is he not such? — is quickly familiar with anyone; within reach and sight of worlds more sublime one does no longer stand on formalities in this mangy one. He complained that his old woman had been forced to look out for a book writer for three days but had not struck lucky till now: but he must have one who would take over, put in order, and catalogue his library and also append, for completion's sake, to his biography his last hours should they now occur; for his old woman was no scholaress, and he had sent his son up to Heidelberg university for three weeks.

His scattering of pockmarks and wrinkles bestowed the merriest highlights on his round little face; each one seemed like a smiling mouth: yet neither myself nor my semiology were pleased by the flashing of his eyes, the twitching of his eyebrows and the corners of his mouth, and the trembling of his lips.

I will keep my promise to specify: on the counterpane rested a baby bonnet of green taffeta, with one ribbon torn off, a toy whip with glued-on tinsel, well worn, a tin finger ring, a box of miniature books in 128-mo format, a wall clock, a soiled copybook, and a finger-long birdtrap.

These were the relics and late fruit of his playful childhood. The art gallery for these, his *Grecian antiquities*, had from the first been under the stairs — for in a house that is the flower tub and propagating box of a single family tree, things stay untouched in one and the same place for half a century — ; and as keeping his toys in historical order had been an Imperial Charter with him from his childhood on, and as no one but he would ever look under the stairs from one end of the year to the other: he could even on the eve of his death surround himself with these funeral urns of a life already past, and rejoice to look back as he could no longer look forward. To be sure, thou couldst not enter into *ancient temples* at Sans Souci or Dresden, there to worship the *Universal Spirit of the Beautiful Nature of Art*, my little Maria, nevertheless thou couldst look into thy Childhood Antiquities *Tabernacle* under the dusky stairs, and the rays of the resurging childhood would play on the gloomy corners like those of the painted Child Jesus did in his manger! Oh, if greater souls than thou would but extract as much sweetness and fragrance from the whole of Nature's orangery as thou didst from the prickly green leaf to which Fate had attached thee, it would be gardens, not leaves, that they would relish; and it would no longer amaze these better yet happier souls that *merry* masterkins can exist.

Wutz said, turning his head toward the bookshelf: "When I have wearied myself reading and marking my serious works, I look at these knick-nacks for hours, and it is to be hoped that it will not discredit a writer of books."

Methinks nothing would serve the world better now than if I presented it with the elucidating catalogue of these artifacts and knicknacks as it was presented to me by the invalid. The tin ring had been slipped on his finger by the previous pastor's four-year-old miss as a pledge when they had been truly and properly wedded by a playmate, and the wretched tin had soldered him to her more firmly than many a nobler metal many a nobler person, and their marriage endured for fifty-four minutes. Later he frequently thought of the ring and the olden times when he, the raven alumnus, saw her — plumed standard nodding — strolling along on the skinny arm of a dappled dandy. Anyway, so far I endeavored in vain to conceal the fact that he fell in love with anything that resembled a woman; a tendency shared by the rest of these merry ones; and perhaps they can do that because their love resides between the extremes of love, and it borrows from both, as the bosom is band and mélange of the platonic and the epicurean charms. — As he used to assist his father in winding the church clock, like the crown princes once escorted their fathers to meetings of state, a little matter like that could nudge him toward drilling holes in a lacquered box and converting it into a wall clock that never worked — like other state bodies — notwithstanding large weights and cogwheels that had been removed from the frame of his Nuremberg horses and employed in a higher service. The green baby bonnet trimmed with lace, the only survival of his former four-year-old head, was his bust and plaster of Paris cast of the little Wutz, who had gone forth now into a large one. His workaday clothes represent a man far more intimately than a portrait; — therefore Wutz contemplated the green baby bonnet with a yearning desire, and from the frozen fields of old age the greensward of a childhood long covered by snow seemed to gleam: "If only," said he, "I had my old flannel petticoat, too, which they always tied under my arms!" — I am familiar with the first copybook of the King of Prussia as well as that of Masterkin Wutz, and having held both in my hand, I can decree that the King wrote an inferior hand as a man, and the Masterkin as a child. "Mother," said he to his wife, "will you look at your husband's hand here [in the copy] and there [in his calligraphical masterpiece of a deed which he had pinned to the wall]; I could eat myself for love, Mother!" His wife was the only person he boasted to; for I must reckon at full value the advantage that accrues from the matrimonial state in that it allows the husband an alter ego to whom he may brag to his heart's content. If only the German public could be persuaded to be such an alter ego for us authors! — The box was a bookcase for the Lilliputian tracts in calendar format, which he had published in his childhood by transcribing a verse from the Bible and binding it with the comment: "Yet another respectable *Cober*[4] produced!" Other authors are capable of this but not before they are adults. While he reported to me on these early endeavors, he remarked: "Is one not truly a fool as a child? Yet even at that stage the auctorial urge was apparent, if in an immature and ridiculous form" and smiled contentedly over the current one. — It was the same with the lime twig: was not the three-inch twig, which he painted with beer and on which he caught flies by their legs, the ancestor of the three-foot-long trap *behind* which he spent his pleasantest hours, while the finches spent their most odious ones *on* it? The bird catcher's craft demands a tranquil, inwardly happy kind of a soul.

It will be easily understood that his greatest invalid comfort was af-

---

4. *Cober's* "Chamber Sermons" — in which is contained more spirit (albeit frequently one of foolishness) than in twenty of today's washed-out sermon piles combined.

forded him by an old almanac with its awful etchings of the twelve months. During each month of the year he derived, without doffing his hat to some curator or knocking on the door of some art gallery, greater painterly and artistic delight than other Germans who doff their hat and knock. For he roamed the monthly vignettes — omitting the month of the ramble — and fantasized into the scenes of the woodcuts all that he and they were in need of. It goes without saying that he felt braced in days of health and sickness alike when he climbed into the tattered black tree in the January winter piece and (in his imagination) stood under the lowering sky, which hung like a canopy over the meadows and fields bound in their winter sleep. The whole month of June drew around him its long days and tall grasses, while in his fancy he brought the landscape vignette to fruition where little crosses, which were meant to be birds, flitted across the grey paper and where the engraver had macerated the lush summer foliage into skeleton leaves. Nevertheless, fantasy fashions each little wood chip into a miraculous medal and each ass's jawbone into a well; the five senses merely provide the cartoons, the outlines only of pleasure or displeasure.

The patient skipped May, which surrounded the house anyway. The cherry blossoms the merry month wears in its green hair, and the May lilies it pins on his bosom as a fragrant corsage, he did not sniff — his smell was gone — but he looked at them and had some of them in a bowl at his bedside.

I have achieved cleverly what I set out to do, namely to lead myself and my audience for six or seven pages away from the sorrowful moment when, in the sight of us all, Death steps up to the bed of our sick friend and slowly with icy fingers pierces his warm breast, alarms the merrily beating heart, captures it, and arrests it forever. To be sure, in the end the moment and its attendant are bound to come together.

I stayed the whole day and in the evening offered to sit with him through the night. His restless brain and his twitching features had firmly convinced me that the stroke would recur in the night; this did not happen, however, to the greatest relief of myself and the Masterkin. For he had told me — and it says so in his last little treatise — that there was nothing more beautiful and more easy than to die on a bright day: that through the closed eyes the soul still saw the sun up in the sky and rose from the withered body into the great blue ocean of light out there; whereas having to leave the warm body in a dark tempestuous night, to effect the long drop into the desolate grave when Nature herself sat there, with her eyes closed, adying — that was too hard a death.

At half past eleven at night, his two best *boyhood friends* came once more to his bedside, Sleep and Dream, to take leave from him as it were. Or will ye abide? Are ye perchance the two friends of mankind who take the slain man from Death's bloody hands and carry him cradled in your motherly arms through cold subterranean caves into the bright land where a new morning sun and new morning flowers will animate him into new life with their breath? —

I was alone in the room — I heard nought but the invalid's breath and the tick of my watch measuring out his short life. — The yellow full moon hung low and large in the south, her lifeless light riming the May lilies of the man and the reluctant clock and green cap of the child. — The gentle cherry tree outside the window traced its quivering silhouette on a background of moonlight inside. — Now and again a blazing star was sent shooting across the sky and, like a man, passed away. — It occurred to me that the very room, which now, draped in black, was the anteroom of the grave, had been occupied by the invalid 43 years ago on the morrow, the 13th of May, the day on which his elysian eight weeks commenced. — I saw that the man on whom this cherry tree had then showered fragrance and dreams was lying there, oppressed by a dream and bereft of smell, and that he might move out of this room even today, and that all, all was past, never to return ... and at this moment Wutz reached for something with his unparalyzed arm, as if trying to capture a falling heaven — and it was at this trembling minute that the hand of the month on my watch clicked and leapt on because it was 12 o'clock, from the 12th to the 13th of May.... Death seemed to set my watch, I heard him masticating the man and his joys, and the World and Time seemed to crumble in a stream of decay into the abyss! ...

Each time my watch gives a leap at midnight, I remember this minute; but may it never again force its way among those minutes that are left to me!

The dying man — this name will hardly fit him much longer — opened two burning eyes and looked at me for a long time trying to recognize me. In his dream he had been a child again, asway on a bed of lilies that had surged up under him and then melted into an upraised cloud of roses, which had sailed away with him through golden dawns and across sweet-smelling fields of flowers — the sun had smiled on him with the white face of a maiden and beamed upon him and finally plunged toward his cloud in the shape of a haloed maiden, and he had been afraid that he might not be able to bring his left paralyzed arm up and around her. — At that he woke from his last, or last but one, dream; for on the long dream of life are the short motley dreams of the night drawn and embroidered like fantasy flowers.

The river of life flowed to his head, ever faster and wider: he believed himself young again and again; the moon he mistook for the overcast sun; he imagined he was a winged cherub attached to a rainbow on a marigold chain, swinging high and low in infinite arcs, swung across chasms and up toward the sun by the four-year-old giver of rings. . . . Toward 4 o'clock in the morning he could see us no longer, although dawn had arrived in the room — his eyes stared stonily — one facial twitch chased the other — his mouth was drawn into an ever-widening smile of delight — spring fantasies never known in this life nor pertaining to the next played with the sinking soul — at last the Angel of Death flung the pale shroud over his countenance and under its cover plucked the soul in full flower and with its deepest roots from its corporeal hotbed of organic soil. . . . Dying is elevated; behind black curtains the silent miracle is wrought by lone Death laboring for the otherworld, leaving us mortals, our eyes tearful but dull, beside the superterrestial scene. . . .

"My poor Father," said his widow, "if they had told you 43 years ago that they would carry you out of the house on the 13th of May, when your eight weeks began!" — "His eight weeks," said I, "are starting again, only this time they will last longer."

When I left at 11 o'clock, the earth was to me as if hallowed and the dead seemed to walk by my side; I looked up to the sky as if I could seek the dead man only in one direction within the infinite ether; and on the crest of the hill with its commanding view of the town I looked back once more on the arena of suffering and among all the houses of Auenthal saw only one whose chimney was cold, and saw the gravedigger doing his work in the graveyard beyond, and heard the bell tolling for him, and thought of his widow pulling the rope in the belfry while her tears flowed: so that I felt the nothingness of us all and swore to disdain such an insignificant life, to deserve it, and to delight in it. —

Well for thee, dear Wutz, that I when I go to Auenthal to seek out thy grass-covered grave, to grieve at the chrysalis of the night moth that was buried in your grave and creeps forth winged, at your grave's being a pleasure ground for tunneling earthworms, sluggish snails, teeming ants, and nibbling caterpillars, whilst thou liest deep below all of them on thy wood shavings, thy head undisturbed, not a ray of sunshine piercing thy coffin boards, and thine eyes sealed by the winding-sheet, to caress thee — well for thee, that then I can say: "while he had life he enjoyed it more merrily than we all."

Enough, my friends — it is 12 o'clock and the hand has leapt forward to a new day and called to our mind the twofold sleep, the sleep of the short and the sleep of the long night. . . .

Hesperus; or, 45 Dog Post Days

THE FOLLOWING EXCERPT IS THE SECOND HALF OF THE
passage "On the Desert and the Promised Land of the Human Race,"
which forms the Sixth Leap Day of *Hesperus* (*W* 2.871ff.). The essay may
have been prompted by the publication in 1793 of the second part of
Herder's *Letters on the Furtherance of Humanity* and by the fact that Christian Otto was working at the time on a study of European reformations
and revolutions (*H-KA* 1.3.424).

For Jean Paul, Hesperus was the star of hope. Hope, the "guarantor
of providence," is, he says in the preface to his late work *Political Fasting
Sermons*, the theme common to all his political writings. (It was probably
the theme that attracted him most to Herder, in whose philosophy of the
history of man an innate hope of immortality is central to humanity's
Bildung.)[1] Nowhere is the sentiment more emotionally outpoured than
in *Hesperus*. In a letter to Karl von Knebel, Jean Paul speaks of the "two
foci" of his work, that "crazy ellipse" on the one hand (the "Schoppe

---

1. 10.1072. Cf. Johann Gottfried Herder, "Ideen zur Philosophie der Geschichte der
Menschheit," in *Sämtliche Werke*, ed. B. Suphan (Hildesheim, 1978), 13:165.

frenzy" of his satirical characters); on the other, his "Hesperus sentiment" (*H-KA* 3.5.126). Yet even here, hope is presented as a question,
and the "eternal hope" at the end is postulated as a moral imperative. But
if the passage does not dispel doubts, it does serve to dispel the suspicion
that Jean Paul's nostalgia, his dreamings and rememberings, were re-
gressive. "All memories are turned into hopes," says the narrator in the
opening chapter of *Hesperus*; and in *Palingeneses*, hopes are said to be humanity's possessions (*W* 1.494; 8, 771).

Jean Paul's work has been — and *mutatis mutandis* can justifiably be —
read in the light of Bloch's principle of hope.[2] This passage in particular
is an example of progressive, as well as realistically prophetic, "dreaming
ahead." In this it is characteristic of the future-directedness in Jean Paul's
work as a whole. Myths of a golden age and of one-time innocence did
not appeal to him, and his increasing unhappiness with the Judeo-
Christian heritage seems to refer especially to myths of the Fall and of
fallen man.

On the Desert and the Promised Land of the Human Race

Mankind has, then, the capacity of eternal improvement; but also
hope? —

The disturbed *balance* of his own forces makes individual man miserable, the *inequality* of its citizens, the *inequality* of its peoples makes the
earth miserable; in the way that all lightning springs from the propin-
quity of the ether's ebb- and flood-tide and all storms from the uneven
air distribution. Happily, it is in the nature of mountains to fill in the
valleys.

It is not the inequalities of possessions for the most part — for the
wealthy is counterpoised by the voice- and fist-majority of the poor —
but the inequality of culture that generates and distributes the political
pressure mechanisms and pressure pumps. The lex agraria in the fields
of the sciences will in the end run in the physical fields as well. Ever since
the tree of knowledge thrust its branches from the philosophical *school
windows* and the clerical *church windows* into the common garden: all
peoples have been invigorated. — Unequal education shackles western

---

2. Dorothee Hedinger-Frohner; *Der utopische Gehalt des Hesperus* (Bonn, 1977).

India to the foot of Europe, helots to Spartans, and the hollow iron skull [1] with its presser bar on the negro tongue presupposes a hollow skull of a different sort.

With the terrible inequalities of peoples in might, wealth, and culture, only a universal storm blowing from all compass points can hope to conclude with a durable calm. A permanent balance in Europe presupposes a balance in the four remaining continents also, which, allowing for minor librations, one may promise our sphere. Discovering a savage will in future become as unlikely as discovering a new island. One people must draw the other out of their callow age. A more equal culture will ratify trading contracts to more equal advantage. Humanity's longest monsoons — during which transplantations of peoples used to take place like flowers transplanted on overcast days — have blown themselves out. One midnight specter remains, reaching far into the eons of light — war. But the claws and beaks of heraldic eagles keep growing until, like boars' tusks, they will curl and disable themselves. Just as Vesuvius was reckoned to contain matter for no more than 43 eruptions, so one might calculate future wars. This long-lasting thunderstorm hovering over our sphere for the last six millenia will rage on until storm clouds and earth have sated each other with an *equal* amount of lightning matter. Only in a *common* flare will all peoples brighten; and the deposit is blood and the bones of the dead. Were the earth to be squeezed to half its size: the time of its moral — and physical — evolution would also be halved.

With the wars, science's strongest drag chains are cast off. Once war engines were the sowing engines of new knowledge as they suppressed old harvests; nowadays it is the press, which scatters the pollen more gently and farther afield. Greece would need to send nothing in Alexander's place to Asia now but a — printsetter; the conqueror grafteth but the writer soweth.

It is one of the Enlightenment's peculiarities that, while still allowing the individual the deception and weakness of vice, it delivers peoples from corporate vices and communal delusions — like robbery on the high seas or wreckage, for instance. We commit our finest and our worst deeds in company; war being one example. Trading in negroes must come to an end in our days unless trading in subjects should start. [2]

The tallest, most towering thrones, like the tallest mountains, stand

---

1. As is well known, the poor negro's head is locked into a hollow iron skull, which depresses his tongue.
2. Written in the year 1792.

in the most temperate countries. The political hills, as well as the physical ones (especially if they spit fire) dwindle day by day, finally coming to rest along with the valleys in *one* — plain.

From all of this follows:

There will be a Golden Age one day, enjoyed even now by every wise and virtuous man, when it will be easier to live well because it will be easier to live at all — when individuals but not peoples will sin — when mankind will have not greater joy (this particular honey being extracted from every flower and greenfly) but greater virtue — when the people partake in thinking and the thinker in toiling[3] so that he might do without helots — when judicial and martial murder are outlawed and cannonballs are only now and again encountered by ploughshares — When that era has dawned, the machine will no longer be clogged by a preponderance of the good — when it has dawned it will not necessarily be human nature to get out of hand again and for a storm to gather (for so far, the noble was only engaged in a running battle with overpowering evil), just as on the hot St. Helena's Island[4] there are, according to Forster, no thunderstorms. —

When this gala time dawns, our children's children will be — no more. Here we stand in the evening and after our dark day behold the glowing sun as it sets and promises us behind the last glow the serene sabbath of mankind; but our progeny will have to pass through a night of high winds and through a poisonous vapor before at last, over a happier earth, an eternal morning breeze, its floriferous nymphs preceding the sun and pushing all clouds aside, breathes on a sighless mankind. Astronomy has promised earth an eternal spring equinox,[5] and history promises her a nobler one; who knows, both eternal springs may perchance coincide.

And we who were thrust down when man vanished among men must raise ourselves before mankind: When I consider the Greeks I perceive that our hopes outpace fate itself. — As we traverse the icy Alps with lights in the night that we should not be frightened by the abysses and the long journey: so fate surrounds us with night and only hands us torches for the *next* part of the way that we should not be distressed at the crevices of the future and the distance of our destination. — There were centuries

3. The millionaire presupposes beggars, the scholar helots; the individuals' higher education is paid for by the multitude's degeneration.

4. Written in 1792. Now the storm, once hovering in the sky over all Europe, rests on the flat earth there.

5. For after 400,000 years, the earth's axis will stand, like Jupiter's now, perpendicular on its path.

when mankind was led blindfold — from one dungeon into another; — there were other centuries when poltergeists walked and wrought havoc all night but naught was displaced at daybreak; there can be no centuries but those in which individuals die while peoples arise, and when peoples decline while mankind rises; when mankind declines and falls itself, and perishes with the shattering sphere . . . what shall comfort us?

A veiled eye behind Time, an eternal heart beyond the world. There is a higher order of things than we can demonstrate — there is a Providence in the history of the world and in the life of each one of us, stoutly denied by reason, stoutly believed by the heart — there must be a Providence following other rules than those we had applied heretofore, linking this muddled earth as a satellite town to a loftier City of God — there must be a God, a virtue, an eternity.

History of My Preface to the Second Edition of Quintus Fixlein

Life of Quintus Fixlein unto the Present Time Extracted from Fifteen Slipboxes

Outing of Headmaster Florian Fälbel and His Primaner to Mount Fichtel

WUTZ WAS FOLLOWED A FEW YEARS LATER BY ANOTHER "Netherlandish" work, *Life of Quintus Fixlein* (*W* 7.16ff., 65ff., 235ff.). Sending it to Christian Otto, Jean Paul said that the main character was "not actually Wutz at a higher social level." Eduard Berend thinks this so patently untrue that he believes "not" was a slip of the pen (*H-KA*1.5.ix; 3.2.48). At the same time, one can enumerate many differences in detail between *Wutz* and *Fixlein*.[1] In general, one can say that *Fixlein* is a more satirical work, even in respect to the hero, who may be of a higher social standing than Wutz but who, by the same token, represents a more petit bourgeois mentality.

Even so, *Fixlein* is often read all too solemnly, as if, for example, Fixlein's deep obeisance in the excerpted passage, "for after all, a nobleman always remains what he is," were a prescription for civil obedience. The nature of the Jean Paul idyll as "perfect happiness within limits" is even more apparent in *Fixlein* than in *Wutz*, but also more obviously ironic.

1. Cf. Anna Kruger, "Wutz and Quintus Fixlein," *Hesperus*, no. 21, March 1961.

When Fixlein finally escapes the life of the schoolmaster and is installed in the parsonage of Hukelum, he feels he has left the valley of tears and been received into the abode of the blessed. "Here dwelt no envy, no colleague, no subrector — here in heaven no one worked for the *New Universal German Library* — here in the heavenly Jerusalem of Hukelum, one did nothing but praise God in church — here the perfected had no need of further knowledge" (*W* 7.138). The Berlin brand of the Enlightenment is a favorite target of Jean Paul's attack, and he could never resist a jibe at Nicolai and his journal. But in fact, nothing would appeal less to Jean Paul than a world in which one did not subscribe to the *Neue Allgemeine Deutsche Bibliothek*. Not that that means losing sympathy with *Fixlein* — to read the idyll unsympathetically would be to miss the point even more.

The *History of My Preface to the Second Edition of Quintus Fixlein* is given here in full; I resisted the temptation to exclude the dated, Age-of-Sentiment-style final section. It is one of two complete Jean Paul works included in this volume (the other is *Wutz*). Although it appears as a preface to *Fixlein*, it has nothing to do with that work.

Jean Paul said he meant nobody in particular with Fraischdörfer, which is probably true, although a reference is often seen to Goethe's friend Heinrich Meyer, and parallels can be seen with Schiller and others.[2] In any case, he parodies the dominant aesthetic, with its principles of play, of the sublime, and of disinterested pleasure — of what Jean Paul sees as all too formalistic and abstract, at the expense of the concrete and material. It is, of course, outrageous caricature, but it is also a matter of deep concern and conviction to Jean Paul, with connotations that are both moral and religious as well as social and political. The subplot of the little narrative is the story of the lady in the vis-à-vis, ending with an invocation that is highly emotional but that is also, and explicitly, sentiment with a purpose. Jean Paul was a percipient champion of women's rights.

To *Life of Quintus Fixlein* were appended several unrelated earlier essays and sketches, including *Outing of Headmaster Florian Fälbel and His Primaner to Mount Fichtel*. This satirical account of the schoolmaster and his school outing is told mostly by the schoolmaster himself, with occasional interruptions, notably in defense of the schoolmaster's daughter,

---

2. Cf. T. J. Casey, "Jean Pauls Schillerbild," in *Friedrich Schiller: Angebot und Diskurs*, ed. H. Brandt (Berlin: Aufbau Verlag, 1987).

from the narrator. The excerpt takes up with Fälbel's account of their arrival in Hof, where he lectures a French republican on politics and his pupils on deportment.

History of My Preface to the Second Edition of Quintus Fixlein

A Switzer (as Stolberg tells us) once vaulted with all his might off the floor onto the armchair and back to the floor again — and when asked about it, declared that "he was vivifying himself." — Norsemen like me need at least half a day's journey to rouse themselves to the point of successfully drafting a chapter. Even *Erasmus* concocted In Praise of Foolishness in the saddle (on his way to Italy); and *Savage*, the English writer, his tragedy Overbury in the streets of London — although his life was a tragedy in itself, if not a domestic but rather an aristocratic one, as he exacted £200 from his natural mother, the Countess of Macclesfield, in return for not making a pasquinade on her, merely being one on her as a result — ; likewise I am known to have done the Grand Tour a few years ago to return like a well-bred young man with the skeleton draft of *Mummies*; yea, and if ever I should decide on an epos like the Odyssey, the bard would, I fear, have to spend as much time on his pittoresque journey of exploration as the hero himself.

Yet on the begettal of a Preface to the Second Edition I never reckoned to spend more than a walking trip from *Hof* to *Baireuth*, a mere stone's throw via three stages. But I find myself at a loss when I arouse the astonishment of my reading posterity and also their forebears by taking them with me over the highway to Baireuth, along which I am traveling — caged in the weaver's loom of the Preface and shooting my shuttle — without coming up with anything decent. For I carried the open notebook before me that I might garner the preface as it would drop from me, sentence by sentence; but few authors have ever been interrupted as frequently in their prefaces. Let me tell you in detail.

Man's moral progress matches his physical one, which is but a continuous fall.

The toll-bar in Hof, where we pay our duty and which had been lowered after the vis-à-vis of a lady who had tendered her own, descended on the preamble's head directly, hard as a predator or an egg cracker: for I was determined to outpace the lady and look at her face; in the pursuit, the fashioning of a preface was therefore sadly neglected, while I dashed in vain after the fugitive carriage. Unknown ladies and unknown books are two quite different matters. I never pick up an unread book without — just like a reviewer — presuming it to be worthless. Whereas with an unknown lady, a man, even suppose he had known and forgotten 30,000 idols[1] already, assumes anew every time that this 30,001st is the unadulterated genuine sacred virgin — the Mother of God — yea, the Goddess herself. And that is what I, too, took for granted out there; at least I could number a lady on whose bepowdered and becurled occiput Aurora alighted so clearly among the cultured heads of the feminine sex who — since according to Rousseau *iron* and *corn* have civilized Europe — owe to the finer products of both, viz, *hairpins* and *powder*, the culture that I expect is commonplace nowadays with the feminine heads of the bourgeoisie. Let no husband resist this external culture of woman if he hopes to possess in his wife a well-built Papinian cooking machine — a Schäferean washing machine — an English spinning machine — and a Girtannerean respiration machine: lest he betray his mistaking an innocent edification for that inner one with which ladies of standing are on the whole unencumbered. Used only externally, culture, like arsenic, lead solutions, and surgeons, is something splendid and wholesome: within the lady's head, so easily flammable the husband should snuff and blow out the *light* with the same circumspection that at night prohibits a physical light within the Imperial Library in Vienna.

Now the forest swallowed the lady, leaving me empty-handed out there on the highway. My loss reminded me of the Preface to the Second Edition, and I made a start in my notebook; and here it is, or as much of it as I achieved on the road hard by Hof.

PREFACE TO THE SECOND EDITION

The poet, like the roast capon, oftentimes carries, beneath the wings by which he rises under the eye of the learned world leaning out of their crowded windows, on the right side his stomach and on the left side his liver. Altogether, man fondly imagines many a time that he has shed the Old Adam, when all he has done is to lift him and fold him back like the

---

1. Varro arrives at a count of 30,000 heathen idols.

crackling on the roast ham, which will just as surely be served in the end, even garnished with flowers.

But now the sun rose behind me. — How pale, how dim and yellow become all those prefaces, those lobster lights of the reviewers and those phosphorescent creatures, the authors, before the enlightenment of the eternal and ever-revolving stage, with its orchestras and its galleries! — I have often attempted to think of printers' blocks, tailpieces, flyleaves, and spacings in the face of this yearly display of paintings in Nature's vast gallery — but in vain, except at midday perhaps, but of a morning or evening, never. For it is in the *morning* and in the *evening*, or rather in *youth* and *old age*, that man raises his earthy head, filled with dreamy and starry images, up toward the stilly sky, gazing at length, and affected with yearning; but during the stifling noon of the day, or life, he inclines his brow, bathed in sweat, toward the earth and her truffles and tuberous plants. Thus the middle layers of a playing card also consist of naught but the printers' waste, while the outer layers are fashioned from first-class material; likewise, the rainbow rises only from morning or evening but never the south.

As the road lifted me higher and higher above the valleys I became dubious as to which I should follow — whether it should be the tree-lined hill colonnade on my left or the magical vis-à-vis with the cultured head straight in front. — I could see that on the Mount Tabor Ridge to my left the spirit would be transfigured, standing first in the rock-hewn footsteps of angels departed, whereas in the coach the descended angel herself was seated.

Preambles were out of the question. Luckily, I perceived close by *Münchberg*, beside Nature's grand structures, which prop up the soul like a vine, an added one, which flattens it to a lowly dwarf bean, to wit, the Gallows Hill, and on it a gentleman botanist. — Incidentally! the greenswards on grassy banks or on glacis or on Wouverman's canvasses cannot hope to compete with the beautiful bowling green of a gallows hill, a harvest- and obsidional-crown (corona obsidionalis) of victorious humanity, as it were. Alas, enough scarlet clouds are gathered on high scattering sanguine rain over the earth! — Now I composed myself for my prefatory task, rebuking myself: "There is no denying the fact that thou art standing outside thy first stage, outside Münchberg, and hast sprouted naught of the preface but the first tiny shoot: this way thou wilt pass through *Gefrees*, *Berneck*, and *Bindloch* not augmenting the preface a whit, especially if thou declinest to say a word but what fitteth a previous

or a later one like a wedge stone. Art thou not free to walk in the footsteps of Herrn von Moser (precursor and godfather of thy slipboxes),
who did not compose a coherent page in his life, but maxims, mottos,
and aphorisms, in short, no lattice at all?" I had to agree with myself; and
therefore continued, in the way of a good pianoforte and in thesibus
magistralibus, *webbingless*, without any connections or hemp plants but
those on the *Gallows Hill* with my

PREFACE TO THE SECOND EDITION
  From time immemorial it has been the tiresome habit of man ever to
have any scratches and pockmarks left by the recently weathered centuries, any burn marks and aftermaths of former barbarities removed
twice — firstly by means of *Time*, and then secondly (although soon afterward, often during the following century) by means of *edicts*, district regulations, imperial ordinances, parliamentary decrees, pragmaticas sanc-
tiones, and episcopal statutes — in such a way that our confounded scurvy,
rusty, moldy, and abject follies and customs resemble the royal corpses,
which also are buried twice, the first time in secret when they smell, and
the second time publicly in an empty double-walled show coffin, followed by doleful funeral flags, black mares, and mourning cloaks. —
  Preface to be continued.

  While I was writing away, the botanist of the gallows flora had caught
up and distracted me. I was amazed to find myself face-to-face with the
Art Councillor *Fraischdörfer*, who was on his way from *Haarhaar*[2] to
Bamberg, where he hoped to observe from some mountain- or rooftop
a major battle, without which, in his capacity as an inspector of so many
battle pieces in galleries, and a critic of Homer's battle to boot, he can
hardly do. — Whereas my face was to him an unknown central Africa. He
cannot be truly at home in the history of the world of letters who needs
to be told that the Art Councillor is a collaborator not only in the new
Universal German Library — but also in the Haarharean, Scheerauean,
and Flachsenfingerean reviewing establishments, being one of their most
accomplished assistants. Just as we lower a pumpkin into a carp pond as
carp feed, he dips his nourishing head as a bouillon ball into many a famished review. And when I recalled the many broad hints of the Council-

  2. As is well known, that is the name of the principality in which the story that I am
about to edit under the title of *Titan* takes place. Whence I am familiar with the Art Councillor Fraischdörfer, although he not at all with me.

lor's, whom I had never done any harm in my life, that he planned to review me presently, I felt sick to death; for there is no greater likeness and at the same time antipathy than between an author and his reviewer, although the same is the case with the dog and the wolf. I therefore turned counterfeiter and forged my own name and introduced myself as quite a different person: "Sir," I addressed the Art Councillor, "You see here before you the well-known Egidius Zebedy Fixlein, of whose Life my esteemed cousin Jean Paul has a mind to present to the world a Second Edition — notwithstanding my daily continued existence and consequent yielding of ever new life to be written about." — Now in contrast to its engraved rendering in the orbis pictus, the Art Councillor's soul was not made of *points* but rather of *exclamation marks*; some souls consist of parentheses or quotation marks, my own soul of dashes. Taking me to be Quintus, he pumped me now as to whether my life and domesticities tallied with what was in print. I imparted many a new feature of Fixlein's, which will appear, though, in the Second Edition, as otherwise he will accuse me in future of giving a poor account of the original. He committed my perorations to parchment forthwith, as he could retain nothing; to which reason he had gathered some headstrengthening herbs on the Gallows Hill for an herb bonnet. He confessed that if his excerpt- and book-filled study should ever be set on fire, Fraischdörfer would be deprived of all his opinions and knowledge at once, as he stored both of them there; therefore, he was right obtuse and ignorant on the road, merely a feeble copy and adumbration of his own self, its dummy and curator absentis.

In fact, the German temple of fame is a beautiful copy of Minerva's temple in Athens, which included a large altar in Oblivion's honor.[3] Yea, just as the Florentines never approach their Pandects except fully arrayed and carrying torches, we from the selfsame respect never handle the works of our poets but when in festive attire and company, holding the works themselves up to candles and lighting not heads but — bright bowls of Meerschaum with them. — I have often been asked why it is that the aging world, which stores in its memory even the earliest works from thousands of book fairs, those by a Plato, a Cicero, even a Sanchunian-thon, forgets the most recent, viz, the latest romances from the last fair, those Kantian, Wolffian, and theological pamphlets, the Life of Bunkel, the foremost inaugural disputations and pièces du jour, pastoral letters, and scholarly journals, oft in the very month it first hears of them. My

3. Plutarch Sympos. I, 9. qu. 6.

answer was good and it went: as there is hardly a mystical person as old as the world, which is truly one of Denner's wrinkled old heads and about to become (and what wonder) marasmically feeble and almost childish: it goes without saying that it, too, is affected by the complaints of old people who have an excellent grasp on all that they heard and read in their *youth* yet forget what they learn in old age in an hour. Wherefore our books resemble the rags in the paper mill whence they come, as the miller ever ferments the fresh ones before the old. —

As a matter of fact, this might have stood as a separate paragraph in the Preface to the Second Edition.

The Art Councillor waxed exceedingly angry at Münchberg: either the houses on top or those at the foot of the hill ought to go; could an edifice ever be aught but an architectonical work of art, he asked me, which must be admired rather than occupied, but we used it improperly as a habitat because it was hollowed out like a flute or a cannon, just as bees would settle into the hollow tree instead of playing about its blossoms. He shewed the absurdity of our billeting ourselves in an artifact akin to using vases by *Heem*[4] as cheese molds or penholders, or scooping Laocoon out as a case for a bass viol or the Medicean Venus for a hatbox. He wondered indeed how the King could stand villages; and frankly confessed that he as an artist could only be pleased when a whole city went up in smoke, as it kindled in him the hope for a newer and finer one.

He was not to be shaken off: now, outside Münchberg, he started assaulting myself instead of the burghers of Münchberg by flogging my opera. Alas, both the Preface to the Second Edition and the fugitive vis-à-vis left myself and my longings ever farther behind, and all that was left for the eye to behold of the lady, as of one who had passed away, was a faraway dust cloud, yet I would not have swapped it for gold dust. Now the Frais Squire and Art Councillor keelhauled and drowned Cousin Jean Paul in a sack, taking me to be Quintus, as mentioned above, and umbrage at his not spreading his biographical pap nice and *smooth* like the peasants, or titivating himself in front of the looking glass of critique. I espoused the wronged and absent man's cause by telling him that as far as I knew from the horse's mouth it was by means of the vaulting poles, climbing irons, and springboards of critical notices rather than the elytron of his own psyche that he elevated himself, that, indeed, he was in the process of penning critical letters, wherein he praised and practiced the art of critique at the expense of the critic — which critical manipula-

---

4. The finest painter of pot pieces.

tion bloated his works to the same extent as noses are *elongated* and stretched by continual blowing. Verily, this is the case: it passes my understanding how a body can write an opusculum barely half an alphabet stout; what is a page at a distance needs must expand into a quire close up, and the quire turn into a ream: an opus, like a new-born cub no more than the size of a rat, when I first throw it off, I will, given time, lick into the shape of a fine brown bear. The critic, of course, sees only what the author has kept and not what was discarded; wherefore one could wish that the authors attached a complete collection of every foolish thought, ruthlessly canceled at the beginning, at the end of their works for the benefit of the reviewers, all the more since, like Voltaire for example, they really do save up and append to their final editions a ragbag of sweepings from the earlier ones, for superior readers, just as a number of Prussian regiments save up the horse dust as a proof of their grooming.

Gradually acidifying from malt- to wine-vinegar, he now told me straight out: "You are ignorant of whom you are shielding, sir: your esteemed cousin has turned your gentleman's likeness into a bambocciad and altogether omitted those virtues of intellect which — as I now hear for myself — in fact you possess. Your Reverence did not arouse the same interest in me on the printed page as he does on the highway." Desiring him to withdraw even that, I dropped out of my role as Fixlein on purpose and said in a pique: "If readers, above all those of the gentler sex, do not appreciate my comical or indeed any imperfect character, I can well account for it: they have no taste for writing let alone for practicing humorists; moreover, a limited imagination will find it more difficult to imagine and take an interest in an incomplete character — and finally, a reader prefers a hero similar to himself to a dissimilar one; and a similar one he ever perceives to be a magnificent specimen." — Verily! For as Plutarch in his biographies balances and compares each great man with a second great man, the reader quietly holds up each character of a biography against a second great character (namely his own), taking notice of the result. And for this reason will maidens set such uncommon store by perfect feminine beauty and grace in a novel's *description* (so greatly does the author beautify the most unfortunate), while showing little desire for it in reality's plastic and sculpture — just as ugly things, lizards, and Furies can only be pleasingly represented in paintings, but not through the art of sculpture — ; for to the maiden the novel is after all a true mirror, and she can see the heroine in it.

Outside the village, which goes by the name of The Three Sausages, the Art Councillor expressed the desire to partake of some goat's milk there. I asked him whether he did as the gentlefolk do, who — because Huart suggests a seven-day goat's milk cure as a homely remedy for the procreation of geniuses — decide on the nannygoat cordial and await the desired result. I dare say their endeavors afterward prove that they, at least royalties, do not take it to cure their consumption. But the Art Councillor shared Jupiter's wet nurse for the sole reason that the Fates had reeled the fatal thread off his spindle legs altogether, leaving him standing, like a flayed, desiccated, and gas-filled bird in Nature's speci-men cabinet, as it were. We needs, said he, must sacrifice ourselves and our books or else our children; in the same way, added I, as the farmer must simply accept one or the other, either dodder or flax.

During the milk cure, the loathing we felt for each other increased as our vitals' moderate heat hatched respectable toads from the swallowed spawn of antipathy. I resented having to linger in The Three Sausages, for it looked as if I were to arrive in *Gefrees* having neither perceived nor conceived aught of beauty (I refer to the vis-à-vis and the Preface), and anyway Fraischdörfer's nature was dull-, sham-, and flash-gold rolled into one, the vilest concoction on earth. Like a dentist, he pulled his incisors while chewing, as only his *canines* were genuine and his own. And when he unbuttoned his coat, did I not clearly discern that his waistcoat's belly was silken and marbled, but its back of linen and white, like the badger, who contrary to all animals wears, as Buffon remarks, his lighter fur on his back and his darker fur on his belly? — And as for his pigtail, we can take it for granted that only its tip shews some of his own hair while the remainder is artificial and long, whereas my own is real and short, as if Nature and Linné had wished to distinguish us like the two well-known animals.[5]

And he for his part likewise blended the lavender acid of wrath with a sound mother-of-vinegar with which to douse me as if I were stricken with pestilence: for he imagined me to be lying, or making a fool of him, and not being Quintus at all, whom I pretended to be, nay, even Cousin Jean Paul himself. This he deduced from my acumen. In order to get at the bottom of me, he unleashed the rag chopper of his mill and attacked all my works simultaneously. I shall be quoting him presently. Although I have often prayed Heaven to send me a cock into the learned journals who should crow if I, a St. Peter of letters, fell, and reduce me to tears

---

5. Myself equus cauda undique setosa — he equus cauda extremo setosa. Linn. Syst. Nat. Cl. 1 Ord. 4.

at the betrayal — or a capon, at least, who in the manner of capons, should sit on my chicks and lead them about; but I never asked for this chicken hawk, and, I allow, I became heated. He started at The Three Sausages and never ceased until we came to Gefrees — all the while calling me Eminence and Jean Paul my Esteemed Cousin — and maintained that "there is no more beautiful form than the Grecian, which is reached most easily by renouncing all matter — .[6] (Hence it is that one now moves best to Grecian choreography by abandoning the scholarly ballast of later centuries and *easing* oneself, so to speak.) — Form is so little concerned with cubic content that it hardly needs any at all, just as pure will had ever been form without matter (consisting in the *willing of willing*, so to speak, as the impure consists in the willing of not willing, so that the relationship of aesthetic and moral forms to their matters equals that of the geometrical to all given real space). — That this explained Schlegel's dictum that as there is pure thought without any matter (the like is utter nonsense) there could be exquisite poetical representations without it (which so to speak strikingly dissemble themselves). — And that in any case we had better rid form of all kernels and spelts if ever a work of art was to achieve that perfection that Schiller demanded, in order to free man and fit him equally for frolic and earnest (which lofty pinnacle, because of the disposition of human nature, could be scaled by the elevated genres of poetry, viz, the epopee, or ode, only through an insignificant vacuous matter or vacuous insignificant treatment of a significant one. Yet as we encounter the latter only in trivial works of art, it appears that the poor ones share with the most perfect the mark that distinguishes them from the mediocre).[7] — Humor, above all, was as reprehensible as it was unpalatable, as it was nowhere to be met in the ancients."

Fraischdörfer shall continue forthwith, once I have noted that some day I shall skilfully set forth in a critical little opusculum how German art critics (barring the latest one) have a deplorable way of dismembering humor and also (to my surprise, as the enjoyment of beauty can only increase with one's ignorance of her anatomy) an even more deplorable way of enjoying it, although as judges in darkness they resemble the Areopagites, who were forbidden to either laugh at a joke (Aeschin. in Timarch.) or to compose one (Plut. de glor. Athen.) — and furthermore that, even though the curved line of humor is not easy to rectify, it is

6. All the parentheses are my addenda, and they explain the Art Councillor.

7. The poorest and the most perfect works of art share this lack of effect, just as, according to Montaigne, *insensibility*, or to Pascal, *ignorance* appertain to two kinds of human being, the *lowest* and the *noblest*, *innate* in the former and laboriously *acquired* by the latter.

neither unruly nor willful else it could not delight anyone but its proprietor — that it shares form and stylistic devices, although not subject matter, with the tragical — that humor (I mean aesthetic humor, which is as different and as detachable from the practical as any other representation from its portrayed or portraying sentiment) is but the fruit of a protracted culture of reason and that it must grow with the age of the world as well as the age of the individual.

Fraischdörfer carried on: "And should this touchstone be used to test the esteemed cousin's works in which such exclusive store is set by their matter, it was incomprehensible how he could have been praised by the critic for choosing such ambiguous matters as divinity, immortality of the soul, contempt of life, and so on."

With these words, we set foot in Gefrees and I saw how the semifamiliar lady once more enveloped herself in her veil like a netted melon and left: which meant that if this crow of carrion of an art councillor had only dispensed with his goatish sherbet in The Three Sausages I should have gained the good fortune of catching her unawares while she was having coachman and horses looked after by Herrn Lochmüller. Instead, I had naught. I wreaked a terrible rage in my heart and lambasted the Art Councillor thus in my mind: "O thou vile frostbitten pillar of salt! Thou hollowed-out shell auger stuffed full of hearts! O thou blown lark's egg, from which fate will never be able to hatch a throbbing, soaring, and rapturous heart! Say what thou wilt, for I shall write what's my wont. — Thou shalt divert neither my eye nor my drawing pen from eternity's glacial peaks on which play the flames of the hidden sun, or from the nebulous star of the other world, which is so far in the past and which has the parallax of but a second, and from all that soothes the hot flushes of life's flight that opens the wing enclosed in the chrysalis, and warms us and wafts us!"

While the graecisising block cutter now sang the praises of the beautiful day and the azure dome of the ethereal hemisphere and averred that here he was speaking not as a painter, who would disdain cloudless skies, but as a poet, who is after all well served in his verses by fine weather: I kept stoking my wrath, all the more as according to Platner the abdomen patently benefits from such fury — and for that reason scholars, who commonly dwell above the most wretched of bellies, ought to incite each other even more zealously in anticritical newssheets — and I activated my lips without misgiving and somewhat harshly berated him sotto voce with these frank if inward invectives: "All that this formless formator in front of me values of the whole universe is that it might sit for him — he would, like Parrhasius or that Italian, subject human beings to torture to provide for himself studies and sketches of pain for a painting of a Prometheus or the Crucifixion — he would welcome the death of a darling son, as the little one's ashes would better profit a Polus in the part of Electra than three rehearsals — the numberless peasantry can after all be of use in pastoral poetry, even comical operas, just as shepherding yields enough for the maker of idylls — Eustathius Nero uses blazing Rome to illuminate Homer's beautiful delineations, while General Orlov offers a helping hand to the painter of battle or naval scenes by providing the needed academies, viz, blasted vessels and battlefields." —

THE DEVIL TAKE IT

Out loud, however, I could not be bothered to utter much more to the Art Councillor. I hastened toward *Berneck* where the queen bee in flight in her vis-à-vis was sure to pull up at The Soup Bowl. I wished in my heart that a couple of carriage wheels might start fuming and for want of tar oil make her stop to collect some black slugs as a substitute for axle grease. My reviewer-to-be became markedly tired and hungry, and because lubricating rather than gastric juices were lacking, he wished to give peristaltic instead of peripatetic motion a try; but I was not to be stopped, and he followed behind with his hunger. "You should be thankful," said I, "for being fully aware of twain states, which to convey from their own experiences seems hard or impossible to painter and poet alike — viz, hunger and weariness. — Whenever I spy a peasant with his shirt in one piece (there is one toiling away over there) I am inspired. I work out how long it will take for the shirt to turn grist for the rag chopper and finally paper, on which some savant may spread his intellectual spawn." As he comprehended my satire, it did not at all concern him: for satires and intimations of death merely touch him who is conscious of neither.

My indifference to the Art Councillor allowed me to stride ahead and resume not only the journey but also the Preface to the Second Edition and set it down on my tablet forthwith.

CONTINUATION OF THE PREFACE TO THE SECOND EDITION[8]

And Kant does indeed enjoy the rare fortune of commanding a stage well edged and bordered by heads that reflect his noises more clearly, as

---

8. The reader may wish to consult the previous continuation and refresh his memory as to the context.

with the ancients who concealed empty pots in their theaters that assisted the actors' voices with resonance.[9] An author who has ideas of his own often adulterates someone else's, which he was meant to disseminate, and suppose that he promised on oath, as once was required of copyists, to copy fairly and squarely, he would all the same differ a lot from the empty head whose upper Torricellean vacuum is, as in physics, the best conductor of sparks. — Yet in the system itself we must obviate blanks, which contain no truths by means of their robes, those lengthy newfangled terms, just as a sensible painter will fill empty spaces with draperies. —

Ethics is a horse of a different color again, where, as in medicine, the theoretician parts company with the empiricist. As on the ancient stage one actor *chanted* while his counterpart furnished the physical *action* to suit, and dramatic art prospered through this separation, in the difficult art of virtue naught will be accomplished until (as now frequently happens) practice is severed from theory, with one merely *pronouncing* on virtue and the other attempting the appropriate *actions*.

Preface to be continued.

For now we descended into the verdant Tempe of *Berneck*, and I put my tablet aside, although I could have writ on with impunity, as addressing myself to the Art Councillor in mind was as good as addressing him in person.

The royal Elijah chariot of the Sun had come to a halt at the post inn, and my journey's directress alighted. I sprang into action — who would have thought it (myself perhaps least of all) that she was no less than a prima donna who had once before acted in one of my prefaces,[10] who but the admirable, the sweet, the familiar *Paulina*, filial relict of the late Captain and general merchant *Oehrmann?*

I was silly for joy, as the good people of Berneck can testify. "Fancy meeting you here, Herr Jean Paul," said the miss, whose countenance in her bridal estate was of a more glowing red than formerly in the shop, the purple sash of the marital service to come, so to speak, the buttonhole and rosette on the conjugal bond.

Fraischdörfer crimsoned as well, like a boiling lobster, when he heard that I was indeed that peripatetically criticized author. He said it was fortunate that I had lied in reality only and not on the printed page, where it was of greater importance for the genuine man's reputation to gain

9. Winkelmann's *Notes on Archit*. Ch. I p. 10.
10. *Siebenkäs*, Part I.

acceptance and endure. He might be gone in a flash like a snowflake in May. Yet he will chalk it up to me and at the very least take a few potshots at his traveling mate from the protective scrub of the Universal German Library. I therefore deemed it expedient to inform the public beforehand: each one of his crossbow's arrows now carries his name (as was mandatory with the Tartars according to Montesquieu), the name of the bow man is Fraischdörfer. He is a man of repute and a decent man on the whole, he observes the afflictions of war in Bamberg and, as I could tell from his fingers,[11] fashions the requisite clear-cut concept and a few pointed ideas to boot, and we hold each other in estimation. — Here is an example and proof positive of how gladly I scatter his laurels: "The file," said the impish Art Councillor "which the authors fail to apply to their works, is used all the more diligently by their publishers on the gold coins with which they are paid." Very prettily turned, this! —

I happily dined with the damsel, whose husband-to-be, her matrimonial pasha and bey and maitre des plaisirs is going to be none other than our old acquaintance, Judiciary *Weyermann*.[12] I admit it was more a matter of seeking the bride out than of fleeing her, and I resembled more the wily Ulysses, who had himself tied to the mast with his ears open, which he lent imperturbably to the song of the Sirens, than his companions, who plugged theirs with wax as if they were hollow molars. She was moreover the Christ Child who silvered the frightful Correggio night, painted into my heart by the Art Councillor, with a splendid reflection: ah, how good she was, how gentle, how innocent and altogether without the *poetic calluses* of sentimentality, and the numerous keen and double-edged sufferings in the house of her father had augmented her heart rather than diminished her mind; on misfortune's sharp lathe she exhaled, like rosewood, the sweet scent of the roses themselves. She had only been granted the outer, the physical foreground refinement by her niggardly father, viz, excellent gowns instead of an excellent education (which was offered gratis in the evening anecdotes of selfless judiciaries), and she resembled most of the maidens around, who, like Vienna, are up to date in their suburbs but confoundedly old world in their inner areas. All the same, the two of us were, like all good friends — and accreted humans, according to Haller — of one heart albeit two heads. That makes up for a lot.

11. According to Buffon, clear notions are derived from separated toes, whence the unindented fish is so obtuse.

12. *Siebenkäs*, Part I.

We made a tardy departure, with myself in the vis-à-vis — vis-à-vis. Behind our verdant hills lay the Children of Israel's desert and before us the plain of Baireuth. Myself and the sun beamed unceasingly and with equal warmth on Paulina's countenance, and in the end I was moved by the still little form. Why should that be? Not merely because of my musings on the general Herrnhutean drawing of marital lots by the maidens who at a certain age possess more emotion than knowledge and in whose untenanted hearts burn anonymous *fires of sacrifice* without *objects* — as in Vesta's virginal temple, which had a fire though no divine image — and who move their altar up to the first deus ex machina who may make his appearance; — nor was I merely affected because she, like most of her sisters, was about to be gathered and crushed like delicate berries by the heavy masculine hand; — or because her feminine springtime held many more clouds than flowers and days, and I compared her, and many another bride, to the sleeping child whom Garofalo painted with an angel holding a crown of thorns over its head, which the angel will thrust on its brow once she is wakened by wedlock: — Nay, what did soften my heart was that whenever I gazed on this gentle, contented, rosy and white blooming face, I was driven to speak to her inwardly thus: "Alas, poor victim, let thee not be so merry! Thou knowest not that thy beautiful heart requireth aught warmer and better than blood, and thy mind greater dreams than those that the pillow bestoweth — that thy sweet smelling *petals* of youth are about to contract into scentless *sepals*,[13] into honey pots for the husband, who henceforth will request neither a tender heart nor a bright mind, nay, only work-roughened hands, nimble feet, the sweat of thy brow, sore arms, and an inert, paralytic tongue. This whole vast talking gallery of the Eternal, the azure dome of the universe, shall shrink into thy household domain, a larder, a woodshed, a spinning room, a parlor perhaps on happier days — the sun will turn suspended balloon stove for thee, a room heater for the world, and the moon a nocturnal cobbler's globe with a cloud for its bracket — the River Rhine will dry up and become thy washtub and copper, and the ocean turn into a herring pond — thou wilt subscribe to the annual Almanac in the grand reading club, and on account of thy cosmological bond, thy curiosity will spur thee on to scan the political journal's gazette for the names of the visiting gentlemen in the Tree Periwigs — while thou imaginest a polymath to be somewhat, although not much, better informed than thy husband. — Thou wert designed to be something better, which thou shalt

13. In the manner of various flowers, viz, the spiky dianthus.

never become (although this is not thy poor Weyermann's fault, who far-eth no better at the hands of the State). And thus Death will come upon thy soul stripped by the years save for its withered buds, and transplant it at last into a kindlier *clime.*"[14] — Why should this not distress me? Do I not see souls week in and week out being sacrificed once they inhabit a female body? And when the richest and best of souls with her heart un-requited, and her wishes denied, her talents neglected and spurned, is being lowered into the walled-up dungeon of wedlock at the dawn of her life — and she can count herself lucky if the dungeon is not an oubliette with a thousand spikes, or if the husband is a gentle arachnid who will allow himself to be tamed by the captive in her Bastille — and the poor thing will be uncommon contented — the earlier dreams and enchant-ments will soon fade away and decay unremarked — her sun will steal un-seen across her cloudy and subterraneous span from one degree to the next, and through her pains and her duties the obscure creature will reach the eventide of her lowly existence — and never will have experi-enced all she might once have desired at the dawn of her day: except now and again during an hour when the resurrected image of a divine heart, adored in days past, or a melancholic music, or a book cast a little warm sunshine on the winter sleep of the heart, she drowsily stirs and, looking about in a daze, murmurs: "It was different once — but that must have been a long time ago, and besides I doubt not I must have been mis-taken." And with that she drifts quietly back to sleep. . . .

Verily, ye parents and husbands, I have not presented this agony im-age that it might squeeze one more tear from the stricken soul whose likeness it is, nay, to ye I am shewing the painted wounds that ye might bind up the true ones and throw your scourges away for good.

As I feel now, and for the same reason, so I felt in the vis-à-vis — the westering sun and the beautiful patient figure before me, and above all my previous discords, with which I regaled the Art Councillor, dissolved them and me in this minor key. Shortly after the lykanthropic act,[15] we turn true lambs of God; having committed a sin, we are (says Lavater) at our most pious; — wherefore those saints who aspire to pious perfection

14. This education, of which daughters of "burgher descent" are so harshly deprived, and in possession of which Hermes and Campe can not see them remaining the *Helots* to our Spartans, I do not conceive as a few paltry French or musical airs, but all that in natural science, physics, philosophy, history, the fine arts and sciences, and astronomy belongs not to the virtuoso but to immortal man. You may look forward to a work from my pen on the topic.

15. Lykanthropists are human beings who bewitch themselves into wolves.

in the hereafter go in for notable sins here below. With the bride, I came out in a lyrical efflorescence of citron blossoms — where I had been a citrate pillar before, one more proof that reviewers ought never to publish their names or set to work but in darkness, else they will not be respected, as Minerva's armorial bird, the nocturnal owl, wreaks havoc at night with impunity, while claiming its place as one of Nature's eccentrics among our feathered friends during the day. But to revert: Man on his journey to the Eden above, and myself to the one in Baireuth, and mankind on its long one toward Judgement Day undergo, like Mumm's Porter, more than one sour stage in the process; yet splendid and sweet do we all, including the porter, arrive in the end: or in other words, half an hour beyond Berneck I narrated to Paulina the Dower for Maidens from Quintus Fixlein.

I was oblivious to all prefaces to second editions. . . . Oh, thou tender bride! I desired to move thee deeply by telling a tale, but thou movest me more by listening. As a matter of fact, there must be other Jean Pauls and Paulinas in Germany, or the present second edition could not have been made at all, and I offer sincerest thanks for it on this opportunity, although not to the Pauline readers, because they did naught for my sake and I profited little, and, what is more, while they sat in front of me, reading, my books on their laps, I was the only one going without, just as at a North American feast the host is the only one not to partake, — nay, my aforementioned thanks are offered to Fate for having created men not *equal* (or we would all die of boredom), nor *dissimilar* (or we could neither endure nor comprehend one another), but prettily *similar*, and I can be taken as one of the rods of the Spartan Skytale, as it were, around which the Great Genius winds lettered sheets, and the reader the other one, around which, because it is turned to match, the sheets can be wound and deciphered as on myself. —

Now that the bride and myself were advancing on *Bindloch*, where I proposed to put up, as I did not consider it seemly to pass through the gate of Baireuth sitting bolt upright beside the affianced lady, and be lodged in print in the gazette as having entered the city to boot, I was, I say, now far too dejected for that very reason, especially with the evening's golden sparkle wafting ahead and the evening chorus warbling above in the open volary of the sky, and about to suffer the loss of the weeping bride, too dejected, I said, to give an account of Quintus Fixlein after the first or the second edition before reaching Bindloch: it could not be done.

But I took out my tablet and drafted a piece. Let ye not, however, expect a continued Preface to the Second Edition. "I am here engaged on an epitaph, my dear," I told her. From her late father and his male cronies she was well used to being bored and neglected: and she gladly forgave me my writing; nevertheless, it was intended to move her, and I proposed to read it to her in Bindloch. And at the close of the story, the epitaph will, with some minor and suitable modifications, be addressed to the reader as well, as recompense for the preface withheld and now unachievable. I wrote on and on, and my eyes darkened, for I had the westering sun in my back and water rather than light in my eyes. Ah, dearest heart! thou knewest not why my eyes were dripping and yet thine also brimmed over! — Descending, the Hill of Bindloch spread before us, we were deprived by the dell of the joyfully dancing sun; yet with the extinguishing of the light we were, just as at an auction in Bremen or Lauenburg, awarded the entire night sky studded with silver suns at the gavel- and bell-stroke of 7 o'clock.

The world reposed — the moon sprouted from the top of the hill like the dormant bell of a lily — my draft was completed — we had swooped down the hill — and I told the bride I would alight and read to her in the open if she were willing to join me, as inside I would have to outmatch the din of the carriage.

We alighted together at the foot of the hill, close by an old pillar, which I have never passed without heaving a sigh at the crushing force with which Fate's monstrous hands seize and transport us tender caterpillars and Gullivers; and these monstrous hands seemed to have set the pillar down here today as a herm and memento for the feeble memory of the human heart. Paulina knew nothing of it; but I led her to the modest pilaster and explained — while first shewing her — the significance of the weathered and brittle female form under the wheels of a coach so pitifully embossed on the pillar. For the neighboring villages tell of a bride who, traveling during a thunderstorm and with shying horses in her bridal coach down the then steeper Hill of Bindloch toward the arms of her bridegroom, was tossed under the wheels and, in front of his agonized eyes — her aspirations betrayed — gave up the ghost. Paulina could barely make out the weathered relief of that bygone calamity in the misty light of the rising moon. Yet her soft stricken heart poured, all the more because of her being so close to a similar situation, the evening sacrifice of a tear flowing over the unknown slain sister whose broken frame, now merely dust — perhaps from a flower's anther — was roaming the valley, while the spirit that formerly quickened it will, should it glance back from the eternal hill path through Time, scarcely behold the eddy of dust that it once aroused and abandoned. And there, close by the triumphal column of martyrdom and under the boundless nocturnal sky, I handed Paulina the composition that I here present to the hearts of her sisters.

THE ECLIPSE OF THE MOON

On the lily fields of the Moon dwelleth the Mother of Man, with her countless daughters in tranquil eternal love. There the blue of the sky, which only sails at such distant height over the earth, has come to rest on the snowfields of anther dust — no frosty cloud will bear a diminished evening through the pellucid ether — no hatred corrode the pacific souls — just as rainbows in a cascade, so all embraces are merged into one in *Love* and *Tranquility* — and when, during her stilly night, Earth floats, unfurled and ashimmer, under the stars, the souls who felt pain and delight on her once gaze in sweet and nostalgic remembrance on the island abandoned, where loved ones still dwell and the discarded bodies repose, and later, when Earth, heavy and soporific, approaches and dazzles the drooping eye, her bygone springs pass by once again in radiant dreams, and when it awakens, the eye is bedewed with the tears of happiness.

But once the shadow reaches another century on Eternity's dial, pain sears the breast of the Mother of Man because the beloved daughters, who have not yet abided on earth, change from the moon to their bodies as soon as the earth touches and stuns them with her earth-cold shade, and the Mother of Man weeps and watches them go, as not all of them, but only the undefiled, will return from the Earth to the immaculate Moon. Thus the impoverished Mother is robbed of her children by one century after another, and during daylight she quakes at the sight of our predatory sphere in the shape of a large solid cloud closing in on the sun.

Eternity's needle advanced to the eighteenth century — with Earth, covered by night, drawing close to the Sun — when, burning with anguish, the Mother pressed to her heart all her daughters not yet arrayed in their bodies, imploring them tearfully: "Oh do not give in to temptation, my dearest, but stay ye pure as the angels, and return!" Now the gigantic shadow had arrived at the century and the dark earth covered the sun — a thunderclap struck the hour — the red-hot scimitar of a comet hung in the darkened sky — the Milky Way shuddered, and from its depth a voice cried: "Shew thyself, thou Tempter of Man!"

Into each century the Eternal One dispatches an evil genius to tempt it. — Far from the little eye, the starry expanse of the infinite stands in the sky, circling around the eternities, an *indissoluble nebula*.[16]

At the Tempter's summons, the Mother and all her children trembled, and the tender souls burst into tears, even those who had been here below and were now transfigured. With the Earth shadow, a giant serpent now reared monstrously up from the Earth and stretched to the Moon and said: "I shall lead ye astray." This was the Evil Genius of the eighteenth century. The lilies of the Moon bowed their drooping and withering bells — the comet-scimitar waved to and fro, as the executioner's sword moves of itself, signaling judgment — the serpent with glittering soul-murderous eyes, with bloodred crest, with moistened and pierced lips, and with tongue ready to strike, twisted its way into the peaceful Eden, its tail flicked malignant and hungry within a grave on the Earth, and an earthquake on our sphere hurled up the sinuous coils and the venomous juices like a fluid and iridescent thunderstorm. Ah, it was the Black Genius who had long ago tempted the wailing Mother. She could not look upon it; but the Serpent began: "Knowest thou not the Serpent, Eve? — I shall tempt thy daughters, thy snowy butterflies I shall gather on the morass. Look ye, sisters, with this I shall lure ye all." — (At this, the viperine eyes mirrored male forms; and the piebald coils, wedding rings; and the yellow scales, gold pieces.) "And for that I shall take the Moon and Virtue away from ye. With silken ribands for toils and lustrous fabrics for snares I shall catch ye; with my ruby crown I shall lure ye, and ye shall covet it; within your bosoms I shall begin speaking and singing your praises, and nestled in a male voice I shall continue and confirm them, and into your tongues I shall slip mine and make them cutting and venomous. — Only when ye have fallen on adverse times or are at Death's door shall I deliver the vain prick of conscience, piercing and hot, into your hearts. — Make thy eternal farewell, Eve; happily, they will forget that which I tell them now, even ere they are born." —

The unborn souls huddled together atremble before the cold swirling poison tree so close beside them, and the souls who had risen again from the Earth, pure as the scents of flowers, clasped one another in timorous joy, in sweet trepidation at a surmounted past. The best-loved daughter, Maria, and the Mother of Man held each other pressed to their hearts and they knelt down in their embrace and lifted prayerful eyes, and the tears welling forth pleaded: "Oh, Ever-loving One, take them into Thy

16. An indissoluble nebula is a complete firmament reflected into infinite distances, where telescopes no longer reveal the suns.

care!" — And behold, when the monster flicked its thin long tongue, forked like a lobster's claw, across the Moon and severed the lilies and, when it had made a black Moon spot, said: "I shall tempt them": behold, there rose in a flash from behind the Earth the first ray of the Sun, and the golden light shone on the brow of a sublime, beautiful youth, who had stood unseen amid the quivering souls. A lily adorned his breast, and a verdant wreath of laurel and rosebuds his brow, and blue as the sky was his garment. He gazed amidst tender tears, radiant with affection on the woebegone souls — like the sun on a rainbow — and said: "I shall guard ye." He was the genius of Religion. The swaying Serpent froze and stood petrified on the Earth and beside the Moon, an arsenal filled with silent, sable death.

And the Sun cast a greater morn on the countenance of the youth, and he lifted his gaze high to the stars and said to the Infinite One: "Father, I shall descend into Life with my sisters and guard all who will suffer me. Protect the ethereal flame with a beautiful temple: she shall not ravage or mar it. Array the beautiful soul with the foliage of Earthly charms; it shall shelter her fruit, not shadow it. Bestow on her a beautiful eye, I shall move it and moisten it; and into her breast place a tender heart: it shall not break ere it beat for Thee and for Virtue. Immaculate and unspoiled, I shall bring back from the Earth the blossom, transmuted into a fruit. For to the mountains and to the Sun and under the stars I shall soar and remind her of Thee and the universe over the stars. Into the snowy light of the Moon I shall transform the lily of my breast, and into the sunset glow of a Spring night the rosebuds in my wreath, and put her in mind of her brother — in the sounds of music I shall call her and speak to her of Thy heaven and unfold it before her harmonious heart — with the arms of her parents I shall embrace her, and in the voice of poetry I shall conceal my voice, and with the form of her beloved embellish my own. — Yea, with the tempest of suffering I shall rage over her and hurl the sparkling raindrops into her eyes and lift her eyes on high to the hills and to her kin whence she cometh. Oh ye beloved, who do not cast out your brother, when, after a splendid feat, after a hard won victory a sweet yearning swelleth your hearts, when in the starry night and the evening glow your eyes melt in an ineffable bliss, and your whole beings rise and thrust upward and open their arms, loving, and tranquil, and restless, and weeping, and yearning: then shall I be in your hearts and give the sign that I embrace ye and that ye be indeed my sisters. — And then after a brief dream and slumber, I shall break the crust off the diamond and drop it, sparkling dew, into the lilies of the Moon. — O tender Mother of Man, do not gaze with such anguish on thy beloved children but part more cheerfully, thou shalt lose but few! —

The Sun flared unocculted before the Moon, and the unborn souls made their way to the Earth, and the Genius of Virtue accompanied them — and as they were winging toward Earth, a melodious cadence spread through the cerulean blue, like swans flying across a winter night and leaving in the air not waves but sounds.

The monstrous Serpent sank back to Earth in the wide arc of an incandescent winged bomb and finally coiled to an incendiary wreath of pitch, and just as a curved whirlwind breaks over a ship, it fell over the Earth and, puckered into a thousand nooses and knots, it twisted, strangling and snaring, through all the peoples on Earth. And the executioner's sword twitched once more, but the echo of the transversed ether lasted longer. —

*

When I had come to a close, Paulina dried her gentle eyes, which she unconsciously raised toward the brighter moon and her faraway scapes. I parted from her — and the wish, which is offered here to all loving sisters of the Genius of Virtue, was my last word to her: "Mayest thou never be other than happy, and may the short spring night of Life pass tranquil and bright for thee — and may the celestial Veiled One grant thee within it some stellar tableaux above thee — night-scented gillyflowers below thee — some night thoughts within thee — and no more clouds than those needed for a beautiful evening glow, and no more rain than what be required, mayhap, for a rainbow in moonlight!" —

Hof in Voigtland, 22 August 1796.

Jean Paul Fr. Richter.

Life of Quintus Fixlein unto the Present Time Extracted from Fifteen Slipboxes

Slipbox Number One.

Canicular holidays — Visitations — An indigent gentlewoman

Egidius Zebedy *Fixlein* had been a working Quintus for barely a week and had taught himself into a glow when Fortune regaled him with four collations and courses, drenched in flowers and sugar, to wit: the four canicular weeks. Even yet I would love to stroke the skull of that good man who invented canicular holidays; I can never go for a walk in them without thinking: now a thousand stooped scholars are raising their heads, out in the open, their heavy satchels abandoned, free at last to pursue what is dear to their hearts, butterflies — or the roots of numbers — or those of words — or herbaceous plants — or their native villages.

The latter was what our Fixlein was after. But it was only on Sunday — for one wishes also to sample vacations in town — that, accompanied by his poodle and a Quinta boy carrying his viridian housecoat, he set out through the city gate: the grass was still dewy, and by the time the trumpetlike vocal cords of the orphanage children rang out with their morning hymn, he had left the gardens behind. The name of the town was *Flachsenfingen*, that of the village, *Hukelum*, and that of the dog, *Schill*, and the date of the year was 1791.

"Manikin" (he addressed the Quinta boy; for, in the manner of Love, children, and Viennese citizens, he was fond of using diminutives), "Manikin, hand me the bundle until we get to the village — have a good runaround and find yourself a small bird, like yourself, to feed over the holidays." — For the manikin was his page boy — polisher-roommate — gentleman companion, and errand girl rolled into one; as the poodle was also his manikin.

He ambled along through the curly cabbage beds, hung with a host of bright beads of dew glass, watching the morning breeze disentangle the bushes, releasing a flock of diamond colibris, such was their sparkle. Now and again he would pull the bell cord — whistling lest the little one should go astray, and he reduced his one and a half hours by meting the way not according to them but to villages. It is more agreeable to the wayfarer — although not at all to the geographer — to reckon by versts rather than miles. On his way, the Quintus committed to memory sundry fields already harvested.

But now, Fixlein, ramble more slowly still through the manor garden of Hukelum, not on account of thy coat, which might perchance brush the anther dust off the tulips, rather in order to give thy mother more time for decking her unwrinkled brow with her black taffeta cupid's band. It annoys me when female readers think ill of the fond woman's wishing to iron it first: they must be ignorant of her want of a maid, and her having to see to the entire master dinner today all by herself — the financial deposit for it having arrived three days in advance of the guest of honor — and without benefit of a family cook. — The Third Estate (she was a horticulturist) does indeed, just like a partridge, carry on its rump even during matins the shells of the workaday egg from which it hacks its way.

One can imagine the doting mother all morning, looking out for her schoolman, the apple of her maternal eye, for there was no one else in the whole wide world—husband and elder son were deceased—on whom she could lavish her heart's abundant affection, none but her Zebedy. Could she ever as much as relate aught about him, of a joyful nature I mean, without several times wiping her eyes? And did she not once dispense her one kermis cake to two mendicant scholars, as she thought God would punish her if she feasted like this while her bairn went without and could only savor a whiff of a cake-, as of any other, garden in Leipzig?

"Gracious! it's you so soon, Zebedy," said his mother, checking her tears with a shamefaced smile, as her son ducked under the window and entered out of the blue and without a knock on the hay-padded door. And as the grand schoolman tenderly kissed her bare brow, while the roast sizzled away, and even said: Mama—which appellation hugged her as snugly as a pericardial cushion—she was so contented that assembling her flatiron was quite beyond her. All the windows stood open, and the garden with its perfume of flowers, the din of its birds, and its collections of butterflies invaded the room: but I might not have mentioned before that the gardener's cot, which was more like a room than a house, was sited in the westernmost tip of the manorial park. The Squire graciously let the widow remain in this dower house, as it would have stood vacant in any case, for he no longer employed a gardener.

Yet in spite of her happiness, Fixlein could not delay, as he was due at the church, the royal maternal court kitchen of his spiritual stomach. He liked a sermon for being a sermon, and also because he himself had preached one once. The mother agreed: these good women believe that they enjoy their visitors if they but give them enjoyment.

In the choir, that free port and pagan forecourt of foreign churchgoers, he smiled at the imparochialized, and as in his childhood he gazed from beneath an archangel's wooden wing upon the vaulted parterre. As if they were children, his childhood years now encompassed him, laced with a winding garland, from which they would now and again pick a flower to fling in his face: for was it not old Senior *Astmann* who stood on the pulpit Parnassus, he who had often chastised him because under him he had had to extract his Greek from a grammar published in Latin, which he could not elucidate, albeit remember by rote? And was not behind the steps to the pulpit the sacristy cabin, where an ecclesiastical library of importance — a schoolboy could not have carried it in his book strap — lay under a pastel Calabar of dust? And did it not even still consist of the Folio Polyglotta, which in earlier years — inspired by Pfeiffer's critica sacra — he had perused page by page, that he might by the greatest of efforts make excerpts of the majusculas, the minusculas, the litteras inversas, etcetera. Although he would willingly have consigned, the sooner the better, this Calabar letter feed to some type box of Hebrew characters, to which the rhizophages of the Orient cling, who in any case subsist almost totally without roughage of vowels. — And stood not the organ bench by his side where the schoolmaster with a nod of his head would enthrone him on the feast days of the apostles that the parish might skip down the stairs to the strains of his rippling murki? —

And the readers will themselves be elated on hearing the news that the Senior, the local divine Elector, while discharging the alms bag, invited the Quintus to call on him during the afternoon, and they will rate it as highly as if they themselves had been asked by the Senior. But wait till they return home with the Quintus to mother and table, both now bedecked in their white-checkered finery, and lay eyes on the splendid cake that Fräulein *Thiennette* (Stephanie) had run off her baking sheet! Although I expect they will want to know first of all who *that* is.

She is — for albeit (according to Lessing) because of the Iliad's very perfection, the personal dates of its author were ever neglected: this may equally well apply to the fates of sundry other composers, for example, my own; yet the cake's lady composer shall not be forgotten on account of her produce — Thiennette is an indigent, insolvent spinster — not possessed of much but her years, of which she has five and twenty — no longer possessed of any close relatives — has little knowledge (as she is not even acquainted with Werther from books) apart from the economical — does not read books, least of all mine — single-handedly peoples, that is to say patrols, as chatelaine the thirteen desolate vacant apartments of the manor of Hukelum, which is the property of Ritmaster *Aufhammer*, Captain of the Dragoons, himself domiciled in the daughter parish of *Schadeck* — commands and feeds his vassals and handmaids — and is entitled to sign herself "By the Grace of God" — which both gentry and royalty did during the thirteenth century — as she lives by human grace, at least the aristocratic one of the Ritmistress, who ever blesses the subjects cursed by her husband. — But the orphaned Thiennette's bosom harbored a sugared marzipan heart, which one could have devoured for love — her fate was harsh but her soul was gentle — she was modest, courteous, and timid, but overly so — she would gladly and calmly accept a cutting humiliation in Schadeck, not feeling the pain, only to ponder it all some days later, when the blood would well forth from the gashes, as a wound will start hurting when catalepsis has passed, and she would weep over her lot, all on her own. . . .

I don't find it easy to strike a gay chord again after this somber note by adding that Fixlein could almost be said to have been brought up with her and that she, his school moiety across at the Senior's, who tutored him for the urban Tertia, acquired the verba anomala with him.

The Achilles shield of a cake with its brown sculpted scales whirled like a flywheel of hungry and grateful ideas in the Quintus's head: of that philosophy scornful of food, or the grand world that wastes it, he possessed not enough for that ingratitude of the wordly wise and men of the world, nay, he could never be done giving thanks for a platter of sausages or a pottage of lentils.

In innocence and contentment the dining quartet — for we must not leave out the poodle, whose place was laid under the stove — now celebrated the Feasts of Unleavened Bread, Thanksgiving toward Thiennette, and the Tabernacles al fresco. One might well wonder how a person could dine with any enjoyment without benefit of — as in the case of the King in France — 448 human beings employed in the kitchen (not even counting the 161 garcons de la Maison bouche), of another 31 fellows in the fruiterie, or 23 ditto in the confectionary, or without a daily expenditure of 387 livres and 21 sous. Meanwhile, I rate a cooking mother as highly as any train of kitchen retainers who would feed on me rather than feed me. The delicious skimmings, which it is the prerogative of the biographer and the world to cream off such a gala occasion, is some table talk of considerable importance. The mother had much to narrate. This evening — she informs us — Thiennette is going to don for the very first time a white muslin matutinal walking habit as well as a satin belt and steel buckle. It will not fit her, however — says she — as the Ritmistress (who festooned Thiennette with discarded garments as Roman Catholics behang their patron saints with discarded crutches and disabilities) was stouter. Excepting gowns, men, and flax, there is nought that good women begrudge each other. In his mind, the Quintus saw angels' wings sprout from Thiennette's shoulder blades and through her clothes: To him, a dress was half a skinned human being, only missing the vital parts and entrails; he adored these wrappings and shells around our kernels, not as a dandy or an arbiter elegantiarum but because he could never despise something that others admired. — Also, she read to him, as it were, from his father's epitaph, who had in the thirty-second year of his life been gathered by the grim reaper from a cause that I shall not treat of until a future slipbox, as I am too solicitous for the reader's well-being. The Quintus never could have his fill of anecdotes concerning his father.

The best piece of news was that Fräulein Thiennette had sent word today that "he might call on her Ladyship on the morrow, as his most gracious godfather was to travel to town." Let me shed light on this first. Old Aufhammer's name was Egidius, and he was godfather to our Fixlein; yet he — though the Ritmistress nightly showered the cradle with a bounty of bread-, meat-, and purse-tithes — bestowed nought but his name as a thrifty christening present; a baleful decision as it turned out. For our *Egidius* Fixlein had only returned from the Groves of Academe with his poodle who, together with other emigrants, had fled Nantes because of the troubles in France, when he and his dog went for an ill-starred walk in the forest of Hukelum. As the Quintus was wont to bid his companion, "Kusch, Schill (couche Gilles)," it must have been the Devil in person who sowed von Aufhammer under the trees just like tares, so that the travesty and corruption of his own name — for Gilles means Egidius — could easily fall on his ears. Fixlein could neither parley in French nor inflict injuria — he had not an inkling of the meaning of couche, which the citizen dogs in Paris now address to their valets de chiens; there were, however, three things that von Aufhammer never revoked, his error, his ire, and his word. The provoked now resolved never to grace the provoking commoner and honor thief with his presence or — presents.

I return. After dinner he gazed from his little window upon the garden and beheld the course of his life dividing into four hill paths and as many ascents into Heaven: one ascension into the parsonage, and one to Thiennette in the manor house — these for today — a third, for the morrow, to Schadeck, and the fourth into all the other houses of Hukelum. After his mother had happily tiptoed about long enough to allow him to study his *Latin Bible* (vulgata) in peace, viz, peruse the Literary Gazette: he for his part bestirred himself, and his mother's humble delight escorted the valiant son who was not afraid to converse unabashed with a Senior. Nevertheless, it was with respect that he entered the house of his former, grey- rather than bald-headed, teacher, who personified not only virtue but hunger as well: for he ate more than His Late Majesty. A schoolman aspiring to be a professor will hardly look at a pastor; but one craving a parsonage as a workhouse and lying-in establishment for himself thinks highly of the incumbent. The new parsonic abode — as if it had taken wing from Friedrichstraße or Erlang like a casa santa and alighted on Hukelum — was as a sun temple to the Quintus, and the Senior its sun priest. To become an incumbent there was an idea coated with linden honey and unique in the history of mankind, save for Hannibal's when he decided to traverse the Alps, viz, the threshold to Rome.

The host and his guest composed an excellent bureau d'esprit: holders of offices, in particular if they be similar, have more to say to each other — viz, their *own* stories — than those indolent June bugs and the court beatified who are only licensed to lecture on the stories of *others*. — The Senior ranged from his stock — in the byre — to the stock articles of his academic career, a topic as dear to such people's hearts as their childhoods to poets. Good man that he now might be, he half relished recalling when he was less so; mind you, wrong doings happily recollected are partly repeated, as good deeds remembered remorsefully are half expunged.

Kind and courteous Zebedy, who did not even enter the name of a gentleman on his tablet without adding an Esq., followed the academic fledgling years of the older man, who had absorbed and imbibed with equal devotion in Wittenberg, and thirsted alike after Guckguck[17] and Hippocrene. —

Jerusalem nicely remarks that the barbarity that often emerges hard by the gaudiest blossoming of the sciences is a kind of strengthening mud bath averting the overrefinement which that very blossoming might otherwise bring about. I believe that he who considers the heights reached in the sciences by a sixth former — in particular by a patrician scion from Nuremberg whom the city must grant a study allowance of 1,000 florins — , I believe that such a man cannot begrudge such a favorite son of the muses a certain barbaric era (the so-called Burschen days), which will steel him enough to keep his refinement in check. The senior had ensured 180 students' privileges — the sum total arrived at by *Petrus Rebuffus*[18] — from lapsing by default in Wittenberg and lost none but his

17. A University beer.
18. I will quote but a few of this Peter's, all in force at the burgeoning of our universities: e.g., a student is entitled to compel any burgher to let house and horse to him; — even his relatives are entitled to be recompensed fourfold for any damages they might have suffered; — he is exempt from carrying out the Pope's written decrees; — his neighbors are liable for aught stolen from him; — should he and a nonstudent lead a disorderly life, only the latter could be evicted from the rented accommodation; — a poor student is entitled to

moral one, which man never makes much of, not even in cloisters. This encouraged the Quintus to expatiate on his own merry sallies in Leipzig, sprung from the pressure of his incubus penury. Hear this: in his walled yard his landlord, who was a professor and also a miser, catered for a whole covey of hens. Fixlein and three feudatory roommates could easily meet the cost of one room; like phoenixes, they had *one* of all the important things: *one* bed in which, like nightwatchmen, one pair would sleep before and the other pair after the hour of midnight — *one* coat, dressed in which they would go out in turn, and which, like a sentinel's coat represented the national dress of the whole company — and several further unities of place and interest. Nowhere can emergency — and obsidional coins be gathered more merrily and philosophically than at a university: the burghers of academe show just how many humorists and Diogeneses are to be found in Germany. There was but a single thing that our Unitarians possessed four of: their appetites. It may have been with too gleeful a reminiscent pleasure that the Quintus recalled how one of the famished coro had invented the means by which the hens of the professor might be levied as duties and taxes. Being a jurist, he requested them to perceive the professor as a fee-tail farmer, entitled to the usufruct of the chicken yard and the house, and themselves as his landlords, to whom he was properly bound to render his duty-fowl. In order that fiction might follow nature — fictio sequitur naturam — he continued: they were bound to capture such carnival fowl in reality. But how to get into the yard? The feudalist therefore constructed a fishing rod, baited it with a bread crumb, and lowered his fishing line into the yard. In a couple of trices the hook grappled a gullet, providing an eyelet by means of which the hen could communicate with the feudalist landlord and be quietly raised, as if from an Archimedean ship, to the starving aero-angling society: where according to the prevailing conditions, their proper liege names and titles of possession awaited them: for the resorption hens were sometimes called smoke-fowl, or wood-, forest-, bailiwick-, Whitsun-, or summer-fowl. "I shall begin," said the angling tenant-in-tail, "by raiding *galloping rents*, the name of the triple and quadruple rents of the peasant who, as in our case, has long failed to render them." Like a prince, the professor regretfully noted the sparseness of population of hens, who, like the Jews, died from their numbering. Finally, he was lucky enough during his lecture — he had just arrived at the *Forest-*, *Salt-*, and *Mint-*

---

be fed by a doctor; — should his murderer not be detected, the nearest ten houses will remain under the interdict; his legacies shall not be curtailed by the falcidia etc.

Regality — to behold from the lecture hall's window a rent fowl, fixed in midair like St. Ignatius at prayer or Juno in punishment; he pursued the incomprehensible vertical rise of the aeronautical animal, finally spying the hoisting mechanic with his animal magnet drawing the dinner lots from the chicken yard. . . . Contrary to expectations, he finished the hen-hawking sooner even than his regalities lecture. —

Fixlein stepped homeward, accompanied by the evening trumpet piece from the belfry, and doffing his hat politely when on his way he passed the empty manor house windows: grand houses were as grand people to him, just as the Indian pagoda means at once temple and god. He delivered invented greetings to his mother, who returned authentic ones to him, for she had been to visit the white-muslined Thiennette during the afternoon, with her historical tongue and *naturalist* eye. The mother had shown her each emergency groschen that the son had dropped into her ample but empty purse, getting him thus into the Fräulein's good books: for women are even more warmly disposed toward sons who affectionately restore to their mothers some of the kindness received than to daughters who care for their fathers, for a hundred different reasons and maybe because they are more accustomed to their sons and fathers being mere five-foot-high thunderstorms, hosed waterspouts, or at least dormant hurricanes.

Oh thou blessed Quintus! on whose life blazes the merit, like the Order of the Black Eagle, that thou art able to tell it all to thy mother, viz, this afternoon at the seniorate. Thy happiness floweth into another's heart to return twofold into thine own. Hearts know a greater proximity, as doth sound, than the mere *echo;* proximity at its closest fuseth both sound and echo in *resonance.*

It is of historical certainty that the two of them supped together that evening and that instead of the dinner leavings, which were to make up a meal in itself on the morrow, they set only the ritual cake or matzoh on their supper table altar of burnt offerings. The mother, who willingly would have sacrificed not only herself but also the rest of mankind for her bairn, proposed to offer the quinta boy, playing outside and provending a bird instead of himself, not a single crumb of the precious baking, but only some of the homemade bread without crusts. But the schoolman was of Christian propensity and declared it was Sunday today and the young fellow just as fond of partaking of a delicacy as himself. Fixlein, being an Antipodean of the great and of geniuses, regaled, endowed, and indulged the assistant housemate in preference to one of those who pass through the gate for the first time and by the time they arrive at the next stage have already forgotten the host and postmaster of the former. The Quintus in any case had a great sense of honor and, notwithstanding his husbandry and coin idolatry, willingly spent it in matters of honor, although unwillingly in matters of some overpowering pity swelling his pericardial sac and thereby depleting his numismatical one. — When the quinta boy had practiced the ius compascui on the matzoh and three pairs of arms rested contentedly on Thiennette's table of bounty: Fixlein read to himself and the company from the Flachsenfingen Directory; he could not conceive of anything nobler, except Meusel's Scholarly Germany — the calendar's courtiers and privy counselors tickled his palate, as the cake's raisins had done before, and on the affluent livings he levied the tithings by declaiming them.

He remained on purpose his own vellum edition, that is to say, he did not even divest himself of his Sunday coat for the vesper bell, for he had plans for the evening.

After supper he meant to call on the Fräulein, when he beheld her, a lily bathed in the evening's purple glow, in the manorial park, whose western boundaries were shaped by his cottage as were its southern ones by the Chinese wall of the manor house. . . . Incidentally, how I came to know this, also what slipboxes are, and whether I was present myself, etc., etc., — shall be recorded faithfully to the reader, so help me God, by and by, and what is more, in this very volume. —

Fixlein skipped like a will-o'-the-wisp into the garden, whose floral perfume skirted his soup bowl's aroma. No one bowed lower before a gentleman than he, although not from the common herd's lowliness, nor a profit-seeking abasement, but from his conviction that "a gentleman ever remains what he is." But his reverence veered to the right (rather than straight ahead) in pursuit of his hat as it were: as he had not risked carrying a walking stick; but hat and stick represented his pressure plant and balancing pole, in short his bowing gear, without which he could not set himself into courteous motion, even were he to be called therefor to the principal pastorate of Hamburg. Thiennette's mirth quickly unfurled and attuned his contorted spirit. He saluted her with a lengthy albeit pleasant harvest thanksgiving sermon on account of the scaly cake, which she found tedious and agreeable at the same time. Maidens not of the grand world account boring pedantry merely like snuff taking — among the unavoidable attributes of the male sex; they adore us infinitely, and just as *Lambert* could only address the King of Prussia in darkness on account of his solar eyes, methinks they often prefer — by reason of our superior airs — to catch hold of us in the dark. — *He* was edified by Thiennette's imperial and caesarean tale of Squire Aufhammer and his gracious lady, who intends to remember him in her will; *she* was edified by his scholar's tale regarding himself and the Subrector, how for instance he had charge of the secunda and held sway over pupils as tall as himself there. Thus they perambulated contentedly in the garden, among scarlet runner blooms, chestnut May beetles, and the declining evening glow, turning about, smilingly, where the lady gardener's head was set into the sliding panel, which itself was framed by a larger one, like a stained glass window.

It is incomprehensible to me how he could not have fallen in love. Although I do know his reasons: in the first place, she had nought of her own; in the second, neither had he but a burden of liabilities; in the third, her family tree provided toll-bar and detention stocks; and in the fourth, his hands were tied by a nobler thought, which for very good reason will be withheld from the reader as yet. All the same — Fixlein! had I but been in thy place! I should have gazed on her and, having recalled her virtues and our schooldays, drawn forth my dissolving heart and offered it like a bill of exchange or served it like a summons. For I should have considered that she followed a nun in two matters, in the quality of her heart and her baking — that notwithstanding her association with vassals of the male sex, she had not turned into a Karl Genofeva Louise Auguste Timothee Eon de Beaumont, but a pretty, fair-haired, crested dove — that she endeavored to please her own sex rather than ours — that in her tears, which she hides rather than boasts of, she shows a soft heart, which has not been first borrowed from the book lender. — With reasons like these I would have been ready to offer my heart before we had reached the third flower bed. — Moreover, had I considered, o quinte! that I knew her as thoroughly as myself, and that (had I been thee) the same Senior would have guided our Latin hands in composing — that as innocent children we kissed in front of the looking glass, looking to see whether the mirror-children did likewise — that we oftentimes thrust our hands of both sexes into *one* muff and let them play hide-and-go-seek there; — and had I finally mused on the fact that we had stopped by the glasshouse, now glowing in the sunset's enamel painting, on whose frigid panes we both (she inside, myself without) had pressed our cheeks toward each other, divided by nought but the vitreous fire screen: I should have gathered the poor soul, crushed by her fate, who sees no higher acclivity sheltering her from the storm clouds than her grave, to my own and warmed her against my bosom and girded her with mine eyes. . . .

Verily, this the Quintus himself would have done had not the nobler thought of a moment ago, which I am keeping from you, forbidden it! — Tender, though ignorant of the cause — wherefore he kissed his mother — , blissful without having enjoyed a learned discussion, and dismissed with a cargo of humble regards, which he was to deliver to the Ritmistress of the Dragoons on the morrow, he arrived at the cottage and gazed for a long time from his darkened windows on the illumined ones of the manor house. — And while the moon in her first quarter was already setting, at 12 o'clock, gently touched by a cool, fragrant, moist little breeze calling his heart by name, he once again raised eyelids already sunk in a dream. . . .

Sleep, for thou hast not committed a wicked deed today! — While the drowsy bellflower of thy spirit has shut and rests upon thy pillow, I will keep watch in the murmuring night for thy morning footpath, leading thee through transparent groves to Schadeck to visit thy benefactress. The Ritmaster will be away by one o'clock. Thou and thy benefactress will have the day to yourselves. Mayest thou prosper in all things, thou foolish Quintus!

Outing of Headmaster Florian Fälbel and His Primaner to Mount Fichtel

On the road to *Hof* I bade my sixth-formers take a note to the effect that the Baireuthian Voigtland was blessed with several products, with rye, oats, potatoes, sundry fruits (fresh as well as dried), and so on; but that one could not record how much.

A bugle call greeted us from the belfry when I and my troop were seen to set foot on the cobbles of Hof. For that reason I shall never, unlike others for some affected fear of self-praise, betraying no mean degree of the same in itself; and, indeed, the motives may not necessarily have been complimentary ones — suppress the fact that on our entry every window flew open and every head behind it popped out: German primary and Latin grammar school boys followed us with their eyes, shop boys stood in their shop doors, caps in hand, and people about to enter their houses stopped dead on their doorsteps. I took pains to ask the way to a carters' inn, as that is where I, like Swift, prefer to put up. It ought to have caused me embarrassment when, on halting our cabriolet complete with its Household Guards at the door of the Saxon post office where I had a franked letter to post, which I had up to now carried myself so as to avail of a reduced rate, when thereupon, as I was about to say, a handsome agreeable man wearing a green taffeta apron stepped among us and — regrettably taking us to be new arrivals; for the post office is housed under the same roof as the great Brandenburg Hostelry — was ready to hand down my daughter and welcome us all. But I was not greatly bothered and merely reiterated my inquiry about humbler quarters nonchalantly; and it was nice of the young man to direct us out of the gate again with a kind laugh — which we put into practice.

I had my beard removed by a sixth-former and my hair crimped by the factotum right there in the spacious taproom amidst the scrunch of carters' crags, while our cook-inheritrix put our smoked entrails to heat by the fireside. God grant that I might soon place the diligent child with a good aristocratic family as a lady's maid!

In the window seat a courier from a merchant firm in Pontak took it upon himself to bedevil and sacredieu the best German political papers and smit Messers S. T. *Girtanner* and *Hofmann* in particular with such foul names and verbal injuriae — which I dare not repeat apart from the lesser ones like fools, perverters of time, spiritual myrmidons — that I wished under my lather it were the procurator fiscal being belabored in my barber's chair and he could haul a scalliwag such as this over the coals. That gallic rogue went to great pains to feign incognizance of, and indifference to, myself and my traveling Philanthropinum, although even the lowliest of my flock has to know more about insubordinations and forms of government — ancient ones in particular — than this sansculotte. Sadly, my jawbones being immobilized by the razor, I could not refute his balderdash; but once released from the blade, I politely advanced on the chap ready to show him the error of his ways and to couch his democratic cataract and enlighten him. I did not disguise from him that I had never got anywhere with the national assembly and that the concepts, which I had taught to my subjects, of the present French foregathering, were altogether different from his. "All the same I will concede" (said I, treating the wretch like a scholar against my will) "that the French mob does not deserve this designation as much as that of a formal Riot, as it did indeed rally not only the number of persons required by law to constitute a rebellion or turba, namely fifteen men (L.4.§.3. de vi bon. rapt.) but an even greater number. But then you for your part must grant me the penalty imposed on rebellions by the ancient, albeit republican, Romans, viz, crucifixion, deportation, throwing to wild beasts; and even if you as a Christian wish to show clemency and, like the Emperor Justinianus, our lawgiver, merely make use of the gallows — as you will be bound to as even the Germans who used to let robbers and murderers live did hang rioters — you only have to consult *Hellfelden* — : you will still be less lenient than the allied forces who wanted to punish the nation, because it has turned soldatesca, merely according to martial law and only harquebuse it." On realizing that I was overtaxing the courier: I abandoned thoroughness in favor of clarity and pointed out to him that descendants could not possibly govern, much less depose, their father (or primum adquirentem), nor grammar school students their rector, and nor consequently subjects their sovereign. I put the question to him whether the Frenchmen's hysteronproteron could have been possible if everyone had annotated and edited his ancient autores instead of the French philosophers; and I challenged him to spell out to me somehow why I of all people had never harbored a refractory thought toward my gracious sovereign ruler. "Because," I countered myself, "I keep plying my classics and treat Paine and his ilk — though I have read the lot — with the contempt they deserve." — It galls me to think that I had intended appraising the fool that even in the animal kingdom the kings, the vultures, the eagles, the lions for instance, devoured their subjects — that a monarch might not be kindly disposed to a whole people and yet look after a few individual citizens and thus was exactly the *opposite* of that divine providence dreamt up by the French philosophers, which facilitates only the *species* but never the *individual* — and that a loyal and patient subject could prove himself best under a tempestuous rule just as the Christian manifested himself in adversity. In short, I was going to deem the man worthy of a public journal instruction; but that hare-brained republican whistled throughout my lecture and without a prosaic word made his exit in such a way that he almost appeared to me to despise both my speech and myself. Meanwhile, I applied this disquisition to my youthful disciples to better effect, and I propose, moreover, when it is time to explore the speech against Catiline, to show them more plainly that it is the Parisians who are *Catilines*, *Caesars*, and *Pisistrateses* thrusting their battering rams into the venerable state edifice. . . .

May I be permitted the following digression: I expended half a day on scouring my library and the reports on the local grammar school teachers as to which one among them might have rebelled against their sovereign ruler. But to my inexpressible joy, I can announce that neither the greatest humanists and philologists — a Camerarius, Minellius, Danz, Ernesti, who possessed Ciceronian speech organs and Roman speech waves, Herr Heyne, the chrestomaths, Stroth, et al., etc. — nor our own late local consistory of educatory custodians, from the rector down to the fifth assistant teacher (inclus.) in particular had ever rioted. Men will never act as or shield insurgents against patri- or matriarchs, men who without exception diligently and delicately dispense instruction in their respective classes from eight till eleven and who do indeed proclaim republics, although obviously none but the two on classical soil, and those only by virtue of Latin and Greek.

Instruction and ingestion concluded, we could easily have donned our hats and inspected Hof's public buildings: had not the responsibility for a certain primum mobile been incumbent on my shoulders — viz, *gestus*. I approached the landlord with a view to borrowing his room upstairs (the few minutes hardly warranting payment), because all we had to carry out there were a few gentle and elegant motions.

For quite some time now I had one of my pupils establish in a public oratorial exercise (to greater effect) that there was more to deportment than met the eye. Other people being pedal and manual, as it were, which it is not possible to work nimbly without a Bachean footing and fingering. I am the first to notice distinctly how greatly I differ in this respect from otherwise learned men who never even suggest these poetical figures of outer man, much less lighten the way with their own. Yet Seneca puts it quite well (c. 3. de tranquill.): "A good citizen's effort is never in vain; for by mere listening, looking, appearing, waving, by silent tenacity, nay by his very deportment he may yield results (prodest)." [19] And why should something like this not rouse a schoolteacher once in a while to ever carrying head, hat, frame, and glove in such a way that his pupils will not lose out by modeling themselves on his classical style? — "To-day," I addressed my mimics in the room upstairs, "we shall have to lay eyes on men of the noblest standing, we shall betake ourselves into the school building and into the billiard hall — in fact, we shall walk the streets of a city long renowned for her exterior polish and where I would least wish you to forfeit your own — for instance: how would you smile should you be required to smile in a superior way in society? Monsieur Scion, pray smile complacently!" He did not wholly achieve it. — I therefore delineated for him on my own lips that delicate standard smile, nicely unfurled, to suit all occasions; I went on to show them the mocking laugh, firstly the *perpendicular* version, where the joke turns up the mouth like a plug propping up the boar's snout on the game cart, and secondly the *horizon-*

---

19. But here is the superior original text: numquam inutilis est opera civis boni; auditu enim, visu, vultu, nutu, obstinatione tacita *incessuque* ipso prodest.

tal laugh, which may well go wide in any event if it should split the mouth open from ear to ear.

My audience copied my smile rather well albeit a bit too noisily. The recapitulation of obeisances followed and I drilled them in the gymnastic exercises of courtesy down to the barest turn. I demonstrated to them that a man of true breeding will rarely present his posterior, though this may cause him enormous trouble. Therefore I passed through the door and returned pulling it shut with my available hand accordant with the syntax of manners and never displaying a thing. "As the tail end of man, or garden," said I, "must remain hidden throughout, it is better to close the door with the rear itself or even to leave it open, as practiced by many." Now a detachment had to march out while facing me all the time and in again in the same fashion. "In my youth" (said I) "I would pivot and maneuver myself backward time and again for hours on end, struggling to take these pas renversés in my stride."

Flower-, Fruit-, and Thornpieces; or, the Married Life, Death, and Wedding of Advocate of the Poor F. St. Siebenkäs

WITHIN THE CLASS DISTINCTIONS SUGGESTED, IN NEO-classical fashion, by Jean Paul, *Siebenkäs* belongs to the middle class of German novels, as distinct from the lowly Netherlandish works like *Wutz* or the exalted Italian novels like *Titan*. Accordingly, it is unusually realistic and with a straightforward story line, as outlined above, insofar as one can ever speak here of the realistic and straightforward.

The first excerpt is Leibgeber's discourse on himself as Adam. Leibgeber is not only Siebenkäs's doppelgänger, he is the eternal alter ego in Jean Paul, sometimes appearing in one of his other guises, like Schoppe or Giannozzo, but always the accompanying adversary, often the devil's advocate. The second passage is typical of the scenes of domestic trials in this story of a hapless marriage. Finally, there is the most famous of the many dreams, doubtless the most notorious passage in Jean Paul, *Speech of the Dead Christ from the Universe that There Is No God*. It influenced the image of Jean Paul, particularly in France; much less so, it would seem, in England. Although Carlyle translated it, the translation had nothing like the impact of that into French by Madame de Staël and her friend Charles de Villiers.[1]

The genesis of the French translation is much disputed, as are the questions of responsibility for the fact that it omits the awakening at the end and of what purpose was intended, and is achieved, by that. (If the intention was to avoid a sentimental happy end, it was surely mistaken. The ending is as realistic as relief after a nightmare — and does not alter the fact that throughout Jean Paul the nightmare remains hovering, or cowering, as a dreaded possibility.) In his own review, Jean Paul not unnaturally objected to the mutilation, leaving out the ending that "closes the wound" (*H-KA* 1.16.LIX,324). At the same time, he appreciated so much French attention and returned the compliment by immersing himself in the study of Madame de Staël — so deeply, as he said, that he felt as if he had married her.

Speech of the Dead Christ developed over about a decade of Jean Paul's life, during which he was wrestling with his own growing skepticism. He was besieged by Ottomarian ideas, he wrote to K. P. Moritz on 9 August 1792 (*H-KA* 3.1). (Ottomar is the unbeliever in *The Invisible Lodge*.) The immediate occasion of the work seems to have been the death of his close friend Adam Lorenz von Oerthel in October 1786, when he wrote the first fragment on atheism. At that time, it was an address by Atheism; gradually, the narrative form was elaborated, at first as "Lament of the Dead Shakespeare to the Dead Listeners in the Church that There Is No God."

In April 1789, Jean Paul's brother Heinrich committed suicide; a year later another close friend, J. B. Hermann, died. In 1792 and 1793 came the deaths of Christian von Oerthel and K. P. Moritz. This was also the period of that "most important evening of my life," 15 November 1790, when he had the vision of his own deathbed. Not that the theme is restricted to that period. It is omnipresent and documented in several similar rhetorical passages, like "Comfortless Lament" and "Annihilation-Faith," in *The Vale of Campan* and *Selina*; or "Annihilation: A Vision," in *Dr. Katzenberger's Spa Journey*, which Jean Paul's two closest friends in his later life, Christian Otto and Emanuel Osmund, found better than *Speech of the Dead Christ* (*H-KA* 1.13.LXXIX). Here, too, the drama of unbelief

---

1. See Byron Libhart, "Madame de Staël, Charles de Villiers, and the Death of God in Jean Paul's 'Songe,'" *Comparative Literature Studies* 9 (1972): 141–51. For a study of Jean Paul's dream passages, generally, see J. W. Smeed, *Jean Paul's Dreams* (London, 1966).

and belief is played out, first in the vision of Annihilation itself: "be terror stricken and die, for I am God"; later in the vision of a God of love: "you cannot die, for I am in your heart."

The pattern is always that of nightmare and cathartic conversion, for Jean Paul based his case on those "secret opinions" he speaks of in "Annihilation: A Vision" on the distinction between what we think we think and what we really think, the latter surfacing once we have truly imagined the consequences of thinking otherwise. In that sense, the heart enlightens the head. (Wherever Jean Paul talks of feeling, it is as a kind of thinking — in that eighteenth-century fashion that annoyed Lessing as an illegitimate blurring of distinctions.) To this end, Jean Paul could, with a good conscience, indulge in every kind of rhetorical exercise to imagine the enormities of unbelief. They include very effective rhetorical devices: for example, trying to imagine that life is a matter not of sixty years but, as relatively it might very well be said to be, of sixty seconds. What hinders belief in immortality, says Jean Paul in his last major work, *Selina*, is lack of imagination — compounded, as he goes on to say there (in his increasing impatience with the Christian tradition), by the narrowness of Judeo-Christian thinking (*W* 12.1120).

In *Siebenkäs, Speech of the Dead Christ* stands out in a way that leads one to view it usually in isolation; but it can be related to the novel through the figure of Leibgeber and that drama of the *I*, the theme on which Jean Paul rings the changes throughout his work, one of the recurring variations being not only a nihilistic one but in the specific Nietzschean sense of a collapse of belief in the Christian God. This nihilistic option is present in Jean Paul whether he is talking about art or politics, philosophy or theology. *Preschool of Aesthetics* speaks of poetic nihilism as being a result of the tyranny of egoism. From Jacobi, Jean Paul learned both his faith philosophy — what Schlegel called Jacobi's "salto mortale into the abyss of Divine Mercy" — and his understanding of Idealism as nihilistic. Jacobi said he preferred his own philosophy of not knowing to the philosophy of the knowing of nothing. He maintains that Kant's *Critique of Pure Reason*, in separating thought from reality, must lead to nothing. And to Fichte, Jacobi wrote the often-quoted sentence: "Truly, my dear Fichte, I shall not be offended, if you, or anyone else, chooses to call a chimera that which I oppose to the idealism which I call nihilism."[2] But however antinihilistic Jean Paul may have intended to be and was,

---

2. *Fr. J. Jacobis Werke* (Leipzig, 1816), 3:44. Cf. Dieter Arendt: "Der Nihilismus . . . Ein Forschungsbericht," *DVJS* 43 (1969): 364–69, 544–66, esp. 355, 556ff.

his own work provides some of the most striking documents of nihilism in European literature. This aspect of his work, with special reference to *Speech of the Dead Christ*, is examined most closely in Walther Rehm's study of the poetic representation of unbelief in Jean Paul and Dostoyevski, the starting point of which is St. Augustine's account of the promethean, self-directed self, of the egoistic "experimentum suae medietatis."[3] Nobody experimented in this sense more than Jean Paul, and nobody anticipated more vividly Nietzsche's vision of man alone in a godless world. (This, rather than mortality and fear of annihilation, is the specific theme of *Speech of the Dead Christ*, the here-and-now consequences of godlessness. Atheism, as Dorothee Sölle says, was never for Jean Paul a painless agnosticism.)[4] Rehm's study puts Jean Paul in the context of that European theme of self-aggrandizement and self-doubt that provoked Pascal's "le moi est haïssable." The context is noteworthy, and yet the very phrase serves to distinguish the quite different world of Jean Paul. There is little of the spirit of Pascal in Jean Paul; for that, the human comedy he constructed around the *I* is much too self indulgent. (The following are taken from *W* 3.119ff., 152ff., 166ff., 270ff.).

Chapter Four, Leibgeber's Adam Letter

Now the postman trudged up the stairs with a new constellation to be set in the serene family sky, viz, this letter from Leibgeber:

Baireuth
21st September 1785

My dear Brother and Cousin and Uncle and Father and Son!

For thy two auricles and thy two ventricles compose my complete family tree; just as Adam, when out on a walk, carried on him his entire subsequent kinsfolk and line of descendants — not yet run out and finally scored — before he became a father and begat his wife. Would to God I had been the first Adam! . . . Siebenkäs, I beseech thee, let me pursue this idea like a man possessed and plead not a word in this letter but what would advance this three-quarter-length portrait of me as the original father of humankind! —

---

3. Walther Rehm: *Jean Paul, Dostojewski: Zur dichterischen Gestaltung des Unglaubens* (Göttingen, 1962).
4. Dorothee Sölle: *Realisation* (Darmstadt, 1971), pp. 251ff.

Those scholars know little of me who presume I wish to be Adam because *Puffendorf* and numerous others assign the whole earth to me like a European crown colony in the India of creation as my rightful Petrine, Pauline, Judine, and all other apostolic patrimony — because I, as the only Adam and human being and in consequence as the first and the last universal monarch, albeit without any subjects for the time being, was entitled to claim the whole world as my own. That kind of thing may be, or may have been, ages ago, in the mind of the Pope, the Holy, though not the first, Father, when he declared himself tenant entail and heir apparent to all the lands of the earth and had the effrontery to pile yet another couple of crowns on top of his crown of the world, viz, the crowns of Heaven and Hell.

How little do I desire! I only wanted to be the old and the eldest Adam in order to saunter with Eve along the espalier of Paradise on the eve of my wedding, in our green fancy aprons and furs, and deliver a wedding address in Hebrew to the mother of all mankind.

Before I begin my speech, let me observe that by the greatest good fortune I had the notion before my fall of committing to paper the choicest morsels of my omniscience. — For in that state of innocence I contained all the sciences, the universal as well as the scholarly history, the various penal and other laws, and the ancient dead languages as well as the living ones, and was, as it were, a living Pindus and Pegasus, a portable Lodge of Light and learned society and pocket seat of the muses, and short golden siècle de Louis XIV — in view of the sense I had at the time it was less a miracle than sheer luck that I jotted down in an idle moment my tutti wisdom: — afterward, when I fell and turned simpleton, I had these excerpts or a reasoning catalogue of my former intelligence in my possession and dipped into it.

"Miss," is how I commenced my homily at the rear of paradise, — "we may be the first parents and of a mind to beget the other parents, but all thou canst think of is sinking thy spoon into some proscribed applesauce. I, being a man and a protoplast, reflect; and I have a mind today to become our perambulating marriage preacher and straw garland speechmaker — I wish I had begotten myself a different one for the purpose — on this solemn occasion and in a short wedding sermon present to thee:

The reasons for doubt and decision or rationes dubitandi and decidendi of protoplasts — or the first parental and bridal couple (which is to say myself and thyself) as they reflect and consider — in fact how they consider

in the first part the causes and reasons for their not seeding the earth but
emigrating instead on the spot, one to the old, the other to the new
world — and in the

second part the reasons for refraining all the same and getting married; —
this is to be followed by a short elenchus or usus epanorthoticus, with
which the night will conclude.

1. PARS

Dearly beloved sister, as thou seest me here in my sheepskin, earnest,
thoughtful and upright: I am not so much full of foolishness as full of
fools, laced with a goodly number of wise men. I may not be tall of stature, and the ocean[1] may have covered my ankles and splashed my new
sheepskin; but by heaven! I do walk about here girt with a sower's cloth,
which contains the seeds of all peoples, and carry the publisher's index
and cashbox of all of humanity, a complete little world and orbem pictum
before me like a hawker's tray on my stomach. For *Bonnet*, included in
the stomach's contents, will, on being delivered, sit himself down at his
desk and disclose that all is encapsulated, each box and parenthesis, stuck
in another, that within the father there is the son; within the grandfather
are both of these two; consequently, within the great-grandfather is
the grandfather, with his own insertion; and within the great-great-
grandfather is the great-grandfather, with his insertion of the insertion
and all his interludes sitting in expectation. Are there not in the present
bridegroom — and this, dear bride, cannot be explained clearly enough
to thee — embodied all religious denominations, even the Adamites,[2]
though excepting the pre-Adamites, and all giants, even big *Christopher* —
each personnel of peoples — all shiploads of negroes bound for America,
and the small package, marked in red, containing the Anspach and Baireuth soldiery England had ordered? Heva, am I not, as I stand here
before thee and if thou lookest at my insides, a living Jews' quarter — a
Louvre of all heads of state, whom I may all beget at my pleasure and
provided the first pars will not dissuade me? Thou wilt admire me and
on observing me closely laugh at me too, as thou layest thy hand on my
shoulder, thinking: within this man and this protoplast are now penned
together all men and all faculties — all schools of philosophy and all sew-

---

1. The French academician *Nikolaus Henrion* stretched Adam to a height of 123 feet,
9 inches, and Heva to 118 feet, 9 3/4 inches. The rabbis report the above, to wit that Adam
had walked through the ocean after the fall. V.II. bibl. discourse by *Saurin*.

2. That well-known sect, who went to church with no clothes on.

ing and spinning schools in perfect harmony — the oldest and noblest dynasties, albeit not yet plucked from the common ship's complement — all of the free College of Knights, albeit still baled together with their vassals, tenants, and cotters — nunneries cheek by jowl with monasteries — all barracks and all deputies, not to mention cathedral chapters complete with their provosts, deans, archdeacons, deacons, and canons each! Ah, what a man, what an Anak! thou wilt add. And thou art right, bless thy heart, I am all of that, a proper luck thaler of the coin cabinet of humanity, the law court of law courts, and fully manned into the bargain, not one associate missing, the living corpus juris of the incorporate civil, canon, criminal, feudal, and public legal profession: Do I not hold the complete editions of *Meusel's* Scholarly Germany and *Jöcher's* Encyclopaedia of Learned Germany, as well as Meusel and Jöcher in Person, not to mention the supplementary volumes? — I wish I could show thee *Cain* — this would, provided the second pars will persuade me, be our first scion and offshoot, our Prince of Wales, Calabria, Asturia, and Brazil — should he be transparent — which I believe he will be — thou wouldst see nested within him like beer glasses the sum total of ecumenical councils and inquisitions and congregations of propaganda and the Devil himself and his grandmother. — However, my lovely, unlike myself thou has not written down anything of thy scientia media before thy Fall, and consequently thou starest into the future as blind as a bat. — Only I, looking through it quite brightly, gather from my chrestomathy that, should I indeed avail myself of my Blumenbachean nisus formativus and risk a few protoplastic peeps at the jus luxandae coxae or primae noctis[3] today, that I would not beget ten fools as normally *one* would beget, but billions of tens and the ones to boot, seeing that all those Arch-Bohemians — Parisians — Viennese — Leipzigers — Baireuthers — Hofers — Dubliners — Kuhschnapplers (complete with their wives and daughters) domiciled in me would be called into being through me, and amongst whom there will be 500 in every 1,000,000 who will not listen to reason albeit they may have none themselves. Duenna, little dost thou know humans so far, only two, for the snake is not one; but I know what I shall beget, and that with my limbus infantum I shall also open a Bedlam. — By Heaven! I shudder and groan when I skim through the volumes of centuries and see nothing but bloodstains and medleys of fools — when I assess the labor it takes for a century just to acquire a legible hand that could vie with an elephant's

---

3. The first night in the actual sense, as according to many scholars Eve turned apple thief during the first morning of her creation.

tusk or the hand of a minister — for poor humanity to emerge from its common- and hedge-schools and resident mademoiselles to take its place with honor in grammar schools, royal or Jesuit colleges, attend a fencing or dancing hall, even, or perhaps a drawing lesson or a dogmatic or clinical lecture. Confound it! I feel uneasy — of course, no one calls thee the mother hen of the future flock, the spawner of codlings, within whom *Leuwenhoek* counts 9 1/2 million stockfish eggs; Evikin, thou wilt never be blamed like thy husband, who ('twill be said) should have known better and begotten naught rather than such a rabble of robbers — crowned emperors on the Roman throne and vicars on the Roman seat, the former of whom adopt the name of Antoninus or Caesar and the latter of Christ and St. Peter and among whom will be those whose thrones will be Lüneburg torture chairs of humanity and a Stein's parturition chair of Old Harry if not, indeed, an upside down Grêve Square serving at one and the same time for the execution of the whole and the delectation of the singular.[4] — Furthermore, they will chalk a *Borgia, Pizarro, St. Dominic,* and *Potemkin* up to me. And even suppose I knew how to counter the charge of these black exceptions, I shall still be bound to admit (and anti-Adams will accept utiliter) that my descendants and settlers cannot survive half an hour without thinking or doing some folly — that the war of giants, which their passions are waging within them, will not observe peace, rarely a truce — that man's cardinal fault will ever be having a host of little ones — that his conscience will serve for little more than a *dislike of his neighbor and a morbid sensitivity to the transgressions of others* — that he will ever be loath to renounce his evil ways unless he be on his deathbed, beside which a confessional will be provided like a commode for children at bedtime — that he will learn and love the language of virtue while showing hostility to the virtuous, like those Londoners who keep French tutors while loathing the French. — Alas, Eve, our espousal will do us scant credit; *red* earth is the meaning of Adam in the original, and verily will my cheeks be so and blush at the mere thought of our great-grandchildren's incessant and indescribable *vanity* and conceit, which will swell with the centuries. No one will tweak his own nose save those who

---

4. It seems almost to indicate an intercorporation of the serious tiger and the playful monkey that the Grêve Square in Paris is at the same time a place of execution for malefactors and a pleasure field for public festivities, that regicides are . . . torn asunder by horses where kings are fêted by citizens, and that the fiery wheels with their broken bodies and the fire workers' St. Catherine wheels whirl side by side and one after the other — horrific contrasts, which we must not pile up here unless we ourselves wish to succumb to copying those who gave rise to our censure.

barber themselves — higher nobility will have their privy lids branded with their families' coats of arms and their initials twined into their nags' cruppers — critics will set themselves above scribes and scribes above critics — Heimlicher von Blaise will permit his hand to be kissed by orphans; ladies, theirs by anybody; and the higher orders, the fancy hems of their skirts. I had only brought my prophetic extracts from the history of the world down to the 6th millenium, Heva, when thou tookest a bite under the tree and I in my innocence followed suit and the whole lot escaped me: — God only knows what the fools and their mates of the other centuries will be like. Miss, wilt thou now activate thy sternocleidomastoidum, which *Sömmering* calls the head nodder, and thus denote thy consent if I tender the question: wilt thou take the present marriage preacher for thy rightfully wedded husband? —

Thy rejoinder of course will be: let us at least attend the second pars, wherein the matter will be considered from the other aspect as well. — And verily, we had indeed almost forgotten, dearly beloved sister, to pass on to

2. PARS

and to ponder together the reasons that might induce our first protoplasts or parents to become the same, join together and serve Fate as the sowing and spinning machines of her linseed and hemp, flax and tow, whose endless network and coils she wreathes around the earthly sphere. — To my mind my foremost reason — and I hope it will also be thine — is Judgment Day. For if the two of us should be the entrepreneurs of the human race: I shall see all my descendants rising from calcine earth in a cloud on Judgment Day and gather upon the nearest neighboring planet for a final muster; and among this abundance of children and progeny I shall encounter people with sense to whom one can talk, men whose lives were passed and lost in a thunderstorm, as according to Roman beliefs those whom the gods favor are slain by a thunderbolt, and yet they would never shutter their ears or eyes in a storm. — Furthermore, I see standing among them those four wonderful pagan evangelists, *Socrates, Cato, Epictetus,* and *Antoninus*, who called to every house with their voices like 200-foot-long fire hoses, which they directed at every blasted blaze of passion, extinguishing it with the purest and finest alpenwater. — All told, I shall become the archpapa and thou the archmama of the most excellent people should we so choose. I am telling thee, Eve, I have it in writing here in my excerpts and collecteana that I shall be the forbear ancestor, Bethlehem, and natura plastica of an *Aris-*

totle, a *Plato*, *Shakespeare*, *Newton*, *Rousseau*, *Goethe*, *Kant*, or *Leibniz*, all of them persons who are going to be even more astute thinkers than their own protoplast. Eve, thou eminent working Member of the present Fructiferous Society of productive estate of the state, comprised of thyself and the marriage preacher, I swear I shall enjoy an hour of several blissful eternities when I fleetingly run through the assembly of the classics and the born again on the neighboring planet and finally kneel down in ecstasy on the satellite saying: Good morning, my children! Ye Jews were wont to utter a secret and fervent ejaculation when a wise man jostled ye; — but what could I utter that would be long enough when my eyes fall at once on all sages and licentiates and blood relations before me, who in the midst of ravenous passion were able to forgo the forbidden apples and pears and pineapples and who, while thirsting for Truth, did not resort to orchard thievery from the Tree of Knowledge, whereas their original parents laid hands on the forbidden fruit although they had never known hunger and on the Tree of Knowledge although they were in possession of all knowledge except that of the nature of the snake. And then I shall rise from the ground, hasten through the crowd of descendants, and fall on the bosom of some choice grandson and hug him and say: "Oh thou faithful, dear, happy, and softhearted son — if in the second pars of my sermon I had shown in the brood chamber no one but thee to my Heva, the queen mother of all the swarms now around us, the good woman would have considered the matter and been open to argument." ... And thou art that good and faithful son, Siebenkäs, and thou shalt ever lie and abide on the ardent hairy breast of

     thy
       Friend.

Chapter Five

The Broom and the Brush as Implements of Passion — The Importance of an Author — Nunciature Disputes on the Snuffing of Candles — The Pewter Cupboard — Domestic Delights and Deprivations

Catholics count fifteen mysteries in Christ's life, five joyous ones, five dolorous ones, and five glorious ones. Having thoughtfully followed our hero through the five joyous ones, which is about the count for a matrimonial linden honeymoon, I am about to arrive with him at the five dolorous ones, with which the succession of mysteries in most marriages will be — concluded. Mind you, I hope his will have the five glorious ones as well. . . .

With the preceding sentence I blithely embarked on this booklet in its first edition as though it were wholly true; but second, and greatly revised, editions demand of their own accord that I should amend it and add that the mysteries mentioned above did not succeed each other like steps of stairs or a series of ancestors but arrived higgledy-piggledy like a mixed hand of cards. But pain is outweighed by joy, at least in duration, in these shuffles of Life, as happened with our own terrestrial globe, which after all has survived several doomsdays followed by all the more springs, hence minor creation days.

— I am setting all this down here on purpose in order to save any poor rogue of a reader who might dread having now to wade through a whole tome of tears, some perused, some shed by himself in sympathy; I am not one of those authors who, rattlesnakes that they are, can watch thousands of mesmerized people jumping with anxiety and alarm before pouncing on them themselves.

On awaking next morning, Siebenkäs straight away sent the devil of jealousy and of married life to join the rest of the devils — for a calming sleep arrests the fever pulse of the soul, and its grains are a fever bark for both the cold ague of hate and the hot ague of love —; indeed, he laid down the silhouette board and with his pantograph took a true reduced copy of yesterday's free rendition of Egelkraut's features, and blackened it properly. When it was finished, he said to his wife for love: "We'll send him the profile at once. 'Twill be a long time before he'll come and fetch it himself." "Indeed, yes," countered she, "'twill be Wednesday — and by that time he'll have forgotten it long since." — "However," replied Siebenkäs, "he could be enticed to come sooner; I would only have to send him the Reuß Trinity thaler of 1679 to purchase: he would never send me a letter but would deliver the money for it in person, as was his wont all along with Leibgeber's coin cabinet." "Or," — said Lenette, — "why not send him the thaler and profile together? It would give him the greater pleasure." — "What would?" asked he. She did not quite know how to answer this frivolous interjection, as to whether she spoke of the black or the minted profile as greater, and in her dilemma she said, "Well, the things of course." He let her off and did not ask her again.

But the Inspector sent nothing except word that he was beside himself with delight at the magnificent presents and would call in person at the end of next week at the latest in order to thank them and settle up with the Advocate. Nor could the dash of wormwood, which flavored the unexpected reply of the carefree and all too joyful Inspector, be sweetened in any way at that moment by the entry of the Inheritance Court Messenger, who handed the Advocate the answer, or the first paragraph, or the defense pleas of the defendant Heimlicher von Blaise, consisting of nothing but a request for three-weeks' grace, which the Court had willingly granted. Siebenkäs, to be sure, being his own poor law advocate, lived in the certain hope that the Promised Land of Inheritance, where milk and honey flow over golden sands, should be conquered by his children after he himself had long since expired on his way to it in the juridical desert. Justice is predisposed to rewarding his children and children's children for a father's virtue and title; meanwhile, it was inconvenient that he had nothing to live on himself during his own lifetime. For he could no longer exist on the Reuß Trinity thaler — for which Stiefel had not even paid him, nor on the only queue ducate still extant from Leibgeber's "Imperial War Chest" for operations against the Heimlicher. For this gold and that silver coin made up (although I have not disclosed this before) the sum total in Leibgeber's cash and redemption chest, and it would be sufficient for none but a disciple of the Redeemer himself. My nondisclosure of the coin cabinet depletion may be considered yet another proof of my wish to refrain from inflicting pain on my reader wherever I can.

"Oh, I shall find a way," said Siebenkäs quite cheerfully and set to with a will at his desk today, the sooner the better to channel by means of his Selection from the Devil's Papers a sizeable honorarium into his house. But a purgatory of quite a different nature is now being stoked up and fanned higher and higher about him, which I had not liked to refer to as yet, although he has been roasting in it since the day before yesterday, Lenette being the roaster, and his writing table the lark spit. For during the wordless squabbling of the last few days he had fallen into the habit of listening to Lenette with a special attention, while sitting there writing away at his Selection from the Devil's Papers: and this wrought havoc altogether with his ideas. The tiniest step, each gentle vibration, attacked him like rabies or podagra, each time putting to death one or two budding ideas, as a loud noise puts to death silkworm or a brood of canaries.

In the beginning, he controlled himself rather well, and he bore in mind that the woman needs must move about, and until she was wielding an astral body or astral furniture, her step on the floorboards was bound

to be heavier than a sunbeam or the invisible angels of good or evil behind her. But while he followed attentively this worthy cours de morale,
this colloquium pietatis of his own, he lost his satirical context and con-
cept, and his writing lost sparkle.

The morning after that silhouette evening, when their souls had
joined hands and renewed the royal alliance of love once again, he could
go about it more openly; and as soon as he had proceeded from blackening profiles to blackening their originals — that is to say, as he toiled in
his satirical soot works — he said to his wife in anticipation: "If you can
help it, Lenette, please don't make too much of a to-do today — it is nigh
a hindrance to me as I sit here and work for the printer." She said: "I
would have thought you could hardly hear me the way I tiptoe about."

A man, although he may long be past the years of his doltishness, will
still have to cover several doltish weeks and fledgling days in the years to
come: and it was truly a doltish minute when Siebenkäs made the request
mentioned above. For now he had forced on himself the compulsion to
lie in wait, while he was thinking, for what Lenette was going to do on
receipt of his supplication. Now she bustled about on spider's feet over
her floorboards and over her web of domestic craft. For like the rest of
her sex, she had not contradicted him for the sake of opposing but merely
in order to contradict. Siebenkäs had to strain his ears if he wanted to
hear her footfall or touch; but he succeeded in hearing most of it. Except
when we are asleep, we take more notice of gentle noises than loud ones:
the scribe now harked to her every step, and his ear and his mind, fas-
tened to her like a pedometer, tripped along with her wherever she
went — in short, in the midst of his satire "The Nobleman with the
Ague,"[5] he had to break off, jump up, and say to his tiptoeing wife: "I
have been listening to this harrowing tripping about for an hour now; I
would much rather you were clumping about in a pair of noisy *crupetias*
with iron soles for beating time with[6] than this — please do me a favor
and walk as usual, love."

She complied and walked *almost* as usual. Having put a stop to the
heavy as well as the gentle walking about, he now would also have liked
to abolish the median step; however, a man is reluctant to contradict himself twice in *one* morning; once is enough. He merely requested that evening that she walk in her socks while he was sketching his satires, espe-

5. Selection from the Devil's etc. p. 41.
6. They were worn by the musici of the ancients. Bartholin. de Tib. Vet. III. 4.

cially as the floor would be pleasantly cool: "As I'll be earning our daily bread in the forenoon, it might in any case be just as well," he added, "if you confined yourself to the barest essentials while I am going about my literary pursuits."

Next morning he mentally sat in judgment on all that went on behind his back, scrutinizing it — while he continued to write, albeit steadily worse — whether it bore the free pass of necessity. The scribe-martyr made light of much of it; but when Wendeline with her long broom swept the bedstraw under the green-painted marriage torus in the chamber: this cross was more than his shoulder could bear. Added to that, he had read in the ancient ephemerids of the natural scientists only the day before yesterday that a divine called Johann Pechmann could not bear the sound of a besom — that its swish nigh took his breath away, and he would run from a street sweeper who happened upon him; such reading matter could not but leave him less tolerant and more observant in a like situation. Without leaving his desk, he called to the sweep in the chamber: "Lenette, please du not swish and curry so with your besom — it keeps me from thinking — There was once an old Pastor Pechmann who would rather have been condemned to sweeping the streets of Vienna than have to listen to it, nay, who would liefer endure a flogging than the confounded noise of its scraping and dragging. And I am supposed to conceive next door to the besom ideas fit for the printer and publisher: kindly bear that in mind!"

Lenette now did what any good wife and her lapdog would do: she fell silent *by degrees*. Indeed, in the end she even dismissed the broom and made no more noise sweeping than her husband did writing when she gently pushed with her brush three straws and some downy fluff under the bedstead. As luck should have it and against all hope, the editor of the Devil's Papers within perceived the pushing: he rose up, made for the door to the chamber, and addressed her within: "Dearest, the hellish agony seems the same once I discern it at all — yea, whether you swish the wretched sweepings under the bed with a peacock fan and an aspergill or blast it behind the chamber pot with a bellows: I and my book in there suffer for it and must needs become crippled." — She rejoined: "I am finished in any case."

Once again he settled down to his work and cheerfully picked up the thread in the third satire "pertaining to the five monsters and their receptacles on whom I had initially hoped to subsist" (p. 46 in the printed edition).

Meanwhile, Lenette pushed the bedroom door gently shut; from this he could only conclude that something else was afoot against him out there in his Gehenna and penitentiary parish. He laid down his pen and called from behind his desk, "Lenette, I can't hear it clearly, but if you are up to something unbearable out there again, I implore you, for God's sake desist, call a halt to my cross-school and its sorrows of Werther — show yourself!" — "I am not doing anything," she rejoined, though puffed with exertion. He rose again and opened the door to his torture chamber to see the good woman brandish a piece of grey flannel, with which she polished the green-painted marriage cot. The chronicler was once confined to one with the smallpox and is therefore familiar with them; but the reader may not be aware that such a green slumber cage looks like a magnified breeding cage for canaries, with its two iron-barred double gates or portcullises, and that this dream balustrade and hothouse is more cumbersome but also more wholesome than our deeply shrouded dungeons of sleep, which swaddle and coddle us from the least breath of fresh air with their stuffy curtains. — The poor law advocate did not gulp anything but a half-pint of bedroom air and embarked in a deliberate way: "I see you are sweeping and brushing all over again — knowing full well that I have been trying in there in the sweat of my brow to toil away for the two of us and that I have not made much sense for the past hour of writing — oh my divine better half, will you for God's sake bring out your grapeshot once and for all but do not ruin me altogether with that flannel of yours." — Lenette said full of surprise: "But you cannot possibly have heard me within, my pet," and polished on at the double. A mite rashly but gently he caught her hands and said in a louder voice: "Enough is enough! — That is precisely my trouble, that I cannot hear it inside but have to imagine it all in my head — and that confounded polish- and besom-thought chases away my finest ideas, which I might have put down on paper! — No one would work away and sit here more blissfully and composedly than myself, dearest angel, if only you were to fire away with your grapeshot, your howitzers, and your hundred-pounders behind my back and discharge your volleys from your domestic battlements; but I am not up to your quiet noise."

Now he was irked by this long speech, and leading her, flannel and all, from the chamber he said to her: "I must say, I find it a little hard that, while I am tearing myself apart in there trying to bring some joy to the reading public, the chase should be unleashed at the same time in my own bedroom, and an author's bed should be converted into a trench out of which he should be pursued with arrows and fireballs. At dinner time, when I have nothing to write, I shall speak sensibly and at length to you on this matter."

. . . .

The following day, Siebenkäs pressed for greater silence around him merely *because* he had pleaded with so much eloquence for it. Our dear Lenette, who was a living sweep mill and washing machine and for whom a bill of fare or laundry donned the attributes of certificates of integrity[7] and confession, would rather let anything pass from her hands — almost including his — than her polishing flannel and broom. She took it to be only his obstinacy, while it was her own, that made her tread on the bellows and thunder and roar on her reed stops behind the poor author's back during the very hours of morn, which were twice precious to him, his Golden Age and Brazen Age, pari passu. She could have pulled out all 32 stops at once during the afternoon had she so wished: but she was not to be budged from her daily routine. Woman is the most paradox amalgamation of stubbornness and self-sacrifice you ever saw, allowing her head to be cut off by the headsman of Paris for her husband's sake but not a single hair on it. Furthermore she can deny herself much for the good of others but nothing at all for her own; she will gladly forgo three nights' sleep for an invalid but not even curtail a catnap to make sure of a good night's sleep in her bed. Neither the blest nor the butterflies can, although they be without stomachs, eat less than a woman resolved to go to a ball or walk to the wedding altar, or one cooking dinner for guests; but should it be merely her doctor or body forbidding her some Esau's pottage or other, she will eat it that instant. A man goes about his sacrifices the other way around.

Lenette, driven by the opposite forces of his exhortations and her inclinations and seeking to walk the female diagonal line, conceived her own Augsburg Interim of suspending her sweeping and scrubbing while he sat writing. Should he step up to the piano for a moment or two, or the window, or over the threshold, however, she would wield her washing stool and polishing implements inside the room again. Siebenkäs was soon to become aware of this deplorable alternation and relieving of the guards and of her *broom;* and her lying in wait for his walking about dulled both himself and his ideas to a dreadful degree. To start with, he showed great patience, as much as a husband can muster, viz, of a short duration: but having pondered silently and at length his and his public's

7. Testimonium integritatis, the priestly certificate attesting that a bride had never been anything more.

joint suffering from this room polishing and a whole posterity's hingeing on a broom, which could so easily do its work during the afternoon while he only busied himself with his documents: all of a sudden the angry boil burst and he became mad, that is to say, madder, and he leapt in front of her saying: "Hang it all! I am up to your tricks at last: you are watching out for each step of mine. Why not have pity and slay me once and for all — starvation and anger are bound to finish me off before Easter anyway. Merciful God! this is beyond me; she can see full well that my book will provide our food cupboard, from which bounties of bread are going to tumble — and yet she is tying my hand all morning so that nothing gets done. I have been brooding for ages and laid nothing but folio E, where I describe the Ascension of Justice (p. 67) — Lenette! Oh Lenette!" — "Whatever I do," she said, "it is bound to be wrong. You might as well let me sweep properly like other women." She went on to ask in all innocence why it was that the bookbinder's little boy — these are not her words but mine — who extemporized all day long on his fiddle and scored and performed whole Alexander's Feasts on it, did not disturb him with his screeching discordant progressions, and why he could bear the chimney sweeping the other day so much more easily than her chamber sweeping. It being beyond his power in such a brief span of time to expound the enormous difference in a few words, he chose to flare up again and addressed her thus: "For Heaven's sake! Here I am supposed to deliver a discourse for you gratis while over there one municipal thaler after another slips through my fingers! Neither Roman Pandects nor Civil Law will let a coppersmith move into a street where a professor toils — yet my own wife would be harder than a man of law? Nay, would be the coppersmith? — Lenette, look here, I shall have to consult the Inspector on this!" — That was a great help.

And now the sum for the Trinity Thaler arrived even before the Inspector; a courteous consideration, which nobody would have expected from a man of such learning. My readers will surely be as delighted at Lenette's being an angel all afternoon as if they themselves were her husbands; — her manual labors were no more audible than those of her fingers or needles — some expendable ones she even deferred — and a sister oratress with a heavenly headdress — albeit held in her hands, for mending, was ushered downstairs, not so much from politeness but with the gentle intention of talking over again the principal points of sewing, which had already been settled, out of the advocate's earshot.

This moved the old eavesdropper and gripped him by his weakest and softest spot, viz, his heart. He ransacked his mind for a proper oblation until he hit upon a quite novel one. "Listen, my child," said he, taking her by the hand in an indescribably friendly manner — "would I not prove myself a sensible man if I practiced my wit and my writing at night, that is to say, if the husband were to create while the wife were not doing the laundry? Consider beforehand such a hydromel and ambrosia life: we would be sitting across from each other, a candle between us, — you would be wielding your needle — and I my satirical one — all the artisans in the house would have exchanged their hammers for beer mugs — the bearers of bonnets would not be abroad at so late an hour in any case. — Not to mention the fact that the lengthening evenings would accommodate longer writing and satirizing. — What do you think, or if you would rather, what do you say to that, to such a new moving and being? And add to that, above all, the fact that we are in funds at the moment and the Reuß Trinity Thaler, our windfall, as it were, will recoin us all altogether, Stiefel and myself, into Father and Son, and you into the Holy Ghost, who emanates from the two of us!"

"Oh, very charming," she countered; "for I should be allowed to go about my affairs in the morning as befits a sensible housewife." "Indeed," added he, "I would write away peacefully at my barbed matin papers and look forward to eventide and taking up where I had left off in the morning."

The hydromel and ambrosia evening came to pass and was without rival among the evenings heretofore. A young married couple facing each other over *one* candle across *one* table, engaged in their harmless and quiet tasks, can count themselves lucky indeed: he full of ideas and kisses; she full of smiles; and her pushing the frying pan impinged on his ear no more than her plying her needle. "If people," — said he in his delight at the domiciliary Reformation — "double their wages in the light of *one* candle, I for one do not see any need for them to restrict themselves to a paltry worm of a dip, which lights up nought but its simple self. To-morrow we shall invest without further ado in a molded candle."

Taking some pride in the fact that in this history I select and narrate only events of universal importance, I shall not dwell on the molded candle's appearance that evening and its sparking off of a lackluster dispute, for in its light the Advocate once again displayed his new theory of candle lighting. For he held the somewhat schismatic belief that it was only rational that each candle ought to be lit at its fat end — and especially a fat candle — and not at its upper, slim end, and that for that reason two wicks protruded from every candle; "a law of combustion" — he added — "in whose support there remains nothing further to add, at least not to women of sense, but the obvious one that a burning candle — like a glutton consumed by dropsy and adiposis — does thicken increasingly at its base; if it be lit on top we should experience down below a superfluous and useless lump, plug, and stump of tallow in its stick; but with what beautiful symmetry does not the liquid candle grease gently settle around its thin end, feeding it up as it were, and giving it equipoise if we but light the fatter part first!"

Lenette put up a compelling defense against his reasons, to wit, Shaftesbury's Touchstone of Truth, the Ridiculous. "Really," she said, "everybody would laugh who might call of an evening and see that I put my candle the wrong way round in its holder, and all the blame would attach to the wife." As a result, a peace formula had to establish parity in this candle discord to the effect that he lit his candles below and she hers above. For the time being, and with their coincident candle, which was fat at the top in any case, he tolerated the interim of incorrect lighting.

But the Devil, who blessed and crossed himself at such things, managed to play into the hands of the reading Advocate that very day the touching account of how his wife would hold the lamp for Pliny the Younger that he might see while he was writing. Now, while he was happily penning the Selection from the imaginary Devil's papers, it occurred to the Advocate how wonderful it would be and how it would save interruption if Lenette instead of himself were to snuff the candle. "Why, I would love to," she answered. For the first fifteen to twenty minutes all went, and seemed, quite well.

Afterward, he lifted his chin toward the candle like an index finger as a reminder. — Another time he silently touched the snuffers with the tip of his pen to the same effect; later again he moved the candlestick the tiniest bit and said gently, "The candle!" Now things turned a little more serious as he started to watch more keenly for the darkening on his paper and thus found that the very snuffers, which in Lenette's hand had promised so much light on his work, were to check his progress as crabs' pincers had checked a Hercules in his fight with the Hydra. That wretched lean pair of ideas, snuffers and snuff, skipped boldly across the whole range of letters of his sharpest satire, hand in hand, and took shape in front of his eyes. — "Lenette," he soon repeated, "would you do us both a favor and truncate the silly black stump, please!" — "Did I forget it?" said she and pruned speedily.

Readers of a historical turn of mind, as I would wish mine to be, will easily anticipate a steady deterioration and dislocation of matters. Indeed, he would often restrain himself now and, while dabbing letters a foot high, wait for a beneficent hand to deliver him from the black thorn in the rose of light before he uttered the words: "Snuff!" — He aimed for a multiplicity of verbs and would say, "Enlighten!" — or again, "Decapitate!" — or"Snip!" — Or he would attempt an agreeable variation in a different part of speech and say: "Trimmers please, Miss Trimmer! — there is a long sunspot in the sun again." — Or "A pretty nightlight for night-thoughts in a pretty Correggio's night; meanwhile snuff it!"

Finally, just before supper, when the charcoal pile in the flame had risen to a great height, he gulped half an airstream into his lungs and, dispensing it drop by slow drop, said with grim mildness: "I see you are not snuffing or trimming anything, never mind that the black stake meanwhile reaches the ceiling. Very well! I'll be my own theater candlesnuffer and chimney sweep until the table is laid; but during supper I, being a rational man, will tell you what has to be said." — "Oh, please do," said she happily.

"I certainly had" — he commenced after she had dished up for him and herself, two eggs for each person — "expected great benefit from my nocturnal toil, assuming you to take care of the easy snuffing at the right moment, as after all a refined Roman lady turned, speaking commercially, into a lamp, holding the wick for her husband, Pliny Junior. But this is no way to be going on, as I cannot write like a fortunate arm cripple with my foot under the table, or totally in the dark like a clairvoyant. All I get out of the candlestick now is that it is an old Epictet's lamp, while I act the Stoic. The candle frequently shows a twelve-inch eclipse, just like a sun, so that I longed in vain, dearest heart, for an invisible eclipse, which often obtains in the sky. Those obscure concepts and night thoughts produced by an author are the very ones hatched by these blasted cinders. Oh God, why couldn't you have snuffed properly!" —

"You must be joking," she countered; "my stitches are much daintier than your strokes, and I could see quite nicely."

"Let me enlighten you then, psychologically and psychoscientifically," he went on, "that in the case of a poor author and thinker it does not matter one whit whether he sees more or less well, but the snuffers and trimmers, which lodge in his mind, will get stuck 'twixt his mental legs as it were, like a horse's clog, and impede progress. — As soon as you have snuffed thoroughly and while I am still living in light I start lying in wait for the forthcoming snuffing. Now this lying in wait, being invisible and inaudible, cannot exist but in thought, each thought, though, preventing one from having another instead — and thus an author's superior thought will all go to the dogs. — And yet I am still only discussing the most insignificant evil — for I need no more think of the candle snuff than of that for my nose; — but when the keenly awaited snuff does not ensue at all — when the black ergot of the ripe candle ear grows ever taller — when darkness grows visibly greater — when a veritable funeral torch feebly shines on a writing semicorpse — and he cannot rout at all from his brain the conjugal hand, which could with *one* single snip free him from all those fetters: then, my dearest Lenette, it really takes a lot for an author not to write like an ass or to plod along like a camel, and I at least have a tale to tell on the topic." Thereupon she assured him that if he was really serious she would certainly do it tomorrow.

This history must indeed commend her for keeping her word on the morrow, for not only did she snuff much more often than heretofore but practically without ceasing, especially since he had proffered acknowledgment a few times with a nod of his head. "Meantime do not" — said he in the end, though with uncommon gentleness, — "curtail too often. Go too deeply into the finer subsubsubdivisions (snip-snip-snippets) of the wick and we shall be back to our former dilemma, as a pinched-off candle burns just as dimly as one with an overgrown wick — which, if you were capable, you could apply figuratively to leading ecclesiastic and wordly lights also — ; but just a little *after* and a little *before* snuffing, entre chien and loup as it were, is when that beautiful median tide of the soul falls, when vision is splendid; this, to be sure, a truly divine life, a perfectly measured twofold black on white, in book and candle!"

Neither myself nor others will be pleased at this new turn of events; the Poor Law Advocate patently placed yet another millstone around his neck, viz, during his writing, albeit superficially, to calculate and observe the medium range or mean term between the short and the long wick; what time will this leave for his work then?

A few minutes later, when she may have snuffed a little too soon, he put the question, although somewhat more doubtfully: "Dirty laundry again?" Afterward, when she may have snuffed almost a little late, he gave her a questioning look: "Well, well!" — "By and by!" said she. — Finally, when he was almost too deeply immersed in tilting his pen and his wife in wielding her needle, his eye, on awaking and looking up, fell on one of the tallest snuff spears to date and, what is more, the whole thing surrounded by more than one sprout. — "Merciful God, if this isn't a life of misery!" cried he, grimly snatching the snuffers and snuffing the candle — out.

During this darksome holiday he could now rant and rave to his heart's content and reproach Lenette at leisure about her plagueing him no matter how good his arrangements, and how, like all of her sex, she could do nothing in moderation but would shear either too much or too little. While she silently lit the candle, he inflamed himself even further and brought up the question whether he had ever demanded of her anything but the merest trifles and whether he had been refused the lot by anyone else ever apart from her, his darling wedded wife. "Answer me!" said he.

She did not answer but set the lighted candle upon the table with tears in her eyes. It was for the first time in their married life. At that moment he perceived, like a mesmerized man, the whole morbid edifice of his inner self, diagnosed it, and cast off the Old Adam on the spot, flinging it with contempt into the furthest corner. This was an easy task, as his heart stood so wide open to Love and Justice that the minute these Goddesses showed their faces his angry voice in the protasis was heard as the gentlest in the apodosis — he was able to halt his battle-axe in mid-air.

Now the Domestic Peace[8] was concluded, a bright and a wet pair of eyes being the instruments thereof, and a *Westphalian* Treaty accorded each party *one candle* and absolute *snuff freedom.*

But this peace was soon to be soured by the sensation that Penia, the household goddess of penury, who has an invisible church and a thousand silent disciples and can call most houses her lares, altars, and tabernacles, once again made her physical presence and infinite power manifest. There was no more money.

First Flowerpiece

Speech of the Dead Christ from the Universe that
There Is No God (1)

Prolegomenon

The object of this fiction is the excuse for its audacity.[9] People deny the Divinity's existence with as little feeling as most accept it. Even into

---

8. Would that Market of Köthen had invented his excellent lamp at that stage (much less expensive and more salubrious for the eye than that by Argand), which has to be snuffed but once during a St. Thomas's Eve, and which, fed with rape oil, has bestowed on me a tranquil and pure light over the years, as on the billiard tables of others.

9. If my heart should ever be so wretched and extinct that any feelings in it that affirm God's existence were destroyed: then I should rouse myself with this essay of mine — it would heal me and restore my feelings to me.

our true systems we never gather anything but words, counters, and medals, as the acquisitive stock their coin cabinets; — and it is only much later that we convert those words into feelings, those coins into pleasures. We may have believed in the immortality of the soul for twenty years — and only in the twenty-first, in a sublime minute, we marvel at the riches contained in this belief, at the warmth of this naphtha well.

Even so was I aghast at the poisonous vapor that threatens to suffocate the heart of him who enters the atheistical edifice for the first time. I will deny Immortality with less pain than it would cause me to deny the Deity: there I shall lose nothing more than a world shrouded in mists, whereas here I shall lose the present world, that is to say, the sun thereof; the whole spiritual universe is smashed by the hand of atheism and shattered in countless quicksilver dots of selfs, flashing, running, straying, converging, and scattering, without unity or consistence. No one is more alone in the universe than an atheist — he mourns with an orphaned heart, which has lost the greatest of fathers, beside Nature's dead body, which no universal spirit moves and contains, and which grows in the grave; and he will continue to mourn until he himself crumbles away from the corpse. The whole world reposes before him like the great stony Egyptian sphinx, half buried in sand; and the All is the cold iron mask of shapeless eternity.

Furthermore, it is my intention to spread fear with my essay among some professors, reading and read, as verily these people, now that they have become convict laborers in the hydraulic construction and timberwork of critical philosophy's mine shafts, weigh up God's existence with as cold a mind and a heart as if they debated the existence of the kraken or unicorn.

I would add for the benefit of those others who have not progressed as far as an aspiring professor that to the belief in atheism the belief in immortality may be allied without contradiction; for the very necessity, which in this life tossed my bright dewdrop of self into a flower calyx and under a sun, can surely repeat this in the second; yea — the second time it can embody me even more easily than the first.

When we hear tell in childhood that at midnight, when our own sleep reaches nigh to our souls and darkens our dreams, the dead arise from theirs and in the churches ape the divine services of the living: we shudder at death on account of the dead; and in the nocturnal solitude we avert our eyes from the tall windows of the silent church and fear to investigate whether their luminescence does originate with the moon.

Childhood and its terrors, rather than its delights, don wings and luster once more in our dreams and frolic like glowworms in the lesser night
of the soul. Pray do not crush these fluttering sparks! — Leave us our dark
painful dreams even as the brightening penumbra of reality! — And what
will take the place of *those* dreams, which raise us from the roar at the
foot of the waterfall to the quiet level of childhood, where the river of
life still in its little plain, silent and a mirror of heaven, drew close to its
chasms? —

Once on a summer evening I lay in the sun on a hillside and fell
asleep. And I dreamt that I woke in the churchyard. The whirring wheels
of the church clock striking eleven had wakened me. I looked for the sun
in the desolate night sky, for I believed an eclipse was hiding it behind
the moon. All the graves stood open and the iron doors of the charnel
house opened and shut by invisible hands. Along the walls shadows
glided, cast by no one, and other shadows walked about erect. In the open
coffins slept none but the children. In the sky only a grey sultry fog hung
suspended in heavy folds, drawn by a giant shadow like a net ever closer,
tighter, and hotter. I heard the distant plunge of avalanches above me,
and below me the first footfall of an immeasurable earthquake. The
church heaved from two incessant discords battling against each other
within and striving in vain to converge in mellifluous harmony. Now and
again a grey gleam flitted athwart its windows, melting iron and lead in
its wake. The net of fog and the swaying earth drove me into the temple,
at whose gate brooded two basilisks with a malevolent glint in two poisonous nests. I walked among unknown shadows, which bore the impress
of bygone centuries. — The shadows foregathered around the altar, and
instead of their hearts, their breasts beat and trembled. Only one dead
man, who had just been buried in the church, lay on his pillow without a
trembling breast, a happy dream lingering on his smiling face. But as one
of the living entered, he awoke and smiled no more. He opened his heavy
eyelid with a painful exertion to reveal but an empty socket, and there
was no heart in his beating breast, only a wound. He lifted his hands and
joined them together in prayer; but his arms grew longer and loosened,
and his folded hands fell away: Above in the church's vault stood the dial
plate of *Eternity*, showing no figures and being its own gnomon; only a
black finger pointed to it, and the dead sought to read *Time* on it.

Now a sublime noble figure, bearing an imperishable sorrow, sank
down from on high to the altar, and the dead all cried: "Christ! is there
no God?"

He replied: "There is none."

Each whole shadow of the dead, not only their breasts alone, shook, and one by one they were ripped apart by their quaking.

Christ went on: "I traversed the worlds, I ascended into the suns, and soared with the Milky Ways through the wastes of heaven; but there is no God. I descended to the last reaches of the shadows of Being, and I looked into the chasm and cried: 'Father, where art thou?' But I heard only the eternal storm ruled by none, and the shimmering rainbow of essence stood without sun to create it, trickling above the abyss. And when I raised my eyes to the boundless world for the divine *eye*, it stared at me from an empty bottomless *socket*; and Eternity lay on Chaos and gnawed it and ruminated itself. — Shriek on, ye discords, rend the shadows; for He is not!"

The pallid shadows dispersed just as a white vapor formed by the frost will melt in a warm breath; and all became void. Then came into the temple a heartrending sight, the dead children who had wakened in the churchyard, and now cast themselves before the sublime form on the altar saying: "Jesus! have we no father?" — And he replied with streaming tears: "We are all orphans, I and ye, we are without a father."

Then the discords screeched more harshly — the quaking temple walls sundered — and temple and children sank — and the entire earth and the sun sank after them — and the whole immeasurable fabric of the universe sank past us, and high on the summit of boundless Nature stood Christ and gazed down into the universe, pierced by a thousand suns, as into a mine dug out of eternal night, where the suns are pit lamps and the Milky Ways the veins of silver core.

And when Christ beheld the grinding convergence of worlds, the torch dance of heavenly will-o'-the-wisps, and the coal banks of beating hearts, and when he beheld how one orb after another emptied forth its ember souls on the sea of the dead, as a water globe scatters floating lights over the waves: he, the highest of finite beings, lifted his eyes sublimely toward Nothing and Void Immensity, saying: "Mute, inanimate Nothing! Chill, eternal Necessity! Insane Chance! Know ye that which lieth beneath ye? When will ye destroy the edifice and me? — Chance, knowest thou when thou stridest with hurricanes through the flurry of stars and exstinguishest one sun after another, and when the sparkling dew of the stars will be quenched as thou passest? — How alone each one is in the vast sepulcher of the Universe! Only I am next to myself — Oh Father! oh Father! where is thine infinite breast that I may rest upon it? — Alas, if each self be its own Creator and Father, why can it not be also its own destroying angel? . . .

"Is that beside me a human being still? Thou poor man! Thy little life is Nature's sigh, or but its echo. A concave mirror beams its rays among the dust clouds of the ashes of the dead to thine earth below, and then ye come into being, ye clouded tottering images. — Look thou down into the chasm across which the ash clouds drift — fogs full of worlds come swirling out of the sea of the dead, the future is a mist rising and the present a falling one. — Dost thou recognize thine earth?"

Here, Christ looked down, and his eyes filled with tears, and he said: "Alas, I was on it once: I was happy then, I still had my infinite Father, I gladly lifted my eyes from the hills to the boundless heaven, pressing my pierced breast against his soothing image, saying even in bitter death: 'Father, divest thy son of his bleeding winding-sheet and lift Him to thine heart!' ... Alas, ye delirious earth dwellers, ye credit Him yet. At this very instant yere sun may be setting and ye fall upon yere knees among blossoms, radiance, and tears, raising yere blessed hands high and calling with a thousand tears of joy toward the open heavens: 'Thou knowest me also, Infinite One, and all my wounds, and after my death Thou wilt receive me and heal them all.' ... Ye wretched ones, they shall not be healed after death. When man of misery lays his weary frame into the earth to slumber toward a lovelier morn full of Truth, Virtue, and Joy: he shall awaken in turbulent chaos, everlasting midnight — and no morning will come, no healing hand, no Infinite Father! — Oh thou mortal at my side, if thou be living still, pray to Him: else thou shalt lose Him forever."

And as I sank down and gazed into the shining fabric of the Universe: I perceived the raised coils of the giant serpent of Eternity, which has couched itself around the galaxy of worlds — and the coils fell away and it encompassed the All doubly — and then it wound itself around Nature a thousandfold, squeezing the worlds together — and crushingly compressed the infinite temple into a churchyard chapel — and all became close, dark, and fearful — and a bell clapper, infinitely extended, was about to strike the ultimate hour of Time and shatter the Universe ... when I wakened. My soul wept for joy that she could again worship God — and the joy, and the weeping, and the belief in Him were the prayer. And when I rose, the sun glowed deep behind the full purple ears of corn and peacefully cast the evening glow's reflection to the little moon, which rose in the east without an aurora; and between heaven and earth a happy transient world stretched its short wings and lived, as did I, in the sight of the Infinite Father; and from all Nature around me flowed peaceful sounds as if from faraway vesper bells.

The Vale of Campan; or, on the Immortality of the Soul, together with an Explanation of the Woodcuts under the 10 Commandments of the Catechism

IN A TYPICAL EIGHTEENTH-CENTURY FRAMEWORK, THE discourse of friends in an affective natural setting, *The Vale of Campan* is on the theme of immortality. This is taken up again more elaborately in the last major work, *Selina*, from which an excerpt is included later. The excerpts here are from the parodistic appendix, *An Explanation of the Woodcuts underneath the 10 Commandments in the Catechism*, modeled on Lichtenberg's *Detailed Explanations of the Hogarth Engravings*, which appeared in five parts from 1794–1799, and taking as subject the primitive illustrations from the Bayreuth catechism of Jean Paul's childhood. *The Vale of Campan* was well received, even in the *New Universal German Library*, but *Woodcuts* gave offense, not least because it was linked to such a solemn work, although in fact it was Jean Paul's regular practice to add irreverent tailpieces. With Lichtenbergean ingenuity and stretches of the imagination, the hidden designs and even dogmas behind the catechism pictures are discovered and, as one of the little figures turns out to be Jean Paul's great-grandfather, a family narrative unfolds as well. The first passage is a digression from the sixth chapter, illustrating a typical Jean Paul perspective. The longer passage is from the final, twelfth chapter. (The excerpts are taken from *W* 8.672ff., 705ff., 710.)

Chapter VI
Woodcut of the Sixth Commandment

Consequently, I shall embark on the performance of my third promise. I take it to be generally known that we all speak of the sacred, the *chaste* moon; an adjective well deserved by her pure white light, her chill, and her mythological relationship to Diana. Now, I have often looked up at the sky during daytime when the moon was new, at the spot where it has to be, albeit unseen, not far from the sun. And once, with the spring feet of imagination, I even ventured a leap into the moon myself. Needless to say, I found everything proven up there that I knew down here from astronomies, viz, that when the moon was new it was nighttime on the side where I landed, and that when I looked at the earth ablaze under the sun, I had to take this daylight at that distance from the pitch-dark moon for a magical moonlightlike earth light. It afforded me uncommon pleasure to amble about on the magical moon disk: for on my right the most breathtaking ranges of moon mountains faced me — the lowest of them consisting of nothing but Montblancs and St. Gotthards — and on my left, amidst a flower-decked plain, an immense dry bay, not unlike a drained lake Ladoga, and above me the most sublime and deepest blue. I thought that the sky there was even more magnificent and intense than an alpine sky; and I ascribe this to the extremely thin mountain air (ours is linseed oil in comparison), for which three little summer clouds would be too much to support. What shone forth most brightly in the cerulean arch of the sky, however, like a large silver clasp (ceinturon) on a blue sash, as it were, was our radiant earth, which reached — if it did not surpass — the circumference of a large bobbin wheel. I was only just feasting my eyes on the pure white, full earth when a Selenitus and a Selenita (they were to be joined in wedlock soon after my departure) came wading along through the dewy and fragrant flowers. He was a good bucolic writer and had published "Views into Eternity"[1] up there, and she was

---

1. According to the earliest philosophers and the latest North American savages, everything is present twice, the first copy being on earth and the second in the sky. Hence, the Lavater on earth postulates one in the moon, and their views differ in nothing but their vantage points.

his reader. The man in the moon and the maid in the moon bore, on account of the mountain air, a great resemblance to Switzers, most especially did they show the same cheerful and unaffected candor of countenance, which presupposes a calm life and the same number of pleasures as virtues, and which I never encountered without its unfolding before my delighted soul all the years and dreams of my youth and a whole arcadia. The maiden, enthused with loving and longing, looked toward the bright, full earth: because there is no life on any world that does not require a second, and on every orb does the tight membrane and seedpod of solid earth press on the eternal heart. The youth addressed her gently: "Whither thy longing, dearest?" — She replied: "I know not — is it not true thou believest that, having passed away, we shall go to the blessed of the beautiful earth?" — The bucolic poet said: "Truly, I have proved it, and not without all precision, in my 'Views into Eternity.' For here, on this vitrified moon full of craters, full of the graves of prehistory, as it were, here is not our lasting city — but up there, *on the pure chaste earth*, that is where we are at home. Look thou at that silvery sparkling belt[2] adorned with which it wends its way through the stars, a wreath of white roses, or a diminutive galaxy twined around it. Splendid, splendid! There, on the silent earth our souls' imperfections will cease — there the pure heart will be gently warmed but never sullied and never inflamed — there virtues and joys and truths will be three eternal sisters, and arm in arm they will meet man and, united, throw themselves on his breast. . ."

At this point, the Selenites heard a sigh behind their backs: it was me. It was no longer feasible to remain hidden; I therefore showed myself with stricken mien to the bucolic writer and said: "The present person is himself a Terrenus engaged in a journey here from German parts, being a heavenly citizen from Hof in Voigtland. But, my dearest Selenita, things look shakier with us up there than one might presume on the moon: thieves — dens of thieves — desecrators of Sabbath — and weekdays — personae turpes — Yahoos — long-armed, shortsighted, and crowned gibbons — several who do nothing — several who think nothing — brutes and even reviewers who do not always reflect on what they write . . . those are some of the blessed and beatific among whom earth has her pick. That white rosary circling our globe, the stellar belt mentioned by ye above, is woven from clouds and raindrops, and the numerous *earth spots*[3]

---

2. Ducarla proved that the sun draws across all countries, whose zeniths it passes, a belt of rain clouds 200 miles wide, which, like a Saturn ring, always encircles them, only in other zones. Lichtenberg's Magazine etc. 3d issue.

3. This is how the oceans of the earth appear to the moon.

we behold cannot, unlike the *moon spots*, bear the names of great scholars but the names of great scoundrels, for out of our earth spots we make freckle- and liver-spots of our inner beings, traversing those spots on water sleds designed to steal either people or goods or life, whence come the divisions of slave-, pirate-, and war-ships. Finally, most worthy bucolic poet, most worthy bucolic poetess, as to the pure chaste earth, people who live on it know best what it amounts to; although it is harder for many a scion of our nobility to break his marriage vows than his word; all the same, we do not lack *great* ones either, who abhor excess to excess, I am here referring to — elephants. Should ye indeed eventually enter our heavenly *Zion*, whose *lookouts* are even now in position: in that case. . ."

Then I myself reentered this Zion. For the postman delivered the Zweibrücken Times, which however was, this time, of unusually small interest and only (if I remember right) served up a dead nomenclature of the guillotined and of dismembered Polish provinces.

Chapter XII
Second and Last Block of Joys

The Chymical Relationship of the Dream, the Birthday, the Deathday, and the Finis

Nothing affects me more cruelly and leaves me more jaded than a discourse with people of unusual fame and shrewdness, and for half an hour's colloquium with Voltaire, with Frederick II, or with Lessing my stomach will drench me with acid and my head with congestions. I find it particularly repugnant if I have heard the eminent man before, who pays me a visit in bed (I am referring to my bureau d'esprit in dreams). I may say that during the past year I was forced to brew and imbibe more sorrel (that excellent prophylactic for migraines to come) and found it harder and harder to drag myself from my bed of a morn, and that only because Mr. H. made a habit of calling night after night, using my pillow as a reception room: for not only was

I forced to exert myself to the utmost during my sleep, when nature desires to rest, in order to shine in the discourse, but also to prompt each word uttered by Mr. H. Hard work, indeed, and especially so in bed. Luckily nothing of what he says, or of its origin, will ever come to his ear; but I would rather converse with him in his parlor a *million times* than *once* in my head, because there I need only say what I know, whereas here, its complement also.

Should the Comptroller make an appearance, one can hold one's own, though; last night, he approached my bed and under cover of other dreams made his way into my brain. The bedmaster seemed to me to be suspended inside a phial of ethyl alcohol like an egg yolk (he was about the size of a fetus) and about to address me in spirit. It is easy to see here how deeply my imagination, which all day long beholds the comptroller in those woodcuts in the nonagesimo-sexto format of a diminutive manikin, fitting a jeweller's scales rather than a weighing machine, invaded my dream and, like Pedrillo, lent it the size of his miniature likeness.

The bedmasterkin said he could no longer float silently in his spirits without having thanked me for scratching open, scraping out, and cleaning up the blocked-over name on his pillar of honor and righting his cockeyed posture — and (with reference to my works) weaving his name, after the custom of ancient Athens, into Minerva's veil. The fetus was well read, I could see, and I wished to appear the same: "My dear intendant des lits et meubles," said I. "Your works remained eternal like the Smaller Catechism; but the images of your conquered provinces marched forth into posterity as in a Roman triumphal procession, and the triumphant victor, again as in Rome, brought up the rear and only appeared in 1797 A.D. Only when the whole play is over does the audience of the world call: 'Author, author!'" — He went on to hold forth on his purpose in appearing to me in his ethyl alcohol, viz, to inform me that it may have been on a hidden urge that I had dragged out his tombstone, buried under debris and church pews, and installed it into the pantheon of undying glory, for he was a kinsman of mine, viz, my great-great-great-etc.-grandfather on my mother's side, and I could have the family tree extracted from the parochial registers in Wittenberg. — I wanted to interrupt the alcohol swimmer; but the aquarius continued: he was confident that his great-great-etc.-grandson should paraphrase and illuminate the 12th woodplate with particular zeal; for he had always been particularly fond of it and whittled away at it for a very long time: and that only because the block represented the celebration of his 34th birthday, which coincided with the first day of spring, in the boxwood pantomime. Yea, in the steeple ball of St. Michael's in Hof there had been laid down and was lying in state a clear and never-used impress of the same block instead of an ancient coin, from which a great-great-etc.-grandson might create a thousand matters, which the world deserved to receive — But at this point my great-great-etc.-grandfather phosphoresced and dissolved in his ethyl alcohol — as if he were alive — setting the rectified spirit alight with his sublimated one, and the whole phial went up in flames. . . .

I awoke, and only my economy night-light flickered more than usual in front of my eyes.

. . . .

Little Gerg, whose descendant I am — he being my great-grandfather — reveals that my great-great-grandfather is in the process of saying grace before meals at the table here, and he himself is the little boy standing beside the table (his parents are seated already), whose progeny, as we said, I am, according to the baptismal certificate of the dream. Even during my childhood, when I had to learn the legend or marginal note of this block by heart, my imagination would skip happily around the printed room, opening wide its window, whose casements turn outward like those in Jena. And this cosmopolitan imagination, which transmogrifies all humankind into my cousins, brothers, sisters, carousing- and feasting-sisters and -brothers, free-board brethren, and litis consorts, has accompanied me through laneways and villages up to this present birthday. I would rather die than make do and be satisfied with that slim and narrow segment of loved ones, a fragment of a degree, which fate and merit allot us from the immeasurable circle of the brotherhood of mankind. Or may a human heart be so tight as to leave only room for a matrimonial bed and a cot along with an old grandfather chair? And our inner arms should embrace no more beings than our outer ones? And there should be no chance of at least appreciably increasing the committee or panel of 20 or 30 beings, to which our portion of loving is bound by our ratio out of the wealth of 1,000 millions of souls? — I cannot agree: can we not (it would be something, at least) declare ourselves to be the distaff- and spearside and cousin of anybody we meet in the street and pursue him in imagination to his 4 walls, 4 chair legs, and between his 4 bedposts? Why not make common cause with the blue- or green-coats coming out of the bakery, with their regulation loaves under their arms, or the cloth maker on his way to the fisherman's hook to collect his carp as early as 3 o'clock on a profitable market morning, or the aristocratic dressing gown with the watering can in his garden looking forward to a refreshing lettuce, and, without having to wait for an invitation, cheerfully sympathize and share their repast in our minds? Can I even pass by an apprentice boy in his finery, hopeful today of his graduational and promotional box on the ear and due to run across me tomorrow as a fully fledged classical journeyman, without turning up (in my mind) at his high-living evening feast and pleasure fraternity? I look forward with the children galloping out of their school to their first rec-reational hour after so lengthy a session; — with the solemn father to the riotous evening full of apocryphical waters of baptism — with the maid-servant to the christening party leaving the church and a more detailed church visitation of each and every bib and tucker — with the schoolmas-ter writing a dreadful division exercise up on the blackboard, which is to result by way of its figures in a house, a ship, or a donkey. I look forward to the latter's development; — with the peddler and gingerbread woman whose slow cooker, portable kitchen, and petit souper is ever a pot, I enter in passing into a trade relationship and as her colleague and partner reap (in my mind) a certain benefit, although our firm should produce from any purchase from her no more than 1 Pfennig's worth of pure profit. And thus rivers of joy and streams from the Garden of Eden flow toward me in every alleyway — pleasure bowers and crocks of gold dance before me — and the city of Hof is my heavenly Jerusalem and mankind my confrère and intimate friend.

May such a blessed man, however, beware of allowing his eyes or fan-cies to follow a chance execution bailiff to the workrooms of poverty or a doctor into the torture chambers of sickness. . . .

But let us continue! Here, as we have said, the reader is about to be dished up the second block of pleasures, and on the block itself things have also been served. All shall be viewed and described under the guid-ance of my plumb line and beacon, viz, the typographical Little Gerg. The dining table is a so-called double-bed–table, as evidenced not only by the table curtain below but also the magnificent drapery and rigging of the bed firmament or palankeen, through which cousin Serenissimus had wished to present my Great-great-great-grandfather with a little keepsake and memento of his bedmastership — and perhaps of the casus in the 10th Commandment as well. Thus sayeth Gerg. Standing behind Gerg himself we see on the block his playmate, a humble squashed La-zarusienne, drawn into table neighborhood with his son by the benevo-lent artist for the joyous occasion. Her hunger is greater than her devo-tion, and the motions of her heart are less fiery than the peristaltic motions of her stomach. Gerg, who was to become my great-grandfather

in more mature years, lifts his prayerful hands up too high, neither from
piety nor affectation but simply because he wishes to be, in the manner
of children, a bishop in partibus, and so of a Sunday climbs on his *bed-
table* and exhorts from up there. That is why in the house of Krönlein
he was never called anything but *Little Bishop*.

Let the public now take a good look at my Great-great-grandmother,
the ex silver servant. Oh Regina, hadst thou ever remained queen of thy
inclinations and true and good, there would be no need for thee to look
on my Great-great-grandfather with such imploring eyes, with thine
head turned hisward rather than heavenward! What a blaze of birthday
wishes! "Dear Heaven! Preserve to me my good honest old bedmaster
for many, many years to come, yea, take myself rather than my Lorenz!"
That is her prayer before her soup bowl. — Better, a thousand times better than on the preceding blocks she is surely on this one. Firstly, there
is only — *one* child. Secondly, my little Great-grandfather and the table-
bed are decked so prettily, the curtain dusted so cleanly and tucked up so
daintily, and the whole room and setting in such good order that the same
can be taken for granted regarding her heart: women tidy the chambers
of their hearts and their houses in one. Thirdly, my Great-great-
grandfather looks exceedingly happy, and my Grandmother like a repen-
tant Magdalen: she had not even — easy though it would have been —
persuaded him to invite to the feast, apart from the pauvre honteuse and
almshouse inhabitant, a guest of her heart, not even an entertainer and
parasite who will be a faithful companion and lackey until he has had his
fill, as the cupping glass will drop away once it has drawn enough blood.
The way my Grandmother looks upon her spouse here, she soars ever
higher above those women for whom the *wedding bell* is the very counterpart of the Catholic *consecration bell*, the former announcing the transformation of their *God* into a *breadwinner*, while the latter heralds the
transsubstantiation of the *bread* into a lord and master. I can foresee that
the reviewers — and above all the revieweresses — will inveigh against me
in public and say I had awarded Regina quite a different score in the 12th
block were she not my Great-great-grandmother. But I retort: on the
contrary.

On the bed-table we encounter two settings for the pair of children
but only one for the married couple. How charming! Linné reports in
his Swedish travel account[4] from the Province of Schonen that in bygone
days they had hollowed out a plate the length of the table and feasted
from it — no great difference between the prolonged plate and a trough
being apparent. It is even more widely known and more graceful indeed

that during those grand erotic days of French chivalry, beloved and knight would ever dine from *one* plate. — And on the 2nd Block of Joys we have the latest case: my Great-great-grandmother lacked a plate. Of the meal offering itself, all we can make out is the soup bowl and a ladle, which would do as a soup bowl for me, and a bread roll in the shape of a pair of spectacles, or an 8.

But let us now take another look at the happy and open countenance of our curly-headed intendant des lits et meubles and remember, once the book is finished, the upright stature, which, like a Viennese banco bill, does not show on the outside any more than is written within. Here, his cap over his right hand, he offers in blithe good humor his grace after meals; he is ever hopeful of getting a better deal next time, but in case this should not come about, he will hope for the same again, anyway. He does not see life as a game of whist, where a new deal is called for should one card not be right, but as a game of piquet, where one calmly accepts the wrong card and plays it as best one can. Solitude and company both are all right with him; nay, he is not even lonely among the multitude, where we are wont to enjoy least company, just as on *sea* we might most easily *die of thirst*.

I wonder what my dear Great-great-grandfather might have done on a day like this? Likely, this 2nd Block of Joys.

4. Linnaeus's Attempt at a History of Nature, Art, and Economy, gathered during journeys through several Swed. Prov.

Palingeneses
Jean Paul's Letters and Biography to Be

THE FOLLOWING PASSAGES SHARE THE SUBJECT OF
philosophy in general and critical philosophy in particular and are taken
from two works of the same period, between 1797 and 1799, the *Palingeneses* and *Jean Paul's Letters and Biography to Be* (*W* 8.735ff., 929f.,
1014ff.). The *Palingeneses* are a revision of the early work *Selection from
the Devil's Papers;* the title was intended to cover the further "rebirth,"
which never materialized, of the still earlier *Greenland Lawsuits.* It begins,
Jean Paul fashion, with an "Open Letter to Leibgeber Instead of a Preface" and continues with the "Old Preface by Siebenkäs Himself," from
which the first excerpt, the apparition of Kant, is taken. The criticism of
critical philosophy, which aroused in Jean Paul a fascinated *horror vacui,*
is a recurring concern. In *Little Postschool to the Preschool of Aesthetics,* he
speaks of "that philosophical dissolution of all material through continuous abstraction into transparent form, although for the most profound
philosopher there adheres to form itself, as the delineation of distinctions, too much material, so that he must perforce dissolve being into
nothing" (*W* 9.498).

When Jean Paul wrote *Letter on Philosophy,* the beginning and end of

which are translated here, he did not yet have children; his only son was
born about five years later. It is, in a poignantly ironic way, an extraor-
dinarily prophetic letter. The most heartbreaking episode of Jean Paul's
life was the death, at the age of seventeen, of his son Max, "my ideal in
heart and mind." Jean Paul's daughter said to Voß: "O, the state my father
was in then! He wailed, I never saw him so before." Rightly or wrongly,
Jean Paul attributed the death to the depressive and debilitating effects
of an excessive religiosity. In later years, Jean Paul reacted impatiently
toward religious dogmatism, feeling more in sympathy, as he says, with
the old woman in Rousseau, whose prayer book consisted of the vowel
O. He derides the "mystical influenza" and the etymological fantasies of
theologians who were as incapable of exegesis as they were ignorant of
Church history. (Jean Paul believed Church history was the best cure for
excessive Christianity) (*H-KA* 3.8.113ff., 163, 266).

Here he has in mind in particular the later works of piety of his one-
time protégé, the theologian Johann Arnold Kanne, who had, said Jean
Paul in a phrase reminiscent of Nietzsche on Wagner, nailed his extraordinary talents to the Christian cross. Jean Paul had his own quarrel with
aspects of the Enlightenment, but he had much less sympathy with the
various forms of religious reaction against the Enlightenment that came
with the Romantic period. He was alarmed by the activities of Julie von
Krüdener, who had once so captivated him and who, now born again,
was crusading through Europe in the cause of Restoration and Christian
renewal, even trying to convert Madame de Staël.

He was dismayed by the later instalments of Jung-Stilling's great
autobiography, with its growing self-abasement and dogmatic emphasis
on a fallen nature. (One has only to contrast that most remarkable example of practical enlightenment, Jean Paul's treatise on education, *Levana*, with, for example, Jung-Stilling's pathetic interpretation of the daily
beatings of his childhood as a wonderful example of God's Providence.)
So the planned work on the excesses of piety, his "Counter-Kanne" or
"Overchristianity," became one of the main concerns of his last years.
There, he upholds his own brand of a natural and perennial religion behind and beyond any particular revelation. Put in Jean Paul shorthand:
"Christ presupposes Kant." It is not the Bible but the principles behind
the Bible that sustained him: "It is better to read Herder on the Bible
than to read the Bible" (*H-KA* 2.4.xiiff., 38ff., 62).

This work became most urgent when what he regarded as a spreading
disease struck nearer home. Max, now a student at Heidelberg, had come
under the influence of Kanne and a circle of zealots, and his letters home

became increasingly dejected and self-rejecting. In one letter after another, Jean Paul tried to wean Max away from the "gushings of melancholy" that made him "think so faintheartedly" of himself. "My good Max, in every letter you seem to me better and more mature and more aspiring. On that matter, believe me and not yourself." Jean Paul's letters to his son are affectionate and supportive and he was an indulgent father. But he balked at the request for permission to change over to the study of theology. He himself had long ago abandoned the old doctrines of the Fall and Justification "to the dark corner to which Lessing banished them," and his advice to Max, much as in the *Letter*, was that the true science of God is not to be found in orthodoxy, "but in astronomy, natural science, poetry, in Plato, Leibnitz, Antonin, Herder, indeed in all sciences at once." Jean Paul campaigned regularly against narrowness, and to his mind the trouble with Kanne, as with Fichte, was simply that they did not read enough. "Lessing and Leibnitz were different" (*H-KA* 3.8.96, 109f., 113ff.).

Not that Jean Paul was necessarily all that logical. It is remarkable that he leans so heavily on the philosophy of Jacobi, who is hardly a philosopher of wide-ranging interests, nor, by all accounts, of much humor either. "He [Jacobi] lacked the natural sciences," said Goethe to Kanzler Müller (26 January 1825), "and with the little bit of morality you cannot arrive at any large view of the world." Nor is Jean Paul all that consistent in insisting on a developing revelation and at the same time on the original Christian message whenever the later developments were not to his liking. But then, Jean Paul was much too emotionally engaged to be logical.

His son died in 1821, and in the months before, one gets a sense in Jean Paul of panic with respect to his work on overchristianity, which he now had such personal need to write. On Christmas Day 1820 he wrote his wishes for the New Year to Max, warning him once again not only against Kanne's "spoutings" (a pun on the name), as opposed to the writings of an enlightened theologian like Paulus, but also against the "narrow sectarianism" of the Apostles themselves.

He went on:

In all the utterances of Christ there is not a word about the crazy doctrine of the fall of all souls with Adam or, indeed, about justification. May God convert you to the cheerful Christianity of a Herder, Jacobi, Kant. Read Paulus's commentary on the three gospels; or ask himself. Kanne is a bad exegesist and historian. Read rather, as I did in Leipzig, (1) Arrian's Ep-

ictetus, (2) the reflections of the loving Antonin, and (3) Plutarch's biographies. There is no other revelation but the still continuing one; and
a Christian like Herder stands above Peter. Our whole orthodoxy, like
Catholicism, has been read into the gospels, and every century inserts its
own views. Listen to the old Voß on early Church history. O if only I
could get down soon to my work on overchristianity! (*H-KA* 3.8.86f.).

Palingeneses

Old Preface by Siebenkäs Himself

There can be few readers of my book — at least, not two. For to speak
Kantwise, no more than *one* is possible, and that one being myself. It was
only this morning that it dawned on me, with a shock of a degree I would
love to observe in others, sometime. For out of a dream of potentates I
had risen and was, while assembling the bits and pieces of my mounting
equipment, counting cities where I was to be read: when the devil escorted a critical philosopher into my chamber who — in envy perhaps at
the seeds of my laurel groves — infused me with the corrosive sublimate
of his system and debilitated me on the spot. He expounded that Space
and Time and Categories were nothing at all per se or to other creatures
but everything to the human race and that with the help of those modes
of thought we created for ourselves the whole material world (so that we
perceived it at once, either upon or beneath them). — Meanwhile, all
these outward appearances created by us within related quite unexpectedly to true and genuine things per se, to real Xs, quite unknown to him
(although it was not ascertainable *how* and *why*), and he himself, being
his own optical illusion, related to one such X domiciled within himself,
which was the very granite core and the self of his self. — But as he was
never, not after death either, going to get to see any of this whole incognito universe, not as much as Hogarth might have sketched on his fin-
gernail, he saw no reason why he should worry about a Something eternally hidden like the Nothing, an eternally invisible mirror foil of visible
forms, as much as about decent pretty appearances, which he at least
knew as such. — If this was so, he was left with no world but the one baked
in his three-dimensional (thinking) molds, viz, those figures and appearances knitted and stitched by him into the hidden transparent ample X
amongst whom he took the liberty of placing me. But I turned the tables

on him on the spot by relegating him among the phenomena solely domiciled in my mind and created by me as a favor through the prime-, pre-,
and sub-forms of my sensuousness and my reason. We had a stormy set-
to, each one insisting on being himself the idealist and turning the other
into his nestling and scion and not tolerating him outside his mind —
until I had the philosopher outside the door and thereby could think him
the way I wanted.

Meanwhile, along with his idealist system he had left behind an ugly
predatory bird preying on the whole universe and choking and plucking
everything — my critical basilisk eye dispatching all Kuhschnappel, the
patricians, Venner, my landlord, my dear Lenette, and very nearly myself
in front of a mirror — all the continents of the world, even the undiscov-
ered ones, and the reigning heads in the genealogical registers, with their
court bellows treadlers, and all *guardianship courts*, and the four *faculties*, and
the four great *monarchies*, and the *Wandering Jew* complete with wandering jewry had been dispersed by the philosopher's foul Samiel's wind —
and there remained standing hardly more beings than could be fitted
under one nightcap, which meant but one, to wit, myself under mine.
The whole reading public also fell victim to these noxious smelter fumes,
apart from one — even the critical philosopher was beyond help, as he
lacked existence in order to pore over me. — Verily, nevermore shall the
philosopher thrive who, within a matter of hours, reduced me in the
deadly arsenic smelter of his system to being the short quintessence and
distillation or residue of all volatilized readers and the representative of
the vaporized corpus. Whence I sit here, writing immoderately and read
by no one: for I myself have little time for it, hardly enough for writing.

Jean Paul's Letters and Biography to Be

Preface

Today is Shrove Tuesday — and fancy dress ball — and mask and
lenten veil[1] will be displayed together, and I would be entitled to come
to a stop; however, tomorrow will be Ash Wednesday, and I wrote something to a renowned scholar of our day that quite fits into this little opus
and that may be inserted here (particularly in view of the fact that this is

---

1. A cloth painted with biblical scenes and exhibited by the Papists from Shrove Tuesday to Good Friday.

going to be my *last* book of the century), although I do not remember it all too clearly, not having made a copy of it at the time. The renowned man is herewith requested to state in the popular gazettes whether I did address him as follows:

Sir (I believe I said), all hell has broken loose in this century and the Holy Ghost as well. Alas, hard times are upon us; *dolinas* and *avalanches* coincide! There will be a few decades — for man's eternal heart will not be able to cope with more — during which Chemistry, Physics, Geogony, Philosophy, and Politics will make common cause and declare the Isis veil of the still and sublime godhead to be itself a form and negate the Isis behind it. The heart, obedient to Nemesis and taught by devouter and humbler times, will quail at a brazen, infamous titan era, when commerce and acuity will reign supreme and intellectual cudgel law will sit in judgment. The present is populated by riotous *shadows* who will, like Homer's, only gain strength and voice once they have tasted *blood*. Mankind has awakened indeed, — I know not whether in its bed or its grave — ; but like an awakened dead body it is recumbent yet, *on its face* and staring into the clay.

The moral revolution (a political revolution is the daughter rather than the mother of the moral one), this forwardness of the spirit of the time extends down to the critics who warn the writer away from the moral code and prefer him, should he deal with matter at all, to go for the lesser evil and delve into the wicked rather than the moral material. Alas, ye destructed destroyers, ye will redouble the sinners but not the poets; do the latter chafe so badly with us under moral theology? And he whom moral teleology would make prosaic, the most immoral would render no less so, as evidenced by the French. Is Hippocrene not a sacred and holy water for Homer and Sophocles, those two great Greek authors, their Parnassus a Nemesis altar and wholly founded on a moral Mount Sinai? —

Meanwhile, our time, too, will come to its solstice. The human heart may scatter like dust, but its object never. Just as the precipitate of a whole plant- and animal-kingdom was needed, the biologists tell us, to furnish mankind with its topsoil and sediment: thus the ashes of harder eons will be the fertilizing agent for better ones. Let each above all revolutionize his own self instead of his time and all will be well, for Time is made up of selfs. Let him toil and dig on, his miners' lamp fixed to his brow, in his own dark space and mine shaft undisturbed by the rushing and roar of the waterworks; and should he be seized by the *flames* of the *afterdamps*, which the *pit lamps* ignite: at least the air will be purified for the pitmen to come. — But we are all alike: we gladly grant to the developments of the universe the infinity of *Space*, but the infinity of *Time* we deny them as if both did not go together. The thousand-year empire of the All shall (so we demand) present itself, freshly disembarked on our doorstep tomorrow, on our birthday, wishing us luck so that we, too, might profit from it. —

But, as we mentioned above, it is not certain if I did express myself in exactly these terms to the renowned scholar; for I jot it down here from memory only.

Weimar, Shrove Tuesday, 1799.
Jean Paul Fr. Richter.

Letter on Philosophy

To My Firstborn Son, Hans Paul, To be Read on Attending University.

Dear Hans Paul, I must write to you in the 18th century as I do not know whether I shall live to see the 19th or your academic coming of age, or even your birth. I surely cannot allow you to wander into the philosophical ghetto unwarned and unarmed, no matter whether they'll press you into the Portico, or the Lyceum, or the Academy, or Epicure's Gardens? — For, I am sorry to say, his *first* system, which offers at least some answers to so many dark questions in a young man's breast, will always be a despotic one; he ought to carry a second one in order to keep the first one at bay. But even if the philosopher, like the young merchant, sets out with the *forwarding department*: they will both of them settle on their own wares in the end.

Before you board the air balloon of philosophy, let me provide you with the following parachutes, or Le Roux caps.

Here take the first parachute, Hans, and grasp it well! Do not mistake a system's logical coherence and the ease with which it answers a lot of phenomena for a mark of its truth, as false ones frequently exhibit the same. Read — and I do not even ask you to read the various hypotheses of the geologists, each of which agrees with a thousand facti — or the logical system of the Catholics or the Orthodox — or those proofs that Homer is only an allegory — or the old ones that the history of the gods merely conceals a biblical one — or the more recent ones that they are an astronomy in disguise — do not bother, I say, to read that, but read those droll essays you inherited from your Father and wherein the man, to his own surprise, pens like a herdsman the pillars of all the sciences for the crazy lies that they are;[2] and then I dare you to try and conclude from the mere harmony and analogy of a system its predestined harmony with the truth! The threefold universe — the physical, the historical, and the spiritual — is so full of lines and outlines that everyone is convinced he is reading *his* ciphers, so full of entwined contours that everyone can, like the wayfarer the stalagmites in Baumann's Cave or the Grecian his mountains, fashion them into creatures of his imagination. If even the Bible and Homer are two such clouds, baked into different shapes by every artist's eye, to how many more optical personifications must the immense cloudscape of the universe provide substance and space considering the distance and multiplicity of its curves? — There is no skepticism in this; for each form that we discover to be erroneous was once a reality, just as being awake preceded its anagram, the dream. Only, you will be asking, what shall I cleave to then?

[What follows is mostly a warning against what Jean Paul, in his championship of the material and the concrete, here calls "the negative philosophy," by which he means the current idealism. The negative philosophers have taken over pure reason, albeit without his learning, from their Holy Father in Königsberg, hoping, by excluding everything else, to keep their critical ark afloat, as Franklin advises buoying up a sinking ship with the help of empty, well-stoppered bottles. They abhor the positive and concrete, having an aesthetic *horror pleni*. Like the lemmings of Norway, they regard objects as hindrances on their direct route, and they prefer to think up a roomy word, open in front and behind, into which they can cram everything. The end of *Letter on Philosophy* follows.]

Enough for now! After all those helmets of Mambrin, you will need Minerva's helmets, and instead of parachute bonnets, Mercury's windlass and wings. — Here they are! Every science, every estate, every age, and every century make one-sided and distort the altarpiece of the universe into a picture puzzle; therefore learn, attempt, experience as best you

---

2. My published proof, e.g., "that the beggars are German bards" or other unpublished ones, "that a thief is a Catholic saint," often lack nothing to validate them as serious proofs than that I should believe them to be such. One might have made up hieroastronomy, for instance, for fun, and it would have been witty; but now it is not, because it is earnest and its author believes in it.

can, all, or at least all sorts! — Protect your higher poetic freedom against
the tyranny of each and every system by studying all systems and all dissimilar sciences. Learn philosophical moderation from the ancients and
from the British colossus, Bacon, who, like the one in Rhodes, lets his
light shine on the ships long after they have passed beneath him. Learn
Socratic freedom and form from Plato, Wieland, Lessing, and Bayle.
Learn matter from Hemsterhuis, Jakobi, Leibniz, and Bacon. And above
all, never go among the philosophers without keeping a royal bodyguard
of physical scientists, historians, and poets about you.

Most especially, the last. All sciences and situations undergo on their
highest Mount Tabor poetical transfiguration, as, according to Makro-
bius, all gods are always Apollo in disguise. The poets reunite the head
with the heart; and without them, that philosophy of yours, which is better at arguing away the joys than the pains, will only become a brilliant
noon, where no *rainbow* is possible and yet the most violent thunderstorms. —

Above all else, act! Oh, there are more sublime truths contained in
deeds than in books! Deeds nourish the whole being from within,
whereas books and opinions are only a warm, nourishing poultice lying
soothingly on the stomach. Instead of the present loveless and enervated
philosophers, friable light magnets, calcined, as it were, by the sun and
loving nothing better than an — audience and having, like children with
scarlet fever, only *hot brows* but *cold hands* (to act with), the tree of knowledge inoculated from the tree of life will under your care flourish and
bear exquisite fruit. And then a god will show you the faith whose roots
lie within you, which will never be felled by the storms of life and under
whose branches you will find shade and fragrance and fruit. — I shall end
my epistle, Paul; indeed, it may have been hardly necessary to begin. For
one day you will read a genius whom in your youth you will neglect for
sheer delight to understand but who will later, with limbs that, like those
of the prophet, are all wings, transport you above the paper orbs of verbal
wisdom. — Oh Paul, once you have scaled the sublime world of this genius, who has never a thought or perception in isolation but who turns
each ring on the waters into a planisphere — who does not lay hands with
his fruit picker on selected branches of the tree of knowledge but who,
like an earthquake, shakes the tree through the ground from which it
grows, — when you scale his world, I say: then you will be on the high-
lands, surrounded more *closely*[3] and more *united* by the peoples below

3. On mountains, distant things are brought closer by the greater purity of the air.

you, and this painter of peoples and eras will grant your heart a greater tolerance than is known by this century — on his alp your soul will be taller, and the refined air of the mountains will draw heaven and earth closer to you, soothing the brilliance of scorching constellations and the uproar of life — fantasy will conjure its Fata Morgana and hang up its rainbow as a full circle — melodies will waft about you when he erects an altar, for on all his building stones Apollo's lyre has rested[4] — And then my dear son, made so happy by him, cherish the thought that your father before you found in him so much happiness and, like myself, never bestow a different name on the man you love and honor most deeply but — Herder! —

J. P.

4. The stone on which Apollo, as he was building, laid down his lyre took from it the gift of sounding. Paus. Att. 42.

Titan

Comic Appendix to Titan

Airshipman Giannozzo's Logbook

Clavis Fichtiana seu Liebgeberiana

THE FOLLOWING FOUR SELECTIONS ARE FROM *TITAN*, AL-
though only the first is from the novel, itself. The others are from the
Comic Appendix to Titan, from *Airshipman Giannozzo's Logbook*, which
forms a part of the *Comic Appendix*, and from *Clavis Fichtiana seu Leibgeberiana*, the appendix to the appendix. (*W* 6.689ff., 844ff., 868ff., 894ff.,
931ff., 949ff., 1004ff.). What unites them is not the novel but their subject matter and their protagonists: Schoppe, Giannozzo, and Leibgeber,
three of those satirical characters who accompany the action throughout
Jean Paul's narrative. These alter egos overlap, even reappear as one another.

In *Titan*, the crazed Schoppe dies when he is confronted by his doppelgänger, who claims to be Siebenkäs. This would make Schoppe Leibgeber, although it is also true that Siebenkäs and Leibgeber are in fact
each other, and there is really no end to the interplay of identities. All
these wild figures are sympathetically presented. In the scene of
Schoppe's death, the narrator bids him farewell as a God seeker driven
frantic in his subjectivity because he was so desperately in search of an
object. *Clavis* is the crazy Leibgeber's commentary on Fichte. Schoppe,

too, fears that from reading Fichte and his Vicar-General, Schelling, he, like the drunkard who urinated in the darkness into the running fountain and stayed there all night because he thought he had not stopped, will "derive" everything from himself, ending with no other object and, like the dying Swift — in Jean Paul's free version of Lord Orrery's account — merely repeating "I am I" (*W* 6.767, 801).

Giannozzo's misogynist outbursts are more diffuse, an element in the mephistophelean half of Jean Paul's world. It is interesting that Jean Paul, recommending to a friend that notorious nihilistic document of Germany's romantic agony, *Nightwatches of Bonaventura*, describes it as an "admirable imitation of my Giannozzo" — going on to add that he finds himself plagiarized by almost everybody, including the ancients (*H-KA* 3.5.20). (The authorship of *Bonaventura* is a perennial riddle in the history of German literature. Jean Paul thought it was by Schelling — evidence, if one needed it, of his high regard for the philosophers he caricatured.) How one interprets *Giannozzo* depends on one's overall reading of Jean Paul: for example, whether one follows Harich in finding a political program in Jean Paul and especially in *Titan*, or whether, like Widhammer, one reads *Giannozzo*, like Schoppe and the rest, in the sense of despair over a world that cannot change.[1] In any event, Giannozzo, himself, is more than ever Jean Paul's alter ego, a fact that is only underlined by letters in which he is at pains to say that he should not be equated with Giannozzo. Probably no other reader of Jean Paul was ever as familiar with the work as Berend, so his comment is noteworthy: that in Giannozzo one hears the voice of Jean Paul himself (*H-KA* 1.8.xcii; 3.4.85, 88).

Schoppe, Giannozzo, and Leibgeber all philosophize about the world in general, but Jean Paul's special topic is German idealism and the subjectivism he rejects. While all of this is work of fiction, it is worth noting that Jean Paul's standing was a good one with the philosophers themselves. Critical philosophy comes off badly in *The Vale of Campan*, but the work was nonetheless highly praised by Kant himself. And of course, there are many tributes to Kant in Jean Paul, either sober comments or comments in his more characteristic fashion, as when he says that all Kant lacked for a Socrates was hemlock or for a Christ a cross.[2] Hegel was instrumental in getting Heidelberg University to confer a doctorate

1. Helmut Widhammer: "Satire und Idylle in Jean Paul's *Titan*," *Jahrbuch der Jean-Paul-Gesellschaft* (1968), 3:69–105.

2. *H-KA* 3.2.127. Cf. Wolfgang Harich, *Jean Pauls Kritik des philosophischen Idealismus* (Suhrkamp, n.d.), pp. 8ff.

on Jean Paul — against strong opposition, for it was said that he would be a bad example to students: his Christianity was doubtful and he drank too much. Hegel even considered collaborating with Jean Paul on an introduction to philosophy for ladies — an intriguing might-have-been of philosophical literature. As for the much-maligned Fichte, Jean Paul read him with as much admiration as unbelief, and in private, that is to say in the public affairs of the period, such as in the atheism controversy that cost Fichte his chair, Jean Paul strongly supported Fichte. In the end, their relationship was one of sparring friends. He got on excellently with Fichte, Jean Paul reported back to Jacobi, even though their dialogue was a "yes-no" one. Admittedly, Jean Paul at this stage believed Fichte was shifting ground from the position of the first edition of *Science of Knowledge* and was moving toward the admission of "something outside the *I*," toward an objectivity that Jean Paul welcomed and that he attributed not least to Jacobi's own arguments, which had to be compelling even for Fichte (*H-KA* 3.3.249, 259; 3.4.63).

Fichte is the main target, but Jean Paul's quarrel is with the whole tendency of German idealism. Fichteanism won't last, he wrote to Jacobi, but what was the use of the devil's death if his grandmother, Kantian critical philosophy, lived on. As for Jean Paul himself, the older he grew the more he believed in "objectivity." When he, as so often, berated philosophy or the philosophers, it was idealist philosophy he had in mind. For example, he said that unlike the poor sinner who pretended her pregnancy was dropsy philosophy pretended the latter was the former (*H-KA* 3.3.315f., 329). Kant, he complained, although unmarried, produced a whole progeny of little Kants. As he understood idealism, every idealist must in the end, as he said in a letter to Herder, become an egoist (*W* 2.800; *H-KA* 3.3.120).

He saw an inexorable development toward the self-centered derivation from self of aseitas (a se), one of the recurring terms for his bête noir. In the *Protektorium* to *Titan*, he says that after the consuming Kant, who at least left things in themselves lying around the place, comes the annihilating Leibgeber, who leaves only the nihilum album of the chemists, and that if one were to follow the lines of Fichte, one would have a black nothing and finally the fohism of nothing at all (*W* 6.102ff.). The Buddhist term *fohism* is another of his recurring terms, not with any serious reference to Buddhism, but denoting the emptiness of content that he sees as the consequence of a philosophy that, he believed, made a basic error in thinking that the "inner eye" is any different from the outer eye, which "always only sees and does not invent" (*H-KA* 3.2.302).

In opposition to the current trend, he maintained the objectivity he found in the philosophy of Jacobi. This was a matter of deep concern to Jean Paul; and for all that *Clavis* is a fanciful work of fiction, it is also at times bluntly partisan. The "right philosophy," he says, is that of Jacobi, who knew that reason is a filter that refines but does not create, or as Herder says, that finds and does not invent. And he added warningly: "But when people like Leibgeber and the transcendentalists of Jena begin to swear by the *Science of Knowledge*, it is time to take note what o'clock it is" (*W* 6.1026ff.).

Naturally, the topic is most often discussed in the letters to Jacobi, the "protector of his faith" against the fohism of the transcendentalists. In one of those letters, he reports a conversation with Goethe, in which he himself said of Fichte that he was "the greatest scholastic," but that that whole sect held the light, or the eye, to be the object (*H-KA* 3.3.106, 129f.). He goes on to complain that Fichte's explanation of knowledge is more in need of explanation than what was to be explained in the first place. Often, Jean Paul's comments on Fichte, as an obscure attempt to explain the obvious, are rather like Dr. Johnson's reaction to Berkeley, kicking the stone and saying: I disprove him thus.

To all of this Kantian critique of reason, Jacobi's philosophy of faith and feeling was, for Jean Paul, the antidote. Jacobi said of himself that he was an atheist with his head and a Christian with his heart, and the phrase can clearly be applied to Jean Paul, too, provided no hasty conclusions are drawn in his case any more than in Jacobi's. It is not a faith that runs counter to reason, any more than in Kant, who says in the foreword to the second edition of *Critique of Pure Reason* that if he removed the metaphysical questions from the realm of reason it was in order "to make room for faith."

If Jean Paul took from Jacobi a philosophy of feeling, it is one that stresses the rationality of emotion, the sense of sensibility. It can be said to be a kind of "wishful thinking," but only on the understanding that the reality of the object of the wish is as reasonable, if as unprovable, as any other object. Jean Paul, like Jacobi, is being, in intention at any rate, altogether "realistic." In a letter to Jean Paul, Jacobi says: "I am a realist as no man has ever been before me." In the context of Jacobi's influence on Jean Paul, it is perhaps most appropriate to illustrate this realism, this acceptance — as it were, on faith — of the objective reality of what is known to the subject, not from Jacobi's philosophy but from one of his novels. In *Allwill*, Clärchen insists on taking nature "at face value." In a letter, she tells of an edition of George Berkeley's *Dialogues* illustrated with an engraving of a child reaching out for its own reflection, while a philosopher looks on in amusement. Clärchen reacts against the implications of the illustration and refuses to be "blinded by reason." Why cannot she be allowed to take the honest face of nature on faith? "I cannot endure eyes that see nothing, ears that hear nothing, a reason busy about nothing for all eternity."[3]

Fichte's own comment on *Clavis* was succinct: the key does not appear to fit, for its maker did not get in. From the outset, Jean Paul was accused of misunderstanding Fichte. Thieriot points out that Fichte's philosophy was not solipsist — but then, Jean Paul never said that it was, although he appeared to suggest that solipsism was evaded only by self-contradictions in Fichte.[4] But asking if Jean Paul misunderstood Fichte is probably asking the wrong question and putting one in the wrong frame of mind for reading Jean Paul. Passages like those below are not an academic exercise. They are both more serious and more comic, for the topic is both a matter of great personal concern and a vehicle for parody. It is bound up with Jean Paul's most cherished beliefs and his lifelong struggle with unbelief. The atheist is defined in *The Vale of Campan*, as the one who "denies the copy its original." In that same work, Jean Paul says that, just as there are idealists of the outer world who believe that perception creates the object, so too there are idealists of the inner world who explain being by appearance, sound by echo, rather than the other way around (*W* 8.611f.).

Jean Paul clung to his "second world" belief with a kind of *senseo ergo est*. In religion he was never orthodox and became progressively less so — witness the fact that of all his contemporaries he exalted Herder most and most consistently. But throughout, he tries to retain, sometimes one feels: to salvage belief in a personal God, not just, as he says in a letter to Jacobi, "a whole deaf-and-blind Spinoza-All." What gives life to the philosophical discussions in these letters is the sense of personal engagement and urgency. Around 1813 the letters of Jacobi suggest a phase of doubt and depression. He recalls the Job story and looks to Jean Paul as a comforter. Jean Paul provides comfort after his own fashion; for example, with the optimistic statistic that every second one person in the world dies, but one and one-tenth are born (*H-KA* 3.6.322f.; 3.7.56).

But idealism generally, and Fichte's *I* philosophy in particular, are first

---

3. F. H. Jacobi, *Allwill textkritisch herausgegeben, eingeleitet und kommentiert von J. V. Terpstra* (Groningen, 1957), pp. 27, 67. cf. Harich, *Jean Pauls Kritik*, pp. 4, 36.
    4. *H-KA* 1.8.cii; Harich, *Jean Pauls Kritik*, p. 274.

and foremost a vehicle for comic narration in Jean Paul. It is both ironic and logical that Fichte should be so pilloried and parodied by a writer who is himself a virtuoso of the *I* and all its apparitions. Self-reflection turns up in Jean Paul in all sorts of bewildering variations. One tries to imagine, for example, the sign of the inn in Flegeljahre, for the inn where the twins meet is called At the Sign of the Inn. Jean Paul campaigns against the egoism of Fichte, but he is just as prone to accuse the idealist philosopher of macerating the *I* into an unknown *x*, as he says in *The Parson in Jubilee*. Jean Paul often suggests that the Germans, especially, have little self-esteem, and he goes on there to compliment the French, who when they say *on*, which appears to mean the present population of 110,375 million, in reality and sensibly mean themselves (*W* 4.653; 7.480f.). The *I* is the central character in all of Jean Paul's playacting, and in the particular case of *Clavis* it must be remembered that it, too, is presented as role play, and that the outburst against Fichte is delivered by a character who is crazy, if admittedly driven crazy by reading Fichte.

Titan

31st Yovel Period. 121st Cycle

[Wehmeier relates Schoppe's sermon to Albano]

   "Were it permitted" (began Wehmeier) "I would now impart to His Lordship a fact with regard to the Herr Librarian, which is — at least in my humble opinion — as striking as many another. The schoolhouse, as you may recall, is hard by the church." This was followed by a long story: Once at the dead of night the organ sounded — he had stood at the church door and clearly heard Schoppe singing and playing a short verse from a capital hymn. — Thereupon, the man had noisily descended from the organ loft, ascended to the pulpit, and commenced an occasional sermon addressed to himself with the words: "My devout auditor and beloved in Christ" — In the exordium, he had touched on the peaceful, but regrettably short, happiness *before* life, although he did not observe homiletic principles, in that the second part was almost a reprise of the introduction; — thereupon, he sang a verse to himself and read from the Book of Job, chapter 3, where Job presents the joys of nonbeing in the 26th verse, which reads: "Was I not blessed? Was I not fine and quiet? Was I not at my ease? But restlessness came." As his topic, he had announced to himself: the troubles and the joys of a Christian; the troubles in the first part, the joys in the second — Hereupon, in eccentric manner and speech, yet using scriptural texts, he had compressed the world's troubles, among which he counted unexpectedly odd matters, long sermons, the two poles, ugly faces, compliments, gamblers, and the stupidity of the world — He proceeded to the comfort in the second part, describing the joys to come of a Christian, which would consist, as he blasphemously put it, in an ascension into the future nonbeing, in death after death, in an eternal deliverance from the *I* — There he addressed, dreadful to hear, the adjoining dead in the church and the royal crypt, asking if they had anything to complain about. "Arise ye" (said he) "take your seats in the pews and open your eyes, should they be wet. But they are dryer than dust. O how quiet and beautiful lieth the infinite world of the forebears shrouded in its own shadow and softly bedded on the ashes of self, not a dream limb left to be injured. Swift, old Swift, who wast in thy latter days so much out of thy reason and didst on each of thy birthdays read the whole chapter from which we have taken the sacred text of today's harvest sermon, how contented art thou now and how wholly restored to health, thy breast's hatred burnt out, the pearl of ransom, thine *I*, corroded and melted at last in the hot tear of life, which alone burns brightly on! — In like manner to me didst thou preach to the sexton." — Here Schoppe had wept and asked, God knows whom, to forgive his emotion — He went on to the practical application, severely urging reform on the listener and preacher, urging pure honest truthfulness, allegiance to friends, proud courage, bitter hatred of mawkishness, abject fawning, and weak licentiousness. — Finally ending the service with the petition to God to let him, should he ever lose his health or his reason or the like, die like a man, and with that he darted out of the church door. "He nearly" (added Wehmeier) "frightened me out of my wits as he hotly abused me: 'What art thou doing here, thou sham body, creeping about the grave?' and I cleared off smartly, as white as a sheet and without making any reply. But what does his Lordship say?" —

Albano shook his head vehemently, without an enlightening word, pain and tears on his face.

Comic Appendix to Titan

3RD JANUARY. ENOCH'S LEAF

Morning Reflection on Little-known Heavenlets of Joy

On an Enoch's Day and an Enoch's leaf a thinking man may observe and measure the heavens as Enoch ascended to the heaven above us — where he must still be ascending, since even if he glided away on a light beam's ferry, he cannot yet have passed the fixed stars of the 19th magnitude, for their beams have not yet descended to us — ; but gaze, o mortal, not only at great vast heavens of joy, throne-, bed-, and carriage-canopies, nay, also at the little parasol above thee, which is of red silk. Then thou wilt sit more easily in small wood-saving hells, in your little portable sulphur slough and pocket Tartarus, and endure.

From time to time, I, too, endure from the years' degrees some evil gradational minutes; thus I have suffered, ever since I know Latin, the anguish of having to stop and think whether to write IV or VI, lest I make a mistake — of calling magahony wood, mahogany — and before my English was perfect, a *ch* instead of an *h* used to slip out after an *s*. — Other black ribbons of mourning are pinned on other men's lives; in Baireuth they receive the Baireuther Zeitung all wet and grey from the presses — or they encounter their slippers facing their beds on arising, and to their annoyance they must turn either themselves or the slippers around before even slipping them on — and with the finest of pamphlets that arrive from the binder's, they first must conquer the evil smell of animal *glue*, which assails them.

And so there is outside the lowliest opera house and chateau de plaisance a ticket collector, who should be called sorrow, worry, and trouble. If gold on the whole impedes progress in studies, how much more does the gilt edging hamper the great in prising apart page by page their copies of dedication, to no great profit in the end. Or for myself, I must have my key in my hand down in the street and carry it all the way up the stairs; yet should I try curing myself of the habit, I would return the key into my pocket ten times and but once into the keyhole.

Whoever must wet his heels in such shallow subsidiary branches of the rivers of Hell — which he may well be doing if he is merely reading a too long description of such — : let him remember that the rivers of Paradise likewise bring forth little warm springs a few steps away from their banks; amongst them is this, that one can, against all expectation, including one's own, break off a morning reflection and wait for the next Loth's Leaf to spin its happy end.

F-k

4TH JANUARY. LOTH'S LEAF.

Heavenlets of Joy, Continued

Loth's heavens of joy, from his wife's *salt* to the *grape*, are not ours, but neither are they unknown.

Small sufferings serve as pebbles, which, like the bird, we swallow to help digesting the feed; small joys are the feed itself. Life loves, like the Austrians, diminutives;[1] or, like the Letts (according to Merkel), diminutives of the diminutives' diminutives; therefore, reverent reader (meaning myself), do thou observe closely whether thou art happy, else thou wilt not be aware of it. Recollect the *traiteur* whom thou sawest at the university, who, already at 9 o'clock in the morning, put out a clean tablecloth — set out covers, two water bottles, and beer glasses in orderly fashion, along with some wine glasses, which were quite unnecessary, as 'twas only young theologians who nibbled his Lenten fare — who then devised with the greatest attention the menus for gentlemen dining at home, thus spending his profitable day in gentle exertion and relaxation — regard this man, I say, who was not in the slightest aware of feeling and lasting better than the Elector, so that thou might be aware of it in thyself. If a pleasure remains year in and year out, it is hardly perceived any longer; friends and delights touch our hearts only when they arrive or bid us farewell. And the cerulean blue in us as well as above us will, having tarried for some weeks, turn quite grey. Yea, thou mayest well have arrived in this world filled with sweet (or bitter) emotions of which thou art never aware, only because they have never diminished. Were it not snatched from our lips each night for seven long hours, we would taste little of the exquisite delight of existing, because awaking is part of it.

Our path through life is provided with so many trees and seats it surprises me if someone gets tired. Let someone add up, if he can — which he should not presume — the exceptional number of goals he reaches on a mere average summer's day, of which each one produces and nurtures

---

1. Quite naturally, as we ourselves are so small. For (according to Modeer) not more than 2 1/2 million ciliates fit into one drop of water; whereas there are ca. a thousand million of us already on our water- or earth-globule; and there is room for more.

Editor's note.

its own little floret of joy. — The typesetter of this morning reflection, for instance, reaches with each type that he sets for it a goal and therefore a little (I grant you it isn't a big one) garden of Paradise; now, if he delivers only *one* folio in *one* day to the printer (which we expect of a deft one) through letters alone — I am not even counting page, punctuation, and catchword — he is daily awarded an import of 8,000 joys, the indescribable bliss not to speak of with which he is now setting this record and harvest register of joys here — a veritable flowerpot orangerie of sweetly blossoming minutes we can barely take in at a glance.

The orangerie extends even farther for readers and authors, but that would need adding machines and calculating chambers. Yet it is precisely the joys that are, unlike votes, not counted but weighed; we only affix a pedometer over a miry and rutted path through life, not on a smooth green one. — How would it be otherwise thinkable that so many men and divines have neglected the joy to be drawn from our name being that of another and so getting into print — or from the printed name of our town — from the mere sight meal of the tablecloth — from the sight of the tools of our trade — from the green of the church tower's verdigris, and the green shutters in midwinter — from the printed word Frenchmen, if we are a democrat, or Allies, if an aristocrat — from counterreviews — from the mere J. J. (Jean Jacques) if a student — from the cut cards with gold pieces *in* them, not *on* them — from the two melancholically beautiful bridge processions marching against each other if we are in Dresden — from those arches of triumph, the bridges without balustrades, if we are in Venice — from the golden letters over the vaults, if we are in Leipzig — and from the happy lot of the common people if we live in a capital town like —

F-K?

13TH JANUARY. HILARY'S LEAF.

Hafteldorn's Idyll on the Gentle Life (Imparted by Matthieu von Schleunes, Esq.)

Musical children and lyrical farmers exist, but they are rare; they are exotic fantaisie-flowers of Nature. One such flower is the peasant prodigy *Hafteldorn* in St. Lüne. On a meager diet of reading — which is confined to the lyrical prosaists Moser, Gessner, and Ebert — and an even more meager diet of viands, he would on many an evening, after his toils in the field, on a page torn from his interleaved calendar, work out prosaic idylls, which Ramler could turn into verse were he with us still. I have perused forty-five of them. I shall impart one of them — neither the best nor the poorest — in the hope of attracting the eye and the hand of the court, for since the cattle plague, he has nothing but debts. It seems that, just like the jockeys in England, our riders on Pegasus's back must be kept famished and light and, thereby, *fast*. And were not, according to Voß, the *winged* gods of the ancients merely *subservient?*

The idyll selected treats of the court itself. To Hafteldorn the plough-share, the cow sheds, the flail, and the harvest-tanned back could never be part of the Arcadia so fondly extolled by the poets; and if a tender pale lady watched Hafteldorn from her castle as he hewed and hefted the oats and refreshed herself through the picturesque labor and rustic tranquil-ity, happily noting how close the tanned peasant thus came to the beau-tiful paintings of landscape painters and poets: the tanned peasant for his part wished for nothing more dearly than to be a pale courtier. In his idyll he therefore encounters the pastoral life and golden age in urban or court life only; an error that hardly takes from the substance of the work itself.

I had better warn those of the gracious ladies who wish to visit him now that, externally (like others, morally) the bard somewhat resembles the Trojan pig, which used to appear on the Roman table, enclosing one delicacy after the other, the final one a roast nightingale, but externally, as I said, remaining a pig.

Matthieu v. S.

Cut, o muse, a hole in the oaten halm and sing of the townsman! — There roam the courtiers, contented Arcadians, smiling. No toil comes near them, no hunger, no war. When the devil enters the countryman with the wine, as he got into Judas with the bread: those sit in harmony at the long table and dine amply; and the swords they carry are, like the trigger and powder pan on the air gun, only shams. Not one of them wants to stand out. They only long to be equal, like cobblestones for the prince, who steps on them. — O the equality of those *first* folk! How help-fully they unite now to rescue a fallen fan from the floor. How affably they bear each other's opinions! How they love man, and always have his image around them, either as statues or busts or as heads on their breasts!

Only their retinue, the comet tail of servants a little more closely re-lated to those exiled from Eden, may be somewhat coarse, as the radish's tail end is most biting and the fishtail boniest.

O what an ever-smiling tranquility! Under the silken parasol's palm leaf and beside the prettily painted stove screen, they know no change of

seasons. These first children, like the first parents, toil not, and the cumbersome pannier is a far cry from their neat little workbaskets. Neither
want nor thirst nor hunger torments them, but ever indulging, they rest
and sit like the heathen all day and all night and know not Time; they
live through the lighted night like yellowhammers[2] and always partake of
a morsel. — They hear not the cannons of war and the buffets of life in
their pleasuring, as the capercaillie is deaf to the shot while he courts.

It is not in the rough, gusty, dusty, and sleety Nature outside that
these shepherds spend their poetic lives, but in the beautiful Nature that
blooms on wallpaper or diorama. They gaze at gentle Nature in displays
and in paintings, thus weaning themselves of the brutish reality, as plaster
of Paris eggs cure chicks of sucking the real ones. A little flower of silk,
a tree painted or modeled in wax, replaces for them what is outside, as
the small conifer does for the caged linnet. And when, after the bright
colors of day, they see, like the strangled, the dark one of night: they stay
up till near morning to enjoy either the starry heavens or the rising sun,
and then fall asleep placidly.

There is no money among these impec-cable Arcadians; like saintly
monks, they do not carry it on them, and they gamble playfully only for
colored ivory.

And on the shepherdesses each night the red and white gillyflowers
of modesty and innocence blossom, lilies, painted on their bosoms rather
than stamped on their backs. Thereupon, the whole shepherdland dallies
in love: the gems flash on the shepherdesses, and the shepherds follow
the lustrous gems, as female insects glow in the night to lure on the
males.

May this innocent joy never forsake the courtmen's and courtwomen's
shepherdland, but may it increase!

Hafteldorn here.

25TH JANUARY. PAUL'S CONVERSION LEAF.

Paul's Conversion through Migraine

If there be a man in whom the beneficent force of inertia (vis iner-
tiae), which is after all ingrained in the lowliest creature and is fully developed in some others, like the great or persons of private means, mold-
ers away undisturbed: alas, I am that man. I need but raise my head from
the pillow of a morn, when I seem to offer at once to the universe the
antechamber, auction room, and Pembroke's cabinet into which it may

2. Ortolans are always surrounded by lamps to make them feed all the time.

stream in full spate. Anything calling itself an idea or a thought comes sailing along on the nerve juice, disembarks, and (following the familiar nepotism of ideas) brings with it its distaff- and spear-side namesakes, neighbors, and friends, complete with antipodes in pursuit — and in a matter of minutes I find on looking around me unpacked in the closets of my brain not much less than the world — all of the Royalists and Electoralists — pia corpora ac desideria — titles from the Pandects, from directories and from Meusel's Encyclopedia — large dictionaries with billions of words in as many tongues — dicta probantia, and Epiphanius with his 80 yapping heretics on a lead — crocodile- and other 18th-century syllogisms — visiting cards of the cardinal virtues, and the cardinal sins in person — nuncios with their nunciature squabbles — rogues, for example Nickel List — celebrated masters — notions that make me laugh — several judicial benefits — bottoms not even attached to a Venus of Medici — dancing dots that are barely alive, and dying swordsmen who are in fact dead — the Devil and La Negresse, his grandmother, or the virgin Europa and the reader and myself and the awareness of it all. —

Macrocosm has settled on microcosm and presses it down. — Last but not least arrive the things that I have to do, the countless letters — the pleasure trips — the visits — the toilet — the excerpts — Hauber's bibliotheca magica (which will help me to write myself into a great light), not to mention the renowned university- and other-libraries, which I shall have to explore with the best.

To come to oneself in such states of affairs and to stride unconcerned over such bales of wares and worlds lying around would be too much to ask of even the best head had it not something that sweeps away the whole clutter — a headache.

That is a different story.

Once I have that: I do not write, neither do I read (for it is not possible), but I pace up and down and spend the best part of the day walking around my self and my life, and under this tranquil sky gaze deeply into the calm sea within me, down to its green fields and to the old ships, which sank a long time ago. It is less the decisions than the grounds for them that are renewed, confirmed, and revived that they might bear me along on the current of action with new vigor; for the best axioms, especially if we act on them, tend to turn dull and feeble and need to be born again now and then.

Therefore, I pity those men who forever thrust forward and rush ahead, the minister, general, man of affairs, whose moral calendars do not include a quiet Good Friday, Ash Wednesday, or any red-letter day, and who desecrate their own inner Sabbath. *Fast* rivers are the *uncleanest*, but they are purified when they flow gently. As so many dog stars rule our lives, each of us ought to award himself frequent canicular feast days. Serious ailments, like the total exhaustion after yesterday's revels, force such Ash Wednesdays upon us, which once in a while sift and direct our whole life. Most people postpone that said Wednesday to a time when they have achieved a house in the country or their hair has turned grey; yet what good is a resting place so close by the great, deep, place of repose? Much better one on the way!

Our soul is never more free, our vigor more keen, life more open and versatile than on the day after completion of a large work, for example a quarto volume, and before we have embarked on a new venture. — It may be her quieter life that shapes the purer moral design of a woman, just as any regular crystallization can only take shape in repose.

The other matter I like about migraine is that it works on the male cornea of the heart until this detaches and it has the heart dangling, naked and soft beyond all. I wonder, do all men have the long, cold saltpeter needles scraped off their north face by migraine as I do? As a matter of fact, and looked at from a physiological aspect, the sickness should always have that effect, as it belongs to those weakening ones that soften and move us. What a balmy hour when we walk up and down in the room — and several angels of light hover around us — and the heart swells even without being wounded, and the breast heaves with such nameless emotion that something to weep about would be welcome — until in the end we dig up a suitable reason, and the well runneth over to our heart's content! What birthdays of childhood remembrances are celebrated! — What castles and alpine huts does our fantasy now construct on the faraway peaks around. — What noble and amiable figures who are dispatched to us and descend from those ruined palaces or from the nearby gardens of the present! — If we have a sister, we ask her for something more gently; if a wife, we give thanks to God that we have one. — A mere chord on the pianoforte becomes a Creation of Haydn; and if, to crown it all, I alight on something old and artless, like "I loved but Ismene": there is no holding me.

Let no Kantian disciple slander this softness as physical, for the hardness against which it helps us is physical, too! — Yet this sweet manna is also a medical remedy. Can any man who has thus been softened continue for long without becoming his own flying field hospital (hospital ambulant), since all must appear to him, as to one who climbs from a warm bathtub, even lukewarm normality, like ice, and nothing can please him but what teaches men to love and endure and makes them more beautiful? Was it not during one of those migraine afternoons five years ago that it suddenly came into my head to reckon in one full swoop that humanity's countless errors and heresies during the last six millenia — on the different continents and their island subsidiaries — in the various tribes — divers religions (of which a Frenchman reckons 184, each of which may in turn have 184 deviations) — with Epiphanius's 80 heretics — in the different sciences (the philosophers frightened me); had I not a headache, say I, when I tackled this infinitesimal calculus and suddenly sat down mollified (I had been incensed before) a virtuous convalescent with the words: "And yet, hothead, thou wouldst, in the face of this host of erratis, beat the battle drum and create a commotion over sixteen or seventeen errors, which thou didst encounter in the Literary Gazette or the Voigtland? Consider that!"

Airshipman Giannozzo's Logbook

SECOND JOURNEY

Termination of the First — the Knights of the Toad — the War of the Frogs and Mice in the Principality of Vierreuter

We must have order in the logbooks of airships; I will begin again. The day before yesterday, on ascension day, nothing in the world could have brought me down to this world again; I allowed myself to be buffeted all over Saxony by the changeable gusts. I or the new satellite circling the earth might have appeared to those below of roughly the same magnitude as the old one. My grace before meals was said in front of a softboiled egg, which I served to myself in inkwine.[3] I would lead a life of plaisance up here were I not incensed all day long by the things I think and detect. Even below I have been known to pace up and down, clenching my fists for days on end while I reflect on the evil Two (the evil Seven, to me), Injustice and Braggadocio, and count to myself the horrendous amount of crowcocks and cockcrows I must allow to do as they please in so many countries and ages, without being able to clip a wing here or chop a comb there, or break a few heads or a window. O brother Graul, dost thou not also know the wrath of a man who wishes

3. Vin tinto, the finest of the Algarbia wines, almost the color of ink.

in vain for a couple of floods or doomsdays or a moderate sulphur slough, and has to watch, like an idle dog, as countless leeches and blood suckers, church- and state-hawks — in every country and county and the three dimensions of time — suck, sting, push, and pluck with impunity — as they, like the green frog who digests inhabited shells, assimilate houses and lands; — as they (the above mentioned beasts) even convert, like Phalaris's bull, the cry of man's misery into the roar of a wild animal? — O, if one could but sweep over their heads as a fully fledged thunderstorm for a week and touch them now and again from on top, I would not complain!

The day before yesterday, when I floated across a dozen market towns and a half dozen townlets and espied through my glass floor and my English war telescope in the gardens and streets and through windows the visiting comedies with their choral accompaniments, ye poor sinners all, quoth I, would God that I were a cloudburst! — Graul, thou wilt not believe it. To be watching one sextodecimo town, that is bearable; but the full view of a complete oyster bank of sextodecimo towns from above, that is chagrin indeed. In 22 gardens of several pygmy towns at once I saw the curtsying and fidgeting, the fawning, preening, and toadying, the lorgnetting, raillery, and raffishness of innumerable pygmy-town persons, all of them (and this is so deplorable) with the pretensions, habiliments, china, and furnishings of the metropolitan. — Here lined up for the dance are the sextodecimo ladies, with their leaden limbs and ideas, yet swaddled in cultured shawls and aswim in their grecian lion skins, many, like hens[4] or officers, sprouting a sickly panache, elderly ones festooned in a colorful garb, the mementos of youth, the way roasted peacocks used to be served up in a garnish of feathers. — They are faced by a rank and file of such dandies and rakes as no residence town could show for itself; the Narcissus disciples of commerce, army, and law, their overbaked, modish crust with lumpish, unbaked insides, conversing on manners and high society, full of banter and badinage at the dowdy ones in the town; not to mention a collection of delicate, powdered, young squires, peeping from billiard tables and castles like so many white bunnikins from the holes of their burrow. — Graul, over one of these fully stocked Saxon gardens, a warren seeded with elegant Sansculottes in long trousers, I extended my arm in transit and anger, as Xanthippe stretched hers over her Socrates within her own house, and poured it — ὡς ἐν παρ-οδῳ — over the pleasure train — Heaven grant, to good effect! Thus did

4. According to Doctor Pallas, feather tufts on hens' heads are caused by the consumption of bones.

I make my maiden appearance as hunt baptist and shower of rain in the Saxon Electorate atmosphere.

But such is the whole unholy earth. One always imagines one's hometown to be the filiation and outlying outhouse of a distant sun city; yet if one could only perceive all the streets on the globe at one glance and thus find the same pedestrian commonage in each hemisphere, one would ask: so this is the famous earth? "That little cuspidor below, the little pisspidorlet, that is indeed that planet," I would tell any seraph flying past me and seeking directions.

And what is my second hell — I recalled my first one above — but to have to conceive of such countless imbeciles who arise of their own accord like an air bed after any deflation — those billions erecting their own stages of homage for months on end — those watches repeating again and again how far they *advanced* — all those drum addicts in thousands of villages, court- and dispatch rooms, schoolrooms, townhalls, backdrops, and prompt boxes who distend happily, and no one around to deliver a prick with the trocar — that is my hell[5] that I am forced to imagine so many windbags whom I can never get at because some of them are a geodetical distance away. — Dear God, just *one* doomsday of universal abasement — and I will gladly bow out! —

But back to my other journeys! Yesterday, Whit Monday, I woke up over the piccolo principality of *Vierreuter*,[6] while being driven straight to its capital and residence town. I decided to have coffee in both of them. Shortly before the Paris Gate, I opened both cocks of my sphere, for the outflow of light and the intake of heavy air — and dropped down like a bird of prey inside the border. This stunned and enraged the sentry, who called out the gate catechist, who in turn was determined to learn my name, business, and where I was going to lodge and for how long. I replied quite civilly that he would be entitled to put blunt questions, as the sentry would be to straighten the crooked barrier and stand grimly in front of it — because small principalities and their residence towns are, like jewels, more easily lost — if I were sitting outside the gate in a carriage and looking in at it; however, now I had, as he could readily see for

---

5. This computation, which drives Giannozzo wild, pacifies others. It is precisely the thought of the inflated army, whose floats and flippers we cannot tear out, that allows us to bear more easily with each proud individual sailing before his own *wind* or with those vain ones who live on the *air* that others exhale, as just *one* more fool.

The Editor

6. The real name is, however, provided the censor does not put asterisks instead* * * * *.

himself, crossed it and entered. He would not give way; neither did I.
The militant stand that I took drew half of the military estate of the
guardroom around me, household troops in the true sense, who had
never amounted to a big noise in the world except to their own ears while
they munched gherkins. Thou didst once say, Graul, that thou wouldst
venture if thou stoodst in front of the coat of arms on the border, to piss
easily over the whole principality, 'twas that narrow. I indicated something along the same lines by asking could one not — just as a certain
town has a living sentry guarding a dummy gate — as easily have here in
front of a real gate a dummy or painted sentry, thus doing away with the
need to relieve it.

FIFTH JOURNEY

Herr von Gehrischer — The people of Mülanz — Blueprint of a Gallow's Jubilee complete with Jubilee Speech

Who could endure a day among the people of Mülanz if it weren't
for a porthole that had to be taken to the glazier's? I did Herrn von Gehrischer, hotel acquaintance encountered in Europe at least thirty times,
the honor of accepting his hospitality, a guest among twelve others. It
would be hard to care less about someone than we did about each other;
"Giannozzo is a very amusing clown, not without talent, although malicious and impertinent withal!" said he; I say, von Gehrischer represents
mankind. Out of a head filled with languages and information — from his
genealogy full of great names — from a picture gallery, a music room, a
bookstore and a money chest, from all of these pearls of mankind he can
but compound a threadbare and passive figure, a nutcracker, who merely
hands others the kernels, a thing that produces nought (excepting his
like), no work, no fortune or misfortune, not even a stroke. Strike out
this living dash, and you will not even see the correction, as the longer
stroke is still there. As I said, he is mankind's pocket mirror. — Radiantly,
the genius descends from Heaven, and the clouds shine far and wide in
his wake — and as the ethereal spirit touches the earth: all is transformed — the rocks open and reveal great grave figures — walls and can-
vas catch the reflection of distant gods and their heavens — all bodies re-
sound, wood, sinew, and gold, and the air is pervaded by song — ; but the
dull human herd barely looks up from the pasture in wonder and bends
down again to graze on; only a few are hallowed and kneel in transfiguration.

As to the people of Mülanz, no god would dislodge this placid choir and cud orgy from their commonage; but would ye care to assess them more closely, without being out by more than three pounds? Come with me to the grand ball, which Gehrischer gives them today. All Mülanz of rank is present, albeit they pride themselves — and this is their only title of any worth — that they, like the old German books, have no title. There is not only a scholarly aristocracy but also a golden one, which keeps open table for those who are *to the manner born.*

They came, they saw, they conquered — what the tables could hold. Heavens, they were the enlightened Eighteenhundreders — wholly in favor of Frederick II, moderate freedom, quality reading for recreation, and a moderate deism — a moderate philosophy — they declared themselves very much against apparitions, enthusiasm, and the extremes — they liked reading their authors as stylistic exercise to the benefit of their business and as a relaxation from substance — the nightingale they enjoyed, as the Italians the real ones, roasted, and with the myrtle they heated, as the bakers in Spain, their stove — they had killed the great Sphinx[7] who sets us the riddle of Life and were carting the stuffed skin about and must have thought it a miracle that anyone else could believe in one. — Genius, they said, we certainly never reject, we only file it a little — and only *one* thing kindles their chilly spirit: the body; for it is solid and sound, their state, religion, and art, and what the *Berlin Monthly* must serve. —

O how I loathe that burnished lead of the polished commonplace, that distilled water and clarified vin ordinaire! I have forded this shallow humanity long ago and become a misanthropist of the heads far more than the hearts,[8] as in the end each head shakes and affrights us with its seashores and ocean floors; but ye, my universal German librarian lot, ye copy machines of the copies, ye who never divine nor guess anything but your likenesses, happy are ye; for if Madame des Houlieres in her idylls calls a mouton happier than a man, how happy must be he who is both! —

Yet the lack of uncommon people in Mülanz does not go so far as to

7. As is well known, Oedipus put the slain animal on the back of a donkey, etc.

8. For the heart is boundless and eternally new. While we may cloy ourselves with the greatest beauties and truths, and crush their charm and form in our own gratification, no beautiful deed appears obsolete or too frequently, nor is moral magic and enjoyment subject to Time. This soul-sustaining unchangeability is founded not only on the boundlessness of the free heart but also on our own disposition, in that we can find moral beauty and freedom and merit only outside ourselves and therefore *love* it, while within us we meet only with moral truth and necessity and *approve* of it. I hope to pursue this difference, which permeates our whole inner being and life, more closely some day.

                                                                    Editor's note

preclude some common ones from arising now and again to repeat the complaints of the Fichtean School as to the superabundance of triviality; even at Gehrischer's ball there were three of those Titus heads leaping about; equally, Piemont does not lack dogs with goiters the same as the Piemontese, nor Asia, monkeys with the pocks of humans.

Tomorrow — and that is the only thing pleasant about her — Mülanz will celebrate in a long civic, canonical, military, and aristocratic procession the centennial of her city charter. But now, since the Germans have nothing more soulless, boring, frigid, liveried, and nightgowned — apart from their comparatives — than their jubilees, processions, coronations, and similar ceremonies: I will sit up a while longer burning the midnight oil as I pen this and compose something ironical that can be dropped on the procession tomorrow, when I shall interrupt the rejoicing by publicly sailing up and away, addressed to the local authorities and reading as follows: ...

FOURTEENTH JOURNEY

Last —

The wind blows so fresh and straight that I find it easy to alight on an alp in the evening after a day's writing and dining aloft. Such is my occupation, my ship being a proper sturdy provision ship. Eating and drinking will lift a man and his ship, eventually.

Yet inside me is oppressive weather in the wake of the painful dreams along which, as over treacherous hot Vesuvian ash flowing back under my feet, I endeavored in vain to work my way up to a firm plateau all through the night. Thus I dreamt of a cock, black as coal, which stood on my breast and scratched for my heart. — Furthermore my little posthorn kept screaming as if alive and in pain through four dreams in the most piercing high notes, glowing bright red from a hot breath, which a dream named in a whisper "the silent thing." Even thou, my dear Graul, wast dispatched to those manes of wakefulness; I ran to meet thee, but thou couldst by no means turn around, thou only couldst reach for me with thine arms turned backward, like a jointed doll, and hugging me to thy back and pigtail didst utter these words without much connection: "A joke is a joke — thus the dear man. — Do but come to me, dearest Giannozzo!" Yet thou didst not allow me to face you, but didst squeeze me more tightly, calling more loudly: "Where dost thou live, Giannozzo, my lambkin? Canst thou not appear to me? Truly, poor devil, I do remember thee!"

Perhaps I shall find thee in Switzerland, Graul, if thou keepest thy promise.

Below me I spy several running guides telling me where I am like street signs on corners; several concert artists of the Vienna contingent are working as soloists in the woods, all playing tunes of their own, so we must be in Swabia.

How green are the vineyards! How bright is the Neckar! — But I feel ever more strongly that I have traversed these plains in past dreams. —

Yes, I am right; now I am sailing across the unknown magic- and morning-ground, where the dark eye of exalted Teresa glowed at my side and I gathered roses out of her bosom. Here, receive them again, Teresa, I am tossing them back onto thy pleasure grounds. Alas, thou standest not now on the lighthouse of Pharos. May the wing of thy wonderful spirit never be wounded! —

A semicircle of jagged storm cloud volcanoes builds up on the horizon, and I can hear thunder afar. The midday sun lies as a long beautiful flash on the glaciers, and I hope to hover over the mountain myself ere the storm does.

Westward I now see the Cathedral and, I believe, Strassburg's telegraph, whose index finger of Death is sublime and awful; like a Goddess of Fate, it raises its scissors — the tongue of the scales of peoples, the in- and declining compass of Time.

Although the mountainous storm clouds are still low in the sky, the thunder comes rumbling ever more loudly and fully. Damnation, it comes from a battle! — Troops come thundering over the hills — countryfolk running — a village goes up like a beacon — horses lie dead in a garden, and I see a child bearing off a severed arm.

Now I can see the plain and the billows of smoke that the burning inferno spews forth. How I crave to be there! My breeze takes me straight over the somber vast deathbed of nations; and I long to lower myself into the fiery clouds and seethe with wretched humanity. — All I can hear is the thudding axe as Death slaughters his cattle, not a sound from the cattle themselves — and the storms of the cerulean sky at rest all around waiting in readiness until they, too, can rise and join in the battle. — What seekest thou on my sphere, thou heavy, oppressive predator? Didst thou carry away a child from a peaceful alp[9] to devour it here, as Directeurs devour a pastoral country? Be off, thou art the black cock who dug for

9. He perceives the bearded vulture, which in Switzerland frequently seizes children.
The Ed.

my heart in the night — O, how much has misery grown during the last few minutes.

Horrible! — Now I could really hate them, the human beings, those ridiculous hoot- and wise-owls of daylight, who turn into savage predators as soon as they gain the least bit of darkness. Their panacea is gunpowder; they use it for cleaning the dungeon air of the countries, to widen and heal the wound that rabid evil inflicted on them. Greed labored for centuries in her silver mines and has at last stored enough arsenic in the poison fangs of your hearts to make waste and wan all that lives and blooms with its smelter fumes. Heavens! how the gem of the second world greedily drew the chaff of souls today! And below stood the Devil, where he had opened a little market stall of limbs for those (viz, directeurs and princes) who like to give thanks for their own being salved by votive members attached to their saints.

Suddenly, I was tossed directly above the smoky field of fire and gleaming weapons; I opened the air cocks and buried myself in the steam, where only the squinting basilisk eye of Death opened and shut his *silver glances*. — I was not low or near enough to the gleam of the bayonets — the artillery's hail of fire — the rain of blood on the ground — the voices of pain — the pale forms of the bleeding. — Only soothing music, harbinger of love's sigh and joy's tear, must sound like mockery in the misery down below, and the kettledrum of the cannons pounded among the gentler, kinder sounds, and the drum rolls of the smaller guns continued. — O God! — Pain paced the earth below and trod on our faces and buried the dead beneath the dying — my heart resounded — then I heard the innocent horses neighing. — Now I, too, flew into a rage, for was I not also one of those down below? And I fiercely hurled all my stones straight at the embattled crowd, whom an evil spirit had jumbled and pitched into this madness of fighting. — God forbid that I hit an innocent horse! — [10]

Then a sudden weight loss lifted me high into the azure sky.

How calmly and coldly the sun shone in his still sky above the sultry inferno on earth, as if humanity's conflagrations of war were naught but sickly sparks flying past his large eye. I looked back on the battle clouds, tears of rage filling my eyes as I imagined the peoples' teardrops gathering to make gleaming crowns into a proud arch of triumph and victory. Alas, the worst in humanity or inhumanity is that no man, no prince, no

---

10. O Giannozzo, the madness with which thou helpest to wound is the same madness that drives nations against each other.

The Ed.

censorship, be it ever so dictatorial or impudent, will forbid even the bitterest rebuke of war, and yet neither honor nor length of the same will diminish on that account.

O wonderful day! Brightly, the shining Swiss mountains draw near, with their valleys and pinnacles, and pour out the Rhine; but behind me the storm clouds pile hastily up in the sky in grim silence; the breezes are slowing down and barely keep me in motion.

Now all is still. What a world to be becalmed over! The Rhine rumbling in front, and behind me the thunderstorm — the city of God with her numberless shining spires spread in front of my eyes — on the distant horizon, white shining statues of gods and their High King Montblanc crown the eternal temples, and the River Rhine tumbles down from on high to rise again, a white giant spirit, robed in the heavenly rainbow and floating, silver and light.

What is this? Does my fate draw near? — Is the black cock scrabbling? — I wished now to lower myself before the splendid new world resting on the old; but I could not, the cord between air cocks was severed when I ripped it too hard in the battle; unless I am swept to an alp by the gusts ere the storm clouds engulf me, my only salvation will be to rip the balloon.

Now a gust carries me straight to the heavenly splendor. But the clouds are beginning to drown the voice of the river, the black serpent of cloud is uncoiling astern and already hissing and iridescing next to me in the east — The chariot of the sun travels low in the earthly dust. O how the sun and the glacial peaks, the abashed River Rhine and the poisonous cloud are encircled by the golden eagles of flame that are spreading their wings in repose on the green alpine pastures. I believe that I shall die today; I shall be seized by the grand thunderstorm. I shall die happily thus, thou Veiled One above me; my spirit is pleased to leave this imprisoning cot in the sight of the mountains, the sun, and the azure dome, and to soar into the boundless free temple. This sun-crimsoned hour, this rugged country, I shall engrave on my tumultuous heart, and after that it may break of whatever it will.

O how beautiful! In the east roar thunder and torrents, and suspended from them hangs, instead of a rainbow, a large, tranquil, multi-hued wheel, a flaming ring of eternity, fashioned of jewels — Not far from the jagged storm, the warm sun shines gently, where the golden green alps bathe their breasts in his light, and the lights and the nights of Switzerland's towering worlds interact in magnificent promiscuity; towns are hidden by clouds, glaciers are glowing, chasms brimful of vapor, pitch-dark forests, and lightning, evening rays, snow, vapor, and rainbows all reside together in the unending circle.

Now the clouds open their jaws to the sun; I can still see a herdsman with his inaudible alphorn on the purple slope over there amidst his white cattle, and a shepherd boy sups from his goat his evening drink. — O how tranquilly ye live in the Tempest of Being! — Alas, the black cloud gnaws at the sun! The lofty land is transmogrified into a churchyard of dolmens; only the tall white epitaphs of the glaciers are still to be glimpsed. —

I am divorced from the world — Switzerland and all else are screened by the boundless storm cloud — beneath the black shroud, rain splatters onto the earth below — the lightning has long ceased, and there is a dreadful delay. — Stars well forth from above, and their feeble reflections seem to float like silvery spangles on the funereal background — Ha! now the wind changes direction and blows me straight over the mute, loaded mine, whose fuse already glimmers. How sinister it is! Ah, but under the clouds there must still be pinnacles bathed in soft golden evening light.

Not a single flash, nothing but sultriness! — But I can feel the cloud drawing me closer. Ah, now a second storm is visibly brewing above me; I begin to see: the two shall collide, and I shall fall prey to one of them. —

I am determined to write up to the last minute stroke, perhaps my logbook will not be destroyed.

Now the ends of the thunderstorms clash and are joining in battle. — O hellish heat! — Oho! now my Charon's bark is dragged into the vaporos whirlpool — my sight is gone — what is Life — the fainthearted cowards below are sure to be singing hymns, and the wretches are sure to admonish each other beside my corpse — O the buffetting — My last day was, I knew it, in Wörlitz — Heavens! today's dream did, after all, clearly portend myself and my end; and to make it come totally true, I will now blow my horn furiously into the storm, like their Mozart down there in Don Giovanni, and make those hypocrites on the ground think their Doomsday has dawned —

Addio, dear Graul, truly thou canst not embrace me . . . . . .

*

Giannozzo's friend (Graul or Leibgeber) imparted to me in the simplest of terms — his heart was still sore with pain — this report of the death of the high-minded youth:

"— Meanwhile, there is no need for the public to learn all of this; suffice it that he be named Giannozzo. It is an unusual providence that this, my most stalwart, if not my oldest, friend encountered me twice unbeknownst to himself. For I was the dancing somnambulist whom he saw dancing the minuet on Mount Brocken; and during my journey to Bern — where I had manufactured my Clavis — I happened to stand at the Schaffhausen Falls while he was blowing above. A terrible thunderstorm raged close to the ground and came plunging down with the Rhine. Indeed, I myself and several others heard a strange, though discordant, staccato and piercing sound emerge from the black canopy over us. Finally, this was rent by a deafening thunderclap: the shredded balloon came hurtling down with its basket into a meadow close by. I knew my dear friend immediately. His right arm and his mouth had been severed, his horn partly melted, his beetling eyebrows burnt clean away from their high ridges, and his face twisted in anger; but the rest was unscathed. I repeat the sensible words that his dream had put into my mouth: "Where dost thou live, Giannozzo, my lambkin? Canst thou not appear to me? Truly, poor devil, I do remember thee!"

Second booklet concluded.

Clavis Fichtiana seu Leibgeberiana

§12

Leibgeber: "I astonish myself," said I, casting a cursory eye over my System, while my feet were being bathed, and looking significantly at my toes while their nails were being cut, "to think that I am the universe and the sum of all things; one can hardly do more in the world than become the world itself (§8) and God (§3) and the spirit world on top of that again (§8). But really, I should not have dawdled away so much Time (another of my handiworks) before I lit on the fact, after 10 Visthnus avatars, that I am natura naturans, demiurgos, and the bewind-hebber of the universe. I feel like the beggar who wakes up from the sleeping draught and finds himself king. Oh what a being, who creates all but himself (for it only *becomes* and never *is*), oh my absolute, all-bearing, -foaling, -lambing, -hatching, -whelping, -throwing, -dropping self!" [11]

At this point my feet refused to remain in the tub, and I paced up and down, barefoot and dripping: "Make thee a rough estimate," said I, "of thy creations — Space — Time (now well into the eighteenth century) — what is contained in those two — the worlds — what is within those — the

---

11. The last three participles are taken from venery.

three realms of Nature — the paltry realms of royalty — the realm of Truth — that of the Critical School — and all the libraries! — And consequently the few volumes written by Fichte, because it will only be after I shall have posited or made him first that he will be able to dip his pen — because he will only live courtesy of my ethical politeness — and secondly because, even if I do acquiesce, neither of us, being antifluxionists, can ever auscultate our selfs, but each must himself invent that which he reads of the other, he my Clavis, and I his publications. Therefore, I make so bold as to call the Theory of Science my work and Leibgebereanism, even *supposing* Fichte existed and nursed similar thoughts; in that case, he would merely be Newton with his fluxions to my Leibniz with my differential calculus, two men of similar greatness! Likewise, there is a like number of philosophical messiahs (Kant and Fichte); and Jewish ones, of whom the first is supposed to be the son of Joseph and the other the son of David.

§13

Polytheism or *Polyselfery.* To have other gods or selfs beside myself is prohibited with the same rigor by the Mosaic decalogue as it is commanded by the Fichtean One. The author of this Clavis must roundly confess to all those who may read or review it, that he, being a strictly logical *Theoretician*, finds it impossible to believe in more beings beside his own, as with it all that was ever discussed and disputed is amply explained, extrapolated, and integrated, viz, the existence of the imagined (§8) and the imagining (§7) universe, and the action of the pure Self or Deity. Else beings — and what is more, the infinite ones — will be needlessly multiplied, as *one* creator and primate of all things will do very well. Millions, nay, trillions of absolute selfs,[12] primae causae, causae sui aliorumque, unconditional reali- and aseities, or deities — viz, Weimaraners, Frenchmen, Russians, Leipzigers, Pestizians, Iroquois, people from all countries and ages — all these primates come and regenerate incessantly, equipped with their own universes (which, moreover, I am expected to buy as authenticated copies of my own); yet as a strict Unitarian and Singularis I must ask: wherefore, and by what right, and within which limits of their populace and coinvestiture? — I ask you, shall I find said selfs anywhere but in that natura naturata bred by myself, in my wide nonself as figures woven into this infinite Hautelisse tapestry, as limitations and

12. The absolute precludes number and, therefore, plurality and, by the same token, unity.

definitions of my noumenon, but never noumena themselves? — And if I allow it, these my own emanations and triplet-, nay, sextillion-births can, if they wish, reduce me to an offshoot of theirs, their derivative or adjective, a little tessera in the mosaic of their nonself. And the old question of St. Augustine's, whether the Son could also beget the Father[13] would be repeated and answered in the affirmative.

To this, Fichte on his part retorts, every time I personally explain to him that he could not — according to pure reason — always be that which he has printed in his Ethics[14] and all over: that it is imperative for him to detach other selfs, although they be merely heraldic figures in the painted nonself, and allow them to step forth animated and embodied, simply in order to have someone to keep moral company with. Just as the Kantian postulates God and Immortality, thus Fichte's self postulates selfs.

I beg him to remember what I said, with my pipe in my mouth as we walked up and down in the closet in Jena, and then decide for himself if he be.

§15

THE SORROWS OF A GOD IN THE GARDEN OF GETHSEMANE

Theopaschist and Patriopassionist that I am, I can sing a song on that particular Passion. It was the Scholastics who raised the question whether God be God nolens or volens.[15] I speak from experience when I say he is nolens volens. Anybody who is one will bear me out when I say that even a mere prince is in a better case. Hearken to my 4 Maestosos on the subject! — My first Maestoso is this: here I sit — looked at absolutely — since time immemorial, which I create, blind, without consciousness, and contracting my invisible vastness into a substance, my ether into a lightning, and have the empirical, somewhat sensible self, which is writing this down as a result, yet carry on creating behind his back, as ignorant of my world as the Stahlean soul (anima Stahlii) of its corporeal abode. This

---

13. de trinit., from which Pet. Lombard, Lib. II distinct 6 quotes it.

14. There we read, p. 214: "That without which there could be no duty whatever, is true absolutely; and it is a duty to hold the same to be true." The first part of this period is circular . . . and actually a question, much as: what if precisely the *opposite Moral were moral?* The second can — as nobody suffers qualms of conscience on account of opinions — mean nothing but: in such a case it is our duty (1) to examine — (2) to act as if it were true — (3) to wish it were true — and (4) if need be, to contradict reason rather than self-respect, to be a skeptic rather than a rogue. For volition and belief are incommensurable quantities, and a transition from one to the other as such is even more difficult than Lessing found the one from historical truths to necessary ones to be.

15. Pet. Lombard. dist. 6. v. c.

must be what the Greeks had in mind when they ordained *night* the universal womb of the gods, and the Egyptians when they rated the mole divine merely because he is *blind*.[16] As a somnambulist creates sermons and other essays subconsciously, I create worlds. I, speaking empirically, have a horror of myself (absolutely speaking), of the hideous *Demogorgon*[17] dwelling within me.

My second Maestoso is that, although I do have plenty of reason, I don't have enough; and in Meusel's Scholarly Germany there are several pages of national gods who have even greater cause for complaint. I will concede that reason is admirable and also infinite and (in the actual sense) not human, which I (as an absolute being) proved by the whole establishment of the universe (nonself); but what was I thinking of when I granted my own subjective reason such a stingy and niggardly slice that it is now itself unable to grasp my objective one? Am I not in the lowly class of animals in whom, according to Herder, the mechanical waxes to the extent that their intellect wanes? — Heavens! I (empirical) ought to have grown into the greatest mind, a universal genius to match such a universe. But as it is, my imagined self grasps of an object, posited there just for its benefit, as good as nothing at all.

Furthermore, the nonself is created (by me as an absolute) at one throw, but the empirical self is frequently hardly finished in 40 years. — And again: while the nonselfs were made pretty equal in value, the selfs differ greatly; now, either this difference or that equality is a miracle. Therefore, the bias is obvious, which (as an aseity) in my bi-incarnation or transmutation into object and subject (§7, §8), I reveal for the object, and to *such* a degree that I as a sun brightly refracting myself in this duplicate rainbow seem to turn the poor subject into a pallid inverted sub-bow and, therefore, to introduce a more cheerful note into this sorry affair, rightly deserve to be called *Leibgeber* (donor of bodies) rather than *Seelsorger* (curator of souls).

True, I am to be comforted by the fact that I (as an intelligent self) am the profoundest of the sages whom Germany nurtures at present. I can freely admit this without playing into my enemies' hands. Kant spent 10,957 1/2 nights, or 30 years, on the begettal of his Critique; Fichte probably needed less than 3 months for it (for reading is also making); but all the more years on inventing his Science of Knowledge, which

16. Plut, quaest. Conv. 4. 5.

17. A horrible old veteran, ensconced on a little ball in the center of the earth, who produced everything, even the gods, and who must not be called by name. Ramler.

heavy tome on the other hand cost me only *one* month to make, or in more popular parlance, read. In this way, we surpassed each other. My Clavis, which cost me at least a fortnight, might be produced by some dunce in 2 hours of what they call reading. But this shows only too clearly that each later self ever produces within a few years or hours, although no one can say *why* or *whereby*,[18] all those developments of previous selfs,[19] the treasures of several centuries; the last will (in the real sense) be the first.

That is one of the disagreeable effects when, like Fichte, we establish several godheads beside our own. We need but agree, for example, to the existence of the innocent fellow in charge of the stove in the library for our one Maestoso to become Legion. For the stoker — who, by the way, represents deity in much the same way as, according to Clemens of Alexandria, a block and a board represent Juno, the heavenly queen, in Thespia and Samos, respectively — has in the meantime created not only Nature complete with her lower and higher mathematical sciences (and continues to do so, indeed)[20] all the renowned mathematical and otherwise erudite works on the world of his making, and all the languages inside the library he faithfully heats week in and week out, are his work entirely so far as the *letters* and *figures* are concerned (being part of the nonself that he produces). Nevertheless, there is no conceivable way in which the boilerman could understand the *content*, the spiritual meaning of the same letters; should he succeed all the same and finally comprehend Euler's Analysis or Ernesti's or Leibgeber's Clavis, or whatever else he may fuel, he will learn nothing but what he had printed before, and invents (like several other philosophers) the concepts *after* the symbols, just like those animal sculptures, which seem to imbibe from the fountain while they really outpour.[21] Or, to use nobler terms, he and every learner

18. This incomprehensibility strikes and punishes all schools, including the one accepting Dualism; for the latter transfers it from the self to the nonself, where it will grow, or it allows it to alternate dazzlingly between the two; i.e. we *posit* ourselves between two stools.

19. For a *past* time is per se posited by the present (Outlines of the Characteristic of the Science of Knowledge p. 106) — little as we ask with regard to the absolute self about any previous one, it is postulated by the Fichtean plurality of selfs itself, and this makes it even more objective than Space (that cube number of the nonself).

20. Because according to the Cartesians (actually according to anybody) beings must be created continuously; according to Origenes the divine Son is always being begotten by the Father; — which is the same thing.

21. For instance in Palermo, animals meant to portray the four quarters of the world appear to drink from the basin that they fill.

resembles that Viennese count of my acquaintance who attached to the naked deserted back of his head an attractive false pigtail, plaited from hair that he himself had formerly shed.

But where are my Maestosos? I have not concluded my second one. I am told, as I mentioned above, that as a Fichtean or Leibgeberean I am a great philosopher, and they call me like the great scholastic Alexander Hales, Doctor irrefragibilis. I go even further and add that only a few can comprehend me or Fichte, and that all those (possibly even myself) who would contradict me (again including myself, should I contradict myself) demonstrate thus most surely that they don't understand me. Students enter into me (I confess it with Fichte). With their stomachs still empty, they are all the more prone to take a malady or a diet and ingest it more potently. Men who are acquainted with previous systems, the great-grandmothers of my own, cannot do that. But what will it profit me to achieve what Alchakim Biamvilla achieved in Egypt, who had himself de-clared God by sixteen thousand with the stroke of a pen, if a system is, like the opera buffa in Naples, performed, transcribed, revised, and re-worked 45 times in a row (because every fool philosophizes)?[22] In that case, the cuckoo clocks cool the ardor we felt for the cuckoo itself. 20 Years on we shall only survive as separate limbs nailed into utterly alien systems. Whereas a poetical work of art is, like an opera seria, performed only *once;* and it will still be whole a 100 years on. —

Third Maestoso. As to this dirge, I expect there are few infinite beings resident in Europe — especially during these troubled times — who will refuse to join in, viz, to the effect that having installed this monstrous all-powerful giant, whom we call nonself, we are now, as was then the God Saturn by his offspring (the Regents of Earth, Sea, and Hell) bound, un-manned, and dethroned by it. Lavater[23] hopes to make his fortune in the other world, provided he can (as he is in a fair way of demonstrating) there create geniuses, plants, worlds, and *heavens.* Although he can see for himself down here what he will get for his trouble; we absolute selfs have created often and much, but on the whole we have gone in more

---

22. At least any energetic person, if he so wishes. The philosopher will not turn poet; but a poet can easily descend to the philosopher, from Plato on to the one I have just this moment received from the binder's. I am thinking of *Bouterwek's* excellent *Apodicics,* this durable rock amidst the present-day logical froth: such is my judgment after reading but the beginning, the apodictical logic. — The ease of philosophizing is derived from the fact that Philosophy is an opera of a thousand connected acts to which it is easy to add one motivation more, whereas all those other works are of no use at all to the poor poet; he must compose a whole new opera. Editor's note.

23. His Views of Eternity II. Letter 12.

for hells. Leastwise, one cannot mistake the old partiality of the absolute self for objectivity, which the new aestheticists copy, as it should have invested the subject with appropriate forces in the interest of balance rather than send the poor mite to do battle against a blind Polyphem. Our divine self's *reflection* is the name Fichte bestows on the world; the out-of-date freethinker *Edelmann* calls it the *shadow* of God. The latter is more to my liking, because the Lilliputean intelligent self is verily darkened and chilled to death by its shadow.

I confess that if the absolute selfdom or freedom, as Fichte will have it, created the world *merely* in order to counteract acting: I can quite see a few things beginning to limp. Do my free religious exercises really need all those stars, which will never tempt me, all those continents, including their islands, all those past centuries, beetles, mosses, and the *complete* plant and animal kingdoms? And if a Sloane proves the existence of God from the stomach — Donatus from the hand — Meier from the spider — Menzius from the frog — Stengel from freaks — and Schwarz from the Devil:[24] can it be said that, conversely, the existence of all those found-lings is equally easily proved from the divine self? — For, let us take es-pecially the latter, the Devil, viz, alien immoral beings. Do I not find wherever I look that the resistance that the free self puts up against itself is far too powerful: And does not Fichte in his Ethics §16 deduce Evil, that is, the defeat of the pure self, from the superior strength of the world of the senses, from the very resistance too greatly postulated by itself to itself?

What, finally, is the relationship of the uniform development of the *astronomical* and the *historical* nonself (in itself quite incomprehensible), which reaches beyond the empirical self in both backward and forward directions, to my freedom of action? Nothing but questions and prob-lems!

Fourth and Last Maestoso. Finally, there is naught more lamentable than the futile, aimless, lofty, and insular life that a God must lead; he has nothing to keep him company. Am I not sitting all the time, and all eternity, condescending as best *I can*[25] and making myself *finite* merely to have *something* around me, yet what do I get around me but the same as those lesser princes — nothing but my own repeating *creatures?* Those two Frenchmen who in Berlin offered — and managed — to hold a whole

24. See Derham's Astrotheology
25. "The self is finite insofar as its activity is objective, etc. (infinite insofar as it is turned against itself). But this finiteness or limitation is infinite because the limit can be extended ever farther." Foundations of the Entire Science of Knowledge. p. 242.

lengthy theological, legal, or indeed any desired colloquium merely by each addressing the other as Monsieur with varied accentuation, — those were, however, as we said, a dualis. But how can I compare myself with them, having addressed myself through a whole eternity a parte ante — and the one a post is not much better — as nothing but Monsieur? — Oh, to be able to turn just the once and be able to say: Madame! or even: Bibi![26]

A being, be it whatever it will, even the highest, desires something to love and revere. Fichtean Leibgebereanism, however, leaves me naught to that purpose, not even this beggar's dog nor that prisoner's spider. For, even positing that they exist, only the *nine* images that I, the dog, and the spider create of each other can have aught to do with each other, not we ourselves. Anything better than myself, which is after all what kindles Love's flames, is not to be had. Love's *cloak*, which has already been worn during the last few millenia to the width of an episcopal pall, will now rot away entirely; all we are left with for loving is our loving. Verily, I wish there were men and I were numbered among them.

All might yet have been well if only myself or Fichte, or both, had not been tempted by Satan to postulate or to reflect. As Jove I was wont to slip into my fine human form and enjoy myself eavesdropping on my own creatures, but now I am past any help. Any divinity, should it still be possible to obtain one by postulation, is ensconced, like myself, in his hermetic ice empyrean of heavens, dreaming perhaps of Uranus or the thirtieth century, while I sit and dream of the earth and the 18th, and is and hears its self-monochord, the singular string of the eternal music of the spheres.

In the words of Jacobi: our acting and insight is an acting of acting and an insight of insight; I might add: a mere *reflecting* of *reflecting* — although *initially* this eternal repeating and reflecting was meant to repeat *something other* than repetition — , and we live a life quite as frugal as that cat of which the "Herald" reported, which a miser in Britain, instead of feeding, merely coated with greasy rinds, so that in order to live it had to keep licking itself from morning to night. To be sure, Schelling admits in his "Philosophy of Nature" that he, too, to begin with felt rather frosty and poorly at the prospect of the infinite nothing surrounding his godhood, yet in the end the inner — creating cheered and refreshed him.

26. The name used by the naive Viennese librarian (oh what a contradictory triad!) *Duval* for all his beloved witty female correspondents.

However, what use is that? — Creating and acting are then no more than a Zimmermann's motion machine, which one moves in order to be in motion. And if, to crown it all — as I fear only too greatly — no one exists but my wretched self on whom that particular lot had to fall, nobody else can ever have been in a poorer case. Any enthusiasm permitted to me is of the logical kind — My metaphysics, chemistry, technology, nosology, botany, and entomology only amount to the old adage: know thyself — I am not only, as Bellarmino says, my own redeemer, nay, I am also my own Devil, Scourge master, and Goodman Death — Practical reason itself (this singular sacred shewbread for a starved philosophical David) wearily sets me in motion, as I can do good to none other but my own self — Love and admiration are void, for like St. Francis I press naught to my agitated breast but the snow maidens I fashioned with my own hand — All around me a vast petrified mankind — no love, admiration or prayer, no hope and no purpose glows in the black uninhabited silence — My self so alone, nowhere a heartbeat, no life, nothing around me, and apart from me nothing but nothing — Conscious of naught but my higher nonconsciousness — Within me the silent, blind, secretly toiling demogorgon I am myself. — So I came out of Eternity, thus I pass into Eternity —

And who is there to hear my lament and who knows me? — I. — Who shall hear it and know me after Eternity? — I. —

Fledgling Years

MOST OF JEAN PAUL'S WORKS CONSIST LARGELY OF digressions, forewords, and afterthoughts; such passages, as well as often being of the greatest interest, can be taken in isolation. *Fledgling Years (W* 4.717f.) is more homogeneous and lends itself less to excerpts. Taken in toto, it is one of the best examples of Jean Paul's narrative practice, which, to be true to life as Jean Paul sees it, can only be rambling and open-ended. As Vult observes in the last chapter, the meanderings of man are like the paths of the heavenly bodies, and all one can do is register their erratic courses like the astronomer Zach in his *Tabulae aberrationis.*

But this cannot really be conveyed in an excerpt. One might take the chapter "Life," referred to earlier as an example of the paratactic construction, or the chapter "Memories," a tour de force of recollection. Vult returns home to find Walt in the act of recalling his childhood, and they join forces in an exchange of memories. (In his old age, Jean Paul liked to have his memories refreshed by his brother Gottlieb.) But this aspect of Jean Paul is adequately represented by passages from the *Self-Life Description* and elsewhere. Besides, it is easy to give a misleading impression, as if escapist nostalgia were the keynote in Jean Paul, whereas he is so much engaged in presenting the crowded life of the present.

The passages following are examples of this; the first is also of interest as one of the most often published excerpts in translation in the period of Jean Paul's greatest popularity in the English-speaking world. Although the English Romantics first introduced Jean Paul, much more was translated in America. It may seem ungrateful to complain about the result. All translations can be faulted, since no one version can satisfy simultaneously the different and never mutually reconcilable criteria of a good translation. But sometimes what has been presented as a translation seems too wide of the mark. Eliza B. Lee was particularly influential, since she translated Jean Paul's autobiography.[1] In the overall, she omits, abridges, and adapts so much that one assumes she was intentionally bowdlerizing. As far as the passage here is concerned, her version of the first few sentences may serve as an example of what some of these more free translations were like. The original reads: "Darauf ging er weiter zur Malerei des Sommerlebens, an welche er sich ohne Furcht mit folgenden Farben machte: 'Schon der Sommer allein erhöhe! Gott, welche Jahres-Zeit! Wahrlich ich weiss oft nicht, bleib' ich in der Stadt, oder geh' ich aufs Feld, so sehr ists einerlei und hübsch.'" In Eliza Lee's translation: "Afterwards he went on to paint his summer life as follows: 'The summer now reigns alone. Ach Gott, what a season. So entirely is beauty diffused around, that I cannot always tell whether I wander in the fields or remain in the city.'[2]

Booklet Two. Number 19. Marlstone

Then he proceeded to painting a picture of summer life, fearlessly going to work with the following colors:

"Summer alone would edify! God, what a season! Verily, often enough I cannot decide whether to stay in town or to walk in the fields, it is all so the same and so very pretty. If one walks outside the gate: one is cheered by the beggars freezing no longer and by the postmen on

1. *Life of Jean Paul F. Richter, Compiled from Various Sources. Together with his Autobiography. Translated from the German*, Eliza Buckminster Lee (Boston, 1842).
2. *Walt and Vult; or, the Twins. Translated from the Flegeljahre of Jean Paul by the Author of the "Life of Jean Paul,"* Eliza Buckminster Lee (Boston, 1846), pp. 146f.

horseback all night with the greatest of zest, and the shepherds sleep out in the open. No need for a stuffy house any more; every shrub becomes an apartment with my good busy bees and the most glorious butterflies keeping us company into the bargain. On the hillside Latin school boys sit in gardens extracting al fresco vocabularies out of lexicis. In this close season there is no shooting, and all living things in bushes, furrows, or trees may revel in safety. Travelers turn up everywhere, coming from all directions, most of their carriages folded back, their horses' saddles adorned with foliage, and the coachmen's mouths with a rose. The shadows of clouds scurry, and the birds flit hither and thither between them, journeymen travel light with their bundles, seeking no work. Even in rainy spells, one enjoys sniffing the freshness outside one's four walls, the wet doing the cowherds no great harm, either. And when night has fallen, one simply dwells in a cooler shade, from which one can glimpse daylight distinctly on the northern horizon and the sweet balmy heavenly constellations. Wherever I look I see my beloved blue, in the flowering flax, in cornflowers, and in the divine boundless sky into which I am ready to dive as into refreshing waters. — And on returning home, there is indeed new bliss to be found. The street has become a very nursery, even at night after supper the tots are allowed out again, albeit scantily dressed, instead of being huddled under their counterpanes, as in wintertime. Meals are eaten in daylight, and one hardly recalls where the candles are kept. Bedroom windows are open all day and all night, as are most of the doors, without ill effect. Even the oldest crones are at their open windows, sewing, and not feeling the cold. Flowers turn up all over the place, next to the inkpot, on top of documents, on conference tables and shop counters. Children raise a great din, and one hears the roll of the skittle alleys. For half the night, one saunters along the streets, conversing loudly and watching the shooting stars high in the sky. The Princess herself strolls in the park of an evening before dinner. Visiting virtuosos make their way home close on midnight and continue their fiddling until they have reached their quarters and the neighbors all dash to their windows. The special mail coaches draw up later with neighing horses. In the midst of the noise, one nods off while leaning out of the window to be wakened again by posthorns, while the vast star-spangled sky has unfolded on high. God, what a joyous life here on this little earth! And that's merely Germany! If I started to think of abroad!

Booklet Three. Number 42. Schiller Spar

Now Life's magic lantern projected right playfully bright running figures along his path; the evening sun being the light behind the panes. They were set in motion, and in the stream down below there had to file past him a surveyor ship — a humble village churchyard at the side of the road, over whose grass-covered wall even a fat lapdog could jump — a special mail coach, four-in-hand, and with four footmen in front — the shadow of a cloud — following this into the light the shadow of a flock of ravens — tall, grey robber castles, walls rent asunder — completely new ones — a rumbling mill — an obstetrician on horseback at full speed — the skinny village barber with his surgical bag full tilt on his heels — a stout frock-coated country parson, with a harvest sermon in writing, giving thanks to the Lord for the general harvest and to his audience for his personal one — a wheelbarrow filled with merchandise and a suite of beggars, both kermis-bound — a subhamlet comprising three houses complete with a man on a ladder, who equipped houses and streets with red numbers — a fellow wearing a white head of plaster of Paris on his head, representing some ancient emperor or savant or other great head — a grammar school boy poised on a boundary stone with his nose in a lending library novel, so that life and youth should be painted for him in lyrical colors — and finally on a distant height, although still nestled in verdant hills, a small town shimmering forth where Gottwald might spend the night, the bright evening sun strongly gilding its gables and pinnacles, lifting them thus into the azure.

"We are scudding rainshowers and descended in no time," said he, looking forward and backward, linking the chain of scattering figures. And there a picture peddler with his picture Bible and picture gallery fluttering from a cylinder across his navel climbed after him making a bid for his custom. "I know for certain that I shall not buy anything" — replied Walt, handing twelve creutzer to him — "but *for this* permit me a quick glimpse at your wares."

"I could not be more delighted," said the man, bending his thorax backward and his picturebook toward him. Here the advocate found his moving pictures again as tableaux, life running riot in color on paper, half the history of the world and its regents, potentates and pottery pictures from Herculaneum, clowns and flowers and military uniforms cheek by jowl and overloading the man's stomach. "What is the name of that little town up there?" said Walt. "*Pancake Parva*, my dear sir, and those mountains yonder are magnificent weather dividers, otherwise the good thun-

derstorm should have set fire to all we possess the day before yesterday"
(countered the picture man) — "As it is, I still have some fine original
pieces to look at," and he unfolded the colorful hanging opus with both
hands. Walt's eye lit on a medley pencil drawing on which almost all of
today's wayside objects seemed to have been captured at random. He had
always considered a so-called quodlibit to be an anagram or an epigram
of real life and looked on it with sadness rather than joy — and now more
than ever before; for there was a Janus head on it, which differed little
from his or Vult's features. An angel hovered over the whole. Underneath was written in German: "What God wills is wrought well"; and in
Latin: "Quod Deus vult est bene *factus*." He bought the crazy sheet for
his brother.

Preschool of Aesthetics

PRESCHOOL OF AESTHETICS IS BEST REGARDED AS A MINE
of ideas, insights, and stimulating and imaginative observations, as Jean
Paul ranges far and wide in his discussion of poetry and its genres, of
genius and the imagination, of humor — defined as "the inverted sublime" — and style, of plot, character, and modes of narration (see *W*
9.77ff., 93ff., 102ff., 125ff., 248ff., 253ff.).

In his discursive fashion, he lectures practitioners with such pieces of
technical advice as that on the introduction of the hero: "Do not surround the cradle of your hero with the whole reading world. Just as the
Gauls, according to Caesar, did not allow their children into their presence until they were nubile — whence perhaps the French custom even
yet of having them educated in the country — so do we want to see the
hero already several feet high; only then should you retrieve some relics
from the nursery, since it is not the relic that makes the man significant,
but he it." He throws out definitions, such as the tidy genre divisions
familiar to generations of students of the theory of literature: "The epic
presents the *event*, which develops out of the *past*, the drama the *action*,

which extends for and into the *future*, the lyric the *emotion*, which is encompassed in the *present*" (*W* 9.267, 272).

Yet, as Margaret Hale says, "Jean Paul regarded all genre classification with great skepticism."[1] So one should not, as a summary by its nature tends to do, systematize the work too much. In *Preschool*, in his discussion of talent and genius, Jean Paul is very dismissive of the merely talented philosopher, dogmatic and intolerant, who has everything pigeonholed and numbered, who "lives at number such-and-such," unlike the great philosopher who lives "in the wonder of the world, in a labyrinth of innumerable rooms." There is nothing the talented philosopher hates more, once he has found his philosophy, than philosophizing. It need hardly be said that this is arguing *pro domo*. To be systematic, *Preschool* is, besides, much too combative and opinionated. Jean Paul enjoys hitting out in all directions, against the nihilists in art, who have no material, and against the materialists, who have nothing else (*W* 9.50, 43).

Even those terms are not that clear and consistent, particularly as Jean Paul seemed to shift position himself during the writing of *Preschool* and between one edition and the next. He started out in opposition to the new trends, for him all too formalistic, in aesthetic doctrines, whether of Goethe and Schiller or of the Schlegels, but gradually he came to have more sympathy with developments during the Romantic period, so that by 1803 he wrote to Christian Otto that his poetic system had "become very Schlegelian" (*H-KA* 1.11.x).

So he finds "the newer school right, on the whole," although this favorable report is once again modified somewhat by the time of the second edition of *Preschool*. If one is trying to identify Jean Paul with one particular doctrine or school, he has not made it any easier by substituting for the originally intended *Nicolaites* and *Schlegelites* the unhelpful terms *stylicists* and *poeticists*. The difficulties are compounded by the overlappings, particularly as they are only partial overlappings, of the different pairs of antitheses, old and new, Greek and Romantic, materialist and nihilist, stylicist and poeticist. Obviously, some kind of ideal fusion or synthesis is implied, an art that does equal justice to the universal and the particular, a spiritual mimesis that neither ignores nature, like the Schlegelites and nihilists, nor merely copies nature, like the Nicolaites and materialists.

---

1. Margaret R. Hale, *Horn of Oberon: Jean Paul Richter's School for Aesthetics* (Detroit, 1973). *Preschool* is the one work of Jean Paul that has in recent years received due scholarly attention in the English-speaking world — in *Horn of Oberon*.

The materialist has the clod of earth, but can breathe no living soul into it, because it is only earth, not a body; the nihilist would breathe in life, but has not even the clod. The true poet, in his marriage of art and nature, will imitate on a higher plane the landscape gardener, who knows how to wed his artificial garden to the natural surroundings as if they were its unbounded extensions, and will surround limited nature with the infinity of the idea so that the former vanishes into the latter as if ascended into heaven (*W* 9.43).

If, in spite of seeming to distribute blame equally between material- ists and nihilists, Jean Paul has a particular prejudice of his own, it is against the nihilists, for he is always in defense of matter and particularly scornful of those who have nothing to say and are expert at saying it. They are like the poor Carthusians, who are allowed no meat in their sausages. They represent a new kind of mysticism, diving into the depths, not to the oyster bank but to the fog bank. This preference is reasserted later in *Little Postschool to the Preschool*, where he reverts to an outright attack on the Schlegel school — fortunately it has outlived its immortal- ity — which regarded "form as everything, including content" and pointed to Goethe as a model; whereas, says Jean Paul, Goethe proves the opposite, since for him every poem was an occasional poem: in Jean Paul's orthography of the time, "Gelegenheit-Gedicht" (*W* 9.423f., 484).

Similarly, if one wishes to relegate Jean Paul's own mode of writing to one side rather than the other in the light of all he says about ancient and modern, Greek and Romantic, objective and subjective, naive and sentimental, then it would have to be on the romantic side. At one point in *Preschool*, he speaks of the straight and crooked lines in nature; and if, as he says there, the endless crooked line represents romantic poetry, it seems apt enough for his own work (*W* 9.85). Referring to *Preschool*, De Quincey says in his essay on John Paul: "One of his books . . . is abso- lutely so surcharged with quicksilver that I expect to see it leap off the table as often as it is laid there; and therefore, to prevent accidents, I usually load it with the works of our good friend — —, Esq., and F.R.S."[2] It is not, therefore, the sort of work from which one can pick a passage that could be said to summarize it.

Reasonably representative and of general interest in the context of so many similar arguments about ancient and modern, pagan and Christian, possession and longing, repose and restlessness, objectivity and subjec-

2. *The Collected Writings of Thomas De Quincey*, ed. David Masson (London, 1897), 11:267.

tivity, are two excerpts from his discussion of Greek and Romantic poetry. Much that he says will remind one of Schlegel and Madame de Staël. The reader will hear other echoes, too. It is ironic that Jean Paul should here refer to poetry as "the gay science," preechoing Nietzsche and reminding us that nobody anticipates as much as Jean Paul the romantic agony of that gay science's "frantic man."

But *Preschool* is above all the theorizing of a practitioner, who, moreover, makes a virtue out of the fact, declaring in the preface to the second edition that the best legislative authority is executive authority. Obvious choices for inclusion here are, therefore, such as most touch upon his own work: from the seventh chapter, what he introduces as "the four components of humor"; and from his chapter on the novel, his Italian-German-Dutch division, and his disquisition on the idyll.

The Fourth Program. On Grecian and Plastic Poetry

§19

THE PEACE AND SERENITY OF POETRY

Serene Tranquillity is the third characteristic of the Greeks. Their supreme God was always depicted as serene (according to Winckelmann), although he had thunder in his hand. Here again, cause and effect blend organically. In the real world, symmetry, serenity, beauty, and tranquillity are reciprocal means and effect, by turn; but in the poetic world that happy repose is a very element and condition of beauty. One external reason for that Greek gaiety, quite apart from their brighter conditions of life and their regular public recitations of poetry — for who would produce gloomy shadow worlds at a public festival and before a crowd? — is poetry's ultimate destination, the temple. The more tender Greek sensibility did not judge the anxious lament, belonging to the dark land of illusion rather than to any heaven, but gaiety to be seemly before God, which can be shared by the infinite with the mortal.

Poetry should be the gay science, as it used to be called in Spain, and like a death, make gods and saints of us. Only ichor must flow from poetic wounds, and like the oyster it should wrap each sharp or rough grain of sand tossed into our lives in mother-of-pearl. Its world must never be anything but the best, where each pain dissolves into a greater joy and where we are like people on mountaintops, about whom the heavy showers of life down below play as a misty veil. Therefore a poem is unpoetic, as a piece of music is wrong, if it ends on a dissonance.

And how is that joy made manifest in Greek poetry? — In the same way as in their representations of gods: through tranquillity. Just as these lofty figures stand in repose and contemplation before the world: thus poet and listener also must stand, blissfully unchanged by mutability. Go and visit a *gallery* with the statues of their gods. Those lofty figures have shed both mortal dust and celestial cloud and reveal a blissful halcyon world within their breasts and ours. Elsewhere, beauty may stir desire and trepidation, albeit gently, but their beauty rests simple and unmoved like a blue ether on the world and time; and it is the repose of perfection, not of fatigue, that stills their eyes and closes their lips. There must be a higher bliss than the pain of desire or the warm, tearful storms of ecstasy. If the Eternal One delights forever and reposes forever, just as finally, be there ever so many orbiting suns around suns in orbit, there must be one supreme sun suspended alone and still: it follows that our supreme happiness; i.e., that which we strive for, is not one more strife — only in Tartarus are wheel and stone turned eternally — but its opposite, an indulgent repose, eternity's far niente, as the Greeks located the Isles of the Blest in the Western Sea, where sun and life go down to rest. The theologians of yore knew our hearts better when they made the joy of the blessed, like the divine joy, consist of eternal immutability and the contemplation of God and granted us one *fixed* heaven after eleven terrestrial *mobile* ones.[1] How much more clearly they divined the eternal if incomprehensible than their successors, who declare our future to be an eternal chase through the universe and accept with pleasure, as merchantmen, ever more worlds out of the stargazers' hands in order to man them with souls who will embark on yet more ships and on new ones sail ever more deeply into creation, so that, as in music, the adagio of their old age or death will be arranged between the present allegro and the future presto. Does that not mean all striving being a clash with the present, declaring eternal war instead of eternal peace, and like the Spartans, arming gods, too?

The ancients embodied unrest, i.e., the pain of strife, in satyrs or personal portraits. There is no troubled repose, no tranquil Week of Passion, but only one of joy; for even a minimal pain remains active and warriorlike. It is the *happy* Indians who place supreme happiness in reposing, as it is the *fiery* Italians who speak of the dolce far niente. Pascal

---

1. According to ancient astronomers 11 skies orbited one above the other while the 12th or crystal sky stood still.

takes the human instinct for repose to be a relic of the lost divine image.[2] With cradlesongs of the soul, the singing Greek draws us out to his vast shining sea, but it is a tranquil sea.

The Fifth Program. On Romantic Poetry

§23

THE WELLSPRING OF ROMANTIC POETRY

Source and nature of all of the more recent poetry are so easily to be traced from Christianity that one might just as well call Romantic poetry Christian poetry. Christianity demolished, like some Doomsday, the whole material world with all its graces, compressed it to a sepulchral mound, a rung on the ladder to heaven, and put a new spirit world into its place. Demonology became the real mythology[3] of the physical world, and devils turned seducers and took up residence in the statues of men and gods; earth-present had altogether vaporized into heaven-future. And what remained, once the external world had thus collapsed for the poetic mind? — That into which it had tumbled, the *interior* world. The spirit entered itself and its own night and saw ghosts. But as finitude clings onto bodies only and as in spirits all is infinite or unlimited: in poetry, the realm of infinity came into bloom on the charred ground of finitude. Angels, devils, saints, the blest, and the Infinite One had no bodily shapes[4] or divine bodies; vastness and boundlessness opened their depths, instead; and that Greek serenity was replaced either by infinite longing or inexpressible bliss — time — and limitless damnation — the fear of ghosts — dreading itself — enraptured introspective love — boundless monkish renunciation — platonic and neoplatonic philosophy.

In infinity's vast night, man was fearful more often than hopeful. Fear in itself is more powerful and more prolific than hope (just as a white cloud will give prominence to a black cloud in the sky, but not vice versa),

---

2. It is the same thing when Fr. Schlegel praises "divine idleness and joy of plant- and flower-life," only he takes too much pleasure in his own verbal exuberance and its counter-effects.

3. We know that according to the Manicheans the whole physical world belonged to the Angels of Darkness; how the Orthodox extended the curse of the Fall to all creatures, etc.

4. Or the supernatural was attached to inartistic embodiments, to relics, crosses, crucifixes, hosts, monks, bells, pictures of saints, all of them speaking the language of letters and symbols rather than the language of bodies. Even actions sought to dispense with the corporeal, that is to say, with the present: the Crusades sought to unite a holy past with a holy future. Thus the legends of miracles. Thus the expectation of Doomsday.

for our imagination knows many more representations for fear than for hope; and this in turn is because the sense and sensation of pain, the physical feeling, can become the source of a River of Hell from any skin point of ours, whereas our senses offer but mean and scanty soil for pleasure. Hell was portrayed in flames, Heaven at best defined by music,[5] which in itself produces yet more undefined longing. Thus astrology was full of dangerous forces. Thus superstition was ominous rather than promising. Added to that the upheaval of peoples, wars, plagues, baptisms by force, gloomy polar mythology in league with an ardent oriental speech — these may also be counted among the mezzotints of the dark hue.

§24
POETRY OF SUPERSTITION

So-called Superstition deserves to be emphasized in its own right as fruit and food of the Romantic spirit. When we read that in Cicero's day the augurs interpreted the 12 vultures, which Romulus had seen, as a sign that his work and empire should survive for 12 centuries; and when we compare the actual fall of the Western empire in the 12th century: our first thought is superior[6] to our later, which calculates the combinations of chance. Let each man remember his childhood — if his was indeed poetic — the mysteriousness with which the Twelve Nights of Christmas were spoken of, the night of Christmas Eve in particular, when heaven and earth, like children and adults, threw open their doors to each other so that they might celebrate the supreme birth together, while the evil spirits roamed in the distance, spreading terror. Or let us remember the trepidation when we first heard of the comet whose unsheathed red-hot sword was drawn each night from its sheath and across the sky over the anxious world below, as if it were leveled by the Angel of Death to point and aim at the dawn of a gory future. Or let us remember a deathbed where most of all we beheld those busy shapes with candles moving behind the large black curtain of the world of ghosts; where we beheld the

---

5. Was not perhaps the indefinite Romantic nature of music partly responsible for the foggy Low Countries having great composers much earlier than serene sunny Italy, which preferred the clarity of painting, as for the same reason the former idealized in indefinite landscape, while the Italians preferred the definite human shape?

6. Even a Leibniz finds it worthwhile to find, for instance, that Christ was born in the sign of virgo. Otium Hanover, p. 187. So a passing observation might be permissible, that when an empty space was left for years for just one more portrait in the Imperial Portrait Gallery in Frankfurt, Fate did fill and conclude it with the portrait of the last of the emperors.

open paws and ravenous eyes and restless pacing awaiting the sinner, but found for the righteous flowery signs, like a lily or a rose in his bier, a strange melody or his double, etc. Even the lucky signs retained their dread, though; like the last mentioned, or the gliding past of a blessed white shadow, or the saying that angels are playing with the child when it smiles in its sleep. Oh how charming. The present author is happy for his part to have spent for several decades his early years in a village and to have been brought up in some superstition, with whose memories he must make do, now that one imputes gastric acidity to him in the place of those playing angels.[7] Had he the advantage of an excellent Gallic education, and in this century, he should have to sense many a romantic feeling in empathy with the poet, which as things are, he can lend to the poet. In France there was at least superstition and poetry from the start; the Spaniard had more of both; the cheerful Italian resembled the Romans and Greeks, about whose superstition there was nothing of our realm of ghosts; but rather it would relate to some good fortune on earth, mostly announced by definable beings; for German coffins, for instance, could never have been adorned with those gay, cruel, wanton groups of those ancient urns and sarcophagi of the Greeks or even the somber Etruscans.

Nordic superstition, which recognized in the skirmishes of the crows and the war games of children the bloody finger indicating the murderous onslaughts of peoples, was all the more romantically exalted, the smaller and more insignificant their portents. Thus the witches in Shakespeare's Macbeth appear all the more fearful the more they shrivel and skulk in their ugliness; whereas in Schiller's Macbeth, the buskins with which he shod them, meaning to elevate them, are the very witches' clogs of Pater Fulgentius to undo their magic. The imbalance between size and supernatural force opens up an immense terror field to our imagination; hence our disproportionate fear of small animals; and he must be a brave general who will sit as calm and motionless at the drone of an incensed hornet as at the roll of a cannon. — In our dreams we quail more in the face of mystical dwarfs than of a tall manifest giant. Now how much of this pseudofaith and superstition is true believing? Not its partial object and its personal interpretation — because either change according to times and peoples — but its principle, feeling, which had to be the teacher of education before it could be its disciple, and which the romantic poet

---

7. We all know that the smiles of sleeping children are caused by acidity in their stomachs, which, however, is not specifically expressed through smiles or angels in adults.

calls, only more transfigured, to life, viz, the terrible feeling of near help-lessness with which the silent spirit stands alone and benumbed inside, as it were, the gigantic mill of the universe. And in that strange mill he beholds countless and unconquerable cosmic wheels whirling without a break — and listens to the roar of an eternal flowing river — thunder is about him and the ground shakes — now and again a brief ringing sounds through the storm — here there is grinding, over there driving and gath-ering — and thus he stands abandoned in the all-powerful, blind, and sol-itary machine, which mechanically roars about him yet does not speak a single word to his spirit; and yet his spirit looks about him, fearful, for the giants who installed this wondrous machine to some purpose and whom, as the spirits behind such a complex construction, he must imag-ine to be far superior to their creation. Thus fear becomes not only the creator but also the creature of the gods; but because within our Self that has its source, which is distinct from the world machine and which flows mightily about and above it, the inner night is, while being the matrix of the gods, also a goddess herself. Any physical or material realm turns finite, narrow, and naught as soon as a spirit world is posited as its ocean and womb. But that a will — consequently something infinite or indefi-nite — penetrates that mechanical determinacy, this we are told not only by our will but also by those inscriptions on the two gates, which lead us *into* and *out of* life; for although there be no earthly life either *before* or *after* life on earth, there is yet a life. And furthermore, we are told so by dream, which we never learn of in *others* without a thrill[8] as a special, *freer*, and arbitrary union of the spirit world with the concrete, as a state when the gates along the horizon of fact stay open all night, although we know not what unfamiliar shapes might flit in through them.

Verily, we may say that the moment we posit a human spirit in a hu-man body, the whole realm of the spirits, the backcloth to Nature with all its points of contact, comes into being, whereupon a different wind will blow and make Earth's Aeolian harp quiver and harmonize. If a har-mony be granted between body and soul, concrete worlds and spirits: then, either with or without physical laws, the spiritual lawgiver must reveal himself through the universe in the same way the body expresses at once the soul and itself; and to err superstitiously only means that we fancy we fully understand the ghostly miming of the universe, as a child

8. We never hear the dreams of others without a romantic feeling; but our own we experience without it. This distinction between the Thou and the Self permeates all the moral relationships of man and it deserves, and will receive, some consideration on another occasion.

fancies it knows the parental, and that we too see everything in relation to ourselves. In fact, each event is a revelation and ghostly apparition, but for the universe and not for ourselves alone. Hence, we cannot interpret it.[9]

The Seventh Program. On Humoristic Poetry

§32
HUMORISTIC TOTALITY

Humor, as the inverse sublime, annihilates not the individual but the finite by contrasting it with the idea. It knows no individual foolishness, no fools, but only folly and a mad world; unlike the common joker, delivering sideswipes, it does not single out a particular folly; rather it hauls down the great, but — unlike parody — in order to put it next to the small, and raises the small, but — unlike irony — in order to put it next to the great and thus to annihilate both, because in the face of infinity all is equal and nothing. Vive la bagatelle, was the sublime cry of the half-crazy Swift, who toward the end liked reading and writing bad pieces best, for in that concave mirror foolish finitude as enemy of the idea would appear to him at its most ragged and in the inferior book, which he read, nay, which he wrote, he would relish the one he imagined. Your common satirist may well pick up a couple of true offenses against good taste or the like on his travels or in his reviews and pillory them and pelt them with sharp ideas instead of rotten eggs; the humorist, though, almost prefers to take the individual folly under his wing, apprehending instead the myrmidon in charge of the pillory together with all the audience, as it is not the bourgeois but rather the human folly, namely the universal, that moves his heart. His Thyrsos' staff is neither conductor's baton nor scourge, and its blows are haphazard. In Goethe's Fair Day at Plundersweiler, one must look for the purpose either in sporadic satires on actors or cattle dealers, etc., which is incongruous, or in the epic assembling and spurning of all earthly hustle and bustle. Uncle Toby's campaigns do not by any means hold up the Uncle or Louis XIV alone as a laughingstock — they stand allegorically for mankind's hobbyhorse and the childly mind nestled inside every man's head as in a hatbox, and which, no matter

---

9. It is most likely for this reason that Moritz, more a visionary than a creator of ghosts, included so many dreams, apparitions, premonitions etc. more often than he explained them, in his Experience-Psychology and thus, with the shield of a collector and exegete, guarded his spiritualism somewhat from the learned and Berlinean corporalism.

how cosily wrapped, will on occasion expose itself and may in the end well be all that is left under the silver hair of old age.

Hence this totality may quite as well be expressed symbolically in parts — in Gozzi, Sterne, Voltaire, Rabelais, for example, whose universal humor endures not *because of* but *regardless of* its temporal references — as in the great antithesis of life itself. Here Shakespeare, the inimitable, steps forth with his magnificent limbs; indeed, in Hamlet, as in some of his melancholy fools, he brings this derision of the world behind a mad mask to its pitch; Cervantes — whose genius was too great for a long drawn-out joke on an accidental derangement and a common simplicity — plays out, though perhaps with less awareness than Shakespeare, the humoristic parallel between idealism and realism, mind and body vis-à-vis the infinite equation; and his twin constellation of folly looks down on the whole human race. Swift's Gulliver — less humoristic in style and more humoristic in spirit than his fairytale — towers on the Tarpeian rock from which his spirit will topple humanity. In merely lyrical outpourings, in which his spirit reflects on itself, Leibgeber limns his world humor, which never aims for or blames the particular,[10] which his friend Siebenkäs is rather more apt to do, wherefore I would credit him with whimsicality rather than humor. Thus Tieck's humor, albeit molding itself rather more on others and lacking somewhat in witty abundance, stands pure and regardant. Rabener, by contrast, lashed one or the other fool in the Saxon Electorate, while the reviewers lash one or the other humorous author in Germany.

If Schlegel rightly maintains that the romantic is not a genre of poetry but that poetry must itself be romantic: then the same goes even more for the comic; that is to say, everything must become romantic, i.e., humoristic. The disciples of the new aesthetic Lyceum display a superior comic universal spirit in their burlesques, dramas, parodies, and the like, without becoming denouncer and gallows chaplain of the individual fool; although this universal spirit often finds a rough and ready enough expression, if the disciple himself is still wrestling with his copies and docimasticum in the beginners' class. However, the comical stimuli of a Bahrdt, a Cranz, a Wezel, a Merkel, indeed most of the Universal German Librarians with their (mostly) false tendencies, embitter good taste far more than the comic heat rashes, blackheads, and freckles (often nothing but exaggerations of the right tendency) of a Tieck, perhaps, or

10. For instance, his Letter on Adam as the matrix lodge of the human race; his other on fame, etc.

a Kerner, Kanne, Arnim, Görres, Brentano, Weisser, Bernhardi, Fr. Horn, St. Schütze, E. Wagner, etc. The false mocker — being a self-parody of his parody — repels us far more with his claims to superiority than the false sentimentalist with his modest claims to sensibility. — *Sterne*, on first being disembarked in Germany, formed and drew after him a long and vapid comet's tail of then so-called (nowadays no-called) humorists who were but babblers of jolly complacency; although I accord them the name of humorist in the comical sense as happily as the Galenists in the medical sense, who dubbed all their diseases vapors (humors). Even Wieland, albeit a true humorist in his poem, strayed in his novels and especially in his footnote prose around his Danischmend and Amadis far into the Galen academy of humorists.

All sorts of phenomena are attached to the humoristic totality. It may for instance express itself in the Sternean construction of periods, which connects not parts but entireties by means of dashes; also by generalizing that which is valid in the particular; viz, in Sterne: "Great men do not write their treatises upon long noses for nothing." — A further outward appearance is that the common critic materializes and suffocates the true universal humorous spirit by hauling it in and imprisoning it in partisan satires — and furthermore, this: that aforesaid insignificant fellow, because he is not equipped with the comic's rebuttal, viz, the world-disdaining idea, is bound to find the former baseless, nay childish and pointless, not laughing but laughable; in his heart of hearts he must with conviction and in more than one regard value the sham whimsicality of a Müller from Itzehoe above the Shandyan humor. Lichtenberg, although Müller's eulogist, who deserved it however with his Siegfried von Lindenberg, especially in its first edition, and too fulsome a funeral orator of the waggish wills-o'-the wisp in Berlin at the time, and somewhat constrained by British and mathematical one-sidedness, did all the same with his humoristic talents rank more highly than he himself may have realized and might, with his astronomical view of the world's hustle and bustle and his witty overabundance, have shown the world something loftier than two wings in the ether, which flutter indeed but whose feathers are gummed together.

Moreover, totality explains humorous tolerance and forbearance vis-à-vis individual follies, for en masse they signify less and do less damage and also because the humorist cannot deny being close kin to mankind; whereas the common satirist, who discerns and depicts, whether in learned or vulgar form, nothing but singular and alien Abderitian capers in the narrow and selfish belief that he himself is different — a hippocentaur among onocentaurs — preaches his capuchin sermon on folly and fulminates from his high horse all the more furiously as matins- and vespers-preacher in our earthly madhouse. Oh how modest the man who merely laughs at it all, himself and the hippocentaur included!

But how to distinguish in this general mockery between the humorist, warming the cockles of our hearts, and the mocker, who chills them, when both of them ridicule everything? Shall the sensitive humorist be neighbor to the old persifleur, who merely parades the inverted deficit of the sentiment? — Impossible, rather do those two differ from each other as Voltaire differs from himself or the French, namely through the annihilating idea.

§33

THE ANNIHILATING OR INFINITE IDEA OF HUMOR

This is the second component of humor, as an inverse sublime. Just as Luther calls our will in a bad sense a lex inversa: so humor is one in the good sense; and its descent into hell paves the way for its ascent into heaven. It resembles the merops, the bird that turns its tail up to heaven, while rising in that very direction, the little juggler who sips its nectar topsy-turvy and *upwards*.

If man, like the old theology, regards our mortal world from the celestial one: it passes by in its orbit, small and vain; but if, like humor, he measures the infinite world by the humble one: then that laughter is born, which yet contains greatness and pain. Therefore, just as Greek poetry, as opposed to the present day, made serene: so humor, in contrast to the old jest, makes partly serious; it walks on the lower soccus while frequently bearing the tragic mask, at least in its hand. Therefore, not only were great humorists very serious, as we just said, but we have to thank a melancholy people for the greatest of them. The ancients enjoyed their life far too much to hold it in humoristic disdain. In the old German farces, this underlying seriousness manifests itself in the fact that the devil is usually the tomfool; and in the French ones, even the grande diablerie[11] makes its appearance, viz, a tomfool quadruple alliance of four devils. A significant thought! I can well imagine the devil being the true inverse of the divine world, the great world shadow, setting off the form of the luminous body, as the greatest humorist and "whimsical man," who as the *moresque* of a *moresque* would, however, be far too unaesthetical;

11. Flögel's History of the Comic Grotesque.

for his laugh would have too much pain in it; it would be like the gaily flowering gown of the — guillotined.

After each pathetic strain, man desires a comic relaxing; as, however, no sensation can desire its opposite but only its scaling downward: the joke sought by pathos must contain a reductive seriousness. And this is inherent in humor. Hence there is, as in Shakespeare a court jester, Madhawya in the Sakontala. Hence Socrates finds in the disposition toward the tragic in Plato's Symposion the comic as well. Hence the English offer a humorous epilogue and a comedy after a tragedy, in the Greek tradition, where *after* the threefold seriousness the tetralogy will conclude with a satire, which Schiller would start with,[12] and where the parodists raised their voice after the rhapsodes. And in French mystery plays, whenever Christ or a martyr was about to be flogged, the old tender kindheartedness would advise in brackets: "Let Harlequin here enter and speak and cheer us up a little."[13] But will anyone ever wish to hurl himself from the height of pathos into a Lucianic or even Parisian persiflage? Mercier[14] says: so that the audience should watch without laughing the nobility of a Leander it must be allowed to anticipate the jolly Paillasse with whom to ignite and release the laughing matter derived from the sublime. A subtle and true remark; but what a twofold abasement of both the sublime and the humor if the latter strains and the former relaxes. A heroic epos is easy to parody and to topple into its counterpart — ; but woe betide tragedy if it does not continue to work even through parody! One can travesty Homer but never Shakespeare; for while the trivial does with annihilatory force oppose the sublime, it does not so oppose the pathetic. When Kotzebue suggests that Benda's music to Gotter's serious Ariadne on Naxos should accompany his own travesty, exalting his jest with solemnity: he forgets that here the music, armed at once with the forces of sublimity and pathos, will conquer, not serve, and as a serious goddess, topple the blithe Ariadne more than once and from a height even greater than Naxos. All the more loftiness arises from undefiled lowliness, as for instance in Thümmel's "common tragedy or paradise lost,"[15] where everybody senses truth and untruth equally forcefully, the divine and the human nature of man.

12. Wrongly, for the comical does no more prepare us for the pathetic than the relief for the strain to come, but vice versa.

13. Flögel's History of the Comic Grotesque.

14. Tableau de Paris, ch. 648.

15. S. Vol. 5 of his Travels.

In the heading of this §, I called the idea annihilating. This is evident everywhere. As reason generally dazzles the intellect, strikes and transports it by force (with the idea of an infinite godhead for instance), as a god does a mortal: likewise humor, which, unlike persiflage, turns its back on reason and falls down in worship of the idea. That is why humor oftentimes revels in its own contradictions and impossibilities, for example in Tieck's Zerbino, where the characters take themselves in the end to be nothing but figures on paper and nonsense, hauling the readers on stage and the stage itself under the impress.[16] Hence humor's predilection for the most vacuous ending, while seriousness concludes epigrammatically with the most weighty, for instance the end of the prologue to Möser's defended harlequin or the pitiful end of my, or Fenk's, funeral oration on an empty royal stomach. Thus *Sterne* for instance several times deliberates assiduously on certain occurrences only finally to decide: there was not a word of truth in it anyway.

Something similar to the boldness of this annihilating humor, an expression of disdain for the world, may be discerned in certain music, like Haydn's, for instance, where whole series may be annihilated by one alien one and that rushes pell-mell between pianissimo and fortissimo, presto and andante by turns. A second similarity is the skepticism that, as understood by Platner, comes into being when the mind reviews the awful throng of belligerent beliefs by which it is surrounded; a vertigo of the soul, as it were, suddenly turning *our* rapid motion into the *alien* one of the whole static world.

And a third similarity are the humorous Feasts of Fools of the Middle Ages, which with an untrammeled hysteron proteron, with an inner spiritual masquerade, but without any impure intention, turn topsy-turvy the worldly and spiritual, caste and custom, in the great liberty and equality of Joy. But for such a vigorous humor our taste is not so much too delicate as our disposition is too poor.

§34
HUMORISTIC SUBJECTIVITY

Comic Romanticism, no less than serious, is — by contrast with classical objectivity — the sovereign of subjectivity. For if the comic consists of the interchange of subjective and objective maxims, I cannot, since according to the above, the objective maxim must be a wished-for infin-

---

16. This he did following in the footsteps of Holberg, Foote, Swift, etc.

ity, think and posit this *outside* myself, but only within myself, where I base it upon the subjective. Consequently, I myself put myself into this quandary — albeit not externally, as happens in comedy — dividing myself into finite and infinite factors and letting the latter derive from the former. This is when man will laugh and cry: "Impossible! This is too crazy by half!" To be sure! That is why Self plays first fiddle with every humorist; if at all possible, he will put even his personal circumstances on his comic stage if only to annihilate them poetically. He being his own court jester and Commedia dell'arte quartet as well as the regent and régisseur to go with it: the reader is asked to contribute a measure of goodwill, or at the least no ill will, toward the writing self and not to make his semblance reality; it would have to be the best reader of the best author who could fully relish a satire on himself. There must be as much welcoming openness toward an author, all the more toward the comic author, as warlike reticence toward the philosopher, to the advantage of both. Even in real life, ill will with its spider's web denies entry to the airy jest as it wings its way; but the poetic humorist stands in much greater need of an open and amicable reception, for he will not be able in the adopted caricature of his art to ply his character cheerfully if it should be weighed down and redoubled by an alien, prosaically antagonistic one. When Swift pretends to be sly and pompous, or Musäus stupid: how can they make any comic impact on him who comes ill-disposed and believing their semblance? — As indulgent goodwill toward the comic author can only be gained through a certain intimacy, which is needed for reconciliation with him, the ever-novel portrayer of ever-novel idiosyncracies, in quite a different way to the case of the serious poet of age-old sensations and beauties; the riddle is easily answered why those superior comical works, still laughed at by later centuries, were received with reluctance by their own age and with stolid faces, while vulgar jest sheets fluttered from hand to hand and from mouth to ear. A Cervantes, for instance, had to attack and denigrate his own Don Quixote in the initial doldrums, so that the crowd should rate it more highly, writing a hostile review called: "el buscapiè," or the rocket, lest he himself should scatter into the sky. Aristophanes was robbed of his laurels for his two greatest plays, *The Frogs* and *The Clouds*, by a long since forgotten Amipsias, who had metaphorical frog- and cloud-choruses at his command. And the reception originally accorded Sterne's *Tristram* in England was as chill as if it had been written for Germans in Germany. And somebody in the German Merkur, which is apt to let pass, nay to lend wings to, anything vigorous, pronounces the following verdict on Volume 1 of Musäus' Physiognomical Journeys:[17] "The manner of writing is à la Schubart and supposed to be droll. One finds it impossible to, etc., and so on and so forth." Wretch, thou, who canst enrage me still in a second edition after so many years as, alas, I preserved thy stupid remark word for word in an excerpt for the benefit of aesthetics. And did not this wretch's twin brother graze at his side in the Universal German Library,[18] matching him fang for fang and weeding the flowers in the beds of Musäus, of the very man with that true German humor, the domestic pater-familiarity that can smile at itself and through whose amicability even the alien admixture of the outpourings of the heart as a comic element is edulcorated? — Further exempla sunt odiosa.

We return to humorous subjectivity. Our distaste for the pseudohumorist is so great precisely because he attempted to *appear* to parody a character who he already is in reality. Therefore, unless an author's own noble character is in command, there is nothing more awkward than having the fool himself in charge of the comic confession, where (as in LeSage's mostly vulgar Gilblas) a common soul, whether confessant or father confessor, in willful vacillation between self-knowledge and delusion, between remorse and insolence, between undecided laughter and seriousness, will put us, too, in that in-between state; and Pigault le Brun in his Knight Mendoza turns even more repulsive with his self-complacent coquetry and his barren and bare unbelief, while even in Crebillon's lye something more than his fools is reflected. How Shakespeare's noble spirit towers when he employs the comical Falstaff as a second assessor of his wild life of sin! How immorality here blends with extravagant folly as nothing but weakness and habit! —

Equally reprehensible is Erasmus's self-reviewer, Folly, first, as it is an empty and abstract self, i.e., a nonself, and again because instead of lyrical humor or severe irony, Folly only recites collegians' notebooks of Wisdom, who screeches even more stridently from its prompter's box than Columbine herself.

Because in humor the self steps forth parodically: several Germans decided to dispense with the grammatical one twenty-five years ago in order to emphasize it linguistically by ellipsis. A superior author went on to cancel it in a parody of this parody, underlining the deletions with

17. Merkur 1779, V. I, p. 275.
18. At a later stage, Musäus had the humility to drive his gold ore into the lead mine of the Univ. German Lib. by presenting it with novel reviews; it is a pity, however, that these comic reviews are now allowed to follow their books and their library into oblivion, rather than picking these pearls from the jumble and threading them.

thick strokes, viz, the delicious Musäus in his physiognomical journeys, those veritable pittoresque pleasure trips of Comus and reader alike. In no time at all, these felled selfs arose from the dead en masse in the Fichtean aseity, selfery, and self-vocality. — But where does this grammatical suicide of the self in German originate, as neither related modern nor ancient languages know it? Probably because we, like Persians and Turks,[19] are much too polite to have an *I* vis-à-vis people of standing. For a German is happily anything but *he* himself. While a Briton will spell his *I* with a capital letter in midsentence, many Germans when writing letters still spell theirs in the lower case even at the beginning, longing in vain for a tiny italic *i*, which would hardly be visible and more like the mathematical dot than the line underneath. And whereas the former goes on to add the self to the My, etc., as the Frenchman the même to the moi: the German will rarely say I myself but rather "I for my part" in the hope that no one will think him bumptious for that. In bygone days, he never referred to himself from navel down without begging forgiveness for existing at all, thus ever bearing his courteous, table- and conventmannerly top half upon a pitiful bottom half reduced to the bourgeois estate as on an organized pillory. And if he does apply his I: he will do it provided it can be conjoined with a lesser one, the Latin school headmaster will address his disciple as *we* in all modesty. The German alone, ever avoiding an I — presupposed by a *ye* or *thou*, possesses the *He* and the *They* as a vocative. — There must have been epochs when not a single epistle containing an *I* would be posted in all of Germany.

§35

HUMORISTIC SENSUOUSNESS

As there is nothing comic at all without sensuousness: it, as exponent of applied finiteness, cannot be gaudy enough in humor. The prodigal presentation through images and contrasts of wit and imagination alike, i.e., through groupings and colorings, should charge the soul through sensuousness and fire it with that dithyrambic song[20] that holds up the world of the senses, distorted and angular in its concave mirror, to face the idea. Insofar as such a Doomsday plunges the world of the senses into a second chaos — merely in order to sit in divine judgment —, while the

19. The Persians maintain: only God can have a self; the Turks: only the Devil, says I. Bibliothèque des Philosophes; par Gautier.

20. The deeper into Tristram the more humoristic lyrical Sterne becomes. Thus his magnificent journey in Volume 7; the humoristic dithyrambic song in Volume 8, c. 11, 12 etc.

intellect can only dwell in an orderly universe, although reason, like God, is not even contained in the amplest temple — : insofar humor might seem to border on madness, which takes leave of its senses naturally, as the philosopher artificially, but like the latter, keeping its reason; humor is, as the ancients dubbed Diogenes, a raving Socrates. —

Let us analyze the metaphoric sensuous style of humor a little further. First, it individualizes down to the smallest particle and the parts of the individualized. Shakespeare is never more individual, viz, more sensuous, than in the comical. And for precisely the same reason, Aristophanes is more of both than any ancient.

While, as we demonstrated above, seriousness ever gives prominence to the universal, spiritualizing our heart, for example, to the point that an anatomical heart reminds us more of the poetical heart than the poetical of the anatomical: the comic for his part affixes us closely to the sensuously defined and he does not, for example, go down on his knees but on both kneecaps, or he even exercises his hams. — Should he or I wish to say: "man's thinking is quite enlightened of late rather than stupid, but his loving is poor": he must translate man into the life of the senses to start with — viz, into a European — and even more strictly, one of the nineteenth century — and confine him once more to a land and a town. — After that, he has to look for a street in Berlin or Paris as the man's habitat. And it behooves him or me to quicken the second phrase organically as well, most expeditiously by way of allegory, until he is in the happy position to speak of someone from Friedrichstadt writing poetry in a diver's bell by candlelight and without a chamber- or bell-mate in the cold sea, connected with life on board ship by nothing but the extended air pipe of his own windpipe. "And thus," the comic may finish, "the man from Friedrichstadt enlightens only himself and his paper, disdaining the monsters and fishes around him." And that is the same as the sentence above.

One might pursue this comical individuation into trivial details. Such as: the English are fond of the hangman and being hanged; we of the devil but as the hangman's intensification, for instance to go hang, more strongly: to go to the devil; likewise, hang it all and the devil take it. One might perhaps write to one's equal: the devil take him, but to a superior this ought to be toned down to the hangman. With the French, devil and dog rate more highly. Le chien d'esprit que j'ai, writes the splendid Sevigné (of all the French, surely the grandame of Sterne, as Rabelais was his grandsire) and loves very much, like all French women, using the same animal. Similar sensuous details are: the choice of verbs of motion at every turn, in plain and in figurative presentation — as Sterne and others assign a short physical one to precede or follow every other, even an inner, action — always to state a definite quantity of money, number, or size, where one would otherwise expect only the general; for instance: "a chapter as long as my arm," or "not worthy a carved farthing," etc. So this comical sensuousness is heightened by the condensing monosyllabism of the English language; when Sterne says for example (Tristr. Vol. XI. ch. X.): that no sooner had a French postillion mounted than he has to alight again because there is forever something amiss with the chaise, "a tag, a rag, a jag, a strap," syllables not as readily translatable into German, especially with their assonance, as the Horatian: riduculus mus. Assonances feature not only with Sterne (for instance ch. XXXI. "all the frusts, crusts, and rusts of antiquity") in the heart of the comic, but also with Rabelais, Fischart, and others, as next-door rhymes, as it were.

Here belong names and made-up worlds, too, for the comic writer. No German can be more saddened by the lack of *one* national and capital city than the one who laughs because it frustrates his individualizing. Bedlam, Grubstreet, etc., are common currency in Great Britain and overseas; but we Germans must content ourselves with a general madhouse and hackstreet, because through the lack of a national city, the names in the different towns are either too little known or of too little interest. — So an individualizing humorist benefits from Leipzig's possessing a university notice board, an Auerbach's cellar, and its Leipzig larks and fairs,[21] all of them well enough known abroad to be used with profit; the same, however, would be desirable for several other matters or cities.

21. One ought, therefore, to make as many named details *of every* German city as possible a matter of common knowledge (as has come to pass with these four), for no other reason than to put a dictionary and land register of comical individuation into the humorist's hand eventually. Such a Swabian league of Towns would soon allow the separate towns to unite to streets, nay, to the boards of a comic National Theater — the comic would find it more easy to limn and the reader to learn. Luckily, Linden — Tiergarten — Charité — Wilhelmshöhe — Prater — and the Brühl Terrace offer fertile soil to any comically individualizing poet; should the present author, however, endeavor for purposes of comic individuation to make use of the names of the foremost, because best-known and -named squares and affairs of the few towns of his own residence, like Hof, Leipzig, Weimar, Meinungen, Koburg, and Baireuth: he should meet with little understanding and less appreciation anywhere else.

The Twelfth Program. On the Novel

§69

ON ITS POETICAL VALUE

The novel loses vastly in purity of formation through the breadth of its form, which may have almost all other forms rattling around within it. It is epic in origin; but occasionally it is the protagonist instead of the author who is the narrator and once in a while its whole cast. The epistolary novel, consisting of nothing but lengthy monologues or lengthy dialogues, verges on the dramatic form, or even the lyric as in the Sorrows of Werther. Sometimes, as in the Ghostseer for example, the action moves with the cramped limbs of drama, while now and again it frolics and skips all over the world, like the fairytale. — Also, the liberty of its prose has a detrimental influence in that its ease exempts the author from the initial effort and deflects the reader from incisive perusal. And even its spread — for the novel surpasses all works of art in sheer paper size — serves to worsen its case; a connoisseur may well study and scrutinize a 12-quire drama, but who would tackle a work of over two hundred? Aristotle decrees that an epopee must be capable of being read in one day; Richardson, as well as our dear writer, comply with this commandment even in their novels and restrict themselves to one day's reading, albeit, being topographically a little bit more to the north than Aristotle, to a day more common at the pole and of 90¼ nights' duration. — But the difficulty of having *one* fire, *one* spirit, *one* attitude of the whole, and of *one* hero extending over ten volumes and the way one decent work needs to be forced, not by the narrow energy of a hothouse pot, which may well bring forth an ode,[22] but with the all-encompassing scorching heat and atmosphere of a complete climate, that is never fully appreciated by the art critics, as not even the artists gauge it correctly; but they start well, continue anyhow, and in the end come to grief miserably.

. . . .

The most indispensable in the novel, into whatever shape it is otherwise beaten or cast, is the romantic. But up to the present, stylists demanded not the novel's romantic spirit but rather its exorcism; the novel was meant to restrain and resist what little glimmer of the romantic might still be alive in reality. As an unversified didactic poem, their novel became a fat vademecum for theologians, philosophers, and materfami-

---

22. It can be produced in *one* day, whereas Clarissa can — irrespective of its mistakes — come into being not even in *one* year. Whereas the ode mirrors *one* world- and spirit-aspect, the proper novel mirrors every aspect.

lias. The spirit became an agreeable habiliment of the body. Just as in the Jesuits' school plays students used to disguise themselves and stand for verbs and their flexions, for vocatives, datives, etc.: thus human characters represented paragraphs, moral applications, and exegetical pointers, words in season, and heterodox extracurricular tutelage; the poet gave the reader, as Basedow did the children, baked letters to eat.

To be sure, poetry, and therefore the novel, does and should instruct us, but only as a flower in bloom will tell us the time of day and the weather through its petals' unfolding and closing and even its perfume; but may its tender sprig never be cut, joggled, and carpentered into a wooden lectern or pulpit; neither the wooden surround nor the person surrounded can take the place of the living fragrance of spring. — And besides, what does giving lessons mean? Giving mere signs. But the whole world and all of time are full of signs; it is the deciphering of these letters that is missing; we need a dictionary and a grammar book of signs. Poetry teaches us how to read, whereas the mere teacher belongs with the ciphers rather than the deciphering clerks.

A man delivering a judgment on the world gives us his own world, diminished and piecemeal, instead of the living wide world, or maybe a sum, not an account. And for this very reason, poetry is so indispensable, for it imparts to the spirit the world reborn in the spirit, imposing no chance conclusion. In the poet, man merely speaks to mankind, not this man to that.

§72

THE POETIC SPIRIT IN THE THREE SCHOOLS OF NOVELISTIC MATERIAL – THE ITALIAN, THE GERMAN, AND THE DUTCH

Every novel must accommodate a universal spirit, which, without hampering the free flow of movement, like a God vis-à-vis free mankind, will stealthily draw the historical whole together and toward a *single* goal, just as according to Boyle every true structure must respond in a particular tone; a merely historical novel is only a story. In Wilhelm Meister, this life- and flower-spirit (spiritus rector) is its Grecian soul meter, i.e., reason's measure and music of life.[23] — In Woldemar and Allwil, it is the giants' war against a heaven of love and justice — in Klinger's novels, a

---

23. After each divine banquet and between the delicate fiery wines a rare ice is circulated in these novels. At any rate, the caves of this Vesuvius will provide our presently burning Italy with all the snow it is going to need.

somewhat unpoetical gremlin and poltergeist, who, far from reconciling reality and ideal, sets them at loggerheads — in Hesperus the idealization of reality — in Titan the spirit appears in curlicues on the title page and through four volumes of the complete war of the titans, but, as is the habit of spirits, it refuses to show itself to the crowd in the marketplace. Should a novel's spirit be an animal soul, a gnome, a tormenting imp: the whole structure will sink to the ground, lifeless or brute.

The same romantic spirit now finds itself faced with three very different bodies, which it has to ensoul; whence a tripartite classification of novels according to subject matter is needed. — The first class consists of the novels of the *Italian School*. (May the lack of an actual art vocabulary pardon the use of an allusive one.) In these the characters and their circumstances coincide with the tone and the eminence of the author. What he depicts and gives voice to does not differ from his own inner being; for can he rise above his eminence, magnify his own greatest? — Some examples of this category will explain what is to come: Werther, the Ghostseer, Woldemar, Ardinghello, the New Heloise, Klinger's novels, Donamar, Agnes von Lilien, Chateaubriand's novels, Valerie, Agathon, Titan etc.; all of them novels belonging to *one* class, albeit of widely diverging worth; for class does not render classical. In these novels, the superior tone demands and selects an elevation above the lower levels of life — the greater liberty and universality of the higher orders — less individualization — more undefined or Italian or ideal natural or historical landscapes — lofty ladies — high passions, etc.

The second category, novels of the *German* School, makes the effusion of the romantic holy ghost more difficult than even the lower, the third. This is where belong — in order to pave the way for my explanations by illustration — for example Hippel, Fielding, Musäus, Hermes, Sterne, Goethe's Meister in parts, Wakefield, Engel's Stark, Lafontaine's Force of Love, Siebenkäs, and particularly the Fledgling Years, etc. Nothing is harder to raise and retain aloft by rare romantic ether than those weighty notabilities. —

I would like to add the third category, the novels of the *Dutch* School forthwith, that I might illuminate them against each other; that is where Smollett's novels partly belong — Siegfried von Lindenberg — Sterne in the person of Corporal Trim — Wutz, Fixlein, Fibel — etc.

Depth as the reversal of height (altitudo) is likewise useful and viable to the wings of the poet; only the middle, the plain, is not, demanding as it does feet and wings at once. Just as capital city and village, or king and peasant lend themselves much more readily to romantic description than does the worthy burgher or the market town in the middle, or as tragedy and comedy can more easily speak with one voice in their contrasting directions than Diderot's and Iffland's in-between plays. For the novel of the German School or the one of the worthies, in particular that written and read by their ilk, presents the great obstacle that the poet, pursuing perchance the self-same path through life as the protagonist and fettered by all its minor entanglements, might limn the hero neither upward nor downward nor with the foils of contrast and yet must bathe the humdrum bourgeois existence in the afterglow of a romantic heaven and lend it radiant color. The hero in the novel of the German School, in the center as it were, mediator between two estates, between their positions, languages, and events, and assuming as a character neither the sublimity of the Italian form nor the depth, comic or grave, of the Dutch, a protagonist of that kind is bound to increase for the poet the cost of being romantic, nay, to put it beyond his means in two directions. — Let him who will not admit this put his own pen to paper and carry on with the Fledgling Years.

§73
THE IDYLL

This is not a lateral shoot, albeit a lateral blossom, of the three branches of the novel; hence no definition is more vacuous than that it represents the lost golden age of mankind.

For the following has not been sufficiently considered: if poetry, through its ethereal echo, transforms *suffering's* discordant note into euphony: why should it not, through the same ethereal resonance, lend more tenderness and sublimity to the music of *happiness?* — It does so, indeed, although not attracting enough attention or praise for it. It is a sweet, nameless sensation with which we receive and share the promised enjoyment and the hero's increasing happiness in epic representations. Pray, gentle reader, allow the appearances of delight in familiar poetical works to fly past with their springtimes, their sunrises, seas of flowers and hearts filled with love and pleasure and, remembering these heavens of art, recall the natural skies of childhood. For it is not true that children are most deeply affected by passion stories — which, in any case, are not to be used but as backdrops and foils for courage, virtue, and happiness; but the ascension into heaven of a downtrodden life, the gradual but abundant blossoming forth from the pauper's grave, the exchange of the steps to the scaffold for the steps to the throne, and the like, those are the scenes that enchant and transport the child to romantic realms, where wishes are granted and hearts are neither exhausted nor broken. And for this reason, too, children love fairytales spreading boundless fortuitous heavens before them and leaving aside the equally boundless available hells. – But let us return to writing pleasure! To be sure, the depiction of happiness easily tires the eye but only because it soon ceases to grow. Pains presented in poetry, on the other hand, entertain us at length, since the poet, like fate unfortunately, can intensify them indefinitely; joy does not possess many gradations, only pain has so many; a long, hard, ladder of thorns finally leads across softer spines to a few roses on top of the rose tree, and in great happiness Nemesis is far more ready to vouchsafe us a vivid and close look at misfortune to come in her mirrors than to allow us a glimpse of future happiness in times of great misfortune.

. . . .

A pleasure play, on the other hand? – We can at least boast of a small epic genre here, namely the idyll. For this is the epic representation of *complete happiness* in *limitation*. The more sublime rapture belongs to Lyra and romanticism; otherwise, Dante's heaven and Klopstock's interspersed heavens would also have to be counted among the idylls. The limitation within the idyll may refer to that of possessions, or of insights, or of rank, or to all of those at once. But as it was linked more with pastoral life by mistake: it was installed through a second mistake in the Golden Age of Mankind, as if that age could move only in an immobile cradle and not equally well in a Phaeton's chariot in full flight. Where is the proof, though, that the first, the golden age of mankind, might not be the richest, the freest, the brightest age?

At least not in the Bible, nor through the assertion of some philosophers that the flowering peak of our combined education should be the repeat of the golden age, and that the nations after due fulfilment of the knowledge and life should regain paradise complete with the two trees of that name. – Pastoral life in itself has in any case little more to offer, apart from quiet and boredom, than the life of the gooseherd, and Saturn's blissful globe is no sheep pen, and its heavenly bed and celestial chariot no shepherd's barrow. Theocritus and Voß – the idyll's heavenly twins – granted the lower orders free access to their Arcadias, the former even to cyclopses, and the latter to worthy burghers, for instance in his Luise and elsewhere. Goethe's Hermann and Dorothea is not an epos but an epic idyll. The Vicar of Wakefield is an idyll until urban misfortune raises the pitch of the *unisonorous* strings of the domestic aeolian harp, producing polyphonic discords and tearing the beginning apart through its end.

Our dear writer's Schoolmasterkin Wutz is an idyll, which I would rate more highly than other art critics, relationships with the author permitting; and the same goes undeniably for the man's Fixlein and Fibel. — Even Robinson Crusoe's life and that of Jean Jacques on his St. Peter's Isle revive us with idyll-fragrance and -sweetness. The slow pace of a carter on a fine day and a good road with his delicious repasts may be raised to an idyll and — although that would be gilding the lily — the bride he wins at the inn. Likewise, a humble schoolman's vacation for instance — or the artisan's lazy Monday — the christening of a firstborn child — nay, the first day on which a royal bride, pursued to the point of exhaustion by court festivities, drives alone with her prince (the train will follow much later) toward a rich resplendent hermitage — in a word, all of those days can become idylls and can sing: we, too, were in Arcadia. —

And why should the River Rhine not be a Hippocrene, a four-branched River of Paradise of the Idylls and, what is more, offer river and riverside at the same time! On its waters it carries youth and future, and on its banks a noble past. Works, which grew on its banks, like its wines, reveal and broadcast idyll delights, and I need hardly evoke the painter Müller here, although perhaps I should mention the undeservedly forgotten novels of a *Frohreich*, so full of Rhenish joyfulness, his Soapboiler and others, for instance.

But what is it, ye ask, that, with such moderate outlay of mind and heart on the part of the actors, moves us so joyfully in the idylls of Theocritus and Voß, and that sways us although it may not transport us? The latter image of the physical swing almost contains the answer; for upon it ye are gently rocked — rising and falling effortlessly — exchanging the air in front for the air behind without any buffet. Thus your happiness with a happy man in a pastoral poem. It is without selfishness, without wishes, and without buffet, for the innocent sensuous circlet of happiness of the shepherd's ye will encircle concentrically with your own superior happiness circle. Nay, ye now lend the idyllically painted complete happiness, which ever reflects your own earlier childish or otherwise sensuously restricted one, at once the magic of your memory and your loftier poetic vantage; the tender apple blossom and the firm apple, otherwise crowned by a withered black remnant of blossom, meet and embellish each other wondrously.

If the idyll presents complete happiness in limitation: two things must follow. First, passion, insofar as it brings angry storm clouds in its wake, is not permitted to invade these tranquil skies with its thunderbolts; a few balmy rain cloudlets may be allowed if we can see broad and bright sunshine around them on hillsides and dales. Therefore, Geßner's Death of Abel is not an idyll.

Second — arising from the aforesaid — the idyll must not be written by Geßner, let alone by Frenchmen, but by Theocritus, Voß, or perhaps by Kleist, and it follows, by Virgil.

For its limitation in complete happiness, the idyll demands the brightest indigenous colors, not only for landscape but also for situation, estate, and character, and it rejects Geßner's hazy and vague banalities where at best a sheep or a ram may emerge from his watercolors while man remains blurred. This severe verdict must not be laid at good August Schlegel's door — who often postdates the harsh judgments, like this one, of others, and shoulders himself the accusations of harshness — but at Herder's, who in his *Fragments on Literature*[24] fifty years ago placed the then ruling and laurel-wreathed Geßner far below Theocritus, whose every word is naive, characteristic, colorful, firm, and true. What delicious natural colors might not Geßner have drawn from his alps — from the cowherds' huts — from the alpine horns — and from the valleys! There is more living Swiss idyll in Goethe's Jeri and Bäteli than in half of Geßner. That is why the French found the latter so palatable and translated him as wholesome fresh cowherds' milk sugar to go with Fontenelle's idyllic superfin. It never bodes well if a German is translated effortlessly into French; hence this, too, among other things is to be valued in Lessing, Herder, Goethe, etc., that someone who does not know German will not know them at all.

By the by, just as its locale is immaterial to the idyll — be it alp, pasture, Otaheiti, parsonage parlor, or fishing smack — because the idyll is a cerulean sky, and the same sky unfolds over the mountain peak and the garden bed, over the Swedish winter's night and the Italian summer's night — : so the choice of the actors' estate is free as long as it does not infringe the condition of complete happiness in "limitation." Consequently, the codicil in its definitions that it ought to cultivate its flowers outside of bourgeois society is useless or wrong. Is a petty society, then, of shepherds, huntsmen, or fishermen not a bourgeois one? or even the one in Voß's idylls? At most, one can understand that the idyll as a complete happiness in limitation must dispense with the multitude of participants and the power of the big wheels of state; and that an enclosed

24. Herder's Works on Belles Lettres etc. Part II pp. 127–42.

garden life is the only suitable life for the idyll-blessed, who have stolen a page from the Book of the Blessed for themselves; for those merry Lilliputians for whom a flower bed is a forest and who lean a ladder against a dwarf tree at harvest time.

Levana; or, Doctrine of Education

LIKE *PRESCHOOL OF AESTHETICS, LEVANA* (*W* 9.557f., 577ff.; 10.821ff., 869ff.) is discursive and unsystematic, which, even more obviously in this case, is essential to Jean Paul's system. One moment he is talking about air and exercise, about the proper clothes to wear (if any), and proper nourishment (including beer), the next about God (defined as: "an inexpressible sigh in the depths of the soul," preechoing the so often misquoted passage in Marx) and churchgoing (preferably a rare event), about sex education (tell them when and what they want to know), or storytelling (it is the story that matters; do not lead off with a moral, like Charles XII of Sweden, who always opened with the king and kept losing at chess). *Levana* is, of course, very high-minded, but Jean Paul never forgets the grim realities, here of the profession of schoolmaster, whether as tormentor or as martyr. So there is the typically bizarre statistical research on the life of one Johann Jakob Häuberle, who in fifty-one years and seven months of teaching administered 20,989 blows on the hand, 10,235 slaps in the face, and 7,905 boxes on the ear. Most teachers, Jean Paul concludes, should be called the Mild, as Cäsarius was because he never ordered more than thirty-six lashes for nuns. Equally,

he reports on the miserable working conditions of the village schoolmasters, worst of all, he suggests, in the district of Bayreuth, with their
"four-kreuzer salary and *solatium*." Fortunately for the state, schoolmasters were drawn from the ranks of Lutheran divines, who held onto the
Catholic vow of poverty. "In short, they have little; all the more can be
taken off them once they are given positions in schools" (*W* 9.578, 584;
10.810, 869ff.).

Based on a fund of experience and observation, his views are strikingly modern and liberal. His concern is for the child's self-confidence.
By all means say, "You told a lie or you did something bad"; but never
say, "You are a liar," or "You are bad." The basic principle of *Levana* is,
the more freedom education allows, the truer the child will be (*W* 9.629;
10.793). Indeed, not always to be educating is one of his main counsels;
a watch is stopped for as long as one keeps winding it. On principle, he
has little use for precepts and none for *edicta perpetua* (*W* 9.619, 622).

A remark in a letter to Emanuel Osmund suggests (although it is not
clear to what exactly he refers) that he found something sickly in Pestalozzi's "pulpit-effusions." Obedience for its own sake is worthless, and
education should never operate through fear, least of all through a God
of fear. Artemidor, the grammarian, forgot everything whenever he got
a fright (*W* 9.585, 624; 10.854; *H-KA* 3.6.46). Much of *Levana* is like an
early Dr. Spock, telling parents to leave well enough alone, or not to
worry. On the one hand, the smallest grief of the child should be respected and should never be the object of mockery; on the other hand,
one should not worry about the moods of children, which change as
swiftly as Rubens could change a smiling child into a weeping one with
a stroke of the brush. Jean Paul sensibly suggests avoiding confrontation.
Do not say no straightaway; say, "Ask me again in five minutes" (*W* 9.623,
639f.).

On the question of women's liberation, he was far ahead of his time.
He was as domestically minded as Luther himself and hardly likely to
neglect motherhood and wifehood. "But before and after one is a mother,
one is a person; the destiny of motherhood should never, and still less
the destiny of marriage, outweigh or substitute for the destiny of humanity, of which they are means, not ends." Equally striking and perhaps
even farther ahead of his age is the emphasis he placed on animal pro-
tection and the reverence for all life: give the child the heart of a Hindoo,
not the heart of a Cartesian philosopher (*W* 10.694, 800f.). *Levana* is a
work of belief in progress. Just as in his time negro slavery was being

abolished, one day man would shake off his stupid anthropos egoism and wake up to the rights of the rest of nature.

Fragment Number Two
Chapter I

§22

Many parents raise their children for their own convenience, namely to become fine standing-still machines, alarm clocks of the soul, whose bells and clockworks are never set nor wound while peace and quiet are required. At any minute the child should be nothing but that on which the tutor can sleep most softly or drum most loudly, sparing him, who has better things to do and enjoy, the need to educate, while providing him with the fruits of education. Hence these secret idlers are so often irritated if the child is not in advance more clever, more logical, and more compliant than themselves. Even energetic pedophiles, like statesmen, frequently behave like inflammable air, which, shining itself, quenches all other lights; at least they expect the child to be, like a minister's pet disciple, one minute nothing but copying hand, the next an anticipating brain.

Closely related to those instructors who would like nothing better than to be engineers are the educators for the external and state convenience; a precept that in its pure application would produce disciples and sucklings and nothing else, all obedient, boneless, well drilled, and all abiding — and there would be no solid hard human core inside the soft sweetish flesh of the fruit — and the childish lump of mortal clay to be inspired by the divine breath of a growing life should remain nothing more than a suppressed and manured receptacle — the edifice of the state should be inhabited by lifeless spinning machines, calculators, sucking- and forcing-pumps, oil mills and models of oil mills and sucking-pumps and spinning-machines etc. Instead of each child being born without past or future but starting out in year one and bringing along an inaugural New Year, instead of this generation, which would rejuvenate it in spirit as well as in body, the state has one made to order, which will clog its wheels and turn them to stone in its icy grip.

All the same, the man precedes the citizen, and our future, succeeding the world and dwelling in us, is greater than either; by what means have parents, who from the start have dressed and straitlaced the human being within the child as a lackey, i.e., as customs official, steward, or lawyer-designate, gained the right to propagate themselves other than physically, instead of begetting spiritual embryos? Can the care of the body entitle one to pinch the spirit, and can a soul be sold for a life of comfort while a body can never match or even approximate the price of a mind? The Teutonic and Spartan custom of doing away with their weak-bodied children is hardly more ruthless than that of raising up weak-minded children.

Fragment Number Six
Chapter IV

§129

Some would even advise that the child must be taught that it is shameful to look at itself; itself? Goodness, they would have to be vile notions, indeed, with which a young body must contemplate itself only to blush at its own sight — it would be a different matter in front of others — blushing for that which is inalterable and involuntary, which is to say, for their Creator! — In later years, too, boys among their own company, or girls among themselves, are almost without shame; only before the others are the sexes ashamed, or before adults even of the same sex. But this gives rise for the stage of mind of those 12th or 15th years of age full of revolution and evolution to the rule: mix the sexes to cancel them out; for two boys will shield and safeguard twelve girls, and two girls, twelve boys, quite adequately against any innuendos, remarks, and improprieties by this precursory dawn of the burgeoning drive, the blush. — A school of girls, on the other hand, altogether among themselves, or a like school of boys — there I will not vouch for anything. But boys do more damage to boys than do girls to girls; because the former are bolder, more confident, coarser, more scientific, more inquisitive concerning matters, as the latter concerning persons, etc.

Folding screens and bed screens of glass planted in front of the minds of children are tools of this false doctrine of shame, the foolish covering of the cover, the sheep's clothing of a — sheep. He who reveals that he is guarding a secret has divulged half of it; nor will he hang onto the second half for much longer. Children's questions concerning pregnancy, where a new baby comes from, are being asked not from any instinct or drive but from innocent curiosity and an inquiring mind; for the former provides the answers, not the questions. In a child the question about the mother's confinement is as far removed from the sexual drive as perhaps the question why the sun, which sets in the West, should reappear in the East on the morrow. But let the educational mystery mongering offer just one of the unknown quantities of this rule of three, and the instinct, sniffing far-off scents, will, combined with a few chance explanations, anticipate and incorporate the obscure into its realm. To this mystery mongering also belong expressions like: this is for adults or when you are big and the whole weighty ministerial misbehavior on the distaff side in the house of a woman giving birth. Secret clauses lead to war; and the secret affiance to sin is not far removed from that kind of mystifying instruction.

But what must we tell the child who asks? — As much of the truth as it demands: "The human mite grows in its mother's womb from her flesh and blood just like the little mite in a nut; that is why she gets sick, etc. As children understand far less of what we say than we think and, just like adults, have a thousand times less curiosity as to the ultimate cause once they get hold of the antepenultimate one than some of us would credit them with, it may be as long as ten years before the child will move the question: but whence the little mite? Answer: "from the Lord God when people get married and sleep side by side." And that is about all we adult philosophers know about the whole matter; and you are fully entitled to tell the child: man may indeed be able to fashion a statue or an embroidered flower, etc., but nothing living, which grows. And thus nothing will be spoiled for the children by the spotless word sleep,[1] or interpreted of what passes all comprehension beyond what the systems of procreation have taught us so far, to which, however, a pretty sacristy was added on by the astute, profound, and versatile *Oken*.[2] I have a time-honored pillar of proof for how easy it is to deal with, restrain, and satisfy children, which at the same time is the familiar stable pillory of religious

---

1. E.g. Heidegger, Burgomaster in Zürich, on learning of the sin of sleeping with a woman, did not sleep a wink all night while lying beside his nurse as a little boy. Baur's Gallery of Historical Portraits, Volume II.

2. "The Procreation of Dr. *Oken*, 1805." The word sacristy denotes that he posits and presupposes Life as something incomprehensible in his "Protozoa of the Infusoriae'; whereby he does not, however, explain procreation of life so much as growth or survival. I also have in mind his brilliantly daring assumption that in the infusorial chaos (the only one in the universe) several lives should fuse and this unit of pluralities in turn solidify in a brighter multiple unit in more advanced grades of life. By the by, I read every word on the infusion creation with a familiar shudder as also the gradation of vivifications arising out of the great infusory of the whole earth; also, I am fully convinced that, there being no bridging of grades between mechanism and vivification, the riddle of universal animation and vivification will have to be solved some place other than in the art of analysis.

instruction: because since the 16th century, and in the course of the 17th and 18th centuries, millions of Christian men and even more women died who had from their childhood days and on each and every Sunday been told that baptism had replaced the Jewish sacrament of *circumcision* — without ever thinking on or even asking what in fact circumcision is. This is how children learn and ask. The present author received instruction on this Christian article of faith only after the age of 18 and from Jewish writings. Ye religious instructors, schoolmasters, tutors, and preachers bear ye in mind circumcision that ye might practice the Pauline one on yere own lips and on the foreskins of yere own hearts.

Army Chaplain Schmelzle's Journey to Flätz

JEAN PAUL HAD A HIGH OPINION OF *SCHMELZLE* (*W* 11.25ff.), regarding it as his most "worked-out" composition (*H-KA* 3.5.217). Not that he could ever think of one of his works as finished. He planned to continue the story with Schmelzle, after the murder of Kotzebue, fleeing in fear of the police to Bayreuth, where he would take refuge with Jean Paul. Like all of Jean Paul's works, it can be read as parody or as satire. Thus it may have been prompted by the examples of neuroses and obsessions that Jean Paul came across in his readings of the odder pietist literature (*H-KA* 1.13.vff.). Similarly, some see in it an attack on the pusillanimity of his fellow countrymen during the Napoleonic period. Maybe so; but most will read it for its universal human story and see reflected in its distorting mirror their own, or in the case of luckier ones, other people's timidity.

The parody is also self-parody, for Jean Paul, too, had a "fearful imagination." Hence his extraordinary modernity. A nice example is near the end of *Schmelzle's Journey*:

So the two of us lovingly arrived home; and after the wonderful day I might have experienced a splendid postmidnight Indian summer had not the Devil led me to Lichtenberg's Volume Nine and in particular to page 206, where it is written: "It might be possible, after all, that our chemists should happen some day on an agent for corroding our air in a flash by some kind of ferment. That way the world might end." Alas, so it verily might! The terrestrial sphere being encapsulated within the larger aerial sphere: all it needs is some chemical rascal on a faraway rascals' isle or in New Holland to discover some air corrosive resembling in its effect the spark and the powder keg: in a matter of hours that terrible global storm, roaring along, will seize myself and us all here in Flätz by the throat; no more drawing breath for me then, no more anything in that asphyxia air — Earth has become one great gallows hill full of gibbets, where even the cattle perish. — In this global fume and global agony there will no longer be any great need for worm- and bed-bug-powders, for Bradley's ant ploughs, for rat poison, wolves battues, and cattle burial funds; and the Devil has taken the lot in that Bartholomew's Night when the accursed "ferment" was haply invented.

First Stage, Attila Schmelzle's Circular Letter to His Friends

To be sure, the mail coach junket and picnic party was not totally to my taste; all of them shady and unfamiliar riffraff, fairground habitués drawn by the scent of Flätz. I am a reluctant acquaintance of the unacquainted, but my brother-in-law, the dragoon, had as usual blown the gaff and bared his heart and soul. Beside me sat a very probable harlot — On her lap a dwarf, who intended to show himself at the fair — A vermin exterminator regarded me from vis-à-vis — And down in the valley a stowaway in a scarlet coat came aboard. Apart from my brother-in-law, I did not like any of them. No one could vouch that the harlot was never going to use my acquaintance for swearing a future statement nor that the sneak thieves among the passengers were not watching my person, my idiosyncrasies, and my circumstances so as to press-gang me under torture. I am careful enough in a strange place and never look up at a prison grill for long in case some rascal inside might shout for sheer spite: "There goes Schmelzle, my brother-in-crime!" Or some fool of a myrmidon might suspect me of having a go at springing my former accomplice. And out of a similar caution I will never look back if a starling behind me calls: "Thief!" As to the dwarf himself, he was welcome to travel with us wherever he wished as far as I was concerned, but he thought to fill us with exceptional cheer by promising that his Pollux and comrade-in-arms, a giant of rare dimensions, also en route to appear at the fair, was to catch up with us with his elephant steps around midnight and either join us inside or mount up behind without fail. The two buffoons make their joint appearance at fairs as reciprocal measuring aids: the dwarf as the convex magnifier to the giant and the giant as the dwarf's concave reduction glass. No one displayed much pleasure at the prospect of the promised arrival of the dwarf's twin exhibitor apart from my brother-in-law, who sees himself as — if the pun may be permitted — made only for *striking*, just like a clock, and indeed told me once "If he were not allowed to belabor a soul now and again and to haul it over the coals up above in the Kingdom of Heaven, he would rather go down into Hell where he could at least be sure of, if anything, too much of a good thing." — As to the vermin exterminator in the conveyance, quite apart from the fact that no one is ever exactly charmed by someone who lives by poisoning like this Grim Reaper of rats and Norn of mice and, what is more, because a fellow like that will increase the kingdom of vermin the moment he is no longer allowed to decrease it, — he looked like a walking disaster in any case, with his piercing stiletto eye, for a start — also his gaunt, sharp, bony face, in conjunction with his enumeration of his outstanding assortment of poisons — and also, for I hated him ever more heatedly, his secretive silence and secret smile, as if he beheld a mouse in some hidden corner that looked like a man — verily, his maw finally seemed to me, who can stand his ground with the best, to be a grotta del cane, his cheekbones bottomless pits and cliffs, his hot breath a calcinator, and his black hairy breast an oasthouse and kiln. —

I doubt that I was far off course, either; because soon he cooly apprised the company, among whom there were a dwarf and a girl, of the fact that he had pierced, not without pleasure, ten bodies with his stiletto — had easily severed a dozen human arms, leisurely split four heads, torn out two hearts, and more in that vein — and not one of them, otherwise men of courage, had offered the least resistance. "But why?" he added venomously, lifting his hat off his ugly bald pate, "I am inviolable — anyone of this company who so wishes may set a fire on top of my head as big as they like, and I shall let it burn itself out:"

My brother-in-law, the dragoon, put a burning spill on his skull forthwith, but the exterminator bore it as if it were a cold blight, and he and the dragoon regarded each other expectantly, each smiling a foolish smile — "it only felt soothing," said he, "like an emollient cold ointment, for this was the winter side of his body, in any case." At this point, my brother-in-law felt around a bit on the bare skull with his hand and exclaimed with astonishment "it felt as cool as a kneecap." Now, after a few short advance preparations, the fellow lifted the quarter-skull off, to our horror, announcing that he had sawn it off a murderer once when his own had been inadvertently broken; and now he explained that the piercing and severing ought to be taken more as a bit of a joke, as he had only performed it in the anatomy theater as an assistant. — However, the clown was not to anyone's taste, nor did he go down well, so that I silently thought to myself as he put back on his capsule top and representative skull: this cesspit cloche may have changed place, but the poison bulb underneath is no different.

In the end I felt it was somewhat suspicious that he and the whole crew (including the stowaway) were all making for the same Flätz that I had in mind; this did not appear to me all that auspicious; indeed, I would as lief have returned as continued, but for my predilection for braving the future.

At last I am getting around to the red-coated stowaway, likely some emigré or refugié (for his German is no worse than his French), Jean Pierre by name, or Jean Paul, or something similar, or no name at all. His scarlet coat would have been all the one to me, notwithstanding its color affinity with the hangman — so aptly called *angstman* in many parts — were it not for the singular factor that he had cropped up five times in five different towns before (in the city of Berlin and the towns of Hof, Koburg, Meiningen, and Baireuth) against all probability and on each occasion regarded me meaningfully enough before going on his way. Whether this be persecution or not, I do not know; but no way can any object be pleasing to one's imagination that keeps one in sight, or in the sights of its muskets, with surveillance troops or from firing slits, moving about for years, and one can never tell where the bullet is going to come from. The red coat became even more distasteful to me when he praised his own gentle nature so obviously; this seemed almost to indicate a standing back and lull before the storm. I rejoined: "Sir, I am returning just now, as is my brother-in-law here, from the battlefield (our last engagement took place by Pimpelstadt), and I may for that reason vote too strongly in favor of marrow strength, breast storm, and thrust ardor, and it may very well be a good thing for one whose heart is a roaring waterspout, or should I say landspout, if his mental state (in which I now am) should make him more mild than wild. However, each mildness needs its own iron bars. If some reckless dog were to attack me intentionally, I should kick him to pieces in my first fury, and my brother-in-law behind me might likely continue twice over, for he is just the man for that. It may seem peculiar, but I still regret (I admit it) that as a boy I did not return with interest the three punches received once at the hands of another boy, and I often feel I should pay them back to his off-spring. Verily, if I merely see a boy cowardly running before the feeble strength of another such boy, I find his running away totally inconceivable and am highly tempted to save him by a stroke of authority. The passenger smiled, albeit not for the best. He pretended to be a legation counselor and seemed a sly enough fox all right, but in the heel of the hunt the bite of a fox turned rabid will make me no less hydrophobic than the bite of a rabid wolf. By the by, I continued my paean in praise of courage imperturbably, only instead of the silly bragging that betrays the coward, I spoke firmly, calmly, and clearly. "I am only," I said, "in favor of Montaigne's injunction: let us fear nothing but fear itself."

"I should" (rejoined the legation counselor with uncalled-for casuistry) "fear once again that I might not fear fear enough but remain too much of a coward."

"And even this fear I shall keep within bounds," I replied coldly. "For instance, a man may well not believe in ghosts or be in the least afraid of them and still find himself in a blue funk at night at the thought of his horror (particularly in view of its aftereffects, epilepsies, strokes, and the like), if nothing else but his too vivid imagination were to delude his senses by dangling some febrile phantasmagoria in front of his eyes." — "That is precisely why," interrupted my brother-in-law, unwontedly moralizingly, "one must never bamboozle the poor sheep of a man with ghostly spooks, or the rabbit may drop on the spot."

An earsplitting thunderstorm, which followed the mail coach, altered the course of the discourse. You, my friends, — knowing me as a man not devoid of all physical science — will have guessed at my measures for warding off thunderstorms: for I will sit in a chair in midroom (and if the gathering clouds should warrant, I will remain in it throughout several nights), and I always protect myself by ridding my person of any conductors, rings, buckles, and so on and so forth and by getting off any likely lightning reflectors so that I might hark to the roll of the heavenly kettledrum in cold blood. — I have never yet been the worse for these measures, as I am still alive to date and I still pat my own back for leaving the city church for the charnel house once without further ado or having received communion, although I had been to confession the day before, because a violent thunderstorm (which did strike the linden tree in the churchyard) hovered above it; but the moment the cloud had discharged itself, I returned from the charnel house to the church and was lucky enough to partake of the love feast after the hangman (who was last in line).

Thus my personal reasoning; but in the mail I was up against people to whom the science of physics is but a bit of tomfoolery. For when appalling storms brewed overhead and crackling fire lumps flitted across the sky as if they were fireflies and I finally had to request that the perspiring mail conclave at least deliver all watches, rings, coins, and the like, perhaps into the carriage bags, so as to rid their persons of lightning conductors: not only did they refuse point-blank, but my own brother-in-law, the dragoon, mounted the carriage box with saber drawn and swore he would deflect the lightning. I cannot say whether the desperate man was in his senses or not; in a word, our position was fearful, and each one of us a likely dead duck. In the end, I as good as quarrelled with two of the human cargo, viz, the poisoner and the harlot, because in their questions they almost hinted that my intentions were less than honest as to the suggested junket of jewels. That kind of thing casts an almighty slur on one's honor, and the storm in my breast surpassed the violence of the one in the sky; and yet I had to conduct the required angry exchange as quietly and as slowly as possible, and I quarrelled gently in case a coachload up in arms might get all hot and bothered and, through their combined perspiration, draw the imminent thunderbolt through the carriage roof into our midst. Finally, I expounded the whole electrical chapter most clearly, although slowly and quietly — for I had no wish to perspire — and sought to frighten them off fear in particular. For each of us might indeed be stricken, nay doubly stricken — electrically and apoplectically — for fear, as it has been extensively proven in Erxleben and Reimarus that the sweat of strong fear adducts lightning; I therefore expostulated, in righteous anguish at my fear and theirs, for the passengers' benefit that amidst our sultry crowd here and with the saber tickling the lightning from our carriage box, and the cloud overhead, and the fear itself spawned by too much perspiring, in short, in the face of this obvious danger, they must not fear anything lest they be killed, each single one of them. "Oh Lord," I cried, "do not lose heart! Do not fear! Do not fear even fear! — Surely we do not want to sit huddled together here like hounded rabbits to be shot dead by our Lord God? — As far as I am concerned, every one of you may be afeared once he has left the carriage, wherever you like in places where there is less to fear, but only not here!"

It is not up to me to decide — as barely *one* among millions die from a thundercloud but possibly millions perish from snow- and rain-clouds and vapors — whether my sermon in the coach might lay claim to a life-saving medal as we drove, undamaged without exception, in the direction of a rainbow and into the town of Vierstädten, where there was a post-master resident in the only street the town could boast of.

Dr. Katzenberger's Spa Journey

THE PASSAGE THAT FOLLOWS, THE DISCOURSE ON MAS-
tication, is typical of the general tone of *Katzenberger* (*W* 11.275ff.). and
comes in the course of the main story line. But Jean Paul is even more
discursive than usual in this work, which includes such seemingly out-of-
place material as the vision of annihilation or the debate on death after
death. In the last, the narrator maintains the reality of the spirit's wishes
without convincing his adversary, for whom longing may be its own object. Although never far from the surface in Jean Paul, the theme is most
elaborated later in *Selina*, as a sequel to *The Vale of Campan*.

It is worth noting how the scene ends — with what is at once an apologia for the writer and a warning to the reader against seeking a conclusion outside the ongoing narrative, with its interplay of persons and opinions:

> We had now come closer in friendship, as before in hostility, and rightly
> ceased; such a dispute can only be interrupted, not terminated, and al-
> lows, like all philosophy, only of armistices, not of settlements. Hence all
> such investigations should, like those of Plato and Lessing, be poetic, that

is to say, dramatic, so that behind the variety of opinions the opinion of the author remains hidden, which the credulous first and so readily seek out and accept as authority, so that in calm possession of all the rest they become its advocates and chargés d'affaires instead of its judges. (*W* 11.167)

38. Summula

The Doctor, bathed in the brilliance, which, light magnet that he was, he had drawn from the royal star, finally took his seat coldly beside his Mehlhorn and his daughter. The money changer had almost lost his appetite in his adoration of the prince and admiration for the Doctor and the ease with which the latter discoursed with the former. During dinner, the Doctor steered the conversation to the topic of eating and remarked that nothing surprised him more than that, in view of the paucity of dead bodies and living dismemberments, the ones inhabited by ourselves should not be pressed into service more often for the sake of science, especially during the summer months, when dead bodies will rot. "Would you mind very much, Mister Mehlhorn, if I were now to harmonize our enjoyment of food with a simultaneous consumption of anatomical facts or soul foods?" — "With the greatest of pleasures, my dear Doctor," said he. "I can only hope to be able to follow your erudite eloquence." — "All it needs is for you to chew while I speak, for what you are about to receive is only a short scientific summary on mastication, which you are to compare with your own, that is to say, living prototype, on the spot. — Very well! — You are chewing; but are you aware that the lever category, which decrees the motion of the masticatory muscles of your two jaws (in actual fact, of only the lower one), is absolutely of the very worst, the so-called third sort, that is to say, the load, or bolus, is at its furthest distance from the lever's fulcrum; hence you cannot crack a nut with your canines though your molars will do it. Let us move on! When you set eyes on that flesh on your plate there: Your parotis, you will observe (which is located just about here), as well as the salivary gland of your lower jaw, will be getting erections and finally pour toward the meat via the Stenonian duct the necessary saliva, whose froth you, like anyone else, owe simply to the expansible types of air. I beg you, dear tollman, chew on, for now all will fall into line from the ductus nasalis and the lachrymal glands, which leads you to hope to digest all you consume

here. This service at sea is about to be followed by the service on land." —
At this point, the tollman laughed quite inordinately, partly in order to
seem polite, partly to hide the unease with which he swallowed everything during this most private of all privatissima; — nevertheless, he was
obliged to continue to consume.

"This is what I mean by service on land: at this point your trumpeter
muscle steps in, driving the forcemeat under your teeth — aided and abetted by your tongue and your cheeks as they dig and shovel to and fro —
there is no escape possible for your forcemeat, nor emigration either,
because it is safely incarcerated and bracketed by two skin flaps (commonly called your cheeks) and also by the sphincter of your mouth (this
being your first sphincter, not to be confused with its counterpart, your
last, which cannot be demonstrated here) — in short, forcemeat is being
splendidly smoothed and moistened and pulped to what we call a bite, as
I can see with my own eyes. All that is left now for you to do (and I would
ask you kindly to oblige) is to discharge the bolus into your pharynx and
gullet. But this, my dear money changer, is where your intellectual omnipotence comes to a halt, at a frontier cordon, as it were, and from now
on it no longer depends on that faculty of freedom, as inexplicable as it
is noble (the distinction between us and the animal kingdom), whether
you wish to swallow the forcemeat-bite or not (which you could have spat
on your plate only a few seconds ago), for now, bound to the cordon or
bit of your gullet, you must needs swallow it. Now it depends on my
esteemed audience whether we keep my Mister Tollman's bite company
on its initial journey and make further progress." —

Mehlhorn, to whom the forcemeat tasted of asafetida, countered: "he
need hardly protest his own predilection for this kind of enlightenment;
but it certainly did not depend only on him." — "I may continue then?"
said the Doctor. "Eminent Sir," rejoined an elderly lady, "your discourse
may be exceedingly learned, but during dinner it drives one almost to
desperation." — "And that, too," he contended, "is easily explained; for I
confess that among all sensations I know none that is stronger, albeit
more groundless and less amenable to reason, than nausea. Just two examples out of a thousand! Last autumn I kept a brace of snipes, and I had
gone to untold trouble to tame them, partly in order to observe and
partly to stuff and skeletonize them. As I am always at pains to serve
something choice to my guests: I offered some gourmets among them
snipe droppings toasted with butter on slices of bread in the usual fashion, as delivered fresh daily by my two snipes. But let me assure you as a
man of honor, dear madam, that not a single one of them displayed the

slightest appetite but only a thorough disgust for the offered droppings; and I ask myself, why? — Only — and here I come to our point — because the trail was not also spread on the toast, and the gourmands saw droppings *netto* instead of *brutto* on their plates. But I ask every sensible man here to judge himself whether I should perchance have slaughtered my marsh birds — who were fed on the very stuff (herbs, snails, and earthworms) that had always been passed by snipes as food for gourmets — whether, I ask, I should slaughter the former (like the man did his goose laying the golden eggs) in order to serve up as it were the laying entrails. — It seems to me as if such devotees could only treasure the hazel locks of the beautiful ladies around our table as long as they were still wound on curlers. — Remember in this connection the Dalai Lama, who used daily to present his admirers, the noblest of his princes, and his faithful, with his own snipe relics; and no one among them ever considered shooting that Pope of Asia like a snipe or wringing his neck just to have him lock, stock, and barrel, but they are content with what he provides.

This is one example of the nausea nonsense. But here is a more compelling one. Nothing, neither wine nor beer nor sweet liqueurs, nor any broth, in short nothing at all is to our mind purer, more indigenous and intrinsic, more calculated to remain (as no extraneous matter can) in our mouth for so long as something of which its owner could not drink half a teacup full were it outside him, that is to say, saliva. If this is not nonsense, then it would not be nonsense either but make perfect sense if I loathed my excellent colleague Strykius out of mere distaste because, though so akin to me in learning and endeavor and part of my inner self, as it were, through friendship, he were standing outside of myself beside my chair."

1811

Political Lenten Sermons during Germany's Week of Martyrdom

JEAN PAUL PUBLISHED THE COLLECTION ENTITLED *PO-litical Lenten Sermons during Germany's Week of Martyrdom* in 1817, bringing together scattered material that had appeared earlier in various journals. The translated passage from this work has, not unusually, little to do with the particular work in which it is embedded. This is *The Twin Military Review in Großlausau and in Kauzen, Complete with Campaigns* (*W* 10.1175f.), an account of the rival maneuvers between Prince Maria Puer of Großlausau and his cousin, the Prince of Kauzen, Tiberius the Ninety-ninth (Tiberius LXXXXIX). In other words, a burlesque on the duodecimo German system of petty principalities. The excerpt here is from the same stable as the *Clavis*, and what was noted regarding the passages from that *Titan* appendix and the foreword to *Palingeneses* is relevant here.

The Twin Military Review in Grosslausau and in Kauzen, Complete with Campaigns

I remember distinctly that I was sitting as studiosus in my study, the Kantian system fixed in my head like my friendly Lodge of the Sublime Light, when a rascally bookseller had a bale of books by Aenesidemus and Fichte and others delivered to my door, about which I had heard from others before that the bale was bound to upset the system. "It is now 1 o'clock," said I, walking to and fro, "and thou art still contented and Kantian, firmly and happily ensconced on thy critical tripod; and it is up to thee now when thou wilt accept the still trussed-up system, which is about to fracture the legs of thy tripod." I made up my mind to remain a Kantian by choice for the rest of the night and to undo the string on the morrow in order to turn renegade later. It would grieve me were I to depict my feelings at the Critique's farewell and how I went over it one last time a believer, while untying the string. But what was the use of receiving another decent system in the shape of Fichte's tabernacle and university and *positing* myself down in it as a tenant when all too soon there arrived on my doorstep a bale of Schelling! — But I threw down the gauntlet and said: "All right, I shall accept this new system, and as if this were not enough, the one after, which will topple this one in turn; but the devil take me if — with my full chair of philosophical faculties — I won't change tack after that."

But I have a different way of dealing with it even now: I allow six or eight systems to accumulate, as a rule, and read the confutation before I get down to the confuted, and by this back-to-front reading I am in the happy position of breaking the spell — like the witches weaving spells by reciting the Our Father backward — so that I just might, if I don't overrate myself, be the man without any system. And when I find myself side-by-side with a systematic mind in a book shop after the Easter Fair surrounded on all sides by systems, which are likely to remint him completely the moment he opens the book and to exchange him as a change-ling of his own self, I cherish a secret compassion. "Alas, my dear inno-cent Sir!" I say to him then.

Life of Fibel, Author of the Bienrodian Primer

LIFE OF FIBEL (*W* 11.378ff.) FOLLOWS ON THE LINES OF *Wutz* and *Fixlein* and is, as Jean Paul said in a letter to his publisher, Vieweg, "a satire on Kantian and other biographers" (*H-KA* 3.5.205). In the year of Kant's death, 1804, no fewer than four biographies appeared, recording Kant's life in meticulous minutiae. For his mock-heroic subject, Jean Paul chose the unknown author, whom he calls Fibel, of the ABC book of his own childhood. (The German word *Fibel*, meaning primer or first reader, is a corruption of the German *Bibel*, bible, from which much of such readers' material was taken.)

If in the end *Fibel* becomes a kind of Parsifal story, and the pure innocent is transfigured in old age, this is probably more than the parody Jean Paul had originally intended. Of course, even as parody it was bound to be affectionate, a tribute to the unforgettable book, with its colorful pictures and its golden lettering on the cover, with which, as Berend says, Jean Paul first entered into his element, the world of words.

The appendix to the *Life* is the primer itself, with its exercises in lettering and in writing the Our Father, the Creed, and the Ten Commandments, and with its alphabet of pictures and doggerel rhymes, beginning with the *Ape* and the *Apple*. It would seem that no copies of the original primer have survived. As Berend puts it: the book, which according to the work itself "ought to be in every library, can be found in none" (*H-KA* 1.13.LXXXIXff.). The translation is of the opening pages, up to the point where Fibel himself begins to read.

1. Judas Chapter

BIRTH

Come, dear Fibel, and step into life at last, tiny and anonymous though thou still beest! Thou wilt reach thy five- or six-and-a-half feet yet in the fullness of time and become named and famed, as indeed we all are! The newborn dwarf will ever remain the primary capsule of the invisible giant who is going to hurl mountains at heaven and hell later on. — My appeal to the unborn author to enter at last into his birth and the world will only seem pointless to those of my readers who are as yet ignorant of the fact that he had not been born until his tenth month.

In the end, his father, a penniless fowler and invalid, stood one day holding out of the window the trap with which he was lying in wait for the finch who was hopping toward him, in order to pull him in, just when the midwife conveyed the good news to him from the wailing room that a living child was to arrive; this caused him slowly to turn his head and say in an undertone: "Quiet!" But the very moment he pulled in the finch on his trap the midwife confronted him, holding Fibel in both her arms out to him; he uttered (while both the finch and Fibel squawked miserably) only the words — reaching for the bird and looking at the babe — : "Have I got *him?*"

2. Judas Chapter

SEASONS OF CHILDHOOD

Man's golden age, namely the earliest years of his childhood, were to tinge even his autumn years with their goldleaf, so happy and golden did they turn out for little Gotthelf. Gotthelf was the baptismal name of a rector magnificus from Leipzig, a distant spearside kinsman (patrilinear relation) of his mother's, whom the old fowler, urged on by the woman in childbed, easily managed to make a godfather, since declining an invitation to the baptismal font is on a par with refusing to pay a coffin bill! The Rector complied affectionately with the request and happily shared, as he did with any beggar or sneezer, his most precious possession, his Christian name: Gotthelf!

The years of little Gotthelf's childhood were beautiful. During that heady season of hope, in spring, the old fowler would always take him and a decoy finch along to the dappled wood on an ambush. While the old man would watch his he-finch luring the jealous cocks on to the lime twigs stuck to his body: the little one watched with him and was the first to run across to where one got caught by the singing catchpoll or living swan's neck;[1] but at times he would follow the bright woodland ranges and pull up foot-high saplings, to replant them crudely only a few steps on in his attempt at a little garden. Or he would hack off their roots and fasten the trees to his oilcloth hat in order later to pin this dainty posy on his mother for want of flowers or strawberries. Now and again he managed to loosen a piece of pine bark with his clasp knife and, making good phelloplastic use of it, he would sculpt and release from the bark block a little cow or a bird or a human being. His soul aglow with the long light of morning, he trotted, full of audible monologues, after his silent father, who, of all possible tongues, employed the human one least but was a walking organ of wildlife and bird-call, himself; there were few birds in the woods with whom he could not have communed in their mother tongue. There are indeed quite a number of citizens who would sooner whistle than speak.

Four fields ahead of his father, Gotthelf embraced and embellished his mother; never mind that *Engeltrut* (that was his mother's name) might have a headache or feel out of sorts or have her hands full: one hand would always be free to caress his cheek. — A different season would offer Gotthelf different pleasures, namely different birds and their trapping methods. Summer was wreathed with nests, true Indian ones to a Henry the Fowler with permission to raid them; not forgetting the quails, which he bags before they can build one. What Ossian is to the youthful dreamer, namely a magical autumn landscape, that in its fullness was autumn to the old fowler, just as to a painter, late autumn in particular; his late summer was a late spring and early summer, a sumptuous farewell feast of the year. The valedictory shrilling of the migratory birds sounded like the tender swan song of spring to his ears; and his son was ever present, helping to carry home the rich booty, be it from limed trees or fowling floors.

To be sure, winter for him bore the greatest profusion of flowers, and

---

1. Name of the gin trap.

every hour was his very flower girl (or bouquetière), provided the cold was bitter and the snow deep and the weather stormy enough. The life of a proper fowler, who calmly pursues his warbling and catching, is in itself filled with tranquil livelong lulling, a lunar rainbow over the sleeping villages. If you add the quiet winter, Nature's siesta, especially in the fowler's den: all will be evident. I can image his house in my mind — and I could see it if I were to get up from my chair —; the ground floor comprises *one* room and *one* stable — its floors and walls hung with songbirds and warblers — a whole vocal springtime confusion, with the fowler providing singing lessons and counterpart in the midst of it all — and outside in the snow lofts and titmouse boxes stand open in order to man more completely the bird odeum. The knitting of quail nets, the weaving of cages and nests for canaries — the feeding of the uncastrated singers (father and son being the galley crew for the animals and the mother the one for the humans) shorten the short days. If on top of all that, goldfinch-canaries have to be dyed Turkish blue and illuminated, starlings taught prose style and bullfinches given lyrical singing lessons in the conservatoire: this will have its effects with true consequences on our little Gotthelf, while the consequences will have their own effects, in due course. This leads us to an easy agreement with Pelz (his first biographer), who asks whether these earliest childhood delights and poésies-fugitives of life among birds might not have drawn the first cartoons and sbozzis for the animal pieces of Fibel's primer in his young soul — for only five human beings appear there — the Monk, the Jew, the Fowler, the Nun, and Xanthippe — as against fifteen animals. I would agree with the matter myself; whereas *one* warm raindrop will bring the hard seed corn of childhood to germination and growth, a whole rain blast does little to fertilize and transform the leafy grown tree.

3. Mobcap Pattern Chapter ·

MUSICAL WEDLOCK SERENADE

His parents' marriage was a connubial Yes-No, yet the most peaceful in the margraviate. The fowler, a tall haggard old soldier — who had brought back from his military campaigns nothing but his honorary discharge and a bullet, still mobile within his body — might talk to himself now and again but hardly ever to others and only Chinese if he did, that is to say, in monosyllables. Calmly and cooly as from a translucid glacial hall, he would regard the external snowstorms swirling about him and say: "So wags the world"; and nothing could change him, not even his wife. She had much against that; in her dreams of a happier married life, she had hoped once to be, like other wives, able to sulk and weep to her heart's content in her own; but the old man cheated her out of that by saying Yes to everything, making no ado, and doing as he wished. "Don't tell me you are saying Yes again?" she would rail, and he would nod yes. Engeltrut, albeit from humble folk (native of a hamlet near Dresden), was yet so delicate, frail, and languid of stature and coloring, so tenderly warm of heart and capricious of mind — which anyway is more often the case in the lower orders than one might expect —, and Wieland must have had historical grounds for giving Xanthippe, whose petticoat fame he himself helped establish, a noble lineage; for the country, too, yields its crop of amicable humors, termagants, and its lively Socratic discourse thereupon.

In the present mobcap pattern, the studious Pelz contributes a story bearing this out. Engeltrut once, having walked about with bandaged jaws and a raging toothache for quite some time and the fowler remaining as stoic as if he himself were the sufferer, blew up at last and let fly at him for standing there like an icicle never showing any emotion, or impatience, not to mention a tear. Yet a tear, and a male tear to boot, is often the very drop to awaken and merrily jolt into life an infusorian dried and dormant for years. "Contain thyself, Trut," he rejoined, "the barber is bound to pass through on the morrow and pull the monster for thee." "Yea, to be sure, on the morrow when all my pains will be over — oh thou cruel man!" she countered. Instead of an answer, he gave a whistle, as was his wont when half in anger at a whole lot of nonsense, namely the finch's so-called sharp wine call, commonly put to the following words by the fowling fraternity: Fritz, Fritz, wilt thou drink the wine with me? — *Siegwart* (for that is his baptismal name) responded to the various goadings to laugh, to rage, to revile, or to forget with his manifold finch variations, of which the Pease pudding, the Large and the Small Trilling, the Musketeer, the Cow thief, and the Sparbarezier were likely his favorites. But there were those rare occasions when he, beside himself with fury, would forget his finch and, playing the nightingale in a short fit of rage, emit love calls.

Engeltrut, however, would gladly have suffered *with* him as well as *under* him, but there was never a hint or a word of complaint. He also let her have what she least wanted — her way; and thus it was only natural for her to complain: "Would God he should turn nasty just once and treat one like another man, at least one would know where one stands with him." And there was no gingering up things by jealousy, either, that spice of matrimony; even though the poor woman, trying for a smack of that zest, would once in a while, when he would offer eggs and rolls to none but his flock, raise the question: "A starling is dearer to thee than wife, then?" He nodded assent in his usual way.

His fault — if the mobcap pattern is to be trusted — may have lain in his name Siegwart, which made him decry any wailing and weeping; for Siegwart derives from guard, werd, and means protector, hence Edward, Burckward, Siward, Weromir, Werner, and (in the diminutive sense), Wernlein.

As far as his wife was concerned, he had another bad habit; he was never at home on the three high Feast Days but out and about disposing of birds and circumventing the church. To make matters worse, he would drag along the little one, consigning mother and son to mutual pining.

Any mobcap patterns restored by the village lads confirm that he did so in order to make him what he himself had once been — a recruit. Gotthelf displayed such a golden extensibility of body — and what else are prince and recruiter, like a magnet, in quest of but *longitude?* — that the long-armed ape and likewise Artaxerxes matched him in nothing but the length of their arms. In order to train him for the life of a soldier, nay, of an officer, he would not permit him to learn anything whatsoever — put mother and church like a court out of bounds — thrashed him to end all thrashings, and forced him into forced marches — and as far as he was concerned, there were never enough racing and standing to attention, of sweat of the brow and chattering of teeth, of winters and summers spent in the open for the boy who was yet to be the author of the future Primer of Saxony.

Oh how much better it turned out! Helf was later to write for his part and I for mine on the same!

4. Bodice Pattern

CHRISTMAS

Once upon a time Gotthelf was to experience the most beautiful Christmas on earth. It was thus:

Engeltrut found herself in the family way and Siegwart thereby in a bad way. She was filled with cravings and loathings, and the 600 complaints, which Hippocrates tells us are caused by the womb, with their 600 shades, cast a grey hue over his life. Above all, she suffered from a distaste for her husband, which even surpassed her erstwhile dislike of sauerkraut and wine — because those are both frequently crushed by the feet of strangers. Then every bird he possessed filled her with horror, his turtledoves were basilisks to her; the village turned avian midden, a Pandora's box open toward all sides; in the end, even God went down in her estimation — all except Gotthelf. She cried for three days once and was not to be comforted, as she could think of no reason for it until Helf fell from a garden wall on which he was riding horseback and luckily sprained a few limbs, which revived her again.

To be sure, she ought to have been a pregnant princess or female nabob: in that case she might have expressed very different desires from a mere craving for roasting a lark's neck or boiling a hen in order to eat her eggs without eggwhite or shell, or for eating chalk in order to deacidify herself like the village beer! Could she not as princess have ordered broth to be served from wren's or elephant's marrow — or the tender stag's horn to be ripened, i.e., roasted for her on its birthplace, the stag's head? — Could she not have requested a sofa of whiskers for her ladies-in-waiting, a city gate as a frame for her monumental portrait, caster sugar instead of flowers cast on her triumphal path, and more exciting presents, like swaddling clothes made from sheer pallia and swaddling bands made from the shredded clothes of shepherdesses, a dressing case conveyed by six horses from Paris, and for the babe-in-arms, a Christmas tree made and ramified from split frontier posts, and the imperial crown jewels as a Christmas present? Should we believe such fancies to be exhaustible: we could easily think of other demands of an imagined *sovereign mother*, e.g., that she might have a penchant for grinding inferior painters and decorators of ceiling frescoes to paint-grains and -drops in her very own cochineal mill — for treating noblemen prisoners to (sugar)bread and (sugar)water — for amalgamating one tribunal with another, perhaps that of law with that of justice, etc., etc., somewhat like enamel with water or oil with water or water with burning oil.

For that reason, fathers in several other societies retire to childbed to be restored from the prior maternal or paternal hardships of pregnancy. The old fowler cured himself of his potter's colic — an apt metaphor, as he was after all the fetus's potter — by means of his usual traveling; but he left her darling behind as maître de plaisirs to the afflicted.

Oh the Christmas celebrations in their little cottage! He had hardly departed the village: when the maternal or oppositional education commenced. To start with, Helf was allowed to feed all the birds himself; whereupon he fed the woodlark so many mealworms that it gave up the ghost on the third day of Christmas. After that he was licensed to be her kitchen soubrette, and he helped to chop many almonds, which disappeared down his gullet, for the festive baking. Throughout Christmas Eve, the carefree chatter of mother and son filled their apartment and closet like the merrily murmuring brook in springtime. She taught him the bowing and scraping and kissing of hands of Dresden society; and he bowed and scraped and kissed his mother without cease. And at his side she bore her old headaches without being aware of them.

The little fellow was a diminutive church triumphant in person, a tripping seat of the blessed, just because he had nothing whatever to fear all day long, nothing to thrash him. The rare maternal blows would always be heralded by the lengthy preadmonitions and forearmings that ran ahead, during which he ran away; the fowler's custom, on the other hand, was to stand tall and still like a dead calm and a cerulean blue, out of which the paternal fist would crash on his shoulderblade.

On this Christmas Eve, Helf was as a boy transfigured, and Engeltrut, a transfigured and supernatural expectant mother! What perpetual delectation! With all their baking passion, they did not bother at all with a midday meal. At three o'clock — so history tells us — all scrubbing was done and the feast day cakes were baked and pervaded the house with their aroma. Helf could sit down beside his own candle and invent five brand-new alphabets at his pleasure, with which he set various experimental exercises, which no one could read, not even himself, without frequent recourse to the alphabet. In the evening he supped blissfully, because his mother enjoyed her food; she, however, enjoyed hers because he enjoyed his. Eucharistic or sacramental disputes between herself and her husband were discontinued; there was no need for her to extol the meal should it prove to be burned or too salty or to belittle it should nothing be wrong.

Children love, like Parisians, staying up late. For once his mother permitted it, and during those calm golden hours he wrote some trifle in almost all of his alphabets — the mother enjoying her nap although it would spoil her nocturnal slumber — from the parsonage sparkled the golden fireworks of the Christmas tree (the peasantry would not exchange gifts until morning) — every star twinkled bright and near, and the lofty sky had come up close to the window — Gotthelf scratched very quietly with his quill so as not to disturb his mother — at last he, too, fatigued by his scholarly toil, rested his head on the table. Later his mother awoke and, awakened, — reminded him of the Christ child and going to bed and asked him to kneel down with her this Holy Night and pray God to grant everything and, in particular, that he would never become a fowler but a rector magnificus like her own grandfather and his godfather. He complied gladly. Thus did Lavater pray to God to correct his pensum for him, and Lichtenberg likewise to answer his learned questions on bits of paper. So each man at prayer is entitled to do; to the Eternal there is no difference between asking for a whole world or for a piece of bread but the vanity of those who pray and He either counts both suns and hairs on the head, or neither.

When he had said his prayers, she allowed him to climb into her husband's bed only in order to make it herself in the morning, a joy out of which she was daily cheated by the old autonomous bed maker Siegwart, who disliked being obliged to womenfolk for anything but his own birth and his children. "I wonder, Helfikins, how our dear Father is settling down now" (said she) "and remember him in your bedtime prayer"; whereupon she blessed her son and folded his hands against any ghosts during the night. — Engeltrut never longed more for Siegwart's presence than while he was absent; so little does distance do damage to love, even in marriage, and so much does a man need to be fixed, like a burning mirror, at the precise focal length from the object he wishes to melt.

Next morning, two of the Christmas presents, viz, a red and white booklet of marzipan and a japanned needle book of his mother's, eclipsed all the rest for Helf; and out of these books, void in themselves — but what are most books but superior book covers — he scooped more manna than I from as many full ones.

Countrywomen would rather miss church than their kitchens on Christmas Day; nevertheless, he did not stay at home with his mother but performed his morning devotions. She put this down in the main to his predilection for lengthy sermons; but the learned Pelz adds that in Church he chose to sit where, when the so-called Master of Saints arrived with the alms bag (the horizontal offertory box, the penny divining rod and cue cum billiard bag), he could relieve the man of the stick, which did not reach to the end of the pew, so that he could rake in his own and the others' donations. This position as subecclesiastical revenue collector, as well as the sermon and the parts thereof, which he would transmit to his mother over dinner, were what drew him to church.

But he liked a return visit in the afternoon, though his edification was gratis then, at his mother's side and with his hands in a little black muff and looking around the temple in a familiar way, to demonstrate that he had been there before. And if he had formerly joined in the adult singing with his hymnbook held upside down: how much more lustily now that he held his hymnal the right way up and could just about manage to read! And what was even more remarkable was the rapidity with which, the moment the white numeral would appear on the blackboard, he found the right page for his mother.

And when he came home and the village's golden hour began, the hour following Evensong, he would have the finest of all in the village, even the parson. And the herring papers are there to paint it for us.

5. Herring Papers

STUDIES

Helf was reading. In front of the fowler's eyes he would not have been allowed to sit over his waste books for even a quarter of an evening; but now he could read anything he could set eyes on in the line of lyrical, legal, or chemical print from the grocer's shop, his free library, and in reading think of all manner of things, losing himself, while munching a piece of cake or an apple with every page, in the most delicious peripheral dreams, the neatly engraved vignettes and etchings and musical notation of his waste sheets as it were. Not for every scholar is wastepaper, not withstanding its lower *shop* price, a suitable reading matter; since it lacks title pages and sometimes starts, like an epic poem, in the middle or at the end, the man cannot quote from it and absorb information to bursting point without being able to discharge with its appropriate quotation a single drop of it out of himself; yet he can make his name only by dropping names.

However, these waste sheets flowed into Fibel's life with the abundance of a second Universal German Library and took its place. They made of him — who got paper bags in all disciplines from the grocer — that polymath as which he appears throughout his Primer on the topics of animal life, the science of education and moral studies, in poetry and in prose. Likewise, the present sages and wiseacres may have arisen out of Nicolai's Library simply because they say that they have not for nothing not only acquired but also read the reviews on anything and everything.

From this Christmas on, Gotthelf discovered reading, and no one could stop him. There are happy people — e.g., himself — to whom a book is more a human being than a human being a book and who truthfully repeat the error of that Frenchman, Mr. Martin, who, in his catalogue of the library of Mr. de Bose, cites the word *printed* as an author Mr. Printed. I know few men of letters for whom the said *Herr Gedruckt* is not the supreme district authority of all terrestrial and celestial districts, your only man to consult, and the new Adam — the manikin of all men and all eons and the absolute Self; I know, as I said, few.

Anything Fibel, the budding scholar, could get hold of by the said author Printed he used to augment his collection of books in the loft — an old page proof — old calendars — a rare miniature calender — the fragment of a catalogue of books — half a sheet of a register — anything whatsoever. The initials that the pastor's daughter as name compositress printed on linen he marveled at as veritable incunabula; and he followed with longing eyes a compositor walking through the village who worked in a — cotton factory. The anecdote from his earlier years is well known, how, in some misconception, having repeatedly read that many a book had flown from a scholarly quill, he hankered after a scholarly quill and pulled several feathers off the tail of a starling, which Siegwart used to refer to as a schooled and scholarly bird! Afterward, so the anecdote says, the fowler coming upon the damage done to the starling's rump, and seeing that his son had drawn a blank, silently added a premium to the extremity that came to hand. His mother applied sauerkraut to the bruise.

An old margravian court and state calendar had the greatest attraction for him, and he read it forty times, as others would read Kant four times and Bardili, five. The ruling house had been torn off, but there were sufficient high ranks, inspectorates, and deputations left to set him beside himself; what amazed and delighted him most was that his village and pastor were also listed in print, as were the tiniest hamlets roundabout with names of their own. Heavens, how he admired the wonderfully intricate clockwork of the state, with a domestic staff under orders and ready to serve the smallest and the greatest alike, Bonnet's animal gradation in spiritual form. He felt dimly that there was nothing more just, more wise, better administered than a state. The present author also remembers with longing this delicious sense from his boyhood years.

It is one of the unrecognized childhood pleasures that in the directory — that spiritual bond book of state administration — one takes the festive and augustly parading celebratory state procession, the saddle- and harness-room of whiskers, wigs, uniforms, and swords, as what it so beautifully appears to be. What is missing in this youthful pleasure, in the way of substance, but permanence? — And does not its recollection so often refresh the cold statesman who later considers the state a rifleman's guild for the purpose of bringing down the prize eagle or a *covey* of partridges, or a nest of *processionary* caterpillars on the oak of state? — Truly, whoever remains unbiased enough will discover in more mature years many a motion in members of state simulating his former views; and he will liken it to that snuff enthusiast[2] who, after an apoplectic stroke, still gestured habitually every quarter of an hour as if taking snuff and thoroughly rubbed his nose afterward, as anyone might.

2. Reil's The Science of Fever Vol. IV.

The Comet

THE COMET WAS JEAN PAUL'S LAST NOVEL; OF ALL HIS major works, perhaps the one that has least got the attention it deserves (*W* 11.605ff., 628ff., 682ff.; 12.994f., 999ff.). As will be clear from the summary, it is more multifaceted than ever, and it would be difficult to assign it to one of the three types, as it is Netherlandish, German, and Italian all at once, although with a bias more toward deflation than exaltation (cf. *H-KA* 1.15.vi, LXVI).

Of the four passages following, three are aside from the main action, only the second passage having directly to do with the story of Nikolaus Marggraf and the search for his true love. This is the scene with the five princesses at the turnstile. Like so much in Jean Paul, it is set in what is recognizably his own local landscape and here reminiscent of the arbor in the Eremitage in Bayreuth.

The first passage is Worble's magnetic banquet. Worble, the hero's majordomo, is a particularly volatile figure, a "veritable J. P., Jean Potage, Jack Pudding." He is poor, but he, too, has a catholic imagination and is able, for example, to sustain himself with cookery books — *crede et manducasti*. He has the name of being a Freemason, but this, the narrator suggests, may be only because the citizens of Rome could make nothing of his unstable character. In his hometown he occupied the lowliest teaching rank of Quintus, and as organist, playing such chorales as "Strike Me in Thy Anger Not," he starts off in the wrong key and — an early Oskar Matzerath — mischievously leads the congregation through elaborate variations into general discord (*W* 12.733, 738f.). In order, he says, to avoid the temptation of a female servant, he employs an under-sized person as cook, who, however, puts on weight and in due course presents him with a daughter, after which they get married.

Later, he establishes a hedge high school for upper-class children, in which, avoiding the four *R*s of reading, writing, arithmetic, and religion, he imparts aphoristic information taken from any and every branch of science, untrammeled by the alphabetic coherence of the French ency-clopedists. Among his gifts are his hypnotic powers — Jean Paul was keenly interested in all forms of magnetism — and so the narrator di-gresses to describe his magnetic banquet (*H-KA* 3.8.55). Like so many passages in Jean Paul, it can be enjoyed simply for its inventiveness. Only slowly does it dawn on the reader that it is also a political satire on a restoration serving the interests of the princes and leaving the people hungry, satire nicely targeted on the Congress of Vienna. It may be that there are other allusions. Berend suspects a reference to the Confedera-tion of the Rhine, in which Napoleon might be said to be the sole ben-eficiary (*H-KA* 1.15.LVIII).

The only passage of *The Comet* known in the English-speaking world was *Dream upon the All*, since this was translated by De Quincey and later by others. The choice is typical of reception history, for there is a marked preference for the more exalted passages. The preference may now be for the more sardonic Jean Paul, and some of what was once so reverently read is now unreadable. Berend rightly observes that some of the least worthy productions, like *The Double Oath* or *The New Year's Night of an Unhappy Man*, were among the most often translated and anthologized (*H-KA* 1.7.XXXV). Not that the value judgment applies to *Dream Upon the All*, which is a highly imaginative essay of his last years. He regarded it himself as one of his "best pieces for a-long time," and one can imagine his enjoyment in writing it "in Miedel's garden" in Bayreuth, as he notes in his "Vita Book" (*H-KA* 1.15.LIX).

In his later years, he became more than ever concerned with "the All," immortality, the "second world," and he makes so many different observa-tions in so many different moods it would be impossible to reduce them to one consistent viewpoint. For all that, there is a consistent trend, though it is more difficult to say what it leads to — more emphasis on change, development, metamorphosis — than what it leads away from, namely narrowness, the static, the prescriptive, and the restrictive, which for him had now come to include Jewish and Christian orthodoxies. There must be a new belief in a new immortality that has nothing to do with graveyards and revelations, as he says in *Selina*. Anticipating much later developments in theology, he was looking for a vantage point for a view out of rather than, in Lavater's phrase, "into eternity"; not a prospect "of" immortality but a prospect "out of" immortality (*H-KA* 2.4.136, 173).

Dream upon the All is one document in this ongoing meditation of Jean Paul and his search for a "spacious" perspective. It need hardly be said that he was at the same time pursuing his otherworldly researches with his passion for out-of-the-way information. He noted from the authorities not only that the entrance to Purgatory is in Ireland but the lesser known fact that Hell is in the north of Scotland. One imagines that it was with his Anglophile sympathies he recorded the case of the Englishman who left all his money to his friends for dinners on the anniversaries of his death, on condition that each time they should first go in procession to his grave, address him by name, and call out: "How do you do?" (*H-KA* 2.4.528f.).

The Comet ends, or rather breaks off, on a note very different from *Dream upon the All*, giving the devil's advocate the last word in the person of the misogynist Leather Man, the somnambulist who calls himself Cain. He is the eternal adversary and Ahasverus — although as antisemitic as he is antichristian, for they are all "Habels" to him. Jean Paul points out that the Bible does not record the death of Cain, and he keeps reappearing in many guises in Jean Paul's novels, forever disputing the arguments of the pious and optimistic.

In the death scene in *Siebenkäs* (in which Siebenkäs provides a model of Christian fortitude in the face of death, except that he is not dying), Siebenkäs refers to Leibgeber as his Cain, dispatching him into a world in which he, Cain, does not believe (*H-KA* 1.5.LII; *W* 3.495). The footnote informs us that Cain, according to the rabbis, slew his brother for disputing his argument against the immortality of the soul. Thus, says Jean Paul, the first murder was an autodafé and the first war was a religious war. In this deathbed scene, Leibgeber makes an observation typical of all these adversarial figures, when he speaks of the Achilles shield that nature provides to the dying: "On the deathbed, one becomes morally sooner than physically cold, a strange courtierlike indifference toward all from whom we must part creeps frostily through the dying nerves, so that sensible onlookers say: look, only a Christian could die with such trust and renunciation."

The Leather Man at the end of *The Comet* is only the last in a line of devil's advocates, albeit particularly satanic and in a more specifically religious context — as if he were driven crazy, not by reading Kant or Fichte like Schoppe or Leibgeber, but by reading the rabbis and Church Fathers. (*W* 12.972). Schweikert would see in this figure a profound skepticism on the part of the ageing Jean Paul toward his own inwardness and art, a final disillusionment with the poetic imagination — which is, after all, unable to alter reality.[1] This may be to isolate too much one figure in Jean Paul's human comedy, as well as reading too much into the accidental ending of *The Comet*, which, if it ended at all, would most likely end at the writing desk in the Rollwenzelei.

Postscript

As we shall recall a certain boy by the name of Worble in this chapter and as he is the one who many years later was to give the notorious mesmeric banquet: I may be permitted to intercalate its description here straightaway; still, it is bound to attract attention.

The great mesmeric banquet of the Prince's Harbinger Worble.

Very few people are capable of giving mesmeric banquets, princes and capitalists least of all. Although I was not among those at his table, I derive great satisfaction from the fact that Peter Worble, the Harbinger, should have been skilled enough to manage the matter, he who liked among all possible tables, not excepting gaming-, writing-, and session-tables, none more than the dining-table, provided it was not a single-seater but accommodated places around as well as set on it. To him, a fellow eater was half the dinner; he used to enjoy several guests along with his food; indeed, he would have asked several guests to join him for one nightingale, so beloved of the tuneful Italians as a — dish, and he would deftly have carved the bird in midair had his pocket been equal to such a roast.

As luck would have it, it came to pass during a phase of middle age,

---

1. *Text und Kritik*, ed. Heinz Ludwig Arnold (Munich, 1983), pp. 204ff.

when he was about to half buy and half borrow, that he stilled his love of humanity and of food by that grand mesmeric banquet, which I am about to describe. We shall read plenty in future of this Peter Worble's being the strongest mesmerizer whom history can come up with after a Puysegur, who subdued a derisive, recalcitrant postillion from a distance or a Pölitz in Dresden, who at a table would make you fall asleep on the dining spot just by putting his hand on your shoulder. To be sure, Worble surpassed them all; he passed over and skipped all the soporific grades in order to start with waking up, that is to say, with clairvoyance. Whether it be on account of his physical strength redoubled in marrow soup kitchens — or the two sixth fingers on his hands, which he, like cats and lions their delicate claws while they pad, would draw in and hence kept charged and safe from exhaustion, or be it his secret mesmerizing by means of his toes — or simply because there are mesmeric Goliaths of whom greater notice will have to be taken in future — or be it, which is the most probable reason, all these together, in short, Worble achieved within minutes through his gaze and omnipotent willpower and invisible teleaspiration and manipulation of fingers and toes, the mesmeric miracles of clairvoyance, hallucination, and forging of links to the mesmerist, which takes others three months at a time.

Among all the miracles, the Harbinger Worble, who was as fond of people and fun as he was of food, loved best that well-known one, where a clairvoyant had to taste every bite and drop consumed by the mesmerist. But never did his kind heart and generous nature and his wonderful mesmeric vigor appear in a more beautiful light than on the occasion of that notorious banquet, which he arranged in the *Town of Vienna* — the name of the hostelry — for a notable company of distempered and hungry men of various ranks.

For he had ordered in the said Town of Vienna a large table laid for 32, if not more, and ordered two courses of the choicest dishes, albeit only one helping per dish, namely, for himself alone. Among the guests of the highest importance (just to mention a few of them) there appeared a Professor Ordinarius of Philosophy, half perished with hunger and chagrin — a Professor Extraordinarius of Law, who had intended to comment his way up, via Napoleon's Deed of the Rhenish Confederation, to a *fortune* at Erlangen on Roman Law, that is to say, to a *fortune* through the neo-German one, but had been left behind together with the Confederation, and was also diseased and indigent — several schoolmen full of desire to eat and deficiency of food — a prelate and a provost and several more monastic men, all of them rather ill, as they had always eaten before as well as after meals — also some courtiers suffering for the identical reason — also some country people of rank diminished and ashen faced through the war — and I could name five or six more guests.

After our purveyor of food and lodging had welcomed his guests with much pressing of hands and scraping of feet — not so much from respect as from mesmeric guile — and placed them in front of openwork napkins, as full of elaborate holes as oaths: he put them to sleep on their dining chairs before the napkins had been unfolded, and they held hands as if they were brothers (as was his silent wish as their mesmerist), and they continued thus throughout the meal, all of them gifted with second sight as a body.

Now he had a delicious anchovy soup served, and he polished off two bowls of that with such relish that the professors and schoolmen agreed with one voice that they had never before tasted such delicate soup when he asked their opinion, while their dry soup bowls were being removed and other plates put in their place. Then followed Muscovite beef and a dainty crab pie, accompanied by baked frogs' legs. Before he even lifted his knife, the Harbinger stated that, with a view to parity and tolerance of both the Roman Catholics and the Protestants being observed at table as well as in Germany, he had ordered today, which was not a meat day, crabs and frogs for those of the Roman Catholic persuasion, but he was going to see to it by a most vigorous willing[1] that while he was eating the Muscovite beef only the Protestants and none of the Catholics should taste it. Here, though, two clairvoyants of the Catholic faith interjected, the prelate and the provost, true oral Christians both of them, albeit in the pleasanter sense, viz, the sense of taste, men who apply the saying: blood (of the martyrs) is the seed of the Church (sanguis semen ecclesiae) to themselves and do their utmost to provide plenty of it through digestion, these two announced that, strictly though they had always observed during their healthier years the rules of fasting, and had restricted themselves to fast day oysters, fast day trout, eel, salmon, and saltwater crab allowed by the Church, they had now obtained a dispensation, and hence he could safely permit them to share his enjoyment of the Muscovite and any other manner of meat. — This way the Harbinger in his capacity of Scottish provender- and lodge-master was able to treat his Lodge of the Sublime Light in the choicest way from the first course on. There would be no telling how they had all savored their food had not the few country

---

1. In the case of several mesmerists, it only depended on their vigorous willing for the clairvoyants not to hear what was being said, etc.

people of rank felt a too great distaste of the frogs' legs, which his munching communicated to them; the plain country folk were simply unable to imagine themselves as Frenchmen or frogs, that is to say have a taste for them, and unfortunately Worble in his hurry had quite forgotten to will that they should not get to taste them.

Thereupon our host of bees — all the more deserving of the name as, whoever the keeper, bees must produce their own honey — regaled the ecclesiastical beehive, the prelate and the provost in particular, by way of an oyster ragoût, which he relished to such an extent that he had to sacrifice himself a second time for the tonsured and the secular gourmets, demolishing another plate and a half, as requested by all around; admittedly, he provided a pleasure as rare as it was innocuous, as the good people, who had up to now quite forgotten to their gastric detriment that, just like purges, oaths, and masses, eating also must be approached on an empty stomach, could all of a sudden enjoy as many oysters through their digestive chargé d'affaires as they liked and not a twinge of gastric complaint. As to the dining courtiers, they were beside themselves over their host, and the sympathetic harmony of their taste buds with his displayed a heart that felt what the other man felt and shared in the other's happiness, which is a far harder thing than to feel pity.

This sumptuous enjoyment of the whole board school of taste and tasting went on and on from one dish to the next; limited country folk, needy schoolmasters and monastics, lean professors ordinarii of philosophy and extraordinarii of the Rhenish Confederation Deed experienced for themselves the flavor of larded pike and roast teal, of giant doughnuts, saddle of venison, and sweet almond cakes. The Harbinger never stopped urging another helping on them, one after the other, and himself followed suit by helping himself to yet one more spoonful, persuading each one of them to forget any fears of overindulgence, with much reference to the mustard, with which he liberally accompanied everything, as the best tonic for body and soul. Withal, he did not stint them in Comet or Elfer wine, a grape that had never before passed most of the feasting and drinking companions' lips, and indeed was not passing them now, either, if the truth be told. — And what on earth were the country- and schoolmen to think and feel when the superior wines of the noble tables wended their way as bravura arias through an opera, namely the wines from the foothills of Good Hope, Hungarian Rising, Vesuvian Lacrymae Christi Spumante? — Enough went even to the Harbinger's head to affect those of the somnolent clairvoyant fraternity in the end.

When the company finally was replete and contented and Worble had taken a last digestive glass of Anisette d'Amsterdam, whose strength set the lot of them aglow: he rose from the table and dismissed his fellow diners, his foster brothers of his taste alma mater, as it were, with the following vivacious and witty after-dinner speech: "May you all have enjoyed my well-meant treat a little, the best you could get in the Town of Vienna! — It might have turned out better, indeed ten thousand times better, and I would fain have (I admit it) dished up Bayonne ham and Strasbourg pies, together with a Polish salad, likewise, stuffed tongue from Troyes and veal from Rouen and chicken from Caux and capons from la Fleche and robin redbreasts from Metz; it would have been a delight, as I said, to treat you to those; but these things were not to be got: it was hard enough to drum up Baked Cats' Droppings and Saxon Yule Logs,[2] Floating Hornets' Nests,[3] and Boeuf à la Mode and Pomeranian Goose in the Town of Vienna. Nevertheless, the repast was (and that relieves me) wholesome and light. If, as the Koran says, aliments will be secreted through the pores of our skin in the life to come: I can promise the same of my own here and now, having offered you, just as, according to Strabo, the Persians offered their gods only the souls of their sacrificial animals, something likewise spiritual at the banquet, namely its *taste*, the only thing, and the best, which the connoisseur derives from a work of art and through which he enjoys it.

For my own person, to be sure, I am obliged to the capital dining society for supreme enjoyment, all the more because I dislike solitary consumption, being therein close to the Manicheans, who vowed at their baptism never to eat by themselves,[4] and also at one with the novelist Hermes, who advises scholars so fervently against eating alone. Verily, he who would deny others a share in his pleasures is as a veritable drone to me, which though it extracts and gathers honey yet does this solely for its own benefit, far better the beekeeper, who also keeps bees and consumes honey but who shares with his working bees during the hard winter months. Thus does the benevolent prince act when he keeps open table and in that way opens the door to Paradise to the hundreds of open mouths of the starving, just as at times the Romans used to leave their precious coins (numismata) to one heir and to the other the pleasure of looking at them,[5] in our case, the gaping folk are the second heir and

2. How to go about making both of them can be found in the Swabian cookery book of Mistress J. Christiana Kiesin, p. 284 and p. 312.
  3. For their recipes v. the Bavarian cookery book of Clara Messenbeck, Vol. I, p. 481.
  4. Fueßlin's Church and Heretics History Vol. I, p. 121.
  5. L. 28. II de usu fruct.

having a thorough look. — And so I wish you all a twofold God bless the meal, viz, not only this one but also your next, for I ask you, after you have been awakened by my counterstrokes, to return home and put in an order with your landlords so as to sate your appetites, which I have done my best to whet with my inferior dishes, just as Plato's meager symposia were praised for his guests' having felt especially hungry afterward."

*

— Thus, then, ended the grand mesmeric feasting congress in the Town of Vienna, the praise of whose splendor and profusion I have heard sung so often. Indeed, it may have been nothing but modesty when the Harbinger likened himself to a prince and his tasty banquet unto an open prince's table of which no onlooker got even a taste. Truly, how did even Napoleon's luncheon at Erfurt, exquisite as it was in itself, benefit that whole congress of Kings, Dukes, Generals, Ministers, and Court Counselors, among whom there was even a Wieland, as we know from his letters; what did that whole congress, close as they were to the table, get out of it but being spectators? And what was that open table but a tableau vivant of the Rhenish Confederation Deed by means of which the Professor Extraordinary hoped to work his way up to his Roman law *fortune?* — The congress in the Town of Vienna, however, where everyone from the courtier down to the school- and countryman indulged in two courses and even became intoxicated, had a different tale to tell of the Harbinger. Indeed, hardly had all of them wakened and finished their meal and the Harbinger left the room: when (while he was paying his portion down below in the taproom) schoolmen and countrymen (they had their wits) had ordinary joints of meat brought upstairs and stilled their splendid appetite (so little had their stomachs been spoiled by the French cuisine) with very little of honest means, whereas the mesmeric expenditure had been needed for the lingual sounding boards, just as the English settle their small bills with coins and the large ones with paper money. — In short, we may repeat once again: where else was there a congress as happy as the one in the Town of Vienna? Where did so much melt on the tongue without reaching the stomach?

Fourth Forechapter

Affairs of the Heart at a Distance and also the Rape of the Princesses

The arrival of three carriages of princesses, however, turned his whole heart around, and all his beloveds came toppling out; besides, room had to be found for a new damsel of such brilliance as to take up two ventricles and two auricles all by herself quite adequately.

It came to pass during that splendid year in the life of young Marggraf, when the earth spread under the budding man's soles like a sun shining up at him, that the five disembarked princesses — none of them seemed to be more than 13½ years of age — strolled arm in arm up and down the linden walk of the castle gardens at Rome. Moonbeams and moonshade, linden blossoms and bees — the latter buzzing even about linden sprays gathered in high-born hands — seemed to flutter playfully in the wake of the five damsels in white; and they for their part were followed by the apothecary Nikolaus. As he could not look in the face of any particular princess and fall in love accordingly: he awarded his heart to the quintet of graces behind their backs and followed behind with his five stigmata. He had that special facility of falling in love at his pleasure provided he had an hour or two at his disposal; for he could move his heart at will as others can twitch the tips of their noses. He had been smitten years in advance and altogether by all princesses, no matter how many of them there might be; because there could, as he knew, exist nothing more beautiful under the sun; therefore, regardless of where one might be or what she was like, his heart gladly subscribed to hers.

Of the royal five damsels, the people — above all the womenfolk, inspired to the warmest praise of the princessly feminine lures and robes by their very envy of those on a more neighborly level — had displayed ceremonial portraits of their loveliness painted on gold ground, which were out of their reach in every street and stall, and the lowliest handmaid vied with her mistress in extolling their beauty. But none of those eulogies on their looks touched his heart as deeply as the eulogies on the five royal hearts, their charity and their graciousness and their unceasing giving of gifts, which common folk praise in their princes more than in any other, less well-to-do, donor. Admittedly, one did not need to be a young Nikolaus Marggraf to succumb to the almighty force of an alliance of beauty with kindness and charity; a union like that of the inspiriting vine with the fructiferous tree, or the luster of a precious stone with its curative powers. — Now let the captivating and philanthropic countenance beam from beneath a coronet — not to mention a royal diadem — and it will raise no one's hackles that Nikolaus said: verily, this is simply too much of a good and a beautiful thing.

All the same, while following the five unseen ones in the castle gardens, stricken in advance though he was, he retained enough sense and respect not to pass the princesses or to cross their path — which could have meant gliding by the gallery of young madonnas at great speed and no feasting of eyes anywhere — rather he ambled ever more slowly, while his pulse raced ever more quickly, as he took it for granted that they should have to turn back up there at the linden walk's turnstile, and thus deliver the entire bouquet of lips and brows into his hands, that is to say, his eyes. "Four or five steps from the turnstile" — he reasoned — "I shall stop, hatless, and they shall have to float past me showing their sunny sides, and I shall receive the full charge. And at the same time, I shall find out which one is the possessor of that beautiful speaking voice." —

It was to turn out differently.

The blithe little goddesses of beauty and charm went past the turnstile; and three had already gone through; but when the two last ones attempted to reel themselves through nimbly, they happened to push the stile in the opposite way and were caught. The diverse directions now threw him into a splendid confusion, two of the ones passed through looking back for the ones left behind, a fifth moving on a bit by herself. He found himself face to face now with two of the graces at once and he was of two minds until the third also turned through the stile thus completing the treble of graces. And so — for hers must be the wonderful speaking voice, thought he — this magnificent one received his heart on the spot and only forfeited it when, to crown it all, the fourth one turned around, a Venus Urania, a little taller, more serious, lofty, and omnipotent than her retinue of graces. "This is a different matter again, and if it is she after all who has that wonderful speaking voice: well!" — thought he, thence bestowing his heart, recalled on the double, on this Venus forever.

Of course, the princesses, on becoming aware of the tall man walking behind them who, moreover, stood guard and waited now, hat almost on the ground, had gone into retreat to avoid having him in the rear, wheeled around and trained on him the full battery of their faces. — Heavens! why had he so few hearts, and in fact only one, instead of a whole mail coach team with which to harness himself to the triumphal chariot of this four-princess tetrarchate — those were his thoughts while the sacred tetraktys had to squeeze through the turnstile close by his eye and his hat.

"Amanda!" called some of the princesses at once to the fifth, who had walked ahead, lost in thought; but the wonderful speaking voice was not among them. Amanda whirled around and flew back, faster perhaps than proper to her lofty position; thus she carried her whole wide-eyed little face, ablaze with a gentle ethereal fire, her full lips combined with her lustrously rounded brow albeit above a nose, which was more a noselet, straight in front of her and exposed toward Nikolaus posted beside the turnstile.

Two minutes earlier Nikolaus would have sworn and given his life as a pledge that neither he nor anyone else could feel the love that infused him now — nothing remotely like it had ever happened around his heart — he was a man transformed, a transfigured Nikolaus, just arisen from the grave of dull mortality.

Beholding Amanda hurry along in order to pass through the stile, he obligingly, and with what little sense he could muster, held it open toward her thus unwittingly keeping her prisoner in its lobster claw. Now he beheld against the background of her wide green hat her charming face in close proximity, which half bloomed in the tender rose-red glow of the evening sun, with her limpid eyes in the shade. But in vain and smilingly she tugged at the lobster claw; he himself tried moving damsel and stile together — bereft of all sense —, when with that wonderful speaking voice she kept repeating without any irony or displeasure: "I thank you, I thank you," so that he should let the cross go and her be. This did finally come to pass; and, released, she thanked him once more with a friendly bow.

Thereby she had dropped her posy, a small orange spray — covered in blossoms and one unripe orange —; and Nikolaus leapt after her and the blossoms in order to hand them to her. But she declined acceptance with a little wave of her hand, robbed, by a kindly look, of any harshness the no might convey. Even I find it hard to decide whether this rendering of a toll charge to the apothecary was attributable more to a proud regality, disdaining owing a debt, or an embarrassed haste, or a rewarding kindness of heart. In any case, the apothecary attributed everything to the latter — and almost melted beside her with gratitude.

There is much to be said in favor of our Nikolaus Marggraf in this connection; for when she flew toward her companions he heard with his own ears Amanda's voice in answer to their question, presumably as to her lost spray of orange blossoms, wafting across: "Never mind, though! our dear Margrave will surely know how to take it." As modest Nikolaus would never connect his family name with the reigning Margrave — as equally none of us by the name of Judge or King or Saint, Taylor, Baker, Wolf, Lamb, or Bull will remember the figurative names in connection with ours —, he could not but, out of similar modesty, believe himself to be meant instead of the Margrave.

Dream upon the All

I was reading the Reflections[6] on that common old error that considers the spaces between one earth and sun and the next to be empty, still more that vast space between one solar system or galaxy and the next. The sun and all its spheres take up of the space between itself and the next sun a mere 3,149,460,000,000,000th little part. Good Heavens! thought I, in what a void the universe should be drowned if nothing were full but a few glinting dust-covered specks we call a planetary system.

Were ye to imagine the ocean defunct and inanimate and its populated islands shrunk to the size of snails' shells: ye should yet commit a far lesser error of scale than that of the world void; and the sea creatures should be committing a lesser one again were they to find living and fullness in the sea only and to regard the vast atmosphere above it to be an empty unlived-in space. If (as Herschel maintains) the most distant galaxies are located so far away from us that their light reaching our eyes today set forth two million years ago, so that whole starry skies beheld by us as still sparkling may be extinct already: oh, what vastnesses, depths, and heights in the universe, compared to which the very universe would be a nothing were it pervaded, and lastly embraced, by a void of such vastness! — But can we ignore for even one moment those forces that must flow hither and yon just to make navigable for our eyes the routes to those far distant coasts of the world? Can ye arrest the pull on an earth or a sun? Does light not flow through the vastnesses between earth and the farthest nebula? And is it not equally likely for a spirit world to dwell in those rivers of light as it is for thy spirit to dwell in the ether drop of thy brain?

After these and similar meditations, I dreamt the following dream: My body — thus went my dream — sank away from me and my inner form emerged into light; at my side stood a similar form, albeit sparkling incessantly rather than glowing. "Two thoughts," said that form, "are my wings, the thought of *Here*, the thought of *There*; and I am there. Think thou with me and fly thou with me that I might display the universe to thee and enshroud it."

And I flew with him. At my headlong ascent, the terrestrial globe hurtled into the chasm behind me, palely surrounded by some South American constellations only, and all that remained in the end of our sky was

6. Krüger, in an excellent treatise in the Archive of Discoveries from the Primeval World, by von Ballenstedt, Vol. 1 Part 1.

the sun, now a tiny starlet with a few little flickers of comets' tails drawn nigh. We flashed past a distant comet, which flew away from the terrestrial sun on its way toward Sirius.

Now we sped through the countless suns so fast that they could barely expand to the size of moons before diminishing into nebulous specks behind us; and their earths made no appearance at all in our rapid flight. At last, the terrestrial sun and Sirius and the galaxy and all the constellations of our sky were below us, a bright nebula among low little cloudlets. Thus we fled through the starry wastes; *ahead* of us, one firmament after another spread out, and narrowed *behind* us — and the galaxies stood erected one after another, remote, like triumphal arches of the infinite spirit. —

Now and again the sparkling form outflew my torpid thought and shone, far away from me, as a spark beside a star, until I thought once more: *There*, and reached his side. But as we submerged ourselves in one starry abyss after another, and the sky above our eyes grew no emptier and the sky beneath no fuller, and while suns plunged unceasingly into the solar ocean as a thunderstorm's cloudburst into the watery ocean: the human heart, filled to bursting, flagged and longed to leave the immense temple of suns for the narrow oratory of meditation, and I said to the form: "O, Spirit, has the universe then no end?" — He replied: "It has no beginning."

But behold, all of a sudden the sky above us seemed emptied, not a starlet twinkling in the immaculate darkness; — the sparkling form flew onward within it — in the end all starry skies dimmed into nebulae behind us and finally disappeared. — And I thought: "The universe did end after all" — but now I took fright at creation's boundless nocturnal dungeon, which set up its walls here, at the Dead Sea of Nothing, into whose bottomless darkness the gem of the shining universe sank unceasingly; and I found only the sparkling form, but not my lonely self, for I was left unillumined.

Then he answered my silent fear: "Oh, thou of little faith! Lift thine eyes! Immemorial light is arriving." I raised my eyes; swiftly a dawn appeared, swiftly a Milky Way, swiftly a whole twinkling starry firmament; no thought could keep pace with those three moments. For dim and distant eons that starlight had been on its way to us and at last arrived from its unfathomable heights. — Now we soared as through a new century, through the new stellar sphere. Once again there followed a starless night passage, and it took longer still before the rays of a distant starry sky reached us.

As we progressively alternated between nights and skies and surged ever farther into a darkness before each stellar vault would turn tiny spark and extinguish below us — as once we emerged all of a sudden from night to be faced by an aurora borealis of flaming suns struggling for globes, with doomsdays burning on every globe around us — and as we traversed the awesome realms of world geneses, where ethereal waters roared above our heads and age-long lightning flashed through the mists of being, where the dark, vast, leaden sphere of a sun only absorbed suns and flames without drawing light from them — and as I beheld a mountain range in the boundless distance, whose brilliant snow was a convergence of suns and yet had suspended above it galaxies in the form of fine crescent moons: my spirit lifted and bowed under the weight of the universe, and I said to the sparkling form: "Desist and lead me no farther; I am too lonesome within creation, and I shall be more lonesome still within its wastes; the inhabited world is vast, the empty world is vaster, the waste grows apace with the All."

Then the form touched me like a warm breath and spake more gently than heretofore: "There is no void before God; around the stars and between the stars lives the true universe. But thy mind can endure only earthly images of the celestial; attend the images!"

And behold, my eyes were opened and I beheld an infinite ocean of light on which suns and worlds were scattered, mere black rocky islets; I was within, not on, the ocean, and nowhere did there appear seabed, nowhere coast. All spaces between one galaxy and the next were filled with light, and sounding seas seemed to flow above seas and below seas, and there was a roaring as from a floodtide and, again, a fluting as from whooping swans in migration; but the two never mingled. The shining and the sounding gently conquered my heart; I was filled with joys, although I knew not whence they arose; it was like a happiness at Being and Being Forever, and an inexpressible love, although I knew not of what, touched me during my contemplation of the new light universe all around me. Then the form spake: "Thy heart now comprehends the world of the spirit; there is none for thine eye nor thine ear; only the world of the body, wherein it creates and reigns. Let thy sharpened eye now behold, poor mortal child; and let thy dreaming heart comprehend!" — And my eye beheld the closest and farthest, alike; I beheld the immense spaces traversed by us and the little starry skies within them; in the bright ethereal spaces, the suns floated as mere ashen-grey blossoms and the earths as black seed grains. — And the dreaming heart comprehended: Eternity dwelt in the spaces, Death in the worlds only. — Upright forms in the shape of man walked the suns but were transfigured on moving away from them and on going down in the ocean of light; and the dark planets were nothing but cradles for the infant spirits of the bright universe. — In these spaces glowed, sounded, wafted, and breathed only Life and Creation within the open All; the suns were nothing but spinning wheels, turning, the terrestrial globes nothing but weavers' shuttles being shot for the eternal web of the Isis veil, which was draped over creation and which expanded when raised by a mortal. There, in the face of living eternity, no great pain could exist any more; there could only be bliss without measure and a hymn of joy.

But in the glow of the Universe, the sparkling form had become invisible or had simply returned to the invisible world of the spirits; I was by myself amidst limitless life and longed for another being. And there sailed and surged from the depth and between all stars a dark world sphere, in full flight across the lofty ocean of light; and a human form like a child stood upon it, neither changing in form nor in size as it drew nigh. At last our earth stood before me and a Christ child on it; and the child looked upon me so bright and gentle and loving that I awoke for love and delight. —

But the bliss remained after I had awoken, and I said: "Oh, how beautiful is dying in full glowing creation, and living!" — And I gave thanks to the creator for life on the earth and the one to come without it.

Chapter Twenty-one
In One Course,
Wherein Everybody Is Ever More Surprised and Startled

The Course
Doings and Disquisitions in the Street — Strange Metamorphoses
Forward and Backward

On considering how the court jester, having only caught up with us in the preceding chapter, enters the plot in the present one without further ado, without any confounded and boring passport queries and inquisitions as to his actions and fortunes since or his sojourns and travels: — I almost look up to myself with a measure of self-content as the historical darling of a story in which I leave even novelists standing who are always so deft at inventing; — and in this I even surpass Walter Scott a little. For what is more tedious in the life of a reader than being — as happens equally often with Scott — plucked unexpectedly from the kindly

familiar present of the protagonist (he staying put himself) and flung into
the haphazard past of some erstwhile or recent arrival, thus having to
undergo pre-Adamite times in the middle of paradise? — And not for one
moment can I ever be safe with Scott in the finest Blücher charge from
a Scott retreat, which by the time the erstwhile or recent arrival's story
has caught up with our hero leaves me with nothing but what I have been
deprived of, viz, the continuation of our story. — By heaven, if there be
none, as I trust, among all mankind who may be diddled and lied to more
readily than one who reads: then I beseech ye, oh novelists, why on earth
cannot ye pronounce to the credulous straightaway: *she* was like this,
while *he* endured that, or whatever ye like, or serve them your crabs —
thus avoiding crab scuttling yourselves — as if they were well done and
really boiled red in the pan, never mind their wriggling still and scrabbling backward like those crabs in the streams of Solothurn or those that
look purple from brandy, although uncooked and lively.

Yea, even men of my craft, viz, history writers, have perpetrated such
novel faults in their presentations, which I am innocent of. Or think ye
I hop, as does the great Thucydides, from the Mitylenaeans to the Spartans before their story is finished — or from those, again minus finish,
to the siege of the Plataeans — and finally back again to the former —
and lastly from thence to Corcyra, in order, nevertheless, to depart for
Sicily with the Athenians forthwith? And can a Dionysius of Halikarnassos, who reproached that old Greek with the foregoing, go on in
the same vein, accusing me in my fifties, as he did him in his seventies, of
skipping to the Peloponnesus after that and on to Doris — to Leukas —
Naupaktus — and to And-so-forth? ... However, without flaunting
these or any other dissimilarities any further, by which I distinguish myself from Thucydides, I would rather return without leaps or bounds to
my history. —

. . . .

Only the court jester laughed. "Why is that clumsy fellow, who can
neither ride nor walk, blocking the merry man's way?" asked Libette.
"He is really looking for me, and I sent for him myself to the house. —
Do come here, Blacky!" she called to him. "See how he comes? I can
twist him around my finger, for it takes a sage to know one. And yesterday
in the little houses" (she was not referring to petites maisons but to Nikolopolis), "I conversed at length and in depth with him on his leanness
and blackness and leatherness."

The court jester's influence on the normally unruly Cain caused amazement; only the Harbinger, who was in the know concerning Libette, thought to himself that the madcap had sensed her sex, the presence of which always assuaged and subdued his hatred of man. Worble was canny enough, by the bye, — as indeed each of us may well be — to see Libette's approach to this complete fool on matters of world government as a political move, whereby she hoped to effect with the help of the complete a healing influence on the partial fool, her brother.

At all events, with such a garrison, Hasencoppen and company could not but match Libette's daring and throw open the fortress to the enemy. Cain walked quietly and silently up to the company without the slightest response to Libette's jests. Equally gently and quietly did he walk past the horseman and up the stairs: once in the Count's room, however, his hairy horns stirred and his ears and nose twitched on his head. He had, with the madman's usual cunning, postponed his eruptions. "Got ye at last," he began, "alive and in front of me within four walls, and ye will have to attend to me now, all of ye. When I have done, ye may leave; whoso sooner departs, deceases. No one will kill me, whereas I shall kill one and the other. Ye desire to ape my subjects, the apes, oh ye subsimians; but ye are a poor copy — ye have renounced Antichrist; and by yere cowardly piety and yere persistent stupidity in the face of a millenium's experiences, ye make yereselves undeserving of Hell. My apes are shrewder, and unlike ye, they do not allow themselves to be ruled by ye, nay, not even by such as themselves. Do not imagine yereselves to be complete apes on account of a certain resemblance in several limbs; the dog, the lion, the pig also resemble some apes, without by any means being apes,[7] and the orangutan laments his kinship to ye.[8] Helvetius's pride in two hands is put to shame by the ape with his four; and yere would-be-lofty form, raised it may be by yere Horace and Herder, cringes and crumbles in the face of the giant constrictor and Serpent of Eden, rearing and towering high above steeples.

Only peel off yere skins and behold yereselves stripped and cut open: and instead of yere charms and human features, there will be cerebral spheres, cardiac lumps, stomach bags, and guts suspended, wriggling in front of yere eyes; that is why ye even cover yere feet and yere hands with animal skins, and yere mangy scalps with animal hair, flaunting black legs

7. The dog head, the pig-tailed ape and the lion marmoset, the baboon and the long-tailed monkey, with their animal likeness permeating their likeness to man, call to mind the physiological tenet that man is supposed to be the animal kingdom's offshoot and apicular flower.

8. As against the other apes, the orangutan is known to be solemn and dull.

and heads and the gaily bright bodices over yere bare-plucked undercoat bodies.

Add to that now yere eternal pitiful dying, and yere not even living as long as the turtle inside its carapace, not to mention myself outside yere Paradise. Are ye not altogether nothing but phantasmagoria people, not even wooden ones, nay, mere aerial marionettes of the kind the bookseller Nicolai in Berlin saw flitting and chattering all around him, until he conducted a bloodbath among this humanity and deployed caudal leeches as destroying angels among those forms, thereby thinning and clearing the whole chamber, until only himself was left, which human being this Nicolai failed to cast to the beasts or maggots, a deed that will only be done with his death?" —

I am sure that the Leather Man span out this simile only because of the common name of Nicolai and Nikolaus. But there was no damming this torrent of words with any retort, and the raging was all the more unexpected, the convict preacher having delivered his earlier sermons in a long-winded manner where the endings had merely bogged down.

"Why don't ye tot up yere nights of *one* year and examine, during the 365th, what is left of those long dream affairs on yere pillows, of the battles, frolickings, convivialities, and conversaziones and the long spooky stories? Not the tiniest feather, not the barest breeze; and now add yere 365 days as well: and ye will come up with the same again, and the devil has the last laugh, ruling yere nights and yere days, and ye all unaware of it.

And yet ye would prefer to be governed by the insipid, the feeble, the transparent men rather than by the Devil, who has a thousand times more sense and life than the whole lot of ye and who only rules yere rulers out of pity. — What kind of beings are ye at all? Yere mothers give birth to yere religion, making ye into Jews or Christians or Turks or Pagans; the placenta being the propaganda, the potter's wheel of yere faith. — Thrones are erected on birth chairs, and a Delphic mother oracle will decide whom ye will adore as a ruler or reprieve as a subject. A boy aged 5 years and 7 months, Louis XV, appoints before Parliament the Duke of Orleans Regent for the duration of his minority,[9] and the Duke submits any state resolutions to the boy for his ultimate approval; and his infant predecessor, the Fourteenth, orders Parliament to declare him of age on the spot and obey him. — Two royal villains, the brothers Caracalla, neither of whom was fit even to be a Roman slave, but both of

---

9. The Memoires of the Duke of Richelieu. Vol. 1.

whom issued the laws for both free men and slaves of two continents, wished to divide up the current universe of that time and one to rule merely in Europe and the other merely in Asia and to supervise their affairs.[10] Such ye were from time immemorial, and Time only makes ye grow pale with fear, black with wickedness and, not until afterwards, blushing with shame. And yere generations are mellowed by nothing but worm caprification under the soil and, as no age is going to bring ye on and develop ye, ye supply yere dead soldiers with spurs on their boots as they are laid out on their pallets. — Yea, go forth and kill each other more often. . . . .always obey them who order ye to the battleground. . . . . and act above and beyond the call of duty by dying at least if ye do not kill. . . . . What is it that hampers my speech now? I feel something, my eyelids are drooping — and I do not want to look much longer on this stupid dismal earth; Hell is brighter." —

To be sure, the Leather Man did feel something, because Worble behind his back had hitherto striven with all his finger levers to transpose him out of the waking into the sleeping state and thereby raised a force of volition sufficient to bring down and put to sleep an army of female invalides. But it was an effort for him to stem and put back Cain's current with his own anticurrent; to quench the fire against all with the fire for some.

Cain went on: "Truly I have been outside eternity for a very long time, and I must swim through the narrow moments of temporality and look upon dying. — The Earth is a foolish place — I am falling asleep."

Worble had just touched the back of his head with his fingers bunched like a brush of electricity, striking him lightninglike, and suddenly sending him into the most extreme mesmeric crisis. In his somnambulist manner, the stricken man attempted the ascent[11] with his eyes closed by thrusting himself into the fireplace and easily upward with the help of little external handholds.

But all were bewildered by a strange, sweet, affectionate voice, which addressed them now out of hiding: "Oh my dearly beloved humans, pray forgive my flight, but I cannot bear my guilt and yere forgiveness face-to-face with ye; yet I see ye all. Oh, thanks be to thee above all who didst turn the black ether blue for me and hast led me out of my burning wasteland into the cool land of the evening glow for a little while. Oh

10. Herodian, Ch. 4.

11. Well known and documented is the skill of several somnambulists of lifting themselves up walls and everywhere with little aids, just like animals.

how my desolate gushing heart has now become still and light and pure! And I love the whole world now, as if I were a child. And I will tell ye all about myself cheerfully, nothing but truth.

In the night I used to walk about angrily as a somnambulist with a closed gloomy mind, and I roamed over the rooftops and broke in everywhere searching for food and drink; and I did so everywhere in my sleepwalking in order to sustain myself. But at the moment of waking, any memory of my stealing and feeding was gone, and I went on to see myself as the imperishable Cain and once more renounced both mankind and God. For I must be punished for my myriad sins, all of them sins in solitude; in my study chamber, I was all that was wicked through thinking — fire raiser — poisoner — blasphemer — oppressive ruler of all countries and all spirits — adulterer — inner actor of satanic parts and, above all, of the lunatic into which I thought myself, frequently feeling that there was no escape. — Thus I am being punished and go on being punished in thoughts about thoughts, and I shall suffer much yet. — Oh ye happy people about me, ye may love the Eternal One, but I must blaspheme against him on waking; and on the first stroke of the christening bell at three o'clock, I shall wake again and be devilish; beware of the wretch then; for my hell will sting and burn all the more scorchingly on reappearing from behind this cool heavenly cloud, the serpent upon my brow will glow all the more poisonously, and should I be able to murder after this truce of evil Nature, I shall do so; — especially thou, my gentle Marggraf, avoid me while thy halo encircles thy head. Once on a rooftop at midnight, I beheld thee with one, and I hated thee fervently; but the moment I wake it will shimmer around thee, on account of thy tender soul, and arouse my ire.

Even now I love all ye mortals with all my heart like a child, and I hate no one on earth. — I hold thee in my heart once again, thou everloving God who looketh comfortingly into the countless deep wounds of mankind and finally taketh either the wound or the wounded. Oh God of Love, be thou loved on by me on my waking. The terrible hour is nigh, bearing my Fury mask toward me and laying it over my face! — Father of Man, I too am thy son; and I will obey thee forever; Father, do not desert me when the little bell tolls.". . . . .

Just then, the clock struck three, and we heard but his weeping, and our souls wept with him within all of us. Suddenly there was the sound of the little christening bell, and the wretch pitched down, awake. Face and hands were blackened, his hair tufts stood angrily on end, and on the swollen skin of his forehead the scarlet serpent writhed, ready to strike, and he cried joyfully: "Oh Father Beelzebub, here I am with thee again; why hadst thou forsaken me?"

They all stepped far away from him, not out of fear but in horror.

Self-Life Description

ABOUT NO OTHER WORK DOES JEAN PAUL COMPLAIN SO much of labor pains as in his letters about his *Self-Life Description* (*W* 12.1039ff.). To the closest friend of his later years, Emanuel Osmund, he said he had become so used to telling lies in his novels, he would rather tell the story of any other life than his own. It afforded him little pleasure, he wrote to Voß, for he had nothing to make up and in no one was he less interested than in himself. It had nothing to do with aversion toward the past, he wrote to his son Max, but with his indifference to "my *I*, as such" and his abhorrence of merely narrating (*H-KA* 3.7.224, 238; 3.8.135). He considered various ways of fictionalizing it, as a necrology, or by coupling it with *The Comet*, to give his own kind of *Dichtung* and *Wahrheit*. In the end, he imagined himself holding a Professorship in the History of Himself and delivering a course of lectures in the winter semester on his special topic. As it turned out, however, it is a very straightforward narrative, lively and graphic in spite of his misgivings. It is a fragment (of which about two-thirds is translated here) of three lectures, the first on his birthplace, Wunsiedel, the second and longest on the scene of his early childhood, Joditz, and the third beginning the period when his father went to the larger parish of Schwarzenbach.

First Lecture

Wonsiedel — Birth — Grandfather

Most Gentle Benefactors and Benefactresses!

It was in the year 1763 that the Peace of Hubertusburg came into the world and also the present Professor of His Own History; — to be precise, in that month that also saw the arrival of the blue-headed and the grey wagtails, the red robin, the crane, the reed bunting and divers snipe and marsh birds, viz, in March; — moreover, on that day of the month when, had his cradle been strewn with flowers, spoonwort and celandine and the aspen burst into bloom to that very end, as did the field speedwell or chickweed, on the 21st of March; — moreover, at the earliest and sweetest time of the day, namely at 1½ o'clock in the morning; but the supreme glory of it all was that the beginning of his life should also be the beginning of spring.

. . . .

But let me return to our history and betake myself among the dead; for they have all departed the world who saw me into it. My Father was called Johann Christian Christoph Richter, and he was third teacher and organist in Wunsiedel; my Mother, the daughter of cloth maker Johann Paul Kuhn in Hof, was called Sophia Rosina. I was baptized by Senior Pastor Apel on the day after my birth. The aforementioned Johann Paul was one of my godfathers; the other was Johann Friedrich Thieme, a bookbinder, ignorant of the fact on how great a Maecenas of his art he was bestowing his name at the time; whence arose the name of Johann Paul Friedrich, amalgamated from both, and the grandfatherly half of which I translated into French, thus elevating it to the full name of Jean Paul, for reasons to be stated during later lectures in the course of this winter term.

But for the time being, we shall let the protagonist and object of this historical lecture rest unobserved in his cradle and at his mother's breast and sleep on — as there is nothing of interest to be gained with regard to general world history from the auscultation of life's long matutinal sleep — sleep on, I say, until I have spoken, albeit only a little and insufficiently, of those toward whom both my heart and my pen impel me, of my forebears, of father, mother, and grandparents.

My Father was the son of Rector Johann Richter in Neustadt on Kulm. Nothing is known of the latter but that he was both exceedingly poor and devout. Whenever one of his two remaining grandsons arrives in Neustadt, he is received with grateful and joyful affection by its inhabitants, and the older people will tell him how conscientious and strict his life and his lessons had been, but how cheerful at the same time. They will show you a little bench at the back of the organ, where he had knelt in prayer each Sunday; and a hollow, which he had dug for himself in the Little Culm as it was called, in order to pray there, and which faced the faraway places where his fiery son — albeit too fiery in his eyes only — was the playmate of both the Muses and Penia. Dusk was to him a diurnal autumn season, in which he would reckon in prayer today's crop and to-morrow's sowing, while pacing the humble schoolroom for a few dark hours. His schoolhouse was a jail, to be sure, if not on water and bread, at least on beer and bread; for a rector's position did not yield much more than those two — together with perhaps the most godly contentment — bringing in, as it did, in conjunction with the cantor's and organist's posts and, notwithstanding this treble-office pride of lions, no more than 150 gulden per annum. And it was at this ordinary Baireuthean schoolmas-ters' trickle spring that the man stood for 35 long years drawing water. To be sure, he would have earned a few more bites or pence had he been promoted to country parson, for instance. When schoolmasters change their gown, for example the schoolmasterly for the priestly cloth, their sustenance improves with it, just as silkworms receive a richer feed each time they slough off their skins; so that such a man can increase his in-come by increasing his labors to the point of approaching, with allow-ances and gratuities or a general pension, the higher retired servant of the state, whose five staves are dotted with notes all the way through the revenue office score, notwithstanding the instrument's many rests. —

Whenever my grandfather called on his pupils' parents during the afternoon, more for the pupils' than their parents' benefit: he would carry in his pocket the bread of the aforementioned bread and beer, on which he existed all his life, and expect hospitality only in the shape of a mug of beer. However, finally it did come to pass in the year 1763 — that is to say, in the year of my birth — on the 6th of August, that, probably thanks to special *higher connections*, he received in passing one of the most important positions for which it was easy, indeed, to exchange rectorship, town, and Hill of Culm; he was in fact only 76 years, 4 months, and 8 days of age when he really was awarded the said position in the — churchyard of Neustadt; his wife having preceded him there 20 years before into the associate position. — My parents had journeyed to his deathbed with me, a 5-months-old infant in arms. And as he was at Death's door, a clergyman (as my Father was fond of telling me) said to my parents: Ask old Jakob to lay hands on the child that he might bless him. I was handed into the deathbed, and he laid his hand on me — Saintly Grandfather! Time and again I have thought of thy dying hand imparting that blessing, when Fate led me out of dark hours into brighter ones; and I may indeed hold onto my faith in thy blessing in this world imbued with and ruled and animated by miracles and spirits!

My Father, born in Neustadt in 1727 on the 16th of December — almost more for the winter of life than for spring like myself, I should have said, had his strong disposition not known how to chisel a decent harbor even from icebergs — could only enjoy, or suffer, the Wunsiedel Latin school, like Luther the one in Eisenach, as a so-called alumnus, or charity scholar; for if one duly divided an annual income of 150 florin between father, mother, and several sisters, nothing whatever was left for him but the alumnus bread, at the most. Thereafter, he entered the gymnasium poeticum in the city of Regensburg, so that he might not only starve in a bigger city but germinate there the true flower of his being instead of the mere foliage. And that was the art of music. In the chapel of the then Prince of Thurn and Taxis, — the renowned cognoscente and patron of music — he was able to serve the saint to whose praise he had been born. Piano and basso continuo were to elevate him two decades later to well-loved composer of sacred music in the Principality of Baireuth. On Good Friday nights, he was often to delight himself and us children with interpretations of divine omnipotence, whose intonations lifted and sanctified souls in Catholic churches during those days. I am afraid I must confess that, on visiting Regensburg a few years ago, none of the local antiquities and past events — not even excepting the Imperial Diet — were as important to me as the straitened paternal existence there; and in the castle of Thurn and Taxis and in the narrow streets where a couple of potbellies would be hard put not to bump into each other, I was often reminded of the strait paths and narrow thoroughfares of the days of his youth. Afterward, he studied theology in Jena and Erlangen instead of music, maybe only in order to toil as a tutor in Baireuth for a time, where his son is collecting all these reports, viz, into his 32nd year. For as early as 1760 he wrested the post of organist and third teacher in Wonsiedel from the state; and accordingly, as a subject of the Margrave

of Baireuth, made his fortune earlier and more successfully than that candidate did in Hanover of whom I read, who lived to be seventy and yet
never gained an ecclesiastical position apart from the one in the churchyard beside it.

Let none of my audience now conclude from the preceding that they
might be offered by me a father who would shuffle along miserably like
some latter-day superchristian swaddled in tear-drenched handkerchiefs;
nay, he was wing borne, and he was welcomed as the most congenial of
companions, full of good cheer, by the best families of all Brandenburg
and Schöpf. The virtue of drawing-room pleasantry stayed with him all
through his life, while in office he was considered the strictest clergyman
and in the pulpit a so-called preacher of the law. In his home town, his
enthusiastic sermons won over his relatives, but in Hof in Vogtland
something still more important, viz, a bride and, even more formidable,
the well-to-do parents-in-law to go with her. If a burgher who has prospered by cloth making and veil selling does not refuse the most beautiful,
delicate, and favorite of his only two daughters to an impecunious third
teacher living a day's journey away in the company of his creditors: then,
on the one hand, this particular third teacher could only have conquered
daughter and parents on the merits of his personal appearance and his
reputation and the mark of great pulpit gifts, and on the other hand,
there must have dwelt in the cloth maker a soul far above his cloth and
his money, to whom the state of talent and of spiritual dignity must have
appeared in a loftier light than the dazzling pile of silver of a common
individual. In the year 1761, on the 13th of October, the loving girl made
her entrance with her possessions as a bride into his cramped little
schoolhouse, luckily unhampered by any furniture of his own. His serene
life, his complete indifference to money, combined with his trust in his
housekeeper, left empty space to spare in his tertiate shell for any mov-
able objects from Hof, which might care to settle therein; — but my
Mother — and that was what married couples were like then and some
are like that even now — took no more notice of that emptiness during
her whole married life than my Father himself. It takes just as much courage for the strong man to marry an affluent girl as an indigent one.

In the course of my history lectures, going hungry will feature increasingly, to be sure, — it is about to rise considerably for our hero — and
I dare say at least as frequently as feasting in Thümmel's Journeys and
drinking tea in Richardson's Clarissa; yet I cannot but say to poverty: hail
to thee, as long as thou comest not too late in life. Riches do weigh more
heavily on talent than poverty, and many a mental giant may well lie

crushed and buried beneath thrones and mountains of gold. Should the oil of riches be poured onto the flames of youth and its burning forces: not much more than ashes will be left of the phoenix; and only a Goethe possessed the strength not to have singed his phoenix's wings at the sun of good fortune. The present poor professor of history would not like for all the gold in the world to have had a lot of it in his youth. Fate deals with poets as we do with birds, when we keep the cage darkened until the singer finally knows the tune he is expected to sing.

Only spare, impartial fate, an old man a life in poverty! He is the one who shall and must be rewarded; his back has been bent too low by his burdensome years, and he is able no longer to straighten up and to shoulder the load as in the days of his youth. Old age needs the peace beneath the ground while still above it; for there is no longer a future of planting and flowering as a foil to the present. Two steps away from his last and profoundest slumber, with only flowers as curtains, he wishes only to rest and to take it easy in the grandfather chair of old age and, between sleeping and waking, to open his eyes one last time and to gaze on the old familiar stars and meads of his youth; and I have nothing at all against it if — having accomplished what was important, even for the beyond — he looks forward to breakfast at night and to his bed in the morning and if, a child for the second time, he is dismissed by the world while enjoying the innocent sensual pleasures with which it had welcomed him at first.

. . . .

I return at last to the protagonist and subject of our historical lecture, laying particular stress on the fact that I was born in Wonsiedel (less correctly Wunsiedel), a town at the foot of the Fichtel Mountains. The Fichtel Mountains, almost the highest region of Germany, bestow on their residents health (they are the first who can do without the spa of Alexandersbad) and a fine physique; and the professor will leave it to his female audience to decide whether he himself appears as living proof or the exception to this in his chair.

. . . .

I was gladly born in thee, little town at the tall mountain range, whose peaks look down on us like the heads of eagles! — Thou hast adorned thy mountain throne with steps leading up to it; and thy healing well provides the energy — not for thyself but for the — sick to ascend to the canopy on high and to hold sway over the wide plains and villages at his feet. — I was gladly born in thee, thou small but dear luminous town! —

· ·

As my Father had been ordained pastor in Joditz by 1765: I can isolate my Wonsiedel childhood reliquary all the more clearly from my first and earliest relics and childhood memories of Joditz.

That parish now is the second act of this little historical monodrama, in which ye, most esteemed Gentlemen and Mistresses, are going to en- counter the protagonist of this play in very different developments in the course of the second lecture. . . . Our hero's ascent has begun, and we have the pleasure of meeting the historical person, whom we had left behind in our first lecture a mere Tertius's son, only two years later, in our second, as the son of a pastor; for in 1765, my Father was called to Joditz by Baroness von Plotho in Zedwitz, née Bodenhausen, the wife of the same Plotho who, in the reign of Frederick the Unique, had, with reason, thrown an Austrian delegate down the stairs at the Diet.

Second Lecture (comprising the period between 1765 and 1775)

Joditz — Village-Idylls

Most Esteemed Gentlemen and Mistresses!
Ye now find the Professor of Self-History in the parish of Joditz where, dressed in a female bonnet and a little girl's smock, he had made his entry together with his parents; the River Saale, springing like myself from the Fichtel Mountains, had followed me there, just as it was to wend its way past the town of Hof before I would come to live there myself later on. The river is the most beautiful, or at least the longest, object in Joditz, flowing around it along the surrounding hills, while the village itself is bisected by a little stream with its footbridge. An ordinary castle and parsonage will be its most significant buildings. The surrounding area is no larger than twice the size of the village, unless one climbs up the hills. — All the same, the village is of greater importance even to a Professor of Self-History than the town of his birth, because he experi- enced there the most important matter, viz, his boyhood olympiads.

I could never applaud the 19 towns, which (according to Suidas) squabbled about the honor of having been Homer's birthplace, no more than the various Dutch locations all claiming to have given birth to Eras- mus (according to Bayle); for even where they lay buried could more merit — or demerit as the case may be — be shared by the inhabitants than where their cradles had stood. But although on the whole a great many princes are born in capital cities, ye'll never hear London, Paris, Berlin, and Vienna boast of it; otherwise all those towns and villages that had produced archscoundrels would have to bear the brunt in inverse ratio. At the most, one might allow native countries to usurp the kudos of native towns provided that a glut of commendable births there has benefitted their regions and their inhabitants quite decisively; but *one* Pindar in Boetia does by no means make it a swallows' summer.

But the real birthplace, that is to say, the spiritual one, is the place of our earliest and most prolonged education; and this even for those world-famous men who rarely require and rarely have recourse to education; but more especially for average men of village- or town-fame, like my hero, who gained so much by both education and spoliation and who really did become thus, in combination with reading (yet another educational and spoliatory institution), the man he now is, viz, a Legation Counselor of Hildburghausen and a Doctor of Philosophy of Heidelberg and, afterward a thrice-affiliated member of various societies and the present unworthy incumbent of this Self-historical professorship.

Let no poet ever be born and educated in a capital city but, if at all possible, in a village, or at least in nothing larger than a small town. To the excitable, delicate infant soul, the superabundance and overstimulation of a large city are a diet of sweetmeats and brandies and bathing in mulled wine. His life will exhaust itself therein in his boyhood, and having tasted the largest, there will be nothing left to whet his appetite but the smaller, a village at most. But there is not half as much to be gained and discovered by moving from town to country as the other way around, from Joditz to Hof. And if, furthermore, I consider what matters most for a poet, loving: in town he will have to encircle the warm equator of parental friends and acquaintances with the wider, frigid tropic and polar zones of unloved people whom he encounters anonymously and who kindle in him as much love or warmth as ships passing each other in the night. But in a village, one loves the whole village; and not an infant in arms will be buried there without everybody else knowing its name and its sickness and sorrow; the people of Joditz are closely attached to each other by habitation and habit; — and this wonderful solidarity with anyone human, including stranger and beggar, is the wellspring of an intensified love of mankind, and its proper heartbeat. — And later on, when the poet takes leave of his village, he will have plenty of heart to share with anybody he might encounter, and he will have a long way to go before his heart will finally have been spent on the highways and byways. —

There is a misfortune, however, that is even greater than growing up in a capital city, viz, the misfortune of having been brought up en route as a wellborn child passing through one strange town after another and from one stranger to the next for years on end and knowing no house but the coach box.

We are about to catch up again with our son of the parsonage, whose life in Joditz I believe I can best represent by letting it file past as a complete idyll yearbook; but I shall let that which does not belong to the bright days go ahead, like foggy weather; that is to say, my lessons; although this fog did lift in the end, to be sure — but only after 10 long years. All learning was life to me, and I would have revelled in being instructed, like a prince, by half a dozen teachers at once, but I had hardly one proper one. I still remember the winter evening bliss when at last I received into my hands from town the ABC reader with its attached stylus as line indicator, on whose cover was printed in truly golden letters (and not without justification) the content of the first page, consisting of alternate red and black letters; no gambler has ever derived more thrills out of gold or rouge et noir than I did out of my book; this is not even counting the stylus. Armed with this now — having gone through enough exclusive tuition and passed all the lower classes within myself — and decked in a bonnet of green taffeta but already in little trousers (in wrestling with which, the schoolmaster's wife was to deputize for my own inept little fingers in public), I made my way to the academy, viz, to the schoolmaster's apartment across the road from the parsonage, and proceeded to recite to all and sundry with the help of my stylus. True to custom, I fell in love with every living thing in the schoolroom, first and foremost with the consumptive, gaunt, but wide-awake schoolmaster, whose anxious anticipation I shared while he was lying in wait for a goldfinch to alight on his trap at the window, or about to throw his snare over the bunting on the fowling floor in the snow outside. And of the Greenlandic winter fug of the crowded schoolroom I remember with pleasure the long stuffed linen bungs, which plugged small air holes drilled into the wooden wall and which one had only to pull out in order to gulp the most wonderful frosty draughts from outside. I was inspired by each new letter out of the schoolmaster's hand, as others might be by a painting; and I envied the ones who were saying their lessons, as I would dearly have liked to enjoy the bliss of spelling as well as singing in concert.

Nothing could please me and my brother Adam — although he would rather have had a bird's nest than a muse's seat any day — more than not finding our dinner ready at 12 o'clock; for we would dash back with our hunger to school so as not to miss even a minute of it and appease the former afterward. Much was made of our devotion to learning; but I know well that the normal child's predilection for a change in the daily routine provided the lion's share; we wanted to eat 3 hours later; and it was for the same reason that we looked forward to the late dinners on fast- and penance-days. Giddy little humans know no greater fun than having the whole house topsy-turvy, whether because rooms were being whitewashed, or we stayed in a strange house, or a lot of visitors were expected, or whatever.

Alas, I locked myself out of the schoolroom forever through an untimely complaint to my Father about a lanky peasant boy (_Zäb_ is his name, for posterity) who had tapped my fingers with a jackknife. And out of ambitious ire, he alone now took over my own and my brothers' schooling; and I had to watch the schoolchildren across the road sailing into a port each winter that remained barred to me. However, there was still the minor pleasure of delivering many a papal bull and decree of his village pope to the schoolmaster and, instead of the Roman agnus dei, or blessed swaddling clothes, or roses, Christmas gifts, a platter of meats or sausages on pig-killing day or some other delectable dish.

For four hours in the morning and three in the afternoon we were instructed by our Father, which meant that he made us learn things by heart: proverbs, the catechism, Latin words, and Lange's Grammar. We had to memorize the long gender rules of each declension, complete with exceptions, as well as the attached Latin paradigms, without understanding any of them. On fine summer's days when he would walk abroad: we would be given such confounded exceptions as panis piscis to be recited next morning, of which my brother Adam, for whom a whole day wasn't long enough for his romps and capers, never remembered more than a fraction. For only rarely did Fortune smile on him when he was made to recite such delightful declensions as scamnum or even cornu in the singular, of which he at least knew how to declaim the Latin half perfectly. Believe me, Ladies and Gentlemen, it was not at all easy on an azure June day, and while the omnipotent lord and father was not at home, to detain and arrest oneself in some corner and memorize two or three pages of vocabulary, all of the same initial and sounding alike; as I say, on such long cerulean days of delight, it was not as easy as on a dim white December day; and it is no surprise that my brother Adam would reap a lot of thrashings on days like that. But the Professor of this Self-History makes bold to put forward the general statement that he himself _never_ received a thrashing during his whole _pupillage_, neither limb by limb nor in his entirety; the Professor always knew his piece.

But we must not let this memorizing put my indefatigable and loving

Father into a false light. He who sacrificed the whole day to writing down and learning by heart his sermons for the peasants, and that only out of an overdeveloped sense of duty, although he had experienced the force of his extempore rhetoric on more than one occasion, and he who, by his weekly visits to the schoolroom and his doubling of public religious instruction for children and in everything else exceeded his duties with his devotion, and who, with his soft, warm, paternal heart was attached to me most of all and was easily moved to tears of joy at small signs of my talents or progress, this Father of mine made no mistakes in his whole mode of education — no matter how strange the ones we may yet come across — save those of reason, not of intent.

This method ought to be recommended even to actual teachers, because no other saves as much time and labor as this truly convenient one, whereby the pupil receives in the book the vicar, or adjunct, or the curator absentis, of his teacher and mesmerizes himself like a vigorous clairvoyant. Nay, this mental self-suckling of children allows expansion to such a degree that I venture by mere letter post to take the helm of whole schools somewhere in North America or at the other end of the world, and I would merely write and tell my schoolchildren what to memorize every day and engage some insignificant person to hear their lessons, and I would enjoy being aware of their beautiful mental reminiscere Sundays in Lent.

I translated much of the beginning of Speccius, as ordered, with the same pleasure with which I would strip any other new branch of learning; the last part I put into Latin under my own steam, but without finding somebody to correct my mistakes. The colloquia (discourses) in Lange's Grammar I divined on my own in German from a longing to know their contents; but my Father did not make me translate in Joditz. In a Greek grammar written in Latin, I avidly and voraciously studied the alphabet and, in the end, quite managed writing Greek, at least with regard to the script. How gladly I would have learned more, and how easily! The spirit, if not the body, of a language easily took possession of me, as will perhaps be demonstrated in public in the course of the third lecture of our winter term.

Only once, on a winter's evening — I might have been eight or nine years old — when my Father wanted to practice a short Latin word book with me, that is, to make me learn it by heart, and I had to read out the first page to him: I read lingua not lingva, but always lin-gua, despite his correction and repeated that mistake in the face of all his corrective gestures so often that he became furious and, in a fit of angry impatience, withheld the book and its study from me forever. I never managed to trace my stubborn stupidity to its source; yet there was no malicious complicity of my heart involved in this — as it assured me all my life — nor in anything else, least of all directed against my Father, who after all offered me a new boyish delight in the form of a different book to memorize. It is with a purpose that we narrate this historic trait in our lecture hall so that the faults, which he points out with something resembling appreciation, in a hero whom, truth permitting, he always presents in a most flattering light, should prove the impartiality of this scholarly investigator and professor of history. — Incidentally, though, how often do not poor innocent people, un-understood and misunderstood, say lingua in life instead of the so correct ling-va, moreover with the tongue (lingua), which at the same time means language! —

History, by the way, — both ancient and modern —, natural history, also the most important bits of geography, likewise arithmetic and astronomy, as well as orthography, all of those sciences I did get to know adequately, although not in Joditz, where I lived to the age of twelve in total innocence — but several years later, in print and in chunks out of the Universal Library. I was all the more parched for books in this mental Sahara. Each book was to me a verdant oasis, especially the orbis pictus and Conversations in the Realm of the Dead; except that my Father's library was like many a public one, rarely open, unless he was absent from it and from home. In any case, I was often prostrate on the flat roof of a wooden cot (not unlike an enlarged animal cage) and, like the great lawyer Baldus, I crawled across books in order to secure one for myself. If ye would just consider that, in a village without population and in a lonely parsonage, books had to be speaking people for a soul so eager to hear, and the most affluent visitors from foreign countries, Maecenases, royalty passing through, the first Americans, or New Worldlings for a European.

Historical greenhorn that I was, I did not understand in the least the quarto volumes of the Conversations in the Realm of the Dead; but I read them, as I read newspapers as a geographical greenhorn, and I was able to quote liberally from both these sources. Just as I told my Father of them — one evening without reprimand on his part the story of Roxelane's love affair with the Turkish Sultan — I treated an old noblewoman to extracts from newspapers. For he was presented with the Baireuther Zeitung by his patroness Plotho in Zedwitz; monthly or quarterly — depending on how often he called at Zedwitz — he would bring home a monthly or quarterly volume all at once, and he and myself would read it to our profit precisely because we received it in volumes rather than sheets. A political newspaper offers true reports only if read not in single sheets but in volumes, as it is only within the space of a whole volume that it contains the sheets that confute its earlier sheets; and like the wind, it cannot show its true color in single puffs and batches but in its larger volume, again as the aforementioned air its cerulean blue only in bulk. I would carry my news atlas into old Lady Reitzenstein's manor and divine one or other item of what I had brought for her during her morning coffee, waiting to be praised for it. I can still recall a certain plural featuring frequently at the time, viz., "confederates." Although it was most likely that the plural belonged to Poland, I cannot recall having taken the slightest interest, as I expect the whole matter was incomprehensible to me in any case. With such a degree of impartiality and equanimity were Poland's affairs viewed in our village, both by myself and my audience.

Our protagonist's avid roots squeezed and twisted in every direction seeking to grasp and to feed. He manufactured clocks, whose dials were their best features and which were equipped with a pendulum and *one* wheel and weights, and which marked time beautifully. He even invented a sundial by inking a clockface onto a wooden plate; and he positioned and fixed the plate with its tin gnomon pointing at the church clock; hence he frequently knew what time it was. Like many a state, he preferred issuing figures on timepieces and beforehand and, like Lichtenberg with his book titles, well in advance of the works themselves. The present author revealed himself in miniature by a box, in which he assembled a pocket compendium of little sextodecimo works of his own, stitched together and cut into shape from the narrow scraps of his Father's octavo sermons. Their content was of a theological and Protestant nature and, in each case, consisted of an exegetical note beneath a verse copied from Luther's bible; he did not bother with the verse itself in his booklet. Thus there was a little Friedrich von Schlegel buried in our Friedrich Richter who, in his excerpts "The Spirit of Lessing" likewise extracted the man's opinions on certain scriptural passages without recourse to the passages.

In like manner, our protagonist launched himself into painting. Several potentates on horseback lay, rather than sat, for him as by means of a fork he conscientiously traced their features through a sheet of greasy, sooty paper and thus strikingly printed their likenesses on a clean page. All the same, I take leave to doubt that he might, in a different clime, have grown into a full-blown Raphael Mengs, who should have been beaten not, like the first, *toward* painting (but) rather *away from* it, notwithstanding conjectures based on the fact that, having been given a little paint box, he had illuminated the whole orbis pictus (the painted world) true to life, as contained in his paint box, never mind how colorfully the first leather balls with red dots and the red building bricks and the slates, which he had fashioned himself, and the glorious paint tray in his box, and the greenish golden beetles glow in his memory. It would be only marginally less justified than concluding from his skill in producing herrings in winter that he should end up a great cameralistics correspondent. His knack of replacing the herring inland and at such great distance from the coast was, when going to buy flour, to wade into the millstream, silently lifting a stone, under which he might catch a gudgeon or an even tinier fish. Those he would stuff into a hollowed-out cabbage stalk (doing duty as herring barrel) and salt thoroughly, and he would have been eating herrings as soon as his little barrel was full had it not been for the odor. And I am afraid the other portents proclaiming the young cameralistics correspondent were even less serviceable, viz, his surrogate inventions, like pretending dried pear halves were little hams, and offering chopped-off pigeons' feet baked in shards as a cooked dinner, or driving snails to pasture. Indeed, I should consider any future historical scholar researching the present one quite ridiculous who would try to make something of importance from the bits and pieces that lie about ready to be picked up in every other childhood as well; nay, that foolish man would seem to be no better than that barber in Paris who, with the help of a Jesuit, assembled sundry elephant bones and sold them as the skeleton of Teutobald, the German giant. A beard does not prove the philosopher, albeit perhaps the sailor or miscreant as they emerge from ship or dungeon, where no razor would have come near them.

As our hero's boundless activity centered on mental rather than physical games — all being pursued with unspeakable transports of delight — : he also invented new letters of new languages. He would simply take calendar symbols — or geometrical ones out of an old book — or chemical ones — or invented ones out of his head and concoct a whole new alphabet. On its completion: he would first of all put his alphabetical solitaire into practice by cloaking a page or two of copied material in it. Thus he became his own cryptographer and hide-and-seek player with himself; and yet — without recourse to Büttner's comparative tables of scripts — he could read off his latest as easily as any common script straightaway, as he had marked the new code with its own handbill letter by letter, and it only needed a peep. For once, we might not take it amiss if the often mentioned historical scholar were to detect in this en- and de-coding, which, even at so early a stage, valued the contents less highly than their investment, a natural disposition toward the future Legation Counselor or possibly legate; and I did indeed acquire Legation Counselor status and could encipher many a thing to this day.

My soul had been receptive to music in every way, not unlike my Father's perhaps, and I possessed a hundred Argus ears for it. When the schoolmaster's final organ cadenzas dismissed the devout of a Sunday: my whole little uplifted being would laugh and skip as into a spring; or when in the early morning after the night's kermis dancing, to be condemned and anathemized by my Father on the following Sunday, the vagrant musicians and the beribboned farm lads marched past our parsonage walls with their shawms and fiddles, much to his chagrin: I would climb the wall, and a bright glorious world would ring through my tight little breast, and vernal desires and springs skylarked within it, heedless of any paternal sermons. I used to spend hours at our ancient discordant piano, whose tuning was strictly left to the weather, strumming improvisations unsurpassed in their daring by the freest rhythms in Europe, especially as I knew neither notes, nor chords, nor anything else; for my piano-skilled Father had never shown me a single key. But if — like any modern composer for ropedances and witches sabbaths and fingers on piano strings — I hit on a short tune, or a tierce, or a sext: I would be in a seventh heaven, and I would repeat the digital find as relentlessly as any decent modern German writer repeats the stylish cerebral one that had earned him applause in the first place; because, acting with greater kindness than Heliogobalus, who had made the cook of an *inferior* pottage eat it himself until he had invented a better one, he conversely treats his reading public to an *excellent* mess for the course of so many Leipzig Fairs that it turns as insipid as the imperial cook's inferior one.

We shall be of two minds, in our hero's cultural history to come, as to whether he might have been destined for philosophy rather than poetry. During my earliest childhood, the phrase wisdom of the world — as also another phrase, land of the rising sun — had been to me as the gates of heaven, open to pleasure gardens as far as the eye could see. I shall never forget that epiphany within myself, which I had never mentioned to a living soul, where I was present at the birth of my self-consciousness, and I can yet quote place and time. One morning, when I was a very young child, I stood on our doorstep looking toward the woodpile on my left when, all of a sudden, the inner vision "I am an *I*" descended from the sky like a flash of lightning in front of my eyes, and it has remained aglow ever since: my *I* had beheld itself for the first time and forever. It is unlikely that memory should play me false, as nothing that anyone else might have told me could have mingled with, and added to, something that happened in man's innermost sanctum and whose novelty alone invested such ordinary concomitant circumstances with permanence.

It seems to me that, in order to give as true an account as possible of our Hans Paul's life in Joditz — for by this name we are going to call him for a while, although we shall certainly ring the changes — it might be well to conduct it throughout one whole idyll year and to divide the normal year with its four seasons into the same number of idyll quarters; four idylls sum up his happiness.

Nobody need be surprised, by the way, at finding a realm of idylls and a diminutive pastoral world in a small village and parsonage. A tulip tree may be grown in the tiniest little patch, but it will spread its flowering branches over the whole garden; and the life-giving air of happiness may be breathed through a window just as well as out there in the vast woods and under the open sky. The human spirit itself (with its infinite heavenly space) is, after all, bound by a five-foot-high body, complete with skins and Malpighian membranes and capillary tubes, and it has only five narrow windows of sensory stimulation that can be opened to the vast universe, with all its orbs and suns; — and yet it will perceive and reproduce a whole universe.

I might find it difficult to decide with which of the four idyll quarters we ought to begin, each one of them being a little preheaven leading on to the next one, were it not that, by beginning with winter and January, our intensification of pleasures should warrant the greatest success. During the cold spell, our Father would, just like an alpine herdsman, descend from the heights of his study upstairs and, to his children's delight, dwell in the plains of the communal living room. In the mornings he would sit in a window corner memorizing his Sunday sermon, and we three brothers, Fritz (that is myself), Adam, and Gottlieb (Heinrich was only to join us toward the end of our idyll life in Joditz), took turns in delivering his full coffee cup and, better still, fetching it back empty, when the carrier was entitled to the undissolved rock candy deposits, which he took for his cough. While the sky had shrouded everything outside in silence, the stream in ice, and the village in snow, there was life in our living room, a pigeon house under the stove, siskin- and goldfinch-cages at the window, at our feet Bonne, our bounding bulldog bitch, the night watchman of the parsonage, and a Spitz, and the affable Scharmantel, a present from Frau von Plotho, — and next door, the servants' room with two maids; farther along, at the other end of the par-

sonage, the stables with all manner of livestock, cows, pigs, and fowl, and
their cacophony; I might add our threshers with their flails, also embraced by the parsonage. Thus in the midst of noisy company, the complete male component of our living room might be spending their forenoon learning by heart cheek by jowl with the female cookery.

There is not a single occupation in the world without the vacation to
go with it; hence I, too, had my air vacation, — not unlike the well vacations — when I was permitted to go through the snow in the yard to the
threshing barn. Indeed, if there was a difficult oral message to be delivered in the village, to the schoolmaster perhaps, or to the master tailor,
I would be called away from my studies and sent there; and thus I got
out into the fresh cold air and could match myself against the newly fallen
snow. At midday, before our own meal and on an empty stomach, we
children could enjoy watching the threshers, how they fell to and polished off their dinners in the servants' room.

The afternoon was to bring more important events and more pleasures. The hours of learning would be shortened and sweetened by winter. Our Father used to perambulate during the long drawn-out dusk, and
we children would trot along with him under his housecoat and, if possible, hold his hand. At the toll of the evening bell, we would all of us
gather and, in a circle and with one voice, pray the hymn: "The gloom
of night with might descends."

It is only in villages — not in cities where there are more nighttime
than daytime labors and pleasures — that the evening bell makes sense
and is of value, as the swan song of the day; the evening bell mutes our
overloud hearts, as it were, and like the cowherd's tune on the plain, it
calls men away from their bustling and toiling into the land of silence
and dreaming. — After the sweet expectation of the tallow-candle moon-
rise in the door of the little servants' room, our living room would be lit
up and fortified simultaneously, viz, the shutters were closed and bolted;
and behind these window embrasures and parapets the child felt snugly
preserved and sufficiently sheltered from all those confounded villains
and from Knecht Ruprecht, who could not get in but was left growling
in vain outside.

And that was the time when we were allowed to undress and to hop
around clad in nothing but our trailing shirts. Idyll pleasures of various
kinds followed each other. Our Father might enter into a quarto bible,
which was interleaved with blank pages, references as to where he had
read a particular verse; or, more usually, he had his folio manuscript book
in front of him and composed a complete piece of sacred music, with its

full score, in the midst of our childish commotion: in either case, but particularly in the latter, I loved to watch him writing and was always delighted if, because of an interval of several instruments, whole quarter pages were quickly filled. He composed his inner music unaided by any exterior sounds — as recommended by Reichard — and without being put out of tune by the children's commotion. We were all sitting and playing at the long writing- and dining-table, nay, even *beneath* it. Part of the joys that forever vanish together with our beautiful childhood was that if the frost turned sufficiently fierce the long table was pushed up to the bench around our stove to keep us warm; and we looked forward to that happy event each winter. For two wooden benches surrounded our monstrosity of a stove; and we profited by being able to walk as well as sit on them and to enjoy the stove-summer next to our skin even at mealtimes.

Oh how the winter's evenings grew in importance several times each week, when the old messenger woman from town stepped into the servants' room, covered in snow, with her cornucopia of fruit and meat and sundry wares, and all of us in the little chamber had the distant city in excerpt and miniature in front of our eyes and our noses, too, in the shape of several butter buns!

During the earlier, and more childish, times our Father would give permission for a delicious dessert after the early winter's evening supper, dished up by the cattle maid at her distaff in the servants' room, which was lit by what little light the pinewood torches afforded, which were ignited and stuck into their holders as needed, as in Westphalia. This sweet course boasted — on top of several biscuit barrels and ice cups filled with folk tales such as Cinderella — the Maid's very own pineapple of a story, telling of a shepherd and his animal fights against wolves, how at one time his danger increased, but then again, his food supply grew. I can still feel the shepherd's good luck as if it were mine; I might mention in passing, based on my own experience, that children are gripped far more by a buildup of luck in stories than by a misfortune, and that they love to pursue ascensions right up to eternity, but descents into hell only as far as is necessary for the elevation and glorification of the heavenly throne. These childish desires become the desires of man; and their fulfilment would be demanded from poets more often if a new heaven were only created as easily as a new hell. It is easy enough for a tyrant to inflict unspeakable pain; but should he wish to invent untold pleasures, he has to offer a prize for the best. The basis for that is our skin; hundreds of hells can pitch tent on every inch of it; while the five heavens of our senses float above our heads, airy and monochrome. —

Only the tail ends of those winter's eves showed our hero their noisome wasps' stings or vampires' tongues. For at 9 o'clock, we children had to retire to our lodgings upstairs, my brothers to a communal one in the closet, and myself to one in the bedroom shared with my Father. Until he completed his two hours' nightly reading below, I would hide under the featherbed bathed in the cold sweat of my fear of ghosts, watching the lightning flicker across the louring spectral sky in the dark, and I felt as if man himself was being cocooned by ghostly caterpillars. Thus I suffered helplessly for two hours every night, until my Father came up at last like a morning sun chasing the specters and the dreams away. Next morning, ghostly terrors and nightmares were quite forgotten; although both would make their appearance again in the evening. Yet I never did tell a soul about it except — the public today.

At the same time, this fear of ghosts was — not so much caused as — fed by my Father himself. He did not spare us a single apparition or foolery, which he had ever heard of or believed to have met with, himself; but, like the theologians of yore, he combined with a firm belief in them the equally firm courage to face them, and God or the cross was their buckler and shield against the ghostly realm. Many a child filled with body fear will yet show ghost courage, but only for lack of imagination;[1] but another — such as myself — may tremble before the invisible world because it is peopled and shaped by his imagination, but will quickly take heart in the face of the visible world, which never reaches the depths and vastnesses of the invisible. Thus an occurrence of physical danger, even a sudden one, — like a bolting horse, a thunderclap, the din of war or fire, would leave me calm and collected, because I only feared through my imagination but not through my senses; and even a spirit shape would solidify into an ordinary live body once I had passed my initial shock, provided it did not precipitate me once more into the boundless realm of imagination through its sounds and features. How, then, can the tragic primacy of the spirit-summoning imagination be curbed by the educator? Certainly not by way of rebuttal or Biester's or Wagner's dissolving of the extraordinary into the ordinary — for a potential undissolved exception will be retained by one's deepest feeling — but on the one hand by a prosaic habituating, presenting and billeting in places and times, which would otherwise kindle imagination's magic incense again, and on the other hand by arming imagination itself against imagination and con-

---

1. Some prose-souls should be inoculated with, or left uncured of, a little fear of ghosts, as religion and poetry.

fronting the spirits with the spirit, and the Devil with God and righteousness.

Even at daytime this horror of ghosts would sometimes attack me on a special occasion. When, for instance, during a funeral, the cortege with pastor, schoolmaster, and children and crucifix and myself wended its chanting way from the parsonage past the church toward the churchyard close by the village, it would be my job to take my Father's bible through the church and into the sacristy. I screwed up my courage and barely managed to race through the dim silent church at a gallop and to reach the poky sacristy; but which one among us can picture the shuddering terrified bounds of flight with the menace in hot pursuit and the awful dash out of the church gate? And who, picturing it, would not laugh? — And yet I accepted the office of bearer each time without a word of demur and bore my agony silently and by myself.

We are now on the threshold of a grander idyll season, of spring and summer in Joditz. There are reasons for both seasons being merged into *one* idyll, above all in the country. In actual fact, spring only dwells within our hearts, whereas in the gardens outside there is only summer, solely designed for fruition and for the present. Snow is the curtain, which has to be raised over the stage, or earth, for the village to commence its summer amusements — the city enjoying its own amusements in winter — ; for tilling and sowing are spring harvestings to the countryman, and each day will produce novel scenes for the pastor, who has his own tillage, and for his ever-imprisoned sons. Then we poor children, locked into the parsonage by the long winter and jailer, will be liberated at last by the heaven-sent seraph of the season, and scattered into the open fields and meadows and gardens. There will be tilling — sowing — planting — mowing — saving the hay — reaping the corn — harvesting — and our Father will be present everywhere, helping, and the children in turn helping him, especially myself, as the eldest. If only ye knew, gentle audience, what it means all at once to escape, and I do not mean escape from the city walls, which after all enclose quite a bit of country as well, but from the walls surrounding a yard, and what is more, to escape to far beyond even the whole village, into wall-less regions and to look down from on high into the village, which one had never looked at from down below.
. . . .

Now life in heaven, viz, under the vault of heaven, began. Those dew-fresh mornings still sparkle for me, as I took my Father's coffee into the parson's garden outside the village, where he sat learning his sermons by heart in the little summer house open to all directions and where we children were to learn our Lange later on in the grass. The evenings used to take us into the garden a second time, but this time with our lettuce-gathering Mother and to the currant bushes and raspberry canes. Eating supper without lighting the lamp is another little-known country delight. Having enjoyed it, my Father would sit in the open, viz, in our walled parsonage yard, with his pipe, and I and my brothers would dash about together in the fresh evening air, robed in our shirts, and pretending to be the swallows that swooped above our heads, and we would flit hither and thither, carrying things to our nests.

The most beautiful thing on wings, however, a delicate blue butterfly dancing about our hero throughout this aestival season, was his first love. She was a blue-eyed peasant girl the same age as himself, of slender appearance, and with an oval face dotted with a few pockmarks yet with a thousand features bewitching his heart like a magic circle. Augusta, or Augustina, lived with her brother Römer, a fine youth, known for his singing voice in the choir and his grasp of figures. Whereas Paul never declared his love — unless my lecture should fall into her hands in printed form — he conducted his affaire-de-coeur so vividly from the distance by gazing at her in her women's pew in the church, not too far away from his parson's pew, yet never getting his fill. But this was only a start; for when she would drive her grazing cattle home of an evening, whose unforgettable bells were familiar to him, he would scale the wall of his yard so as to see her and wave to her, then down again to the gateway in order to squeeze his hand through a gap — no other parts of the children's bodies must leave the yard — and transfer some confectionary like sugared almonds or some other delicacy, which he had brought back from town, into her hand. Sad to say, in some summers he did not even succeed to that extent but had to swallow his sweetmeats, himself, and the chagrin to go with them. If, however, his almonds, instead of falling on stony ground, reached this Elysium of his eye: then a whole hanging garden of blossoms and fragrance would spring up in his head, and he would be strolling in it for weeks on end. For pure love desires nothing but giving, and finding happiness by giving it; and should there be an eternity of ever-augmenting bliss, who should be more blessed than Love? —
. . . .

We are coming to Paul's Sundays, when the idyll waxes considerably. Sundays seem almost to have been created for parsons and parsonage children; and Paul was particularly enchanted by a large number of Trinity Sundays, or shall we say, the largest of 27, although none of the 27 added *one* extra summer Sunday, as far as the world or the church were concerned. In cities royal or official birthdays or Fair days are the true Trinitatises. Paul began his enjoyment on bright Sunday mornings by sallying forth through the village, even before the service, jingling a bunch of keys — thus announcing his presence to all and sundry — unlocking the parsonage garden, and picking some roses for the lectern on his Father's pulpit. — In the church, things looked more cheerful simply by virtue of the tall windows throwing wide bands of light across the chilly floor and the women's pews and because sunlight cascaded over the magic shepherdess Augustina. Nor should we underrate the fact that he (in company with his brothers in office) was given permission to deliver the statutory half pound of bread and some money to the tenants of the week between service and dinner, firstly because his Father would send a generous measure, thus giving happiness to his peasantry, and secondly, because children love delivering pleasant surprises to houses, and Paul most of all. Every once in a while he had to deliver his share to the peasant Römer, as well, and he would look out for the patron saint of his church and his heart — but always in vain; for ten paces more or less made quite a difference in his love's scenography after all; and just think if fortune had smiled on him and he had found himself less than a step away from her! — Alas, not a hint can I give of such bliss manqué — for in that case he would have spoken for sure.

I hold that nobody, not even tenants of judges', princes', professors' or any other chairs can have an idea of how parsonage children relish their Sunday evening suppers (but for the pulpit tenant himself), once both divine services have been concluded, for they will celebrate with their Father his late Sabbath repose, as it were, after his pastoral burdens are shed and his priestly cassock has been exchanged for the lighter housecoat — in a place, moreover, where of a Sunday evening the village is guest performer and audience, pari passu. I might be accused of giving short measure if I omitted another Trinity joy, only because it happened less often; but it was all the greater for that, when Pastor Hagen of Köditz appeared with his wife during the sermon in order to hear our Father preach and to call on him; and Paul's little playmate, the suffragan pastor, turned up on the porch. And if Paul and his brother spotted him through the latticework of their choir stall: a wriggling and fidgeting and a palpitating of hearts and a waving of hands would begin, and any idea of listening to the sermon — and should the combined propaganda society and the ten supreme court preachers and pastors primarii queue up on the pulpit to have their say — was quickly dismissed. But the moment's pre-Sabbath, the foothills of highest hopes, the breakfast of the day had

to be relished mainly at a distance and in the church. He who, after the
first happy rush of filial and parental preparations, still demands to be
given descriptions of the beatific evening zephyrs and calms: forgets that
I cannot provide the impossible. At the most one might add on a little
extra panel that the Joditz pastorate would accompany the House of Köditz far beyond the boundary of the village late at night and that, in consequence this jumping the village fences for the wide world, heightened
by the presence of parents and suffragan pastor, and at such a late hour
to boot, was bound to bestow and entail beatitudes of which more in the
life to come.

And now, gentle male and female listeners, let us advance to such
Joditz idylls as are enjoyed by Paul outside rather than in Joditz, and
which might be most conveniently divided into those where himself is
absent from home and those where his Father is not at home. I shall start
with the latter, because I count it as one of the unrecognized childhood
pleasures where fathers go on a trip. For it is during those very times that
mothers will grant that dazzling release from academic censorship and
the freedom to act to their children. Under the eyes of their Mother,
caught up in her duties, Paul and his brothers ventured in quest of such
a village-boundary game beyond the confines of their own gateway as
butterflies, gudgeon, and the sap of birches, and willow bark for flutes,
or to admit a new playfellow, Schoolmaster's Fritz, or to help tolling the
noonday bell just for the fun of being lifted by the swinging bell rope.
One amusement within the gate was great enough in itself — only Paul
might have easily broken his neck in its execution and thus deprived me
of my whole professorship in advance — as it consisted of climbing a ladder to a free-standing beam in the barn and jumping into the hay two
stories lower down, just for the thrill of flying. Now and again he would
push the piano up to the window upstairs and play it beyond all moderation for the benefit of the village below and any chance passersby. He
used to increase its volume immensely by forcing a quill with his right
hand across the strings tensed by his left on the keys. Indeed, he also
applied a few quill strokes to the other side, where the bridge tautened
the strings, but not much of a harmony could be achieved.

Of course our Joditz summer idylls will be enhanced by walking out
of the village to visit another, or even a town. Can one receive a more
blessed instruction on a fine summer's day and after a Lange's Grammar
recital than hearing the words: "Go and get dressed, you are going to
Köditz with me after dinner"? Never was food less palatable, and Paul
had to keep up with his father's vigorous strides. An hour later, however,

he would have his little suffragan pastor, unrestrained games, his friend's wonderful mother — the sound of whose speech he can still hear ringing across the distance like the strains of a lute and the harmonica bell of the heart — and now and again one or the other tiny laurel wreath just wide enough to encircle his little head. For his Father in his paternal gratification at his grasp and retention of his own sermons, whose main proposition and parts and sundry fragments he could nimbly repeat in the evening, would make him recite the same again for his parsonage friends; — and the little one, I may say, succeeded successively. — It showed courage in a young boy who in the course of his life had never encountered anything grand — earl — general — superintendent — apart from a nobleman twice a year at the most (Herr von Reitzenstein, because he was under arrest for a long time and a fugitive afterward) — it showed courage in such a boy to speak in public before the parsonage family in their living room. But no matter how great his shyness while standing silent, once he opened his mouth he was filled with courage and fire. And did he not venture farther afield? Had he not one afternoon, when his Father was not at home, picked up a hymnal and visited an old crone, bedridden with palsy for years, and stood before her like a fully fledged pastor on a sick call and proceeded to read to her suitable bits from the hymnal? But he was soon interrupted by weeping and sobbing, not that of the crone being moved to tears by the hymnal — she remained coldly indifferent — but by his own.

Once our hero was even taken along by his Father to the court of Versailles, as we may call Zedwitz without exaggeration, for it was after all the Joditz patronate's royal residence. On his return from his court audiences — almost twice monthly during the summer — he would cause the greatest rural amazement in his wife and his child in the evening with his tales of exalted persons and their court ceremonial, and of the courtly dishes, the icehouses, and the dairy cows, and how he himself had soon been sent for from the "domestics" hall into the presence of Baron von Plotho, or even the Fräulein, for whom he would render études and exercises on the piano, and finally to Frau von Bodenhausen, and because of his lively nature his presence would always be requested at table, no matter how many distinguished lords of the Vogtland were dining at it. But like an old Lutheran court preacher, he acknowledged the immeasurable greatness of the estate, as he did the apparition of ghosts, without quaking at either of them. All the same: happy are ye, children of the present time, ye who are educated erect, not prostrated before rank, and fortified from within against exterior dazzle! — The adoration by the Joditz parsonage sons at the throne of Zedwitz an hour's journey away would be especially buttressed once a year through a splendid carriage, which would call each Maundy Thursday to fetch our Father to be the patronate's confessor at Holy Communion. His sons are well qualified to discuss the coach, having themselves been taken, together with their transports of delight, for little jaunts through the village on each occasion before his departure.

Ye may have an idea now of what it meant for our protagonist to walk to Zedwitz with the reigning monarch's father confessor, who had been carried away in extolling his son's virtues to a higher authority, to be presented at court. Having walked the gallery of ancestral portraits downstairs in the castle at length, Paul was received by Baroness Bodenhausen at the top of the stairs, the exhibition chamber, as it were, where he who flew up the stairs caught hold of her gown according to court rule and pressed his ceremonial kiss on it. — And thus the whole audience was duly completed without court-épées or Lord Chamberlains, and the boy was free to scamper about again.

And this he did in the glorious garden. There is hardly another legate, apart from our Hildburghausen Legation Counselor, then at a tender age, who can have absorbed and inhaled such romantic hours as these pergolas, fountains, hotbeds, and arbors imparted to a village child fantasizing within rather than outside himself, who for the first time and all by himself reeled among these splendors with a pressed and sated breast. What brought the elated Paul back to baser reality was a wooden bird on a rope, whose iron beak he could skilfully aim at a target. And a fruit tart sent down from the castle held the balance between standstill and flight, and its delicious aftertaste remained undiminished in the reliquary of our protagonist. Oh, ye beautiful hours and walks in seclusion for the famished village child, whose heart so intensely desired to sate itself with, or at least pine for, the world outside! —

Among the less illustrious summer idylls fall the frequent walks to Hof and his grandparents, which Paul undertook with his knapsack on his back in order to fetch meat and coffee and all those things that either were not to be got in the village at all or at least not at very low city prices. For his Mother gave him only a modest few coins — for the sake of appearance — so that his grandmother, full of generosity toward daughter and grandson, while parsimonious toward the rest of the world, should fill his knapsack with the items currently listed. The two-hourlong walk took him across indifferent and unremarkable country, through a wood and in it across a rushing river full of rocks, until at last on a high plain the town with its twin steeples and the River Saale in the valley below richly rewarded and showered the frugal young bearer. With a childish shudder at the ancient wars and afflictions, he would pass the entrance to a cave close by the suburb where, legend has it, the people of Hof took refuge during the 30 years' war; and the nearby fulling mill, with its continuous roar and its immense girders, expanded his village soul and made it capacious enough to receive the city. Once he had kissed the hand of his tall serious grandfather at his loom and that of his delighted short grandmother and publicly handed over both the official maternal letter — his Father being too proud to ask — and what little money he had, and behind the door in the hall the secret articles of appeal: he could trot off home again in the afternoon with his packed knapsack and with the sugared almonds for his adored Augustina, happy at the parental free board on his back.

He still remembers how on a summer's day as, at about two o'clock on his journey back, he surveyed the bright sunny hills and the rippling waves of the cornfields and the swift shadows of the clouds, he was overcome by a hitherto never experienced vague yearning, a mixture of mostly pain and a very little pleasure, a desire without remembrance. Alas, it was the whole man's longing for the heavenly things of life, embedded still without name or color in the deep, vast darkness of his heart, illumined fleetingly by the alighting sunbeams. There is a time of longing when its object does not yet bear a name, and it can only announce itself. And later on, also, it was less the moonlight, whose silver lakes can do no more than gently dissolve the heart in their depths and, thus dissolved, guide and carry it into eternity, than the light of the afternoon sun on open country that claimed this force of a painfully expanding longing; in Paul's writings, this has been described and imparted several times.

And in the snowy winter, too, Paul had to travel frequently as an impecunious Hof- or Holland-migrant, and to use his wits in negotiating subsidies, even with his grandfather, just as he was allowed to accompany his Father on his visits to the nearest parishes during the coldest spells. It was to these weekly athletic walks that he owed much of his enduring resistance and his best antidote to a nonsensical physical education, which, like any other at the time, did its best, with the assistance of fur hats, purges, and blocking of fresh air, together with keeping warm and keeping still and altogether too much pampering, to advance rather than counteract an adverse future. But precisely this is the good fortune of village children and the children of the poor that summer at last, aided

and abetted by spring and autumn, will demolish the winter weeds; because all of a sudden those plantlets, grown pale in the bleak glasshouse,
will be invigorated and hardened in fresh air and fine weather and by
running about barefoot and bareheaded and by eating fresh and uncooked food. Only the gentle princesses are cheated out of their salubrious summer. But common folk still don't believe that summer makes
up for winter, holding conversely that the indoor season is going to cure
the outdoor one.

. . . .

I am afraid the fact that I have reserved autumn to be the climax of
our Joditz idylls, the season which can lead nowhere but into snowdrifts,
is going to cause comment, and that not only in Germany. But an imaginative being like Paul not only enjoys autumn, itself, in autumn but also
winter in anticipation, with its domestic contentment, and spring with its
lyrical promises, while spring arrived dissolves into summer, which in
itself is truly a quiescent and intermediary stage of our imagination, too
closely related to autumn and too distant from spring. Even now he beholds through the semipellucid trees of Indian summer the ranges of next
year's snow blossom hills and traverses them, honey drunk like a bee,
although they melt away in proximity, and spring journeys and spring
harvests are being designed and enjoyed far in advance, and by the time
spring does arrive, the main matter will have come to pass. And if landscape painters have a predilection for autumn: so do poets, the painters
of the mind, at least in old age.

But our hero looked forward to autumn from a very particular point
of view; he had always a leaning toward the domestic, the still life, a spiritual nest building. He is a domestic snail, snugly retiring into the narrowest convolutions of his shell and falling in love with it, always provided his shell remains wide open, and he will be able to extend his four
feelers, not only four butterfly wings, high into the air but ten times
higher, right into the sky, with each feeler touching one of Jupiter's
moons, at least. We shall hear more in our lectures of this foolish bond
between seeking the far and the near — like a telescope either doubling
the distance or the proximity, depending on which way it is held — than
I ever asked for or mere autumn delivered.

This domestic affection showed in the boy's imagination; he called
the young swallows lucky who could settle so snugly inside their walled
nests at night. — On climbing into the vast dovecot in the loft, he would
feel at home in this roomful of roomlets or pigeons' dens, and its frontage
was as a Louvre to him, or a miniature Escurial. I am afraid I must take

the consequences if I include in my lectures the childish tidbit of his fully furnished fly house of clay, a palace, in fact, which he had built himself, about the size of a man's fist, only a little taller; the whole plaster edifice was painted red and subdivided by ink into blocks, and it had two stories, many stairs with handrails, many closets, and a capacious roof space; but on the outside it boasted bay-windows and overhangs and even a chimney, which was covered by glass so as to keep the flies from coming out instead of the smoke. Windows were plentiful all over, and one might say the castle consisted of more window than wall. When Paul now observed the countless flies rushing upstairs and downstairs in this vast pleasure castle and into the large rooms and dainty bays: he imagined how blissful their home life must be and longed himself to run with them along the windows inside and took the place of the owners who were at liberty to retire from the largest parlors into the daintiest, narrowest closets and bays. How insignificant and how small the parsonage must have seemed in comparison!

Even as a writer he was to continue this love of nooks and crannies in Wutz and Fixlein and Fibel; and the man even now likes the look of every pretty shingled little cot, with its two stories and flowers at its windows and its tiny garden to be watered from the window; and what is more, the dear domestic dupe will happily sit inside the closed coach and look past its side pockets saying, "A splendid little fire-proof room, this! And the largest gardens and villages rushing past out there!" — It has to be said that he would be able neither to write nor to live in a knight's hall or a St. Peter's church — to him it would be but a marketplace with a roof, whereas he could write or live forever on top of Montblanc or Mount Aetna as long as things were properly equipped for the purpose; it is only the close and human that cannot be small enough for him, as against the expanse of nature, which cannot be vast enough; for the smallness of the works of man is diminished by their magnification.

The painting of our Joditz autumn idyll has been almost completed through the foregoing. For autumn leads us human beings into our houses, bequeathing its cornucopia for the winter's nest, which we build, like the crossbill with its ice-month nest and fledglings. That must have been the origin for Paul's even yet listening to the first threshing, the noisy rooks' flights into the woods, the migratory birds screaming or sounding their valediction as harbingers of the snug domestic ensconcement of winter; and he would listen to them with a lingering pleasure. And I must apologize on his behalf for the way he heard the poor gaggles of Martinmas geese with such relish as prologues and leading singers of wintertime, too. I have always thought that he derived such uncommon pleasure from travelogues on winter countries like Greenland and Spitz-bergen out of the same indoor- and winter-penchant; because the mere contemplation of hardship on paper does not explain the concomitant joy, else the selfsame joy would have been felt on reading about the red-hot distress of arid countries. Whereas I should be inclined to ascribe the familiar delight of the man in each quarter hour by which the autumn days waned to his predilection for any kind of superlative — for the infi-nitely great and the infinitesimally small, in short for maxima and min-ima, particularly as he rejoiced at the waxing of days in exactly the same way and wished for nothing as much as for one of those endless Sweden days. All of this makes it obvious with what inestimable frugality and ac-complishment God had prepared and equipped the man for his path through life, which had nothing to boast of along the wayside, so that, no matter how black things were, he could always turn black into white; and with his amphibian instinct for land and sea, he could neither drown nor die of thirst.

These are but autobiographical characteristics, dear sirs, which lend themselves to his biography and which may be acknowledged with grat-itude by his future biographer.

Nor am I conscious of any reason besides that taste for the cozy win-ter interior that would explain why Paul used to ruminate with such gusto on yet another autumn delight lean enough in itself. For during autumn evenings (and overcast ones, at that), his Father, wrapped in his house-coat, would take himself and his brother to a potato field above the Saale; one of the boys would carry a hoe, the other a hand basket. Out there, plenty of new potatoes for supper would be dug by their Father; Paul gathered them into the basket, while Adam was permitted to climb after the biggest filberts. After a while, he had to descend from his branch and let Paul have a turn. And they would happily make their way home with their potatoes and hazelnuts; let each man imagine for himself the plea-sure of being abroad for an hour and the fifteen minutes' walk back with the spoils and celebrating the harvest festival in the candlelit room at home with the same intensity as the original beneficiary.

But two further fresh and green autumn flowers of joy survived in his cerebral ventricles, both of them trees. One is only a tall sturdy muscatel pear tree in the parsonage yard, whose glorious garlands of fruit the chil-dren would try to convert to man-made windfall all during autumn, until on one of the most important days of the season their Father would climb the forbidden tree on a ladder and gather the sweet paradise for house and oven. — The other evergreen tree, flowering on even more gloriously, is smaller; it is the birch, which was cut each year on St. Andrew's Eve by the old woodcutter and hauled into the living room by its stem, where it was planted in a large tub of water and lime so that it should bear its green leaves in time for Christmas and the golden fruit with which it was to be decorated. It was the nature of this birch, which was not a weeping- but a jubilating-birch, that it would scatter its festive flowers on the dark December path up to Christmas with its little forced leaves, each fresh one like the hand of a clock marking another day passed, and also that each of us children celebrated his Sukkoth of fantasies beneath this May tree of winter.

I assume that those of my audience who obtained representations of Paul's Christmas festivities in his writings, which I could not hope to surpass, will kindly dispense me from giving my own description. But two omissions should be made good. For when Paul stood in front of the candlelit tree and table on Christmas morn and the new world of gold and glory and gifts lay uncovered before his eyes and he found and was given a new abundance: the first thing to arise in him was not a tear — that is to say, a tear of happiness — but a sigh — that is to say, a sigh at life — ; in a word, even to the boy, the step or leap or flight out of the surging, playful, vast ocean of fantasy onto the limited and limiting firm coast was marked by the sigh for a larger, more beautiful country. But before this sigh could expire and before happy reality rallied its forces: Paul would feel from sheer gratitude that he ought to show himself exceedingly happy toward his Mother; — and he would assume this semblance instantly and for a short time, for in no time at all, the dawning light of reality was to extinguish and take away the moonlight of imagination.

And at this point we ought to be mindful of a paternal idiosyncrasy, which pertained to the same moment: for his father — always so happily sympathetic, giving and sharing enjoyment so generously — would emerge from his bedroom on Christmas morn into the cheerful bright living- and servants-rooms downstairs as if cloaked in mourning; their Mother denied any knowledge as to the source of this annual sadness, and no one plucked up the courage to ask him. And he left all the labor and pleasure of laying the festive board on Christmas Eve to their Mother, lagging behind Paul considerably in this respect, who always enjoyed lending a hand to his wife, or she to him, with the Christmas opera for his children; — for he had indeed played — especially while they were younger and ignorant — postman for the fraudulent notes, and set designer and dramatist on his sofa for months in advance, and finally on the night, as director and stage-technician-in-chief, set the scene and arranged the display on tables and trees, so full of understanding and light that the whole thing shone as brightly as did his eyes.

This notwithstanding, one can almost explain the Father and the paternal mourning from the son, for the latter has had to cloak a similar sadness with all exterior happiness and activity for many years since. They are both of them stricken by the woeful comparison — chafed through their sacred music and novels — between reality's manly autumn and the childish springtimes that went before, when the ideal puts forth blossoms straight from the trunk of reality, without the deviation of leaves and branches.

And even then the child's nectar and wine demanded an added zest, the ideal ether of belief in a bounteous Christ child. For as soon as his eyes had chanced to convince him that it is only human beings, not angels, who bring and display the blossoms and fruits of joy: their paradisaical fragrance and light had gone out and been wiped away, and the humdrum cabbage patch remained. And yet it is incredible how he, like all children, held off the iconoclasts of his heavenly belief and held onto his angelic revelation against all the insights of his years, and against any hints of coincidence, until finally he came to see and conquer rather than be vanquished. Thus reluctantly does the man of any religion allow himself to be dragged down to men playing bountiful deity high up in the skies.

— So far the Joditz idylls, which had lasted long enough for the parents and children, viz, as long as the Trojan War. Debts and expenses for four sons increased, and the latters' need for the promised superior school grew ever more urgent. And their Father, too, would be exasperated occasionally that his best years and greatest vigor should be strained and drained in so narrow a parish. In the end, Pastor Barnickel died in Schwarzenbach on the Saale, a small city or large market town. Death is the true stage-manager and -technician on earth. He plucks a human being out of the beginning, middle, or end of the sequence like a number, and lo and behold, the whole sequence will reassemble in a new order. On this occasion, that particular living, which was in the gift of the Prince of Reuss and of Baroness Bodenhausen, alternately, fell into the hand of Richter's patroness, who had for a long time and undisguisedly looked forward to being able to reward and rescue the dear, selfless, cheerful, and impoverished parson.

All the same, he did not pay Zedwitz any more visits on that account, rather fewer. And petitioning for the parish, or even just asking, should, in his old-fashioned belief that only the Holy Ghost called to sacred office, have sullied him with the stain of simony. Thus his patroness, proud of birth, had to make do with the upright penuriosus, proud of office, without petition or supplication. And now I shall let you into a secret of the court of Zedwitz — long since forgotten there — by telling ye straight from the old pastor's mouth what transpired there on the day of the appointment. As he was always admitted to the old Baron (von Plotho) first: that man was so overjoyed and delighted that he could not keep the happy news to himself but imparted it, or perhaps even the document, straightaway, although it was really up to his wife, the actual patroness, to hand him the letter. Naturally enough, a certain resentment on the part of the Baroness toward the Baron could not be concealed from the court when the newly created pastor presented himself to her filled with gratitude. At the same time, the two had been of one mind in their desire to save their moneyless friend all manner of douceurs and gratuities for potential messengers — fatal words for one of the parties — by delivering the vocation in person.

Conscious as I am of your benevolent attitude toward both father and son, it should be my guess that ye will now be uttering cries of delight in your hearts: "Oh, how delicious that the moon change of parsonages should have blessed him with finer weather at last, and we behold the genial musician hurrying home with his bulldog bitch, away from his Lord and Lady (whom he would have amused for longer out of sheer gratitude) that he might share his own elation with his loved ones as soon as he could and, above all, with his spouse, who had verily suffered enough with her gleaning and tithes gathering on the parental fields."

My only comment shall be that ye are wide of the mark, and I am surprised at your blunder. It was with a solemn sadness that he imparted the joyous news; not only because the flower- and harvest-crown of happiness is ever sprinkled with a few tearlike dewdrops, as is the bridal wreath, but also because his parting from his beloved and loving parish, his second family for so many years, albeit in the larger family prayer hall of the church, was shedding its first tears within him, and lastly because the tranquil, calm, inconspicuous, simple village still life should in future hang in his memory merely as a painting of yore. To be sure, country life is monochrome, just as life at sea, where little things never change, only important ones; but it offers a kind of monochrome gratification, which gives strength, just as the monochrome sea will invigorate a consumptive, because neither dust cloud nor insects will harm him.

—I believe I have done my self-historical professorial duty with regard to the educational village of Joditz, and the time has come to accompany our protagonist in our next lecture on his family's move to
Schwarzenbach, where, however, the curtain of life will be raised by several feet at once, thus allowing a little more than a glimpse at his earliest
baby shoes. For we shall propel him indeed from today's into the following lecture as a youth more than twelve years of age, yet knowing less
than the three-year-old Christian Heinrich Heineken did when, having
passed his examination, he was put to her breast again by his wetnurse —
so utterly lacking in knowledge of natural, geographical, or historical science, always excepting the particle, which was himself — of French or
music — in Latin clothed but in a little Lange and Speccius — in short, as
transparent and empty a little carcass or skeleton and so devoid of any
learned substance or body that, just like yereselves, I can hardly wait for
the place and the hour when he will begin to know and to pad his skeleton in Schwarzenbach on the River Saale.

We are about to leave the anonymous little village; but although it
has never been crowned with the laurel wreath of some battle or other,
like many another village: he is entitled nevertheless to hold it in high
esteem, I believe, and still address it as if taking his leave today: "Beloved
village!, thou wilt remain dear to my heart! Two little sisters I left in-
terred in thy ground — My contented Father passed his happiest Sundays
upon it — And during the dawn of my life I beheld thy bright rolling fields.
I know that thy inhabitants whom I once knew have departed long ago,
like my Father; but my heart wishes their unknown children and grand-
children well; and may every battle pass them by."

Third Lecture

(Schwarzenbach on the Saale)

Would ye believe, gentle audience, that Paul has no recollection
whatever of the upheaval of packing, moving out and moving away and
moving in, of any leave-takings, either his parents' or the children's, nor
of a single object on a two-mile-long journey, with the sole exception of
the aforementioned tailor's son, to whom he entrusted the soot portraits
of a few kings, intended for his beloved? — But thus is child- and boyhood; it will remember the infinitesimal but forget the most prominent,
and who can tell rhyme or reason. Farewells are, in any case, less mem-
orable than arrivals for childhood, eagerly thrusting in all directions; for

a child will leave the long familiar conditions ten times more readily than the short-lived, and it is only in the grown man that the opposite seems to be indicated. Farewells hardly exist for children, who know no past but only a present brimful of future.

Schwarzenbach, to be sure, had a lot to offer — a pastor and a curate — a rector and a cantor — a parsonage with many small and two large rooms — facing it, two big bridges with the accompanying River Saale — close beside it the schoolhouse, the size of (or maybe larger than) the whole Joditz parsonage — and among the houses even a town hall, not to mention the long-vacant castle.

A new rector took up his post at the same time as his Father, Werner, from the district of Merseburg, a handsome man with a wide brow and nose, full of fire and feeling and of a captivating natural eloquence, bursting with questions and parables and disquisitions like Pater Abraham; otherwise without any depths in either languages or any other sciences. He compensated for the lack in this aspect by a head filled with freedom rhetoric, and his fiery tongue was a lever for the children's minds. It was his precept to make them learn only the most fundamental forms of grammar — by which he meant nothing but declensions and conjugations — in order to have a go at reading an author. Paul had to take the instant high leap across Lange's Colloquia straight into Cornelius; and it worked. The schoolroom, or more properly the school ark, contained raw beginners, spellers, Latin pupils; big girls and small girls — all of them ranged from floor to ceiling as on hothouse shelving or in an antique Roman theater — as well as rector and cantor, complete with the accompaniment of shouting, humming, reading, and beating. The Latin pupils constituted a school within the school, as it were. Soon an attempt was made at Greek grammar, also, with its learning of declensions and indispensable verbs; and without any further dallying over grammar, they were translated into translating the New Testament. And Werner, who when in full spate used to praise himself to the point of being surprised at his own greatness, even considered his faulty method to be an original one, whereas it was nothing but one of Basedow's; but Paul's rapid progress only served as another proof of his theory. About a year later, a gangway was forged from some few declensions and verbs out of Danz's Hebrew Grammar, written in Latin, to the Book of Genesis, whose beginning, the very exposition threshold for the young Hebrew scholars, was forbidden territory for the uneducated Jews.

I shall continue with our protagonist's life in chronological order after *one* moment's excursion ahead of time to sneak a glimpse with you at how much he had to do and to know all at once. After that I shall revert to my statarical self again.

Like a Vulgate maker, he was put to translate the Greek Testament, and the Hebrew one orally, into Latin. While Paul translated (he was the only Hebrew scholar in the whole school), the Rector would take recourse to a printed version at his elbow; and if our hero got stuck in his analytical treatment of certain words, disaster might strike again in the teacher faring no better.

The present novelist quite lost his heart to the Hebrew language and analysis lumber and trivia — yet another hidden aspect, indeed, of his love of domesticity — and he begged and borrowed Hebrew grammars from any sources he could in Schwarzenbach in order to be in possession of anything whatsoever that might throw light on diacritical dots, vowels, accents, and the like, to be dished out by himself in his analysis of each individual word. Thereupon he stitched together a quarto book and, beginning with Genesis, provided over several pages such a wealth of instruction drawn from every borrowed grammar on the first three words, on each of their letters, their vowels, and the first dagesh and shwa, that he decided to end with the word beginning (his intention had been to follow through in this way chapter by chapter). And what is written on the topic of Quintus Fixlein's battue for letters large, small, and back to front in a Hebrew folio bible (in his first notebook) may be literally applied to Paul's own life.

In the same foolish way, Paul proceeded with the by now antiquated Hofmann, a Grand Cross Speccius to any pupil, with its German translation sentences or paradigms of Latin rules, wriggling his way through its convolutions as the man progressed to ever greater syntax ornata into participial bottlenecks of such proportions that the poor Rector was hard put to follow, let alone correct him.

On his arrival in Schwarzenbach — to continue cursorily for a moment — Paul was taught the piano by Cantor Gressel; — and here, too, having learnt to play a few dances and later on the rudiments of the chorale — God grant the poor boy a thorough teacher for once, although there is not a sign of the like on the horizon — he was soon to be left to his own devices, and he freed himself from the shackles of proper instruction by improvising on the piano and picking up and rattling off at sight any music he could lay hands on anywhere in the town. He acquired the grammar of music, basso continuo, more or less the way we pick up the grammar of German in speaking.

At the same time, he immersed himself in German belles lettres; as there were none to be had in Schwarzenbach apart from the novelistic genre, and even of that only the inferior novels of the *first* half of the last century: he assembled his own little tower of Babel out of these blocks, notwithstanding the fact that he could never extract more than one block at a time from it for his perusal. But out of all stories on bookshelves — for Schiller's Armenian has only half the impact the second time — none was to charge the veins of his innermost being — to the point of physical ecstasy even — with such a nectar and balm as the original Robinson Crusoe — : he still remembers hour and place of his ecstasies; it was in the evening, at the window facing the bridge; and one other novel, Veit Rosenstock, by Otto, — read and proscribed by his Father — was to repeat a moiety of that enthusiasm. It was as a pirate and plagiarist only that he enjoyed it in the paternal library until his Father's return — once reading it during his Father's weekday sermon as he lay on his stomach in a deserted gallery. I little envy the children of today, who are being robbed of the first impression of a childish and childlike Robinson and fobbed off by the man's latter-day adaptors, who make a lecture hall of the tranquil island, or a printed Schnepfental Academy, and press a textbook into the shipwrecked Robinson's hand, making him walk about mouthing their own dictatos, setting up hedge schools all over the place, notwithstanding the fact that the man was fully occupied barely keeping himself alive.

Round about the same time, the young Curate Völkel asked his Father whether he might borrow the boy for a couple of hours after dinner each day to teach him a little philosophy and geography. Why I, in my rural awkwardness, was deemed worthy of this sacrifice of his afterdinner rest by him, who was not fired by any particular pedagogical talent, I shall never know.

In philosophy he taught me, or rather, I read out to him, Gottsched's Wisdom of the World, which for all its aridity and vacuity quickened me by its sheer novelty like a draught of fresh water. Thereupon he pointed out to me many a city and border on a map — methinks one of Germany; I cannot say that I recall any of it, however hard I search for it in my memory. I would undertake to prove myself to be among all living authors perhaps — although this may sound a bit much — the most ignorant with regard to maps. For me an Atlas of maps would carry hell in place of the sky of the mythological one, were I asked to transfer it into my head. The little of the geography of cities and countries, which may have stuck, is what came to me in passing during that course of geographical instruction I attended, in part statarically from mail coaches and in part cursorily from their coachmen, if I may express it in decent grammar school German.

I am all the more grateful to the worthy Curate for his guidance toward so-called natural theology. For he would set me the task of proving without the bible that there was a God, for example, or a providence, and so forth. To that purpose I would receive a little octavo-size page with the proofs and indications from Nösselt or Jerusalem and others in unfinished sentences only, or even just single words and dashes. These encoded hints were explained to me; and out of this leaf my own leaves would open, following Goethe's botanical creed. If I began each essay with warmth, I would finish it in a blaze; for every time the end would be loaded with the end of the world and of life, with heavenly bliss and the overabundance pouring forth from the young vine in its spring ardor, which will bear the fruits of the spirit only in autumn. And if those hours of composition meant freedom and happiness rather than toil: who deserves praise and merit more than the selector of the right flower- and fruit-bearing topic? — For we only have to compare those fulfilling and stimulating essays with the run-of-the-mill tasks given by teachers, so vast and so vague and so alien to the young mind, or so far above the youthful sphere of existence, a thousand of which I would hazard to hatch in a footnote[2] for fun, that I would wish in all seriousness a liberal man who understands youth would sit down and, regardless of the most sublime ideas and interpretations he might otherwise furnish, write nothing for the time being but, like those countless dispositions on Sunday texts, a volume of prize questions for teachers, so that all they in turn had to do to solve them was select from them the ones they wished to assign to their pupils.

Better still might be no exercises at all; the youth himself being free to elect the matter as he would a beloved to whom his heart warms generously and only with whom he is capable of begetting life. Only leave the young mind alone for the space of a few hours and pages — as even the older one needs — so that he may sound without interference from

2. On topics as frigid and vacuous and general, demanding all and nothing, as for instance In Praise of Diligence or the Importance of Youth, not even the most prolific and mature mind could produce anything lively. Then again others, too large and too loaded, like A Comparison of Ancient Generals or Weighing Up Ancient Modes of Government, for instance, are ostrich eggs . . . on which the pupil with his tiny wings is going to sit in vain and generating heat only in his head while attempting to hatch them. Between those two kinds there are handsomer ones, those replete with sensual or historical material: as for instance Description of Conflagration, of Doomsday, of the Flood, Proofs of their Nongenerality.

you; else he will be but a bell sitting on the ground and unable to ring unless it be suspended, free and untouched, in the open.

But this is how all men in office act throughout; they have no inclination to make free spirits out of slavish machines and thereby to show their ability to work, to create, to command, but on the contrary, they believe they can prove it by hooking up an intermediary machine to their immediate next or superior spirit machine and, finally, to all those intermediary machines a last one, so that in the end there will emerge a mother puppet, leading a daughter puppet, which in turn will be able to lift a little pet dog. — And all of it but one single hooking up by one and the same engineer. God, the purely free, desires to educate free men only, whereas the Devil, the purely unfree, desires only his own kind.

Selina; or, on the Immortality of the Soul

JEAN PAUL HAD LONG PLANNED A REVISED VERSION OF *The Vale of Campan*, and on the day of his son's death, 25 September 1821, he resolved to complete it forthwith and to dedicate it to Max. In December he wrote to his publisher, Cotta: "The third volume of *The Comet* will soon be finished and I shall immediately begin on my very important work on the immortality of the soul, of which *The Vale of Campan* only gives the valleys, not the heights."

This work had been building up for thirty years, and with it he hoped to reveal to "many damp eyes" bright new prospects "in the future land of being." "Not the Bible, but the right insight into the All comforts and sustains." In similarly confident terms he spoke of his purpose in a letter to Voß, again adding: "All without the assistance of the Bible. There are, through the centuries, greater insights into the All than those of Peter and Paul." At the same time, he made the typical remark on immortality in another letter, that he "will find it easier to experience than it is to prove" (*H-KA* 3.8.146ff., 240).

Selina (*W* 12.1105ff., 1197ff.) became a sequel to *The Vale of Campan*, rather than a revision, with a related cast of characters. Selina takes the place of her mother, Gione in *Campan*, Alex replaces his father, the skeptical Karlsson. To this work, Jean Paul devoted most of the energies of his last years, dictating his "work of hope" day after day, although all this time he was plagued by illnesses. He was going blind, he had chronic breathing and digestive troubles, his feet were so swollen he could scarcely walk, sometimes he could scarcely talk — after a lifetime of walking and talking. By the time of his death, he had completed nine of the planned twelve chapters.[1]

The dialogue between believer and unbeliever is a recurring scene in Jean Paul, on the pattern established in *Siebenkäs*, where Siebenkäs tries to convert Leibgeber, for whom "the planets are licensed only to serve the traveler, not to house him" (*W* 3.68.514). In *Selina*, Henrion is a passionate believer, his brother Alexander, the unbeliever; and if there is any conclusion, it is a matter of personal concern and interplay of relationships, over and above the fluctuations of exalted arguments and deflating rebuttals. As suggested by one of the chapter headings, "Conclusion from Longing and the Higher Predispositions," the arguments for immortality are moral and aesthetic, based on conclusions drawn from man's innate instinct for development — what Jean Paul here calls *Bildungtrieb*, in accordance with the obstinate orthographic campaign he was carrying on at the time.

But he was also conducting a more serious campaign against the "miseries" of the "newer theology," to which, the narrator in *Selina* suggests, the natural sciences are a refreshing antidote, with their teleological zoology. As so often in the late Jean Paul, "torture morality" is his particular target. The doctrine of the resurrection "transfigures the corpse by first crucifying the body." Alexander is the mouthpiece for the mockery of the theologians, who are "more sharp witted than polyhistorical," and whose differing views, as he found them in the eighth volume of Gerhardus's *loci theologici*, he examined in order to find out which organs rise again and at what age — which bodies are selected from the clothes cupboard, as Alexander puts it (*W* 12.1203f., 1224, 1228).

In *Selina*, too, hope is the guiding principle. As Alexander is more amenable to ideas of a world soul or of a transmigration of world souls, the narrator considers the case for metempsychosis in an essay that ends: "And so let us travel and hope" (*W* 12.1126, 1155). Apart from that, the subject has no conclusion except inasmuch as it is enclosed in the frame-

---

1. Cf. Günter de Bruyn, *Das Leben des Jean Paul Friedrich Richter* (Frankfurt, 1978), pp. 362ff.

work of friendships. This is, to be sure, a sentimental conclusion, as indeed *Selina*, in spite of the satirical asides, is altogether a sentimental work. The arguments themselves are by definition sentimental, but then this was always a position Jean Paul defended. Harich wished to forget *Selina* and found it hard to forgive Jean Paul for wasting so much time "tinkering with 'proofs' for immortality" and trying to improve on the *Phaedon*, instead of recognizing that Moses Mendelssohn was passé.[2] But *Selina* and similar works loom so large in Jean Paul it would give a quite distorted picture not to allow them due prominence. Besides, it would not be Jean Paul if there were not something subversive about the sentiment, as well. There could hardly be a more sentimental subject matter than that with which the excerpt here ends, Selina's dream of her mother's deathbed, and yet what surfaces in the dream is a very unsentimental exposure of anxiety and doubt.

Vesta

"Has the Eternal One any purposes at all, and do we know Him so thoroughly?"

"We do," said I, "we know Him better perhaps than our own thin fluid of being. He alone, the Most Holy One — and no necessity of circumstances, no chaos of accident — could have implanted in us that spiritual, organic impulse to education, which nurtures the inner person toward moral beauty; an adumbration by his holy spirit, so that divine images be brought forth, which, however, as the finite one is everywhere infinitely, not finitely, distinct from the Infinite One, possess only virtues but not virtue. Morality is the graceful limb structure of the complete inner person. Once man has graduated to being a moral work of art: Death appears on the scene and shatters the ancient world. Thus the Godhead paints its image into myriad spirits from one eon to the next, only for them, together with the image, to be wiped out forever a few minutes later. — Moral perfection knows only its incessancy, so unrelated to and unsatisfied by Time that it demands no less than eternity. It is true that the noble minded will — as evidenced by so many Greek and Roman believers in Death — in the face of all certainty of his eternal extinction no more desist from the blissful indulgence of his purest being than the

2. Wolfgang Harich, *Jean Pauls Kritik des philosophischen Idealismus* (Suhrkamp, n.d.), p. 46.

nonbelieving man of the world will leave a plate unfinished or a cup undrained of the condemned man's last meal before his annihilation; but if Time, like sin, as it were, finally plucks out the inner man's heart: then too much strength is required to embark on the high endeavor we can never complete. Higher man does, after all, trust in the chance of molding his moral fragments into a whole and a work of art at least at a later, after the present, time; for truly the most beautiful souls can only appear to themselves and to others piecemeal and torn in the violent tempest of life; they are fireworks lit in the rain; even the most splendorous composition igniting in fragments, the loftiest names lose letters, and not a single whole is aglow in the sky.

It is not the lack of a reward — for virtue can no more be rewarded than blessedness, least of all with the latter itself — but the lack of its continuity that threatens the stalwart heart, which must flutter and flinch with its noblest strivings and pleasures beneath the Damocles sword of annihilation. And in the end all shall vanish before it, all that is noblest, not merely virtue, not merely finitude, but even the Eternal One.

"And even the Eternal One," the hitherto silent Selina joined in, on a very emotional note, and went on: "Wondrously enough I had never reflected so often on annihilation as during the few days of our conversations on immortality. And this may also have been behind my curious dream, whose torment had to ease by and by. I saw my beloved mother fading away on her last bed of rest and reaching out to us all with trembling hands for a final farewell. As she and we wept: a harsh cold voice muttered in the corner behind us: the valedictory couch is no victory couch, with death all is over, Death and Nothing and Nothing and All. 'Indeed,' said my mother unexpectedly, disengaging her hands from ours and folding them and trying, albeit in vain, to raise them in prayer: 'Now that I have taken leave from my loved ones, I must take the cruellest leave from the most beloved of all, from Thee, my God! Ah, how didst Thou love me, Thou All-loving One! All my beautiful days didst Thou bestow on me from Thy Heaven, and my tears didst Thou dry or turn into tears of joy, and my heart was ever and ever with Thee. — Alas, now I must perish forever, and never again can I thank Thee through amelioration or by redeeming my failings to Thee! Thou shinest on through the eons, and they shall behold Thee, but I shall be no more. Let me give thanks, then, for a last time; my heart shall love Thee until it ceases to beat!'" ... Selina's voice faltered: "I cannot divulge the remaining words of the dream after all, although one as untrue as that ought not to move me so against my promise," and she departed the room with tears in her eyes.

The rest of us, too, cut short our discourse, for the thought of the All's Most Sublime One inundates us with thoughts that only solitude can accommodate, neither company nor tongue. Let us conclude this little chapter as well, then, wherein a more beautiful light shines from the throne of the Supreme One on our graves and on the far Elysian fields than, so to speak, from the plain of the whole natural world.

Index

(References in Jean Paul, as in Sterne, are not necessarily genuine. At times, Jean Paul may mix fictional names with his out-of-the-way facts.)

Abaelard, Peter (1079–1142), 10

Abraham, 8

Abraham à Santa Clara (1644–1709, Viennese preacher and satirist), 355

Adam, 88, 158, 161ff., 195, 251, 297

Aenesidemus (i.e., Gottlob Ernst Schulze, 1761–1833, Göttingen philosopher, nicknamed after the Cretan sceptic), 287

Alchakim Biamvilla (11th calif of Egypt), 232

Alexander I (1777–1825, emperor of Russia), 67

Alexander the Great (356–323), 117

Ameipsias (comic dramatist, contemporary of Aristophanes), 256

Anak (Deut. 9:2), 164

Antonin. *See* Aurelius, Marcus

Apel, 323

Aquinas, Thomas (1225–74), 37

Archimedes (287–212), 149

Argand, Jean Robert (1768–1813, mathematician), 179

Aristophanes (446–388), 256, 259

Aristotle (384–322), 166, 261

Arnim, Ludwig Achim von (1781–1831, German romantic writer), 70, 252

Arnobius (ca. 300 A.D., African rhetorician), 63

Arnold, Heinz Ludwig, xiii

Arrianus, Flavius (disciple of Epictetus), 195

Artaxerxes I of Persia (nicknamed Longimanus, d. 424 B.C.), 293

Artemidoros (1st c. B.C., grammarian and lexicographer), 270

Athanasius of Alexandria (295–373, church father), 96

Augusta. *See* Römer

Augustine, Saint (354–430), 161, 229

Aurelius, Marcus (121–180, emperor and philospher), 165, 166, 195, 196

Bach, Carl Philip Emanuel ("Berlin Bach," 1714–88), 156
Bacon, Francis (1561–1626), 201
Bahrdt, Karl Friedrich (1741–92, rationalist theologian), 251
Baldus de Ubaldis (1327–1400, jurist), 333
Ballenstedt, Johann Georg Justus (*Archiv der Entdeckungen aus der Urwelt*, 1818), 312
Bardili, Christoph Gottfried (1761–1808, philosopher), 298
Barnickel, 352
Bartholin, Gaspar (1655–1738, Danish medical scientist), 170
Basedow, Johann Bernhard (1723–90, pedagogue), 262, 355
Baumann (miner, discoverer of cave in the Harz), 200
Baur, Samuel (*Zeitgemälde d. denkwürdigsten Personen d. 18. Jhdts.*, 1803ff.), 273
Bayle, Pierre (1647–1706), 201, 328
Beaumont, Charles de (1728–1810, diplomat, allegedly hermaphroditic), 152
Beddoes, Thomas Lovell (1803–49), xii
Bellarmin, Robert Cardinal (1542–1621), 235
Benda, Georg (1722–95, composer), 254
Benn, Gottfried (1886–1956), 77
Berend, Eduard (1883–1973), xii, xiii, 41, 63, 82, 120, 204, 288f., 301
Berkeley, George (1685–1753), 32, 206
Berlepsch, Emilie von (1755–1830), 23, 26, 75
Bernhardi, Ferdinand (1769–1820, satirist and linguist), 252
Biester, Johann Erich (1749–1816, librarian and journalist), 340
Björnstahl, Jakob-Jonas (1730–99, Swedish orientalist), 87
Bloch, Ernst (1885–1977), 116
Blücher, Gebhard Leberecht (1742–1819, fieldmarshal, dubbed "Marschall Vorwärts"), 51, 316
Blumenbach, Johann Friedrich (1752–1840, anatomist), 164

Bodenhausen. *See* Plotho, Luise
Bonnet, Charles (1720–93, philosopher and scientist), 163, 298
Börne, Ludwig (1786–1837, radical journalist), 42, 64
Bouterwek, Friedrich (1766–1837, writer and critic), 232
Boyle, Robert (1627–91), 262
Brecht, Bertolt (1898–1956), 73
Brentano, Clemens (1778–1842, German romantic writer), 252
Brockes, Barthold Heinrich (1680–1747, merchant and poet), 49
Brooks, Charles Timothy, xi
Bruyn, Günter de, xiii
Brydone, Patrick (1741–1818, scientist and travel writer), 87
Buffon, George Louis Leclerc (1707–88, zoologist and botanist), 129, 134
Bunkel (from *The Life of John Buncle esq.*, by Thomas Amory; 1691–1788), 126
Büttner, Christian Wilhelm (*Vergleichungstafeln der Schriftarten verschiedener Völker* 1771ff.), 335

Caesar, Julius (100–44), 155, 241
Cain, 40, 164, 302
Camerarius, Joachim (1500–74, humanist), 155
Campe, Joachim Heinrich (1746–1818, pedagogue), 136
Caracalla (188–217, Roman emperor, murdered his brother and rival, Geta), 318
Cardone, Vincente (1590–1620), 49
Carlyle, Thomas (1795–1881), 4, 27, 158
Carminati, Bassiano (1750–1830), professor of therapeutics in Pavia), 89
Cäsarius, Bishop of Arles (470–542), 269
Caselman, 60
Catherine of Alexandria, Saint (4th c. martyr), 49
Catilina, Lucius Sergius (108–62, Roman politician and conspirator), 155
Cato the Younger (95–46, Roman patriot and stoic), 73, 166

Cervantes Saavedra, Miguel de (1547–1616), 251, 256

Charles XII of Sweden (1682–1718), 269

Charlotte Sophia of Mecklenburg (wife of George III), 67

Chateaubriand, René de (1768–1848), 68, 263

Christ 36, 51, 71, 72, 109, 158ff., 167, 179ff., 194, 204, 208, 247, 254, 315, 352

Christopher (legendary giant and Christian martyr), 163

Cicero (106–43), 47, 126, 247

Clemens of Alexandria (Titus Flavius, 150–218, Christian gnonstic), 231

Cober, Gottlieb (1682–1717, preacher and devotional writer), 84, 110

Coleridge, Samuel Taylor (1772–1834), 4

Comenius, Jan Amos (1592–1670, theologian and pedagogue), 86

Corday, Charlotte (1768–93), 32, 66

Cornelius (?) (Cornelius Nepos, 100–32, chronicler), 355

Correggio, Allegri da (1494–1534), 134, 177

Cotta v. Cottendorf, Johann Friedrich von (1764–1832, bookseller and publisher), 66, 360

Cranz, August (1737–1801, satirist), 251

Crébillon, Claude Prosper Jolyot de ("Crébillon fils", 1707–77, novelist), 257

Dante Alighieri (1265–1321), 265

Danz, Johann Andreas (1654–1727, orientalist and philologist), 155, 355

David, King, 228

Demosthenes (384–322, Athenian orator and statesman), 47

Denner, Balthasar (1685–1741, portrait painter), 127

De Quincey, Thomas (1785–1859), 4, 41, 243, 301

Derham, William (1657–1735, English theologian), 233

Descartes, René (1596–1650), 231

Diderot, Denis (1713–84), 264

Diogenes of Sinope (4th c. B.C. cynic), 149, 259

Dionysius of Halikarnassos (1st c. B.C. rhetorician and historian), 316

Dobeneck, Friedrich Ludwig Ferdinand von (1770–1810, counsellor in Bayreuth), 70

Döblin, Alfred (1878–1957), 31

Dominic, Saint (1170–1220), 165

Donatus, Aelius (4th c. B.C., grammarian), 233

Dostoyevski, Fjodor (1821–81), 161

Ducarla-Bonifas, Marcos (1738–1816, physicist and writer), 186

Duval, Jamerai (1695–1775, emigrant French writer in Vienna), 234

Ebert, J. Arnold (1723–95, translator of Edward Young), 212

Edelmann, Johann Christian (1698–1767, theologian), 233

Eliot, George (1819–90), 4

Elisabeth, empress (of Russia) (1709–62), 94

Ellrodt, Sophie (b. 1795), 10

Emanuel. See Osmund

Engel, Johann Jakob (1741–1802, writer and critic), 263

Enoch (Gen. 5, 21–4), 210

Epictetus (55–135, stoic philosopher), 166, 177

Epicurus (342–268), 199

Epiphanius (315–403, metropolitan of Cyprus, opponent of Origenism), 215, 217

Erasmus von Rotterdam (1469–1536), 10, 67, 122, 257, 328

Ernesti, Johann August (1707–81, philologist and pedagogue, author of Clavis Ciceroniana), 155, 231

Erxleben, Dorothea Christiana (1715–62, first woman doctor of medicine in Germany), 280

Esau, 173

Euler, Leonhard (1707–83, Swiss mathematician), 231

Eustathius of Constantinople (12th c. archbishop of Thessalonica, Homer commentator), 132
Eve, 162ff.

Feder, Johann Georg Heinrich (1740–1821, professor of metaphysics in Göttingen), 86
Feuchtersleben, Karoline (1774–1842, Jean Paul's fiancée), 23
Fichte, Johann Gottlieb (1762–1814), 9, 26, 27, 31, 160, 195, 203ff., 222, 227–35, 258, 287, 303
Fielding, Henry (1707–54), 263
Fischart, Johann (1546–90, Alsatian satirist), 260
Flögel, Karl Friedrich (1729–88, cultural historian), 253f.
Fontenelle, Bernhard Le Bovier (1657–1757), 267
Foote, Samuel (1720–77, English actor-dramatist), 255
Forster, Johann Georg (1754–95, scientific explorer and writer together with his father, Johann Reinhold Forster, 1729–98), 87, 118
Francis, Saint (1181–1226), 235
Franklin, Benjamin (1706–90), 200
Frederick II of Prussia (the Great, 1712–86), 46, 60, 61, 187, 221, 328
Frederick William III of Prussia (1770–1840), 67
Frohreich, Heinrich (pseudonym of novelist Karl Heinrich Bardeleben, 1775–1852), 266
Fueßlin, Johann Conrad (Neue und unparteyische Kirchen- und Ketzer-historie mittlerer Zeit, 1770–74), 307

Galen (129–199, physician), 252
Garofolo, Benenuto (1481–1559, painter), 135
Gautier, Hubert (Bibliothèque des Philosophes, 1723), 258
Gedicke, Friedrich (1754–1803, Berlin headmaster), 95
George, Stefan (1868–1933), 13

Gerhardus, Johannes (1582–1637, Lutheran theologian), 361
Geßner, Salomon (1730–88, Swiss writer of idylls), 212, 267
Girtanner, Christoph (1760–1800, physician and historian), 123, 154
Gleim, Johann Wilhelm Ludwig (1719–1803, anacreontic poet), 23
Goethe, Johann Wolfgang von (1749–1832), 4, 5, 6, 16, 18, 26, 43, 66, 75, 76, 82, 121, 167, 195, 206, 242f., 250, 263, 265, 267, 327, 358
Görres, Joseph von (1776–1848, cultural historian), 252
Gotter, Friedrich Wilhelm (1746–97, poet and journalist), 254
Gottsched, Johann Christoph (1700–1766, professor of literature in Leipzig), 357
Gozzi, Carlo (1720–1806, commedia dell'arte dramatist), 251
Gressel, 356

Hagen, Christian (1688–1766), 343
Hale, Margaret L., 242
Halensis, Alexander (d. 1245, English scholastic theologian), 232
Hales, Alexander. See Halensis, Alexander
Haller, Albrecht von (1708–77, physician and poet), 134
Hamann, Johann Georg (1730–88, Sturm und Drang writer, the "Magus of the North"), 58
Hannah, Richard W., 81
Hannibal (247–183), 148
Hardenberg, Karl August Fürst von (1750–1822, Prussian chancellor), 67
Harich, Wolfgang, 4, 16, 17, 60, 61, 65, 82, 204, 207, 362
Hauber, Eberhard David (1695–1765, preacher and geographer), 215
Häuberle, Johann Jakob, 269
Haydn, Joseph (1732–1809), 216, 255
Heem, Jan Davidsz de (1606–84, Dutch painter), 127
Hegel, Georg Wilhelm Friedrich (1770–1831), 204, 205

Heidegger, 273

Heine, Heinrich (1797–1856), 42

Heineken, Christian (1721–26, child prodigy, whose biography appeared in 1726), 354

Heliogabalus, Emperor (204–222), 336

Hellfeld, Johann August (1717–82, jurist), 155

Heloise (1101–64), 10

Helvetius, Claude Adrien (1715–71, French philosopher), 317

Hemsterhuis, Franz (1722–90, Dutch philosopher), 201

Henke, Johann Christian (*Neuentdeckte Geheimnisse in Erzeugung des Menschen*, 1786), 52

Henri, 65

Henrion, Nikolaus,163

Henry the Fowler (13th c. Tyrolean minstrel), 290

Herder, Johann Gottfried (1744–1803), 16, 18, 30, 58, 70, 77, 115, 195, 196, 202, 205, 206, 207, 230, 267, 317

Hermann, Johann Bernhard (1761–90), 10, 11, 44, 159

Hermes, Johann Timotheus (1738–1821, theologian and novelist), 136, 263, 307

Herodianus (170–240, Greek historian), 319

Herold, Karoline (b. 1779), 10, 18

Herschel, Friedrich Wilhelm (1738–1822, musician and astronomer), 312

Herz, Henriette (1764–1847), 31

Heyne, Christian Gottlob (1729–1812, classical philologist), 155

Hieron I of Syracuse (5th c. B.C.), 54

Hilary, Saint (315–367), 212

Hildburghausen, Charlotte Herzogin von (1769–1818), 67

Hippel, Theodor Gottlieb von (1741–96, statesman and novelist), 263

Hippocrates (460–370, Greek physician), 293

Hoffmann, E. T. A. (1776–1822, German romantic writer), 33

Hoffmann, Gottfried (author of popular Latin textbook, first published in 1705), 356

Hofmann, Leopold Aloys (1746–1806, journalist in Vienna), 154

Hogarth, William (1697–1764), 184, 196

Holberg, Ludwig von (1684–1754, Danish dramatist), 255

Höllerer, Walter, xiii, 26

Homer, 38, 90, 125, 132, 198, 199, 200, 254, 328

Horace (65–8), 10, 260, 317

Horn, Franz (1781–1837, novelist and literary historian), 252

Houlieres, Antoinette du Ligier, Madame des (1633–94, poet), 221

Huarte, Juan de Dios (b. 1530, physician and writer), 129

Iffland, August Wilhelm (1759–1814, actor-dramatist), 264

Ignatius of Loyola, Saint (1491–1556), 51, 72, 150

Jacobi, Friedrich Heinrich (1743–1819, philosopher), 22, 24, 26, 27, 58, 61, 66, 77, 160, 195, 201, 205, 206, 207, 234

Januarius, Saint (martyred A.D. 304), 52

Jerusalem, Johann Friedrich Wilhelm (1709–89, abbot in Wolfenbüttel, theologian and pedagogue), 148, 357

Job, 207

Jöcher, Christian Gottlieb (1694–1758, librarian and lexicographer in Leipzig), 164

John, (the apostle), 107

Johnson, Samuel (1700–1784), 206

Joseph, Saint, 228

Judas, 213, 289

Jung-Stilling, Heinrich (1740–1817, physician and writer), 194

Justinian I, Emperor (527–565), 154

Kafka, Franz (1883–1924), 19, 28, 54

Kalb, Charlotte von (1761–1843, patron of Schiller and Jean Paul), 18, 23

Kanne, Johann Arnold (1773–1824, orientalist and theologian), 58, 194, 195, 252

Kant, Immanuel (1724–1804), 37, 58, 87, 126, 132, 160, 167, 193ff., 200, 204ff., 216, 228ff., 287f., 298, 303

Karoline, Queen (of Bavaria, 1776–1804), 67

Keller, Gottfried (1819–90, Swiss writer), 39, 83

Kerner, Justinus (1786–1862, Swabian poet), 252

Kiesin, 307

Klatt, Fritz, 64

Kleist, Ewalt von (1715–59, soldier and poet), 267

Kleist, Heinrich von (1777–1811, dramatist and narrative writer), 35

Klinger, Friedrich Maximilian von (1752–1831, Sturm und Drang dramatist and novelist), 262f.

Klopstock, Friedrich Gottlieb (1724–1803, epic and lyric poet), 265

Knebel, Karl Ludwig von (1744–1834, translator and poet), 115

Kommerell, Max (1902–44, literary historian), 38, 81

Korff, Hermann August (1882–1963, literary historian), 16, 17

Kotzebue, August von (1761–1819, dramatist), 32, 254, 275

Krogoll, Johannes, xiii

Krüdener, Barbara Juliane von (1764–1824, novelist), 194

Krüger, Johann Gottlob (1715–59, scientist), 312

Kuhn, Johann Paul (1710–80, Jean Paul's grandfather), 323

Lafontaine, August Heinrich (1755–1831, novelist and preacher), 263

Lambert, Johann Heinrich (1728–77, astronomer and mathematician), 151

Lange, Heinrich Arnold (*Das geistliche Recht der evangelisch-lutherischen Landesherren und ihrer Unterthanen in Deutschland*, 1786), 96

Lange, Joachim (1670–1744, schoolmaster, grammar- and textbook writer), 331f., 342, 344, 354, 355

Lavater, Johann Caspar (1741–1801, pastor, poet, and phrenologist), 52, 86, 136, 185, 232, 296, 302

Lee, Eliza Buckminster, 237

Leibnitz, Gottfried Wilhelm von (1646–1716), 37, 87, 167, 195, 201, 228, 247

Lesage, Alain René (1668–1747, novelist), 257

Lessing, Gotthold Ephraim (1729–81), 58, 71, 145, 160, 187, 195, 201, 267, 282, 334

Leuwenhoek, Anton (1632–1723, Dutch scientist), 165

Levin, Rahel. *See* Varnhagen, Rahel

Lichtenberg, Georg Christoph (1742–99, physicist, essayist, and aphorist), 35, 184, 186, 252, 276, 296, 334

Linné, Carl von (1707–78, Swedish botanist), 129, 192

Lipsius, Just (1547–1606, humanist), 57

List, Nickel (1656–99, notorious outlaw), 215

Lombardus, Petrus (1100–1164, scholastic theologian), 229

Longfellow, Henry Wadsworth (1807–82), 4

Lot, 211

Louis XIV (1638–1715), 52, 162, 250

Louis XV (1710–74), 318

Lucian (120–180, satirist), 254

Luise, Queen (of Prussia, 1776–1810), 31, 51

Lukács, Georg (1885–1971), 4, 81

Luke, Saint, 49

Luther, Martin (1483–1546), 8, 61, 68, 72, 253, 270, 325, 334

Macclesfield, Countess of, 122

Macrobius, Ambrosius Theodosius (5th c. Latin writer), 201

Malthus, Thomas Robert (1766–1834, English economist), 38

Mann, Thomas (1875–1955), 47, 77

Market, 179

Martin, 297

Marx, Karl (1818–83), 269

Mary, (the Virgin), 52

Maximilian I, King (of Bavaria, 1756–1825), 67

Mayer, Karoline. *See* Richter, Karoline

Meier, Georg Friedrich (1718–77, philosopher in Halle), 233

Melanchthon, Philipp (1497–1560), 52

Mendelssohn, Moses (1729–86, philosopher), 362

Mengs, Anton Raphael (1728–99, painter), 334

Menzius, 233

Mercier, Louis Sébastian (1740–1814, dramatist and theorist), 254

Merkel, Garlieb (1769–1850, journalist), 211, 251

Messenbeck, 307

Metternich, Clemens Fürst von (1773–1859), 67

Meusel, Johann Georg (1743–1820, historian and lexicographer), 151, 164, 215, 230

Meyer, Heinrich (1760–1832, Swiss painter, Goethe's art adviser), 121

Miller, Norbert, xiii

Minder, Robert, 34

Minellius, Jan (1625–83, Dutch pedagogue and classics editor), 155

Modeer, Adolph (1738–99, Swedish economist), 211

Moeller van de Bruck, Arthur (1876–1925, conservative cultural historian), 64

Mohammed, 51

Montaigne, Michel Eyquem de (1533–92, essayist and philosopher), 53, 130, 279

Montesquieu, Charles de Secondat de (1689–1755, writer and political philospher), 134

Moritz, Karl Philipp (1757–93, novelist and writer), 17, 75, 159, 250

Moser, Friedrich Carl von (1723–98, minister in Darmstadt, lawyer, and writer), 212

Moser, Jakob von (1701–85, jurist), 125

Möser, Justus (1720–94, statesman and writer), 255

Mozart, Wolfgang Amadeus (1756–91), 226

Müller, Friedrich (1749–1825, "Maler Müller," painter and Sturm und Drang writer), 266

Müller, Friedrich von (1779–1849, "Kanzler Müller," Goethe's confidante), 195

Müller, Johann Gottwerth (1749–93, "Müller von Itzehoe," comic novelist), 252

Musäus, Johann Karl (1735–87, satirical novelist and folktale writer), 256ff., 263

Napoleon I Bonaparte (1769–1821), 66, 301, 308

Nerrlich, Paul (1844–1904), 16

Newton, Isaac (1643–1727), 167, 228

Nicolai, Christoph Friedrich (1733–1811, bookseller and center of Berlin Enlightenment), 58, 59, 67, 87, 121, 242, 297, 318

Neitzsche, Friedrich (1844–1900), 72, 161, 194, 244

Nodier, Charles (1780–1844, writer and scholar), 5

Nösselt, Johann August (1734–1807, theologian), 358

Novalis (i.e., Friedrich von Hardenberg, 1772–1801, German romantic poet), 13

Oertel, Friedrich Benedikt von (1767–1807, writer), 43, 75

Oerthel, Adam Lorenz von (1763–86), 10, 11, 159

Oerthel, Christian Adam (1775–92), 159

Oken, Lorenz (1779–1851, scientist and philosopher), 273

Origines (185–253, gnostic theologian), 231

Orleans, Philipp II, Duke of (1674–1723), 318

Orlov, Aliksey Grigorjewitsch (1737–1808, Russian general), 132

Orrery, John Boyle (5th earl of Cork and Orrery, 1707–62), 204

Osmund, Emanuel (1766–1842), 12, 17, 18, 31, 33, 60, 61, 75, 82, 159, 270, 322

Otto, Christian Georg (1763–1828), 3, 10,

Otto, Christian Georg *(cont'd)*
18, 26, 31, 43, 63, 66, 67, 72, 115, 120,
159, 242
Otto, Johann Friedrich. *See* Sintenis

Paine, Thomas (1737–1809), 155
Pallas, Peter Simon (1741–1811, zoologist
and travel writer), 218
Papin, Dionys (1647–1712, physician and
scientist), 123
Parrhasios (440–390, painter), 132
Pascal, Blaise (1623–62), 130, 161, 245
Paul, Saint, 360
Paulus, Heinrich Eberhard Gottlob (1761–
1851, theologian), 195
Paulus, Sophie (1791–1847, daughter of
above, m. A. W. Schlegel), 33
Pausanias (2d c. geographer), 202
Pechmann, Johann, 171
Pembroke, Philip Herbert, Earl of (1584–
1650, patron of Van Dyck), 214
Perthes, Friedrich Christoph (1772–1843,
bookseller and publisher), 70
Pestalozzi, Johann Heinrich (1746–1827,
Swiss educational reformer), 270
Petau, Denis ("Petavius," 1583–1652,
Jesuit theologian), 57
Peter, Saint, 37, 66, 129, 165, 196, 360
Petrus Rebuffus (i.e., Pierre Rebuffe,
1487–1557, jurist), 148
Pfeiffer, August (1640–98, orientalist and
bible scholar), 145
Phalaris (6th c. B.C tyrant of Crete), 218
Philip II of Spain (1527–98), 57
Pigault-Lebrun (1753–1835, novelist),
257
Pindar (522–448, Greek lyric poet), 329
Pisestratus (d. 528 B.C, tyrant of Athens),
155
Pitt, William the Younger (1759–1806), 63
Pizarro, Francisco (1478–1541, conqueror
of Peru), 165
Platner, Ernst (1744–1818, physician and
anthropologist in Leipzig), 131, 255
Plato (427–348), 126, 167, 195, 201, 232,
254, 282, 308

Pliny the Younger (61–113, Roman orator
and statesman), 177
Plotho, Erich Christoph von, 328, 345,
353
Plotho, Freifrau Louise Eleonore (d.
1810), 328, 333, 337, 345f., 352f.
Plotinus (205–270, neoplatonist), 44
Plutarch (50–125, Greek biographer), 126,
128, 196, 230
Pölitz, Karl Heinrich Ludwig (1772–1838,
aesthetician), 304
Polus (Greek actor), 132
Pope, Alexander (1688–1744), 10
Potemkin, Gregor Alexandrowitsch, Prince
(1739–91, statesman), 165
Pufendorff, Samuel von (1632–94, law
professor in Heidelberg), 162
Puységur, Armand-Jacques de Chartenet,
Marquis (1751–1825, physicist, student
of Mesmer), 304

Rabelais, François (1495–1553), 251, 259,
260
Rabener, Gottlieb Wilhelm (1714–71, sati-
rist), 251
Radcliffe, 51
Ramler, Karl Wilhelm (1725–98, poet and
essayist), 212, 230
Rehm, Walter, 161
Reichardt, Johann Friedrich (1752–1814,
composer), 339
Reil, Johann Christian (1759–1813, profes-
sor of medicine in Halle), 299
Reimarus, Hermann Samuel (1694–1768,
philosopher and theologian), 280
Reitzenstein, Frau von, 334
Reitzenstein, Herr von, 345
Reuß, Fürst von, 352
Richardson, Samuel (1689–1761), 261,
326
Richelieu, Cardinal (1585–1642), 60, 318
Richter, Amöne Odilie Minna (1804–65,
daughter), 31
Richter, Emma (1802–53, daughter, M.
Förster), 31
Richter, Johann (grandfather), 324f.

Richter, Johann Adam Christian (1764–1816, brother), 330f., 337, 350

Richter, Johann Christian (1727–79, father), 8, 323

Richter, Johann Gottlieb (1768–1850, brother), 236, 337

Richter, Justus Heinrich Wilhelm (1770–89, brother), 11, 159, 337

Richter, Karoline, née Mayer (1777–1860, wife), 23, 31, 33

Richter, Max (1803–21, son), 31, 42, 58, 194, 195, 322, 360

Richter, Sophie Rosina, née Kuhn (1737–97, mother), 323

Rilke, Rainer Maria (1875–1926), 72

Robespierre, Maximilian de (1758–94), 66

Rollwenzel, Dorothea (1756–1830), 31

Römer, Eva Justina, 342f., 347

Romulus, 247

Rousseau, Jean Jacques (1712–78), 8, 12, 58, 85, 88, 123, 167, 194

Rubens, Peter Paul (1577–1640), 270

Sachsen-Gotha, Emil August Herzog von (1772–1822), 67

Sanchuniathon (ca. 1250 B.C., Phoenician historian), 126

Sand, Karl Ludwig (1795–1820, radical theology student, executed for assasination of Kotzebue), 32

Saurin, Jacques (1677–1730, Huguenot Hebraist), 163

Savage, Richard (1697–1743, satirist and dramatist, died in prison), 122

Scaliger, Julius Caesar (1484–1558, humanist philosopher, philologist, physician), 44

Schäfer, 123

Schelling, Friedrich Wilhelm Josef von (1775–1854), 204, 287

Schiller, Friedrich (1759–1805), 5, 6, 16, 18, 26, 37, 43, 77, 82, 87, 121, 130, 239, 242, 248, 254, 357

Schlabrendorff, Henriette von (1773–1853), 31

Schlegel, August Wilhelm (1767–1845, cultural historian and Shakespeare translator), 242, 267

Schlegel, Friedrich (1772–1829, brother of August, novelist, philologist, literary theorist), 31, 70, 77, 130, 160, 242ff., 246, 251, 334

Schleiermacher, Friedrich Ernst Daniel (1768–1834, theologian), 31

Schramm, Wilhelm von, 64

Schreinert, Kurt, 64

Schubart, Christian Friedrich (1739–91, Sturm und Drang musician and poet), 257

Schulz, Friedrich (Über Paris und die Pariser 1791), 103

Schütze, Johann Stephan (1771–1839, critic and journalist), 252

Schwarz (?) (Friedrich Schwarz, 1776–1837, theologian and pedagogue), 233

Schweikert, Uwe, xiii, 21, 26, 28, 41, 303

Scott, Walter (1771–1832), 51, 55, 315f.

Seneca (5–65, stoic philosopher and poet), 156

Sévigné, Marquise Marie de (1626–96, French epistolary writer), 259

Shaftesbury, Anthony Cooper, Earl of (1671–1713, philosopher), 176

Shakespeare, William (1564–1616), 10, 11, 159, 167, 248, 251, 254, 257, 259

Simon (of Cyrene), 51

Sintenis, Hieronymus Friedrich (1750–1826, theologian and novelist under pseudonym Joh. Fr. Otto), 357

Sloane (?) (Sir Hans Sloane, 1660–1753, physician and naturalist), 233

Smollett, Tobias George (1721–71), 263

Socrates (470–399), 166, 204, 218, 254, 259

Sölle, Dorothee, 161

Sömmering, Samuel Thomas von (1755–1830, anatomist and anthropologist), 166

Sophocles (497–406), 198

Speccius, Christoph (1585–1639, grammarian), 332, 354, 356

Spinoza, Baruch de (1632–77), 207

Spitzweg, Karl (1808–85, painter), 81
Spock, Benjamin, 270
Staël-Holstein, Germaine de (1766–1817), 4, 159, 194, 244
Stahl, Georg Ernst (1660–1734, Berlin chemist and king's physician), 229
Staiger, Emil (1908–87), 4
Stein, Georg Wilhelm (1731–1803, physician), 165
Stengel, 233
Sterne, Lawrence (1713–45), xii, 6, 12, 250f., 252, 255, 256, 258, 259, 260, 263
Stolberg, Friedrich Leopold Graf zu (1750–1819, poet and translator), 122
Stourzda, Alexander (1788–1854), 63
Strabo (63–26, Greek geographer), 307
Stroth, 155
Sturm, Christoph Christian (1740–86, pastor), 87
Suidas (10th c. Greek lexicographer), 328
Swift, Jonathan (1667–1745), xii, 9, 10, 37, 153, 204, 209, 250, 251, 255, 256
Sydow, Josephine von (1758–1829, writer), 31

Theocritus (300–260, Greek poet), 265ff.
Thieme, Johann Friedrich, 323
Thieriot, Paul Amiel (1780–1831, philologist and violinist), 39, 48, 207
Thucydides (460–400, historian), 51, 316
Thümmel, Moritz August von (1738–1817, novelist), 254, 326
Thurn und Taxis, Prince Alexander Ferdinand von, 325
Tieck, Ludwig (1773–1853, German romantic writer), 30, 31, 70, 251, 255
Toricelli, Evangelista (1608–47, mathematician and physicist), 133

Varnhagen, Rahel (1771–1833, writer of letters and memoirs, literary salon in Berlin), 31
Varro, Marcus Terentius (116–27, encyclopedist and philologist), 123
Vieweg, Friedrich (1761–1835, Braunschweig publisher), 288

Villiers, Charles François Dominique de (1765–1815, critic), 159
Vincon, Hartmut, 81
Virgil (70–19), 267
Vogel, Erhard Friedrich (1750–1823), 10
Völkel, 357
Voltaire, François Marie de (1694–1778), 10, 32, 57, 58, 128, 187, 251, 253
Voß, Heinrich (1779–1822, philology professor in Heidelberg, son of following), 33, 42, 322, 360
Voß, Johann Heinrich (1751–1834, Homer translator and idyll writer), 33, 194, 196, 213, 265ff.

Wagener, Sigismund Christoph (Die Gespenster. Kurze Erzählungen aus dem Reiche der Wahrheit, 1797), 340
Wagner, Ernst (1769–1812, novelist), 252
Wagner, Richard (1813–83), 194
Warren, Austin, 6
Weisser, Friedrich Christoph von (1761–1836, satirist), 252
Wellek, René, 6
Werner, Karl August (schoolmaster and pastor, model for Magister Wehmeier in Titan), 355
Wernlein, Konstantin Friedrich (1765–1830, pastor, married to Christian Otto's sister), 293
Wezel, Johann Karl (1749–1819), novelist), 251
Widhammer, Helmut, 25, 204
Wieland, Christoph Martin (1733–1813, novelist, poet and translator), 16, 201, 252, 292, 308
Winckelmann, Johann Joachim (1717–68, archaeologist), 133, 244
Wölfel, Kurt, xiii
Wolff, Christian (1679–1754, philosopher), 126
Wolke, Christian Heinrich (1741–1825, philologist), 33
Wouverman, Philips (1619–68, Dutch painter), 124
Wuthenow, Ralph Rainer, 81

Xantippe, 38, 218, 291, 292

Young, Edward (1683–1765), 10

Zach, Franz Xaver von (1754–1832, astronomer), 236

Zäh, 330
Zelter, Karl Friedrich (1758–1832, musicologist), 76
Zimmerman, Johann Georg Ritter von (1728–95, writer, physician to the English king at Hannover), 235

Designed by Martha Farlow

Composed by Graphic Composition, Inc., in Janson Text

Printed by The Maple Press Company, Inc., on 50-lb. Glatfelter Eggshell Cream and bound in Holliston Kingston Natural with Rainbow Antique endsheets